Secrets of Award-Winning Digital Artists

Jeremy Sutton and Daryl Wise

Wiley Publishing, Inc.

Secrets of Award-Winning Digital Artists

Published by
Wiley Publishing, Inc.
909 Third Avenue
New York, NY 10022
www.wiley.com

Library of Congress Control Number: 2002108432
ISBN: 0-7645-3691-5

Manufactured in the United States of America

10 9 8 7 6 5 4 3 2 1

1K/SR/QY/QS/IN

Published by Wiley Publishing, Inc., Indianapolis, Indiana
Published simultaneously in Canada

For general information on our other products and services or to obtain technical support, please contact our Customer Care Department within the U.S. at 800-762-2974, outside the U.S. at 317-572-3993 or fax 317-572-4002.

Wiley also publishes its books in a variety of electronic formats. Some content that appears in print may not be available in electronic books.

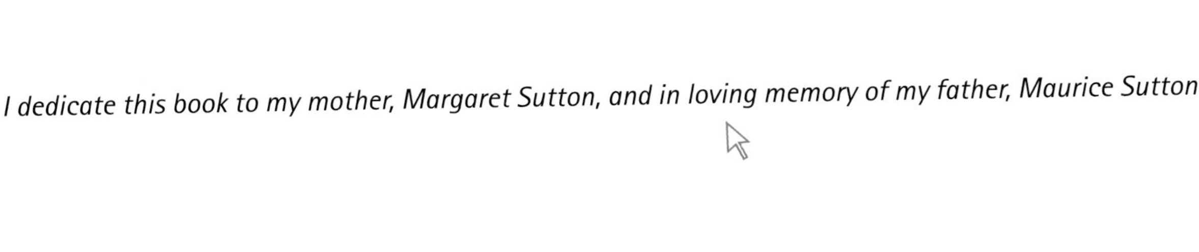
I dedicate this book to my mother, Margaret Sutton, and in loving memory of my father, Maurice Sutton

Foreword

My art training began in the school of realism. It was really traditional art in that painting realism meant painting things as they were. The idea was to paint realistic images so that water would look like water, and silver would shine like silver. Additional thought was given to the composition of the painting, to the positive and negative shapes (foreground and background), the positioning or location of objects, and so on, within the piece.

During my second or third year of art school, new types of paints emerged on the scene. They were called acrylics. I remember the numerous debates and conversations about whether or not acrylic paintings would be considered fine art. I thought to myself that art is not so much about the medium it's done in than it is about the creativity. In acrylic paint, I was able to paint thicker, and more spontaneously, with many layers. The paint dried faster, so it was an obvious advantage. The debate, however, raged on.

A couple of years passed by, and I began to hear another debate. This time around, it concerned the question of whether or not television and video imagery would be considered fine art. I thought again, yes, because art is about creativity. The medium is an artist's inspiration and simply acts to bring out different types of creativity. At the time, there was an exhibit at the Museum of Modern Art where I saw TV sets piled upon TV sets with looped images. It stimulated my thought. To me, it was art.

Now we are well into "the personal computer age," and the question of the moment is whether or not computer or digital art is legitimate. Once more, my answer is yes, of course it is. If the medium, in this case the computer, can help to create something even more difficult to do by hand, then by all means use it. Digital tools for artists have gotten quite sophisticated, and still images on computer screens, if arranged in the right way, can make interesting installations. I myself enjoy "mixing and matching" my pen and ink with my digital tools, meaning art created by hand, scanned into a computer, worked on and tweaked, printed out, and embellished once again by hand. The "painterly" capability of digital tools continues to open new doors of expression, and obviously a lot of things can be done.

The most important thing of all — a word of caution even — is to create positive imagery. It is easy to play with computer-based media, as you can with pen and ink, to draw negative images. I suggest that artists use their talents to create works that are not only provocative, but also beautiful and uplifting. In my view, that is and always will be the challenge, whether it be with oil, acrylic, television sets, or pixels.

These pages are filled with a great many works living up to that standard. The artists showcased here have attained a high level of technical and creative virtuosity, and they have graciously agreed to share their beautifully realized perspectives with us all. The result is a delightful showcase of both inspiration and craft.

With that said, enjoy the book, and remember that creativity is art.

Peter Max
New York, New York
August, 2002

Preface

Secrets of Award-Winning Digital Artists gives you both creative and technical insights into the beautiful artwork of some of today's top artists working in the digital medium.

Each chapter features an artist's award-winning artwork accompanied by background text and illustrations. Headings located in each chapter make it easy for you to quickly access the information that most interests you. Each chapter is designed as if you were having a conversation with the artist in his or her studio, asking the artist questions about the artwork, the creative process, the views that influenced their work, and the tools used to create the art.

In embarking on this exciting project, we imagined what questions you would want to ask each artist. First, you might want to hear the story behind their artwork. Why did they create it in the first place? What was their inspiration and motivation? These questions are answered in *The Story Behind the Artwork* section in each chapter.

You might want to understand the over-all creative process — how did the artist go about making the vision become a reality? This information is in *The Creative Process* section.

There's always something in a picture that draws us to ask "How did they do that?" The "how-to" is addressed in the *Technique* section of each chapter. Here you find a step-by-step technique used in the award-winning artwork. The *Technique* sections are a great opportunity to learn and implement a wide variety of practical and creative techniques in your own artwork.

The collective experience and wisdom of all the artists featured in this book form a powerful resource that is shared in the *Artist's Creative Insight and Advice* sections. Learn from the rich diversity of the artist's background, interests, and approaches to making art.

The conclusion of each chapter's "visit" to the artist's studio is a summary of their background, artistic influences, tools, and contact information, all contained in the *About the Artist* section.

The artwork has been divided into two main groupings, Fine Art and Photography. Some of the artwork could equally have fit into either category. In determining the sequence in which the artwork appears, we imagined that we were curating an artshow in a gallery. We imagined the reader as a visitor to the gallery, strolling from artwork to artwork.

This book has been written for both "artists" and "non-artists" alike. While there is in-depth technical information that is useful to the digital fine-art professional, there is also creative insight that will be of interest to anyone with a desire to learn more about art, and who wishes to further their understanding of the creative process.

The book is cross-platform, with commands first written out as menu commands and then followed by the Macintosh/Windows keyboard shortcuts in parentheses. File sizes are generally described in inches and pixels per inch (ppi). Dots per inch (dpi) is used when referring to print resolution.

Writing this book has been an enjoyable learning experience. We hope that you will find reading it both educational and enjoyable. We invite you to e-mail us with any comments or thoughts about this book.

Cheers,

Jeremy Sutton
San Francisco, California
`Jeremy@portrayals.com`
`www.portrayals.com`

Daryl Wise
Watsonville, California
`dsw@surfnetusa.com`

Acknowledgments

We wish to sincerely thank all the artists who agreed to be featured in this book. Each artist generously contributed a great deal of time and effort preparing answers to our questions, making screen shots to illustrate their techniques, and locating source materials, files, and illustrations. Thank you artists, for sharing your beautiful artwork, techniques, and insights, and for your patience in answering our multitude of questions and queries!

Jeremy Sutton: I wish to thank Daryl for inviting me to be his co-author on this project and for all of his behind-the-scenes organization, research, project management, public relations, and his work with the artists and judges. In dividing our responsibilities, I did the actual writing of each chapter, while Daryl was responsible for initially contacting the artists and judges, and following up with getting permissions. We both worked on selecting the artwork and the content structure. Thank you Daryl for all your support and for being such a pleasure to work with.

Thanks to Elizabeth Fenwick who took the photograph of Daryl and me.

Last, but not least, I wish to thank the great team at Wiley Publishing, Inc., that believed in this project and supported and encouraged Daryl and me throughout the process of writing the book. That team includes our Acquisitions Editor, Mike Roney; Project Editor, Mary Goodwin; and Technical Editor, Colin Smith. Thanks for everything you have done.

Daryl Wise: I would like to acknowledge a few individuals who helped make this book possible. First, my partner Jeremy Sutton. Jeremy and I have known each other for many years, and we make a good team. His unwavering passion for digital art played an important part in making this book unique and informative. Besides being an accomplished digital artist, Jeremy is also a good dancer. You should see this guy do the Lindy Hop! I mention this because, like dancing, writing takes a lot of energy, finesse, and style.

Thank you to the art judges, who unselfishly loaned their time, experience, and expertise to the various digital art competitions. Thank you to the artists who are featured in this book and artists everywhere for making the world a better place. Thank you to all of my friends from the "good ol days" at Fractal Design. That was fun and rewarding! I still remember John Derry saying, "Can you believe it — they pay us, too!"

Thank you to the good folks at Wiley Publishing, Inc., for making the entire book process an enjoyable experience, including Acquisitions Editor, Mike Roney; Project Editor, Mary Goodwin; and Technical Editor, Colin Smith, who made sure that Jeremy and I stayed on course and that, together, we created a book that is interesting, well written, and inspiring.

Contents At A Glance

dS

Contents

Part I

Fine Art

As you look at the work featured in this part of the book, we want you to feel as if you are strolling through a fine art gallery, having the opportunity to view a wide variety of artwork in a single place. Better than a simple visit to a gallery, this part of the book allows you the unique opportunity to hear the creative thoughts and learn about the techniques that contributed to making each piece of art.

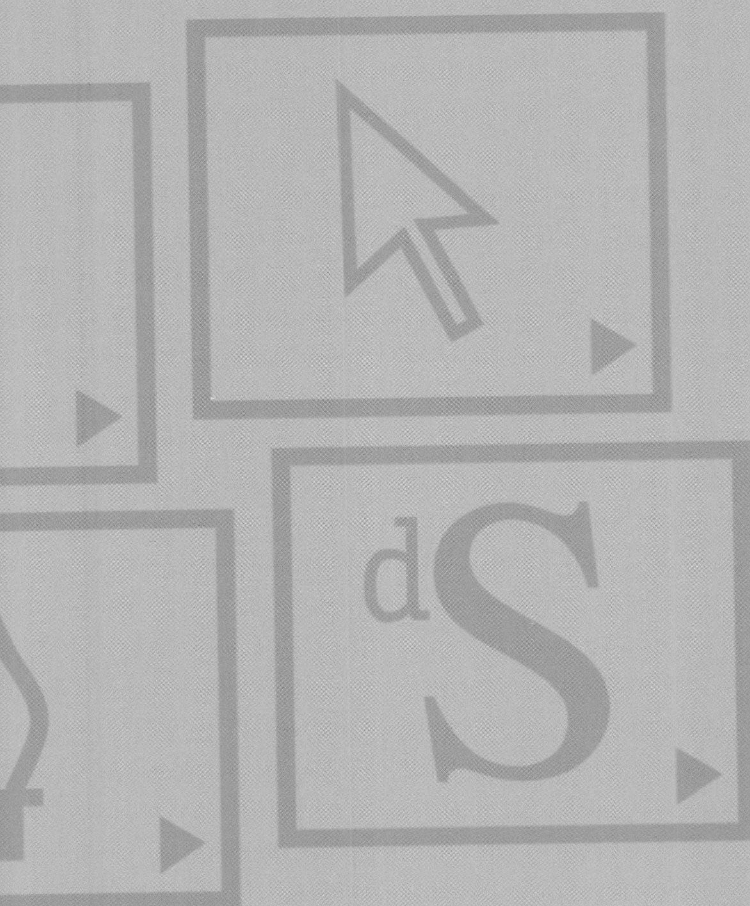

WHO GOD BLESS NO MAN CURSE

Chapter 1

Street Scene

by John Trevino

Artist's Statement

When I look at someone like Mos Def, I see someone who moves fluidly between different styles with ease, and yet is able to bring them all together in the end. That's how I want to be as an artist.

The Story Behind the Artwork

Street Scene (1.1) was made during a time when John and his girlfriend were staying with a friend while looking for studio space. John was getting more and more discouraged because he had just relocated to Los Angeles and didn't have the job and rental history landlords wanted to see. Also, as a painter, John was having withdrawal symptoms, being unable to paint for months. He did have his computer set up, though, so he began experimenting with how he could create a digital piece in a manner that would feel similar to how he would approach creating a traditional painting.

John wanted to create something that dealt with his feeling of temporary transience, of being between places, of anticipation. He kept thinking, "If someone would just let us get our foot in the door, we can make the rest happen."

The figure holding the plant represents that feeling of having something that you're eager to put down and watch grow. The text "I want to believe" is something that John borrowed from the UFO poster in Mulder's office on *X-Files.* For John, it captures the struggle between faith and doubt. It's ultimately a kind of optimistic affirmation against those circumstances

◀ 1.1

that may be trying to tell you different. Along with that text is the line, "Who God bless, no man curse," which is aimed at those folks who John felt were standing in the way of what he was put here to do.

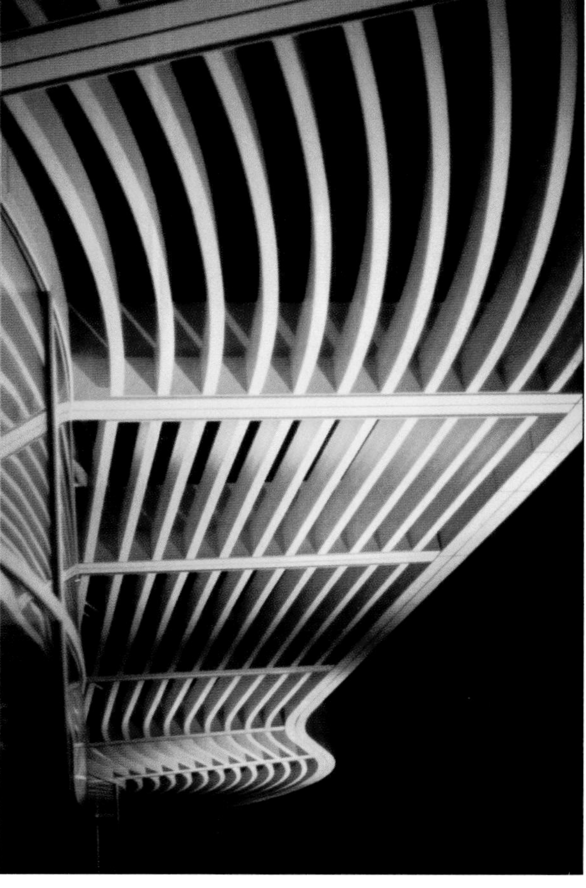

1.2

The Creative Process

John wanted to approach this piece in a way that would be close to how he was used to working on the traditional canvas. As in his traditional paintings, John built up layers, painted over certain parts of these layers, and then recovered the layers, making use of the Layer masks in Photoshop.

The source material for these layers included scanned photographs, such as images of curved wood from the Getty Museum in Los Angeles (1.2), and of skeletal dried leaves (1.3).

1.3

About the Artist

Biography

John graduated from University of California Santa Barbara with a BA, and from Howard University with an MFA. At Howard University, he was awarded Best of Show at the student exhibition as well as a commission for a collaborative mural project. In the past three years, John has been teaching himself different programs as they applied to him as a painter. He started with Photoshop to help with printing his portfolio, moved to Illustrator to design a logo that could identify him as an artist, and then bought a Wacom tablet and began using the Painter Classic it came bundled with.

Influences

Everyday experiences, exchanges between people, relationships with friends, and direct observation from his surroundings. The work of Aaron Douglass, Charles White, and John Biggers. The work of graphic artists and their manipulation of text. Music is also a huge source of inspiration for John, especially hip-hop.

1.4

1.5

John also recycled segments from his other artwork, such as the text "Who God bless, no man curse" from a painting titled *We Be Clubbin' #4* (1.4), and circles from the background of a preliminary sketch for a mural (1.5).

John developed a multi-layered image in Photoshop. He copied a layer and then opened it in Painter Classic (which doesn't support layers). After painting on the image in Painter Classic, he then reopened the altered image in Photoshop and played with the changed layer against its previously unaltered version, using the Layer mask.

John introduced the appearance of flickers of light in the pyramids by painting in Photoshop with the brush set to Color Dodge (see the technique described later in this chapter). John played with all the different scanned images, manipulating their opacity and blending modes, along with basic choices on color and composition. John experimented and explored, saving those things that visually resonated with him.

John began with a rough pastel and acrylic piece that he did with the intention of working on top of it in the computer (1.6). The picture evokes the feelings John had while looking for a studio space. He initially thought he would have the central figure pregnant, to signify being pregnant with possibilities.

Studio

Computer System:
Micron Millennia 600
28GB hard drive
512MB RAM

Monitor:
19-inch

Software:
Adobe Photoshop
Illustrator
Painter Classic

Tablet:
12 x 18-inch Wacom Intuos tablet

Input Devices:
Linotype-Hell Saphir Ultra 2

Removable Media:
100MB Zip drive
CDRW drive

Printer:
Epson 2000P

Contact

John Trevino
Los Angeles, California
j.art@netzero.net

By this stage (1.7), John had layered images over themselves to form the background as well as the pyramid forms. He dropped a detail of a sketch, one that he had originally created for a mural, into the background at this point. The circles in this sketch communicated things like the path of planets around the sun and a sense of the passing of time to John.

John then introduced some text and the leaf forms that would make the main figure's wings (1.8). He also drew in a young boy also with small wings that was connected with the main figure. Also, a scan of some fabric was brought into the woman's dress and for the texture of the boy's hair.

This stage (1.9), which happened in Photoshop, shows how he painted whole sections out on layers, similar to how he would paint a traditional painting, only in this case, he turned this layer off and on, or worked parts of it into the underlying layer through a layer mask.

1.7

1.6

1.8

The piece was basically finished at this point (1.10). However, John was still considering some decisions about the colors in some areas. He masked off this area, made it a separate layer, and filled it with different colors, a working method unique to the digital medium.

John knew that the painting was almost finished when he changed who the central figure was interacting with from a little boy to the plant. From there, everything else just fell into place and it boiled down to just adjusting the colors.

The image was a work in progress for many months. As John felt the need to paint, he'd pull it out and mess with it, until he got to the point where he felt it was complete.

Susan Levan on John Trevino

"John's piece is evocative and intelligent. He mixes photo imagery, type, graphic composition, and loose, gestural painting. The result is both tension-filled and serene, edgy and luminous."

— Susan Levan, Digital Artist (`www.bruckandmoss.com`)

1.9

1.10

Technique: Creating Flickers of Light (Photoshop)

This technique describes the way John added flickers of light to the pyramid in *Street Scene*.

1. **Open a file that contains an image element where you want to add the look of flickering light.**
2. **Use the Eye Dropper tool to grab a color that you want to have as a hue in the flickering lights.**
3. **Select the Brush tool.**
4. **Set the brush mode to Color Dodge in the Paintbrush options palette (1.11).**

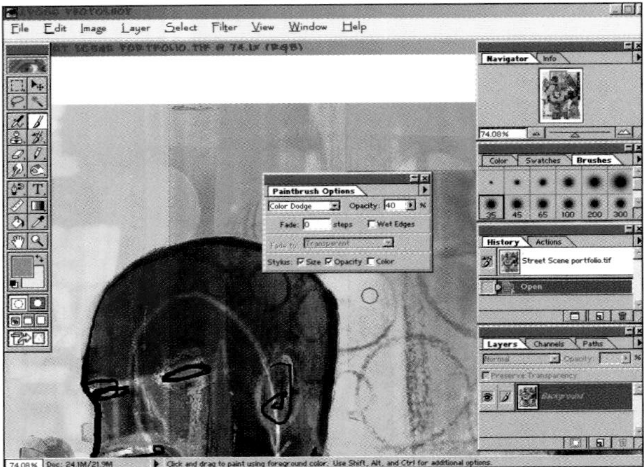

● 1.11

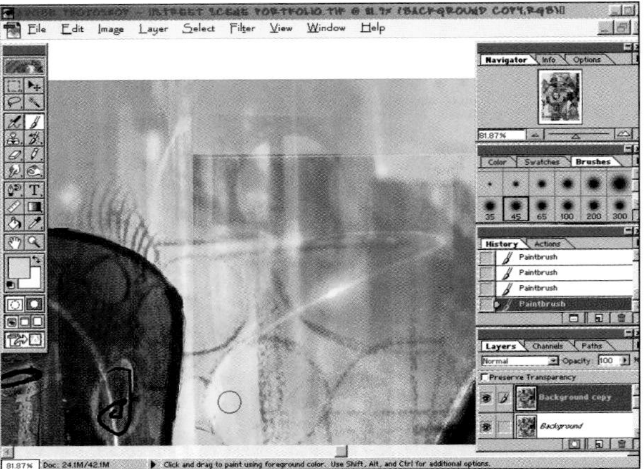

● 1.12

5. **Set the opacity to 40% in the Paintbrush options palette.**
6. **Treat the Brush tool like a highlight brush that you can use to gently brush in the flickering lights (1.12).**

[NOTE]

This technique is equivalent to erasing pastel marks on colored paper and revealing the paper color underneath.

Artist's Creative Insight and Advice

Why Digital?

Painting is my center. Digital is just another tool in the production of a piece. Up until recently, I didn't really bother with anything digital because when I was in undergrad, it always seemed like a shortcut for the people who couldn't draw. Now the digital medium is part of my mix, just like another album for a DJ mixing music.

Although the combination of a Wacom tablet and Painter or Photoshop is an amazing combination, it's not real paint, and for people who love the viscosity and color of paint and other traditional materials, it won't be replacing them anytime soon. This should be conceded. An actual impasto stroke is not the same as what's achieved in Painter. Say no more. It's just not.

What's more interesting to me conceptually is when the "output" becomes the painting. Looking at it this way becomes less and less about whether a traditional artist goes digital, and more about how they *use* digital.

The only thing really hemming me up right now is not having a nice digital camera, because that would really close the loop for me. For instance, I can see working on a painting, hitting that wall where every artist wonders where to go next. Instead of staring at it for hours, I could a take photo of it with a digital camera and continue to play out possibilities in Painter. This is the single best reason artists should incorporate digital into their work: the value it has for strengthening their *process*.

If artists begin to look at this way of working and embrace it, we could see a shift toward some interesting work. It wouldn't be this tired kind of argument some artists make about what the software isn't doing (while really hiding what many people are unfamiliar with and don't want to learn). It would be about looking at what it can do for them. Like giving you 15 different possibilities that you can print out on archival paper, sketch, draw, paint, or collage on top of and take your work 15 different ways without worrying about drying time or losing parts of a composition.

Advice for Artists Working in the Digital Medium

Consider how an awareness of traditional materials or techniques could strengthen and separate your work from the slew of other people generating digital images. It seems like a lot of the digital aesthetic is rooted in the imitation of reality, having evolved over the years from the 2D manipulation of photographs to the generation of 3D environments. From my perspective, this has always produced a kind of soft, seamless feel reminiscent of airbrushed pieces. A jagged lasso selection is out of place in this aesthetic, let alone showing a brush stroke. I think that digital pieces that incorporate a more organic feel, through showing the artist's hand or at least the use of actual textures, can make for more interesting work.

The main lessons I've learned working with digital have been the need to define my creative space and feel confident with it. For me and my work, it's not about the perfect Web button or interface, although something in that information may be useful in another way. Instead, I continue to challenge myself to make art that is not based on the needs of a client, but something I can use as a compass to help me navigate life and give me insights on how to prepare for the future. The most any artist can hope for is that their vision speaks to something unspoken and that people feel the need to support that voice.

Printing

Fortunately, I've been pretty lucky with the colors I'm getting in my prints. For a while I was torn because I wanted to use elements I had generated on the computer as pieces to be collaged into my traditional work, but because of the archival issue, I didn't. Since that time, I've purchased an Epson 2000P and have been very satisfied with the results I've achieved.

Printing out of Photoshop gives me the best results so far. I use their archival matte paper the most for working back on top of with other media, although it seems to buckle easily when wet. I usually use acrylic medium or spray adhesive to glue the paper to a piece of Arches hot press watercolor paper. From there, I work with acrylics, pastel, and oil pastel on top of it. Golden's acrylic ground for pastels is especially good for giving a tooth to work on top of paper that doesn't have much tooth.

Chapter 2

Bullpen

by Richard Harvey

Artist's Statement

My work combines traditional art media and techniques with digital technology. This enables me to analyze the process and experiment beyond the possibilities of traditional methods alone.

The composition of my subject matter reflects the interplay of my graphic design and fine art background, usually portraying single or group figures, capturing emotion through facial expression.

The Story Behind the Artwork

Bullpen (2.1) developed spontaneously as an unplanned visual sequence from two separate faces. The bullfighter image emerged first in the upper half of the canvas, and then Richard created the bull's head in the lower half.

By modifying the digital tools in Photoshop, Richard found a way to duplicate a woodcut look — what he calls his "digital carving technique." This technique is most prevalent in the lower of the two faces (the bull's face).

With a modified eraser as his cutting tool, Richard cut through a solid black layer at different angles, and with different size cutting brushes (modified erasers), to give the carving effect. He increased the hardness and spacing of each cutting brush to give a different edge and special effect to each cut. (For more information, see the technique section later in this chapter.)

◀2.1

The Creative Process

Richard started off in Photoshop with a 12 x 16-inch, blank white canvas in Grayscale mode at 150 dpi (he used 150 rather than 300 dpi resolution because he liked the coarseness of the lower resolution). He scanned in a hand-drawn, black-and-white line drawing as a grayscale image (2.2).

Richard used the Move tool to drag the scanned image into the blank canvas as a layer. He then scanned an ink wash drawing, also in grayscale, and dragged that over the other layer.

He then selected the line drawing layer and chose Filter➔Stylize➔Find Edges (2.3). Richard then flattened the image.

Using the Lasso tool, while holding down the Shift key, Richard drew two free style forms on both sides of the face. Holding down the Shift key allowed him to add to selections. Otherwise he would automatically replace any earlier selections with the last one. He filled the selections with black (2.4). At this stage,

● 2.2

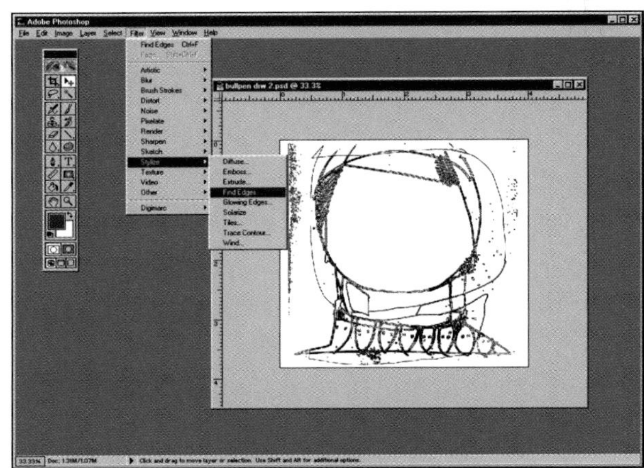

● 2.3

About the Artist

Biography

In 1972 Richard earned a BFA in Graphic Design with a fine art minor in printmaking from the Rochester Institute of Technology (RIT). Since then, he has combined his fine art endeavors with his commercial work as a graphic designer. During the early 1990's he undertook digital graduate study at RIT, and his work came to subtly reflect the influence of the digital world. He has a studio with the Anderson Alley Artist's Group, and bi-annual shows at the Austin-Harvard Art Gallery. He has lately taken up primitive sculpting as his next artistic adventure.

Richard's work has been published in magazines and exhibited in numerous juried events and competitions (digital and non-digital), including the 2002-Seybold/New York City and 2001-Seybold/San Francisco Art Contests. He won First Place in the Digital Fine Art Competition "Pointing Fingers 2000" at the Vanguard Gallery, Milwaukee, Wisconsin.

Influences

Leonard Baskin, artist, sculptor, designer, and fine printmaker. Alphonse Dargis,

Richard converted the color mode from Grayscale to RGB. He then chose Image→Adjust→Curves (2.5).

He changed the grayscale image to a colored image by selecting each color channel (red, green, and blue) in the Curves dialog box to colorize the gray scale image in each individual color. He selected RGB in the same Curves dialog box and continued to rework all three colors (red, green, and blue) at the same time.

He then selected the Magic Wand from the toolbar, holding down the Shift key, and used it to select a couple of regions on either side of the face. He filled these with a solid spot color (red) (2.6). He did the same for the eyes (2.7).

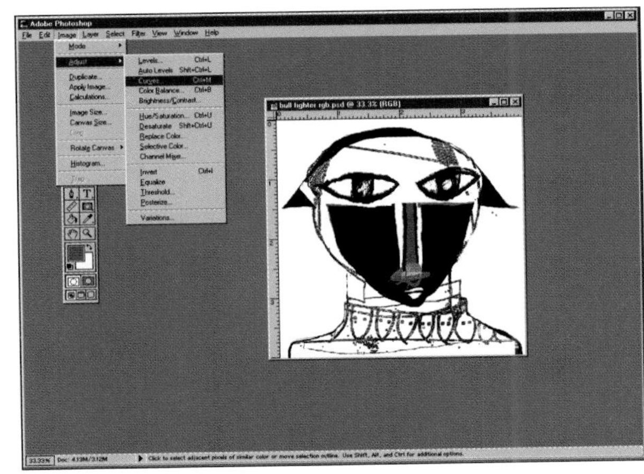

2.5

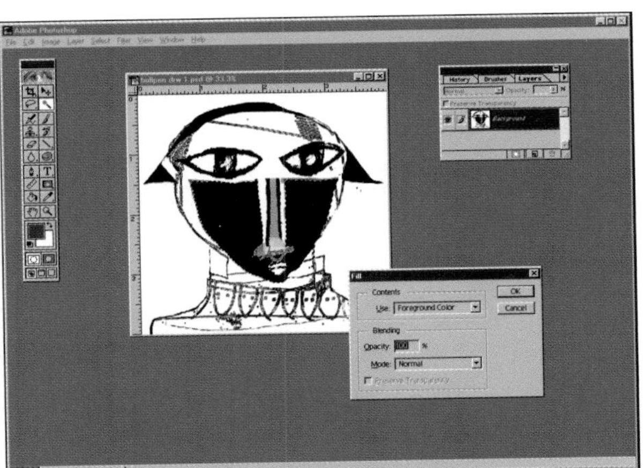

2.4

2.6

inventor, sculptor, painter, and printmaker. Other influences include Picasso's collage techniques, Matisse's drawing line quality, Robert Motherwell's powerful abstract collages, Henry Moore's sensitive, amorphic sculptural figurative forms, the color and form of the German Expressionists, and the works of Robert Marx, all of which infuse their subtle effects on Richard's work.

Studio

Computer System:

Power Mac PC

Gateway GP7-500

Gateway Solo laptop 9100SE

Monitors:

Viewsonic 17-inch and 19-inch

Software:

Adobe Photoshop

Procreate Painter

Tablet:

3 x 5 Wacom digital tablets

Input Devices:

Umax scanners

Slide and print scanner

Removable Media:

Zip drives

Optical disk drive

External 16X CD rewriteable drive

Internal 32X CD rewriteable drive

Printers:

Epson Stylus Photo 750

Epson Stylus 3000

Contact

Richard Harvey

Rochester, New York

Mharv@frontiernet.net

2.7

2.8

The lower image (the bull's face) was created using Richard's digital carving technique on a separate canvas, described later in the technique section. He then dragged the bull's face in as layer, combining the upper and lower images into a single composition. He flattened the combined image, and then cut into the border with his customized Eraser cutting tool to make the edge look irregular (2.8). This final touch helped give the image the rough hewn woodcut feel.

Technique: Digital Wood Carving (Photoshop)

This technique describes the way that Richard modifies and applies the tools in Photoshop to create the look of a traditional woodcut.

1. **Choose File→New.**

   Open a new document in RGB mode with a white background.
2. **Choose New Layer from the Layers palette.**

   This generates a new, blank, white layer.
3. **Choose the Rectangular Marquee tool from the top left of the tool bar.**
4. **Make sure black is the foreground color.**

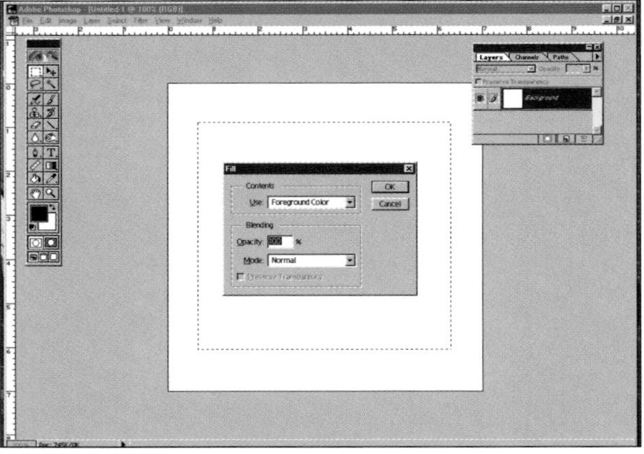

2.9

5. **Drag the Rectangular Marquee tool within the layer to make a large rectangular selection.**
6. **Choose Edit→Fill to fill the layer with foreground color (2.9).**

   This generates a black rectangular block (2.10) in the layer that you will subsequently erase away to carve out your image.
7. **Choose the Eraser from the tool bar.**
8. **Make sure the Eraser mode is set to Paintbrush.**
9. **Choose a round, solid brush shape from the Brushes palette.**
10. **Click on one of the solid brush size previews in the Brush options pop-up to access the Brush Options dialog box.**
11. **In the Brush Options dialog box, drag the control handles on the preview of the brush shape to squash and rotate the shape.**
12. **In the Brush Options dialog box, set the hardness slider to maximum (100%) and the spacing to about 25 (or you can uncheck the spacing).**
13. **In the Brush Options dialog box, set the angle to about 49 (2.11).**
14. **"Carve" out your image from the black block (2.12).**

    Carving out an image from a black block is analogous to the way a traditional woodcutter into a block of wood. Where you carve out wood the ink will not go. Thus you are creating the white spaces against a solid (usually black) background in your final image. This is the opposite to making dark marks over a white background as you would if you use media such as charcoal, paintbrush, or pen on white paper. In your digital woodcut carving you will have to think in reverse and erase out highlights from the black block, rather than add shade or lines to a white background.

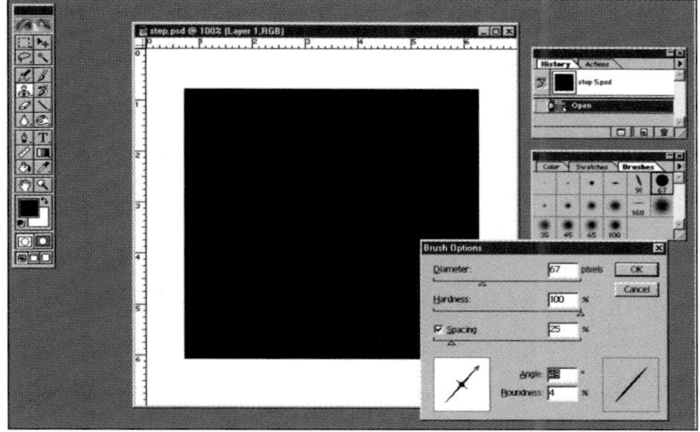

● 2.11

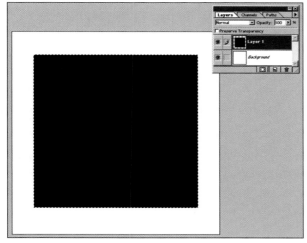

● 2.10

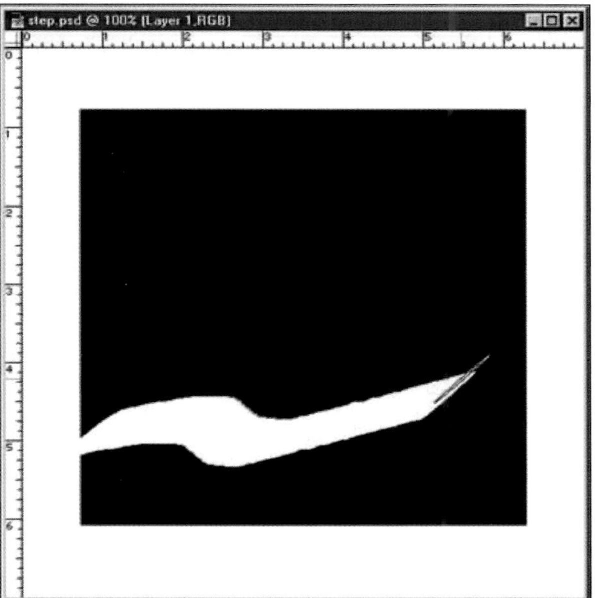

● 2.12

15. **Experiment with different size, shape, and angle settings for the modified eraser** (2.13 and 2.14). These different cutting tools are what add richness and realism to the woodcut effect.

Artist's Creative Insight and Advice

Why Digital?

From my perspective, the digital environment affords more freedom than traditional methods alone, taking the creative process to a level beyond what has existed, especially the ability to capture, save, and understand the creative mind at work. I like the immediacy and flexibility of being able to create spontaneously, return to previous steps in a piece using the History pallet to learn from where I've been. I satisfy my need for the traditional feel by combining hands-on materials and techniques within the process.

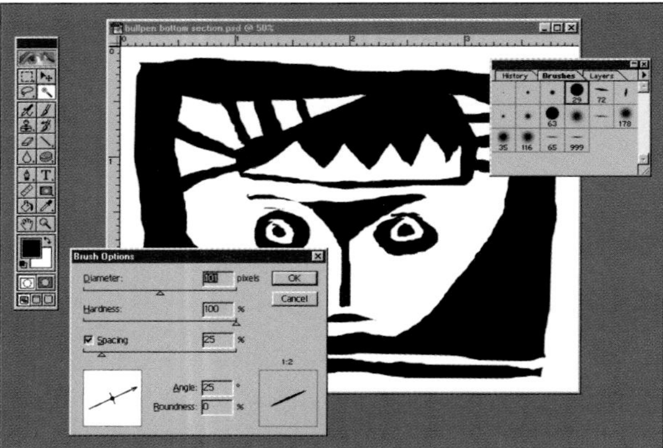

● 2.13

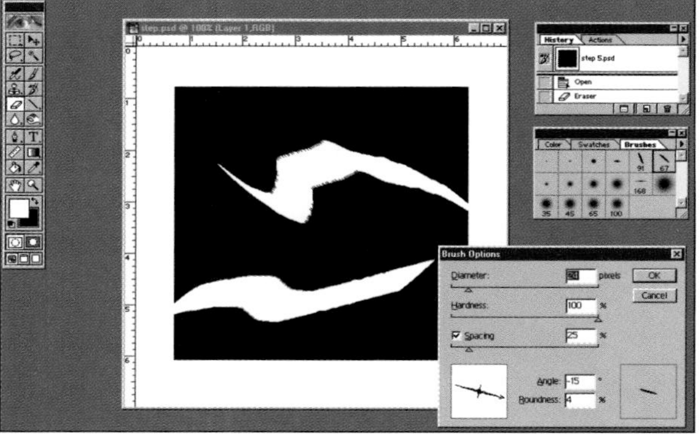

● 2.14

Certain core techniques are fundamental to my work, but the sequence of steps varies. I usually begin with my own pencil drawings, found objects, or photographs, which I scan into the computer. From there I follow where the piece takes me, revising with color and form, using the History palette to give the versatility of draft and redo. After digitally printing the image, I often create monotypes from the same image by adding effects with a variety of traditional materials, such as pastels, inks, acrylic glazes, and colored pencils.

Advice for Artists Working in the Digital Medium

I tend to be very pragmatic and organized in my approach. So first, I would suggest that — rather than random experimentation when using software for the first time — you think about the type of application you are trying to achieve and focus on learning only that application for a particular effect. Practice, practice, practice and save the steps so you know what decisions you made to create that image, and take notes as you go.

Another help has been to purchase the quick "how-to" books, study them, and use them as you play with the software. Also, artists should develop strong traditional drawing and painting skills to apply in the digital program.

Color Management

I work with only the color profiles that Photoshop and my Epson 3000 color printer offer, scanning in my own grayscale drawings, collages, photos, or found objects. When I add color within the computer, I usually work with what I see on the monitor, print artist's proofs, and readjust the color with the Photoshop color tools. Also, after the image is printed, I sometimes continue to modify the image with non-digital materials, frequently making a series of digital monotypes from a single image.

Output

Archival integrity is essential both to preserve work for myself and as a responsibility to my clients and gallery director. I try to stay as archival as possible with acid-free printmaking paper and special digital archival papers and inks.

My favorite output is the Epson Stylus Color 3000 Large Format Ink Jet Printer. In addition to traditional printmaking paper, I have started using professional digital fine art papers from Legion Paper Company. Of the seven papers that I have experimented with so far, my preference is Somerset photo enhanced/textured, which can be reworked with non-digital materials after printing.

Chapter 3

Three Voyeurs

by Alessandro Bavari

Artist's Statement

I prefer to work with a very vague concept, since it allows me more room for experimentation. My final artwork has often changed almost totally from the original idea.

The Story Behind the Artwork

Three Voyeurs (3.1) is one of an ongoing series of images about the biblical cities of Sodom and Gomorrah, which, the Bible story goes, were ultimately destroyed by God in his wrath at their sins and self-indulgence.

Alessandro imagined these two cities as a kind of amusement park for visionaries, where his gaze was neither accusing nor benevolent, but simply amused and curious, open to taking in as much as possible. What emerged was an enormous freak show designed with kitsch and geometrical rationality.

In short, he wanted the people of Sodom and Gomorrah to be happy, creative, and imaginative up to the very day of the apocalypse in which God, omnipotent and vexed by their excessive exuberance, decided to spread forevermore his immense black veil.

Alessandro considers his Sodom and Gomorrah series to be an open-ended project, too stimulating and enjoyable to be concluded, and to which he will continue to add images. It is an always-expanding project, like Sodom and Gomorrah would be if they had survived the Divine Wrath: irrational, chaotic, exuberant, and spontaneous — like all modern cities.

◀ 3.1

The Creative Process

Alessandro first modeled some of the ornate background objects (3.2) in Softimage 3D. The landscape and skyscape (3.3) are from a shot he took some years ago in Marok. The three men peering through the holes in the ground (3.4) are friends who kindly agreed to pose for him.

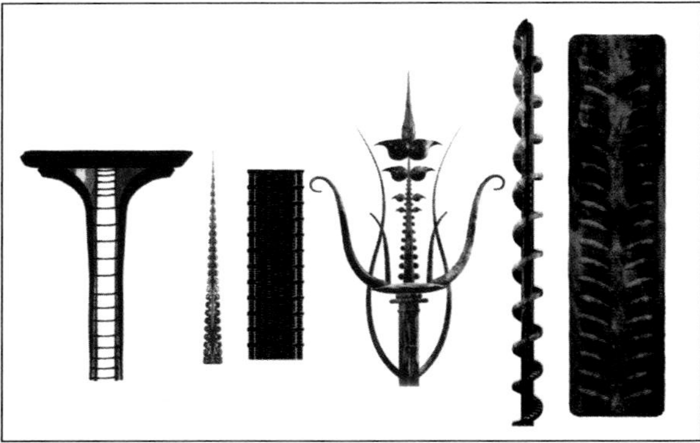

● 3.2

● 3.3

He started with a sketch of the composition. After scanning in the source pictures as grayscale images at 300 ppi, he converted the images to RGB in order to utilize all the parameters of control on the tones and color, such as levels, curves, color balance, selective color, and so on.

He composed everything in Photoshop. He added many different layers (over a hundred) with different degrees of transparency, following the same kind of style as when using oil paint, building up layer upon layer. He applied a variety of effects (such as Multiply, Luminosity, and Sharpen) and filters (sometimes up to ten times on the same part of the image), superimposed textures, added dust and scratches, and blurred and contrasted details. He did not go overboard on these manipulations, just letting the image develop in an intuitive, fluid, painterly way. As part of the process of adding texture and scratches, he scanned in some paintings he had done in oils and ink and scratch techniques (3.5).

Then he blended all the layers and flattened the image. He finally applied some effects on different parts of the whole image, very softly.

Alessandro spent approximately 48 hours on this painting.

● 3.4

About the Artist

Biography

Alessandro Bavari was born in Latina, a coastal town south of Rome, Italy. He studied art at the Academy of Fine Arts in Rome, where he developed a strong foundation in the techniques of oil, watercolors, and engraving. At the same time, he experimented with methods of mixing tar, glue, and industrial paint and explored photographic printing techniques. In 1993, he added digital manipulation to his art and developed a personal artistic language using industrial and organic products from nature. He then combined photographic process with computer digitalization, which he says led to, "Contamination among the art, dissolving the boundaries which distinguish them." Alessandro has had his artwork included in a long list of international periodicals and numerous exhibitions.

Influences

Alessandro is strongly influenced by Indo-European cultural myths and allegories. The works of Giotto, Michelangelo, Caravaggio, and Piero della Francesca and other artists of the 14th and 15th centuries have also

Technique: Creating a Hole in the Ground (Softimage 3D Extreme and Photoshop)

Alessandro created the holes in the ground in less than five minutes. This technique gives you an idea of the way he constructed the hole in Softimage 3D Extreme and integrated it into his main image in Photoshop.

1. **Create a section in your 3D software (3.6).**
2. **Apply a 360-degree rotation to the section (3.7).**
3. **Apply texture, utilizing UV mapping, to the object.** UV mapping is a method of taking a flat texture image and "wrapping" it around a complex 3D form so the texture appears to distort in a realistic way that matches the 3D form. The 3D form is often represented by a mesh, and the texture is mapped onto this mesh. This approach gives a more realistic effect than wrapping around simplified forms like cylinders, spheres, and cubes.
4. **Export the rotated section to Photoshop.**

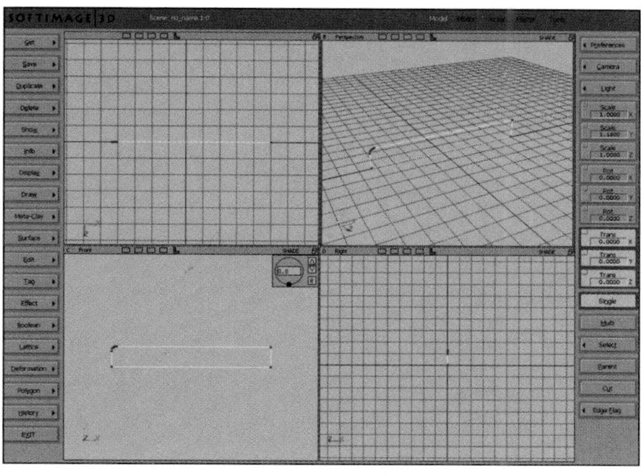

● 3.6

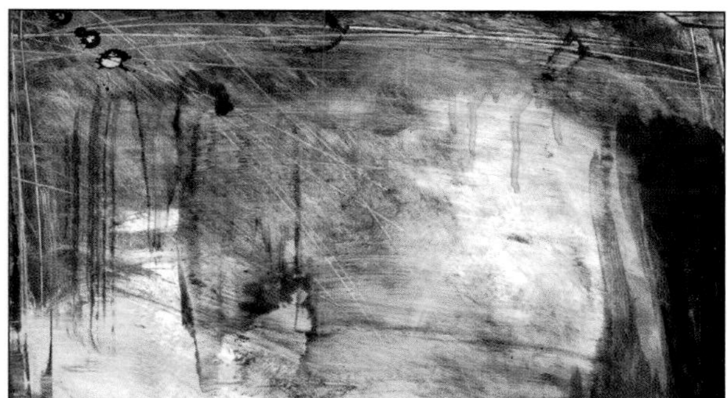

● 3.5

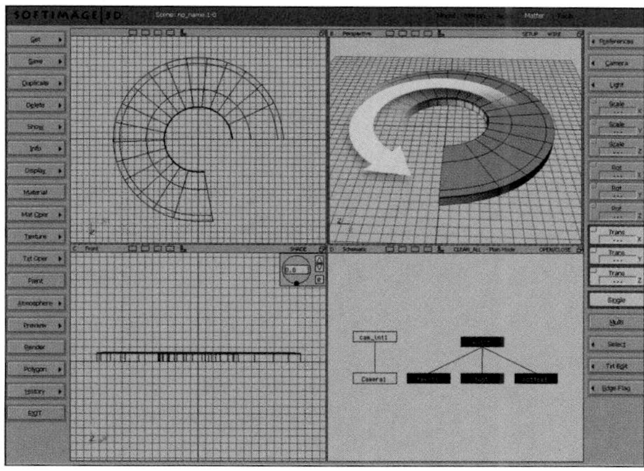

● 3.7

had a large influence on him. Elements such as the distorted perspectives of Giotto's pictures, or the plasticity of Michelangelo's suspended bodies have all had an impact. Even the Gothic and Flemish paintings of Northern Europe have been a reference point, from the surrealistic landscapes of Bosch to the solemn portraits of Van Eyck. The classic architecture of nearby Rome, and the Italian countryside also play a part in shaping his work. His contemporary cultural influences are the filmmakers Peter Greenaway and Shinya Tsukamoto who made the disturbing mechanical body horror film *Tetsuo*.

Studio

Computer System:
Macintosh G3, 350 MHz
40GB hard drive
704MB RAM
PC Intel, 1400 MHz
80GB hard drive
512MB RAM

Monitors:
Lacie Electron 21

Software:
Adobe Photoshop
After Effect
Media 100
Softimage (on PC)

Input Devices:
Umax Scanner
Minolta Film Scanner

Printers:
Epson Stylus Color 740

Contact

Alessandro Bavari
Latina, Italy
info@alessandrobavari.com
www.alessandrobavari.com

5. **Use Photoshop's Rubber Stamp tool to add texture to the imported "hole" image, drawing upon textures already in your main picture.**
6. **Using the Airbrush tool, create the same kind of light in the hole as there was on the main picture (3.8).**
7. **Use the Freehand Lasso tool to make a selection that cuts out the hole.**
8. **Choose Select→Feather.**
9. **Feather the selection by about 5 pixels.**
10. **Choose Edit→Copy (Cmd/Ctrl-C).**
11. **Select the main picture, into which you wish to place the hole, and choose Edit→Paste (Cmd/Ctrl-V).** This makes a perfect transition between the cut-out hole and the photograph (3.9).

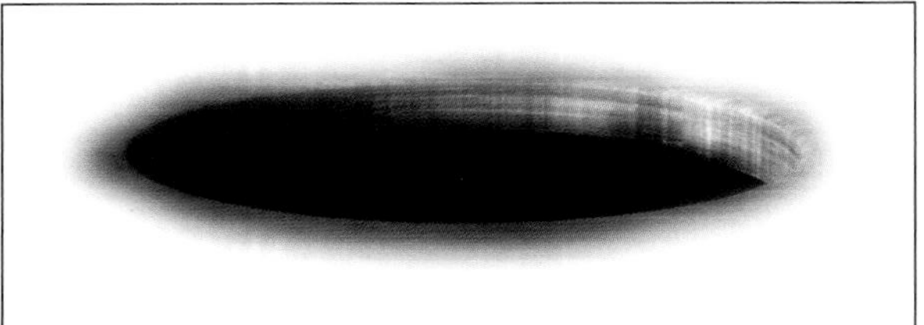

● 3.8

● 3.9

Anders F Ronnblom on Alessandro Bavari

"For excellence in digital art and design, using a mixture of digital tools, both 2D and 3D, for exciting and adventurous photography."

– Anders F Ronnblom, Editor in Chief, *EFX Art & Design* (`www.macartdesign.matchbox.se`)

Artist's Creative Insight and Advice

Why Digital?

I originally worked in the darkroom with traditional photography. When I discovered Photoshop I was really surprised about the total control of the image it gave me, plus the opportunity to undo and edit. I wanted to experiment, and, although nowadays processors are much faster, I really appreciated in those early days of Photoshop how much quicker it was to work digitally compared to traditionally.

I use Photoshop 4.0, rather than newer versions like 7.0. The 4.0 version for me is the better because it is like a true darkroom, with essential tools for the photographer, a very light version without an overload of unnecessary tools.

However, digital also has a downside. I hate that now everyone can be an artist just by applying several filters, one after another. That's why I use filters very rarely. I am very discriminating about the filters I use — they have to be very impressive and used sparingly.

Working in Black and White

Black and white is very useful for understanding shapes and lights, and is also very useful in keeping file sizes manageable when you work on big files. I convert to RGB just at the end, applying then some color balance, tone, and saturation.

Output

My favored output is to print my work on to photographic paper up to about 30 inches by 50 inches, using the Lambda system, which is like a large digital enlarger that writes the image directly to the paper using lasers based on the RGB colors.

Chapter 4

Shrine of ART

by Hiroshi Yoshii

Artist's Statement

I like to surprise people by the picture that my imagination produces.

The Story Behind the Artwork

Shrine of ART (4.1) was created as a facade (wall art) for a PC tradeshow exposition; it appeared on the wall of a booth about PC graphics.

In this piece, Hiroshi tried to show what he calls "caricatured art." There is a fantasy, caricature feel to the objects and creatures depicted. The finish of the surfaces has a slightly granular, chalky texture. The way Hiroshi creates this effect is described in the technique section later in this chapter.

The Creative Process

Hiroshi created the whole piece in Painter 5, using only two brush variants — a customized Large Chalk (4.2) from the Chalk (Dry Media) category and a customized Grainy Water (4.3) from the Water (Liquid) category.

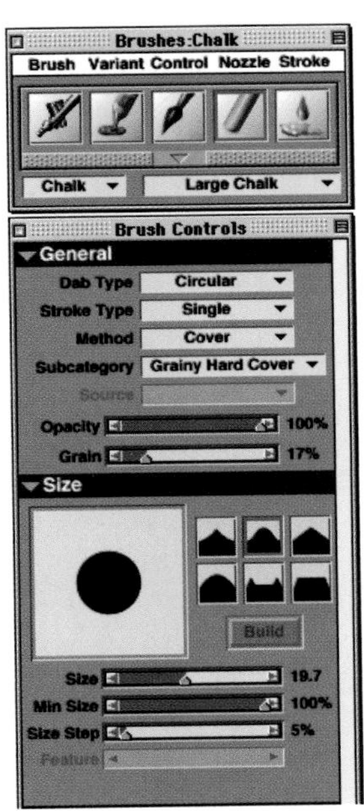

4.2

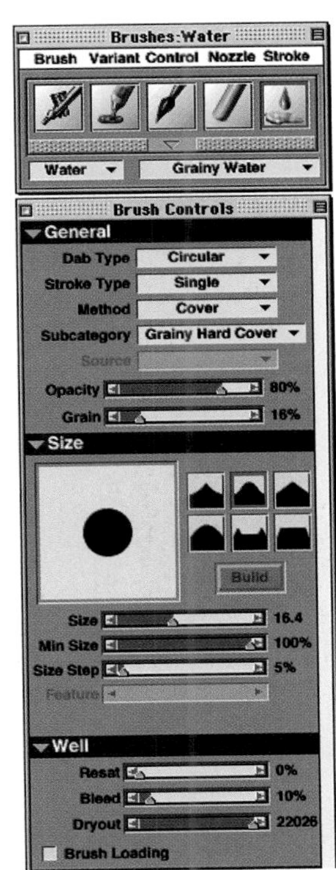

4.3

◀ 4.1

First, he drew a rough black-and-white line sketch (4.4).

At this point, Hiroshi generated a mask based on the black. He did this by generating a selection over the black portion of the image and then saving the selection in the form of a mask, which could be applied at any time in the future.

He then quickly filled in the line sketch with color to produce a rough color sketch (4.5), not worrying too much about precise edges.

He then clicked the "eye" next to the mask listed in the Mask section of the Objects palette (4.6), while making sure the RGB canvas was still active (highlighted in the Mask list) so any paint would be added to the canvas, not to the mask.

4.4

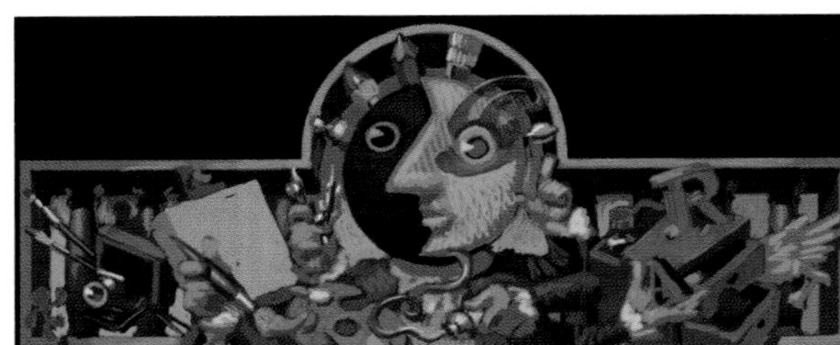

4.5

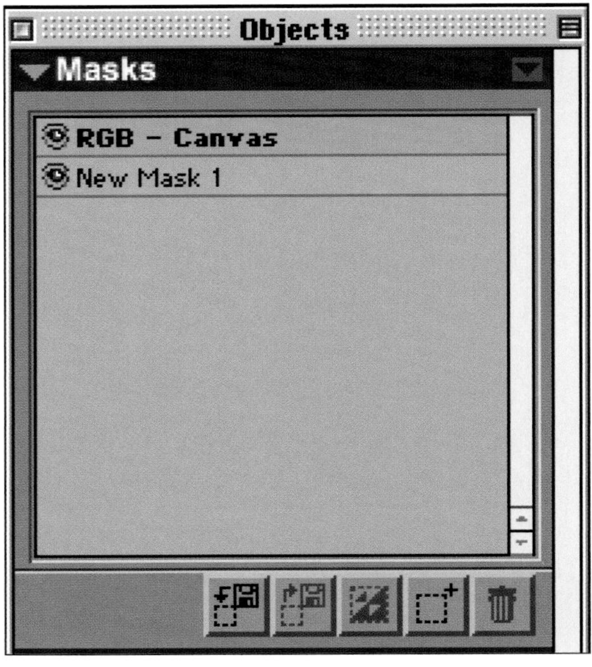

4.6

About the Artist

Biography

Hiroshi is an illustrator for books and magazines.

He was born near Nagoya, Japan, in 1962, and graduated from Nippon Designer Institute Nagoya in 1983. After working as a graphic designer in 1990, he started work as a freelance illustrator. Originally, he painted with Liquitex. In 1992, Hiroshi began to use Fractal Design Painter and the Macintosh computer. He wrote and published the books *Painter Wonderland, Hands on Painter!*, and *Painter Athletics.* He won the Grand Prix of "MetaCreations Beyond the Canvas Digital Art Competition" in 1998 with *Shrine of ART.*

In 2002, he wrote and published a book for Painter Classic. He also created two short animations with Painter for TVCF.

This caused the mask to be displayed, superimposed in red, over the rough color sketch (4.7). In this manner, the visibility of the mask acted as a visual reference while painting on the RGB canvas.

He then loaded the Ver 4 Paper Textures library and selected his favorite paper: Rougher (4.8), adjusting the scale of the paper to suit his image.

Hiroshi then drew in earnest, taking time to build up the shading and work into the precise details. He drew mainly with the Large Chalk, sometimes smoothing it with the Grainy Water. He would paint a dark color, juxtapose it with a light color, and in that way describe a shadow, sometimes inverting the texture as he did so.

● 4.7

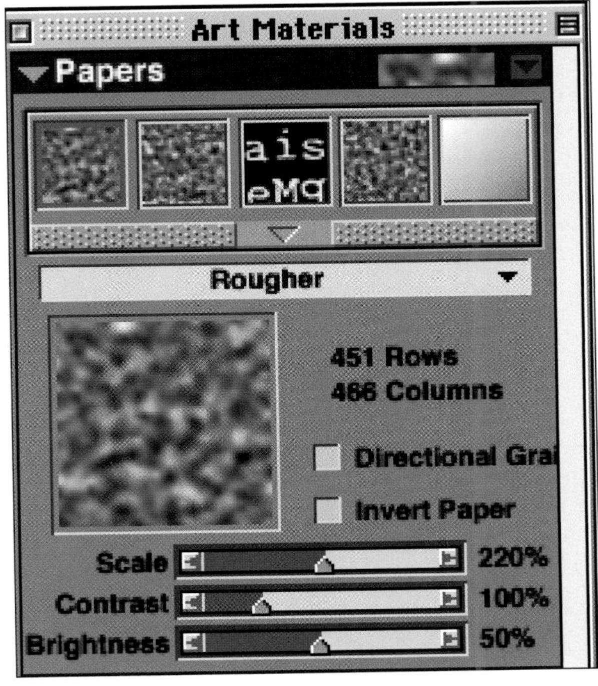

● 4.8

Influences

Many artists, cartoonists, and illustrators.

Studio

Computer System:
Apple Power Mac G4, 500 MHz
1GB RAM
Apple Cinema Display
Apple PowerBook G4, 500 MHz
1GB RAM
Sony PCV-LX91
512MB RAM
Windows 2000
Pen tablet LCD display

Tablet:
Wacom Intuos 6 x 8
Wacom Cintiq

Contact

Hiroshi Yoshii
Tokyo, Japan
hiroshi@yoshii.com
www.yoshii.com

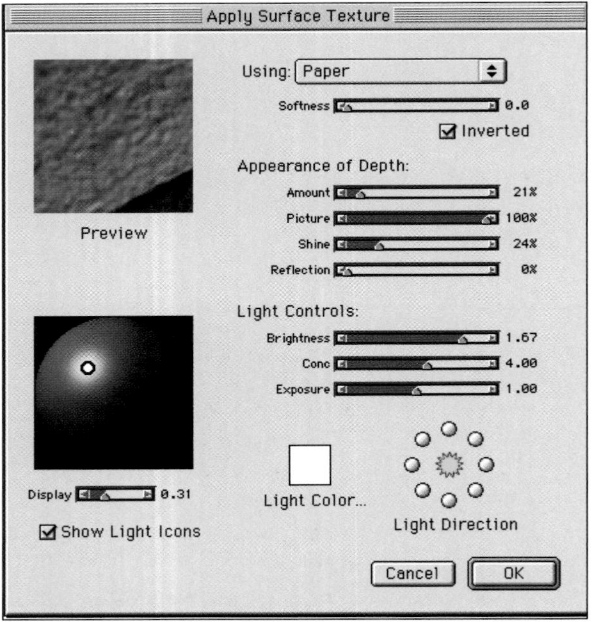

● 4.9

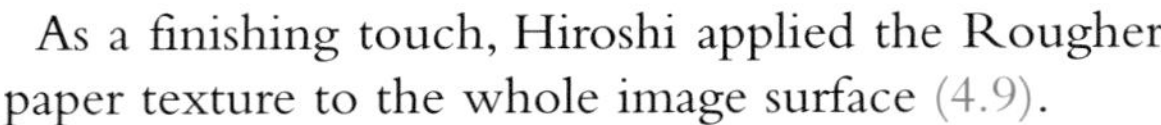

As a finishing touch, Hiroshi applied the Rougher paper texture to the whole image surface (4.9).

This created a uniform rough paper texture over the whole work, one of the elements of Hiroshi's distinctive style.

It took about one week to complete *Shrine of ART.*

Technique: Creating the "Hiroshi Chalk" Look (Painter)

This technique takes you through, step by step, the methodology that Hiroshi followed to create his beautiful and distinctive "Hiroshi Chalk" look.

1. **Open a blank canvas in Painter.**
2. **Choose the Large Chalk in the Dry Media category in the Brushes palette.**
3. **Choose black in the Colors section of the Art Materials palette.**
4. **Choose Load Library from the bottom of the Papers pop-up menu in the Art Materials palette.**

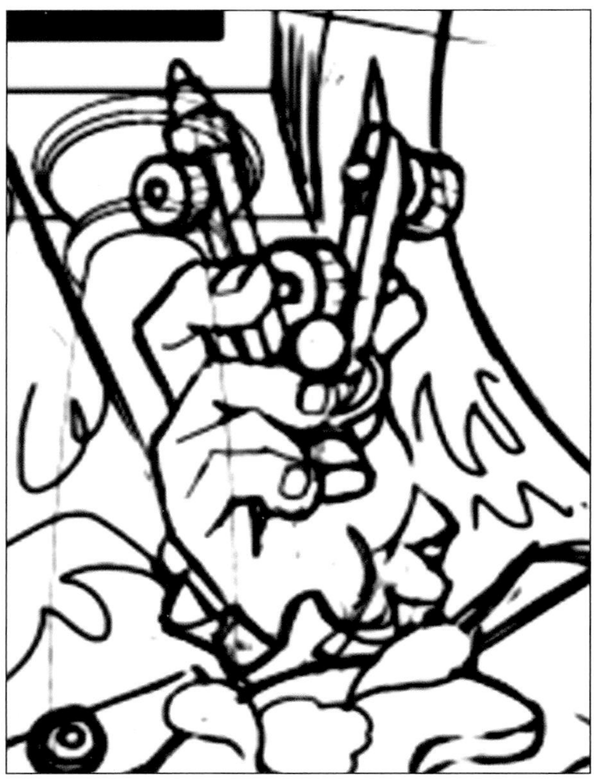

● 4.10

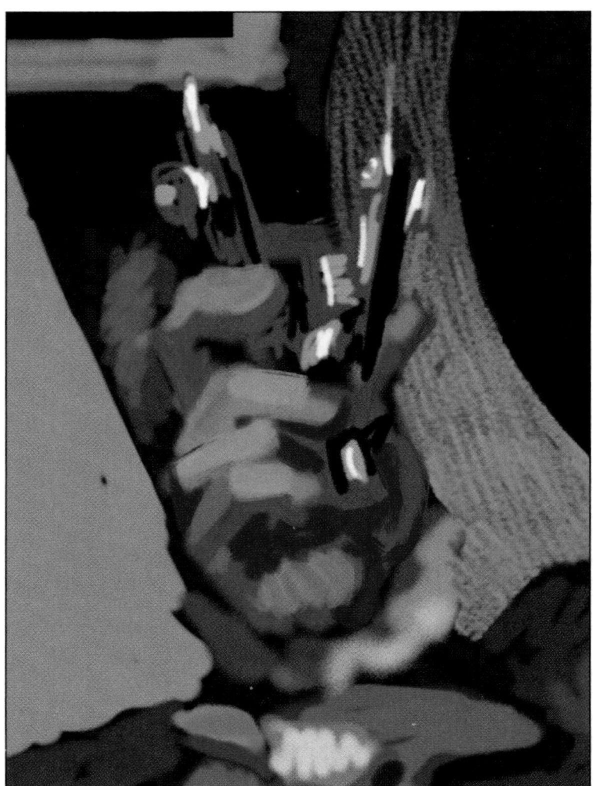

● 4.11

5. **Locate the Ver 4 folder in the Painter 7 application folder.**
6. **Select the Paper Textures library from within the Ver 4 folder.**
7. **Select the Rougher paper texture.**
8. **Draw a rough black line drawing outline of your design (4.10).**
   You can base the design on a scanned, hand-drawn sketch or digital photo, if you want. Otherwise, make something up from your imagination. Adjust the Chalk brush size to suit the line drawing.
9. **Choose Select→Auto Select with Using: Image Luminence.**
   This generates a selection over the black portion of your rough sketch.
10. **Choose Select→Save Selection.**
11. **Choose Select→ None (Cmd/Ctrl-D) to deselect the selection.**
    This saves the selection in the form of a mask. This mask can be applied at any time in the future to paint into, or apply effects, in the black portion of the image, or, by inverting the selection, to paint into, or apply effects, in the non-black portion of the image.
12. **Quickly fill in the shapes outlined in the sketch with color to produce a rough color sketch (4.11), not worrying too much about precise edges.**

TIP

You may want to enlarge your chalk at this stage.

13. **Click the "eye" next to the mask listed in the Mask section of the Objects palette, making sure that the RGB canvas is still active (highlighted in the Mask list) so the paint is added to the canvas, not to the mask.**
    The open eye causes the mask to be displayed, superimposed in red, over the rough color sketch. Use the displayed mask as a visual reference as you paint on the canvas.
14. **Using the Large Chalk for painting, the mask for reference, and, from time to time, the Grainy Water (Liquid category) for blending, build up detail in your image (4.12 to 4.17).**

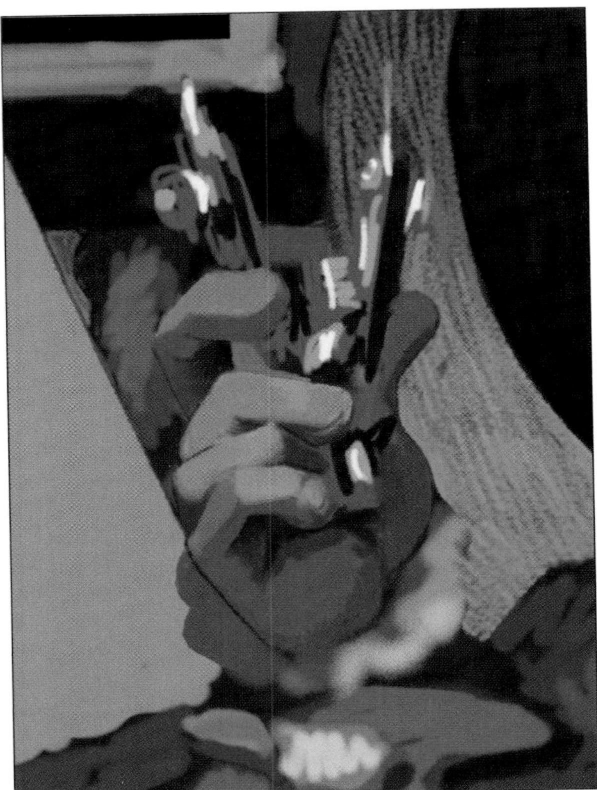

● 4.12

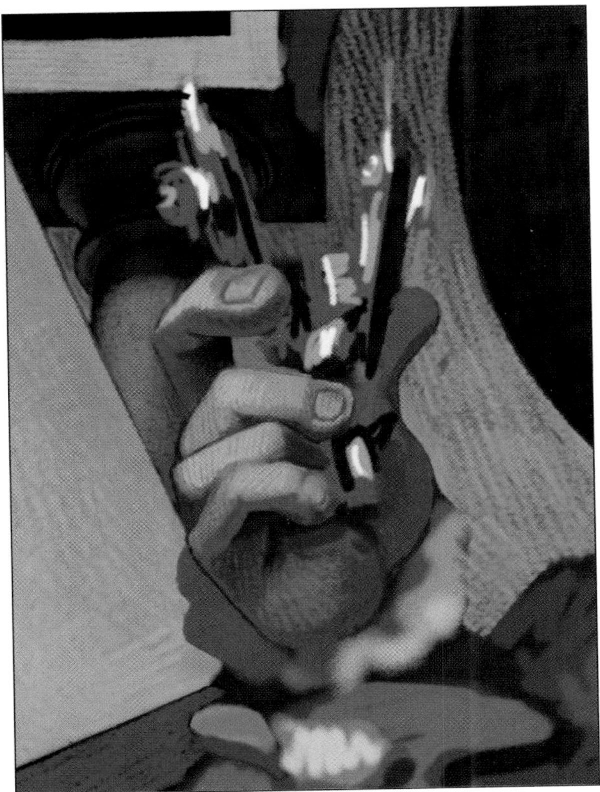

● 4.13

15. **Choose Effects➔Surface Control➔Apply Surface Texture with the Using menu set to Paper.**
16. **Click OK to give the final texturization to the image (4.18).**

Artist's Creative Insight and Advice

Why Digital?

I can't stand traditional techniques because of the very long time they take. Traditional techniques can't keep up with my imagination, where as digital can go just as fast as my imagination!

Advice for Artists Working in the Digital Medium

Take the time you need to create work digitally. Don't be in a rush! Working digitally is many times faster than working traditionally.

Color Calibration

I use a post-script printer with print color simulation. I adjusted the color of my screen to the optimum. I use an Epson Stylus Photo 2000P that produces prints that are beautiful and excellent in lightfastness and quality.

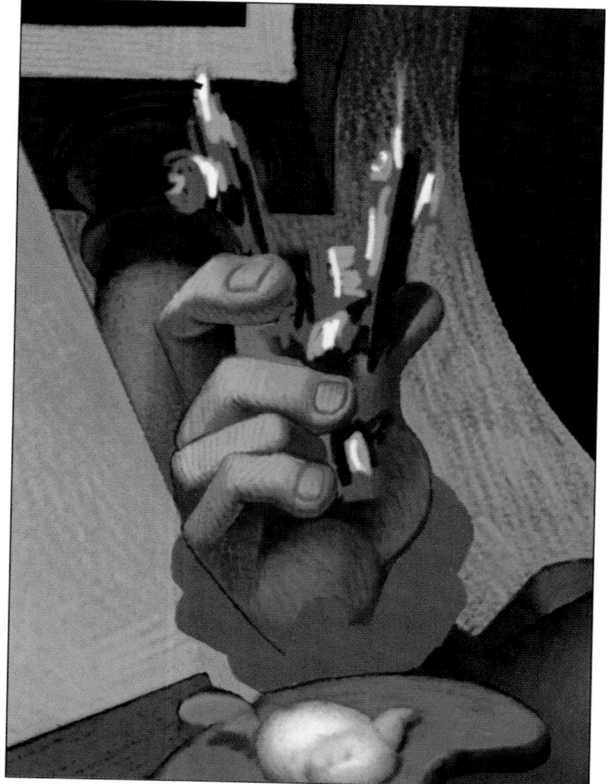

● 4.14

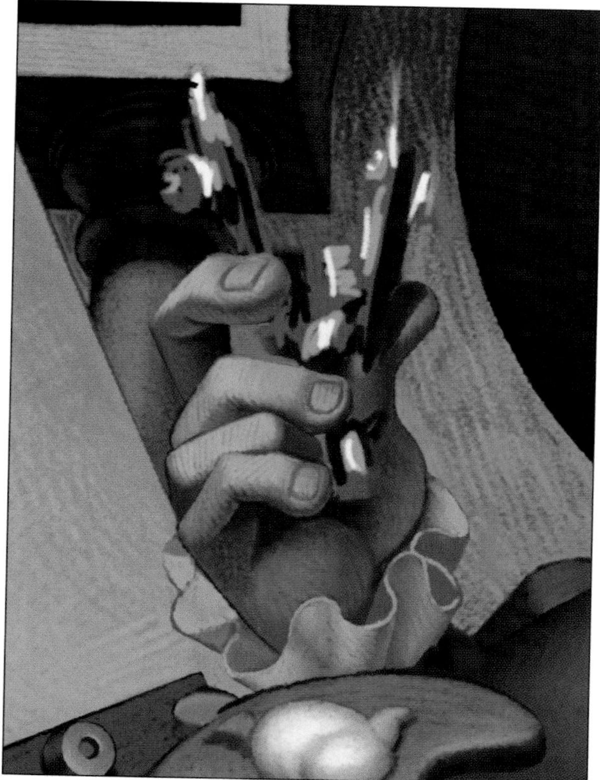

● 4.15

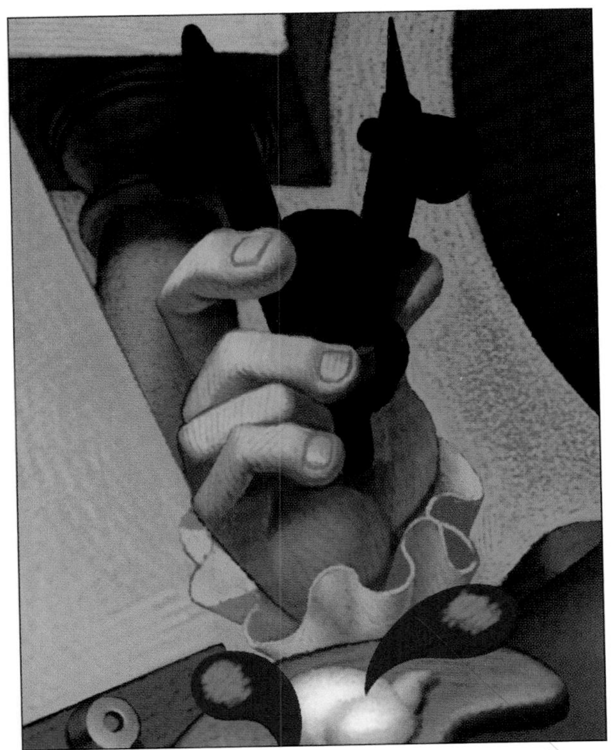

4.16

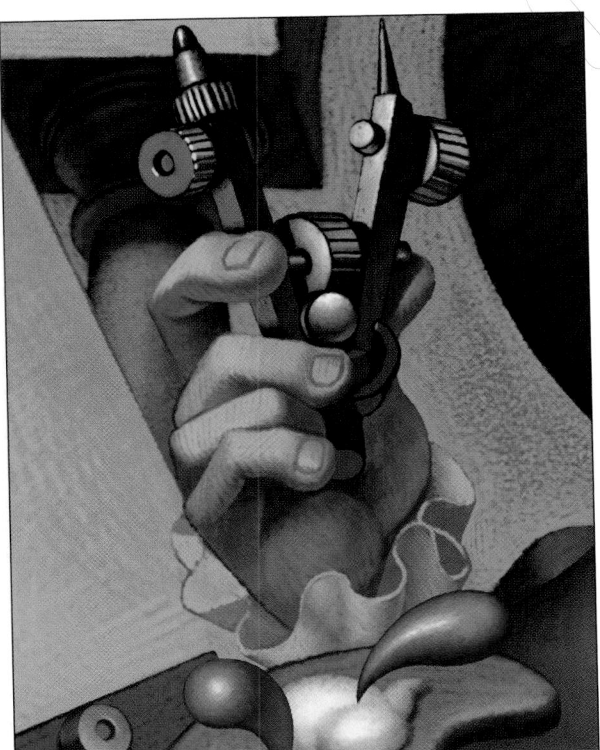

4.17

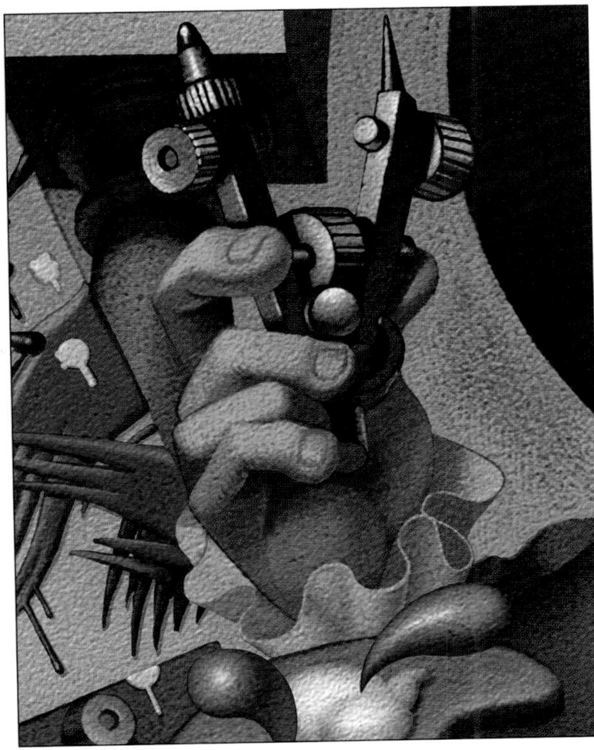

4.18

Chapter 5

The Running Dress

by Kent Oberheu

Artist's Statement

Pixel-based images are just really tiny mosaics with a whole lot of colors; vector art is like film noir — it's based on tension and location. In the end, it's all just a big string of 1s and 0s on a disc spinning around in circles until you turn it off. "Ah yes . . ." you say, "but is it art?"

The Story Behind the Artwork

The Running Dress (5.1) is an image generated by mathematics. In technical terms, it came about from an exploration of a four-dimensional, fractal object in 3D space. Kent used software called POV-Ray, which creates the effect of painting in 3D, as if brush strokes of paint were pulled through space, and the paint was frozen in the air.

Having worked as a traditional artist, Kent wanted to get away from intentional works, where he set out to build a composition from a preconceived notion. After experimenting with several approaches, he discovered a technique that fit his needs.

He could explore a vast amount of visual territory by manipulating some simple mathematical procedures with computer code, instead of using explicit tools, like paint brushes. With this approach, half the process is visually evaluating what has been accomplished (involving looking at many results), and working out the way the controls and adjustments of the procedure effect the visual results. The artistry comes about by steering the mathematical process towards a visual goal.

Kent found that the outcome of procedures takes on a life of its own, and many times, the outcome can't be predicted. *The Running Dress* embodies this. Kent didn't set out to create a dress frozen in space, yet that was what he found, and it was interesting and unique.

◀5.1

The Creative Process

At the time this image was created, between 1996 and 1997, Kent wanted to explore a 3D shape which wasn't visible in any real-time methods then available, until rendered in a 3D program such as POV-Ray's raytracing engine (POV-Ray is open source freeware).

Kent generated a series of preview frames. Each preview frame took approximately four minutes for a thumbnail-sized representation of the 3D form. He spent several days playing with the algorithm (mathematical equation) that defined the 3D form. This algorithm had four variables that determined the shape of the 3D form. Kent started by adjusting the values of these four variables and rendering many preview frames, making educated guesses on new settings for the variables as he went.

Finally, in an act of frustration, realizing that the process was consuming far too much time, Kent decided to use an animation technique to automate his testing of visual results. In technical terms, he took each variable of the equation and ran it through an independently cycling loop over time using sine waves of different frequencies. The effect is similar to several swimmers in the same pool paddling at different rates on the surface of the water. A series of waves emanates from each swimmer and collides with the others waves producing unpredictable results.

Kent set up a three-hundred frame, low resolution animation of the values of the fractal object, then he distributed the frames of the animation to four separate computers to render overnight. After the

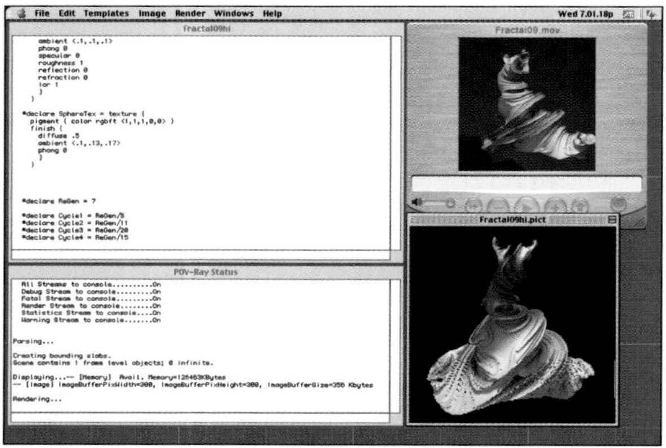

● 5.2

About the Artist

Biography

Kent has a Bachelor of Fine Arts degree in Visual Communication from the University of Kansas, Lawrence. Upon graduation, he worked in the trade show graphics industry, and developed techniques to create very high-resolution illustrations and graphics. Kent has worked with F. Kenton Musgrave, and Benoit Mandlebrot, and won Best of Show at Macworld Conference and Expo 2000 for the piece, *The Running Dress.* He has also exhibited at SIGGRAPH 2001 and IMMEDIA 2002.

Influences

Vaughn Oliver because of his great sense of combining classical and abstract elements. Kent's father, an architect, also had a great influence on his development in the arts. Other influences include Lyonel Feininger, Eliel and Eero Saarinen, Alexander Calder, Frank Lloyd Wright, Giorgio De Chirico, Umberto Boccioni, Lebbeus Woods, Frank Gehry, Saunders Shultz, Ernest Trova, and Henry Moore.

sequence was finished, he compiled the frames into a movie. He played the animation back and wrote down the frame number from the movie where he found the shape that was most interesting. He then retrieved the values that produced the desired shape. Then began the process of tweaking the values and rotating the object into the final position. Five light sources were used in the final scene with some subtle off-axis lighting to create hue shifts around the edges of the form.

When the scene file was to his liking at low resolution, he rendered the image to 6000 x 6000 pixels. The render in POV-Ray took 149 hours on his 120 MHz PowerPC (5.2).

The final render was then composited in Photoshop (5.3) with a subtle gradient and ground shadow to produce the final image at 7000 x 7000 pixels (see the technique later in this chapter).

Kent spent about 30 hours manipulating the scene file prior to the high resolution render, 149 hours rendering the final resolution image, and another 15 hours manipulating the gradient, testing several options, then compositing the final high resolution image. Added together, the "hands-on" hours were approximately 45 hours, and the unattended rendering time was 149 hours.

The background gradient is deceptively subtle. The gradient traverses 5000 pixels with less than 200 shades of red without banding. Kent invented debanding techniques for prepress and exhibit graphics operations that enabled illustrations to be enlarged to the size of a 30-foot wall while maintaining subtle tonal effects. He applied these debanding techniques in this piece.

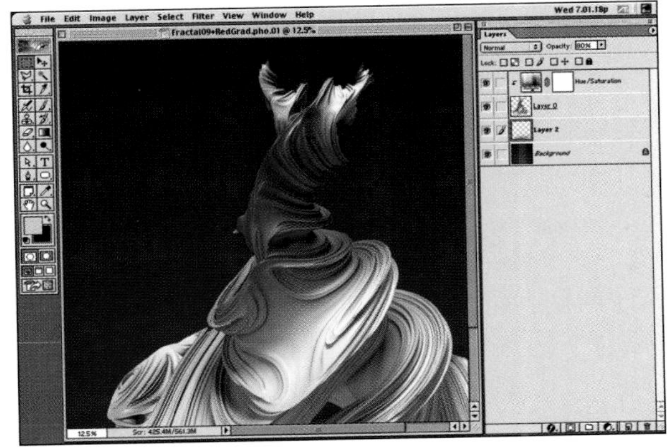

● 5.3

Studio

Computer System:
PowerMac G4, 400 MHz
10GB hard drive
1.5GB RAM
PowerMac G3, 500 MHz
2GB hard drive
684MB RAM

Monitors:
5-inch Pallet Monitor (G4)
17-inch Monitor (G3)

Software:
Adobe Photoshop
Adobe Illustrator
POV-Ray
Adobe After Effects
Maxon Cinema 4D
bhodiNUT SLA and Jenna
Pandromeda MojoWorld

Tablet:
Wacom 4 x 5 Graphire (G3)
Wacom Intuos 6 x 8 (G4)

Input Devices:
Canon Elura

Removable Media:
Iomega Zip
JAZ 2

Archive Media:
DAT DDS-3 backup through Dantz Retrospect

Printers:
Epson Stylus Photo 1280
HP LaserJet 4000

Contact

Kent Oberheu
Berkeley, California
k_oberheu@semafore.com
www.semafore.com

Technique: Adding a Shadow to a 3D Object (Photoshop)

This technique shows the simple way that Kent filled the background with a gradient and painted a realistic shadow onto his rendered 3D object.

1. **Open an image in Photoshop that contains a 3D shape against a black background which has an alpha channel mask.**
   Most 3D programs allow you to export a 2D image like this.
2. **Select the alpha channel in the Channels palette.**
3. **Click the selection symbol (the small marching ants circle) at the bottom of the Channels palette.**
   Doing so selects the background (5.4).
4. **Select the Gradient tool (5.5).**
5. **Select a gradient from the Gradient tool options pop-up menu (5.6).**
6. **Drag the Gradient tool in the background selection.**
   This fills the background with the gradient.
7. **Select New Layer in the Layers pop-up menu (5.7).**
8. **Select the Airbrush tool.**
9. **Select black as the foreground color.**
10. **Set the New Layer to be in Multiply mode.**
11. **Use the airbrush to paint in the shadow on the new layer (5.8).**
12. **Adjust the new layer opacity in the Layers palette to give a satisfactory shadow.**

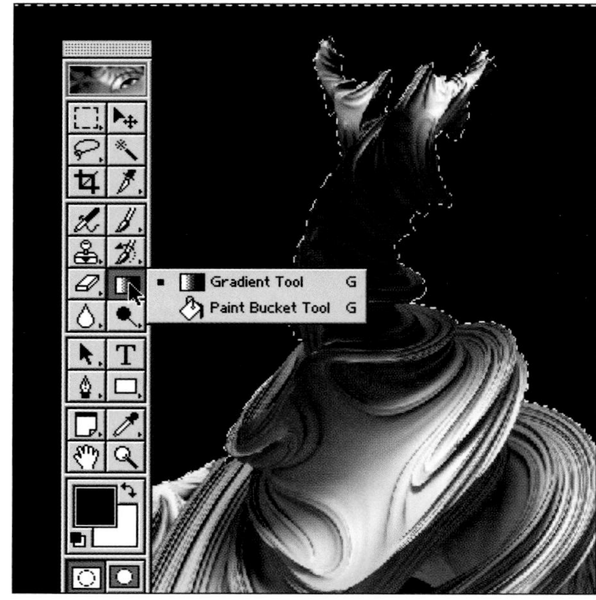

● 5.5

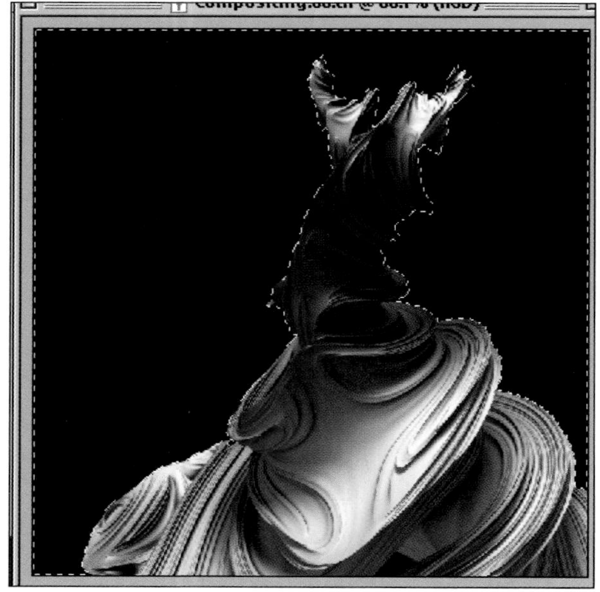

● 5.4

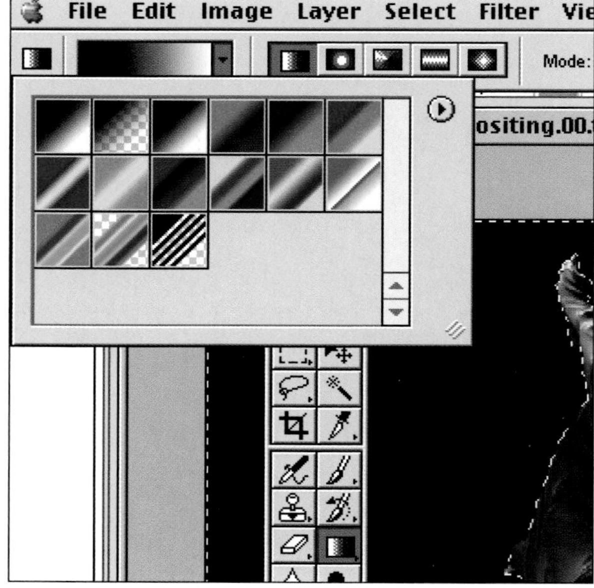

● 5.6

[NOTE]

Kent didn't use the black channel to extract the object, then delete the background from the layer, duplicate the layer, and make this the shadow because, though the silhouette could be used as a drop shadow for the layer, it would make it look like the object was cut out of a 2D plane floating in front of another 2D plane.

The shadow was created as a low-resolution soft shadow, painted with very large brushes in subtle tones to build it up to the desired look. Kent studied the lighting of the model to carefully place the shadow so as to make the object appear suspended over the background, as if frozen in space. The shadow emulates the softness and the direction of the light that using the silhouette would not achieve.

13. **Choose Image→Adjust→Curves (5.9).**
14. **Adjust the curves to add any desired color cast you want to be applied in the shadow.**

[TIP]

Kent used the Curves tool, rather than the Hue/Saturation tool, to add a color cast because the Hue/Saturation tool creates a lot of banding. The subtle gradation across the span of this image is 7000 pixels across. Curves can remap each of the Red, Green, and Blue channels independently giving far greater tonal subtlety than the Hue/Saturation tool.

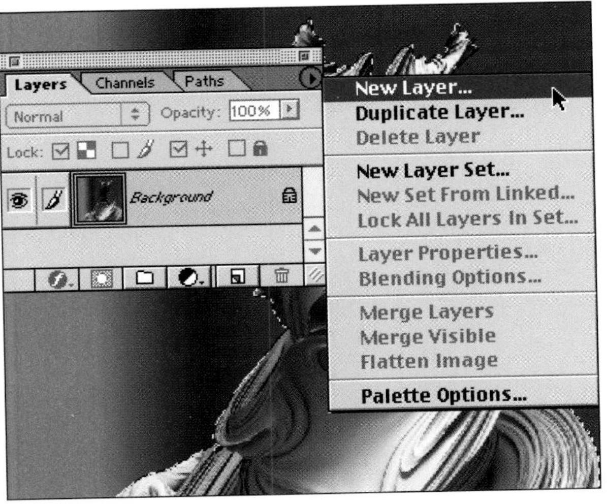

5.7

Artist's Creative Insight and Advice

Why Digital?

Working in the digital medium, an artist has flexibility that extends creativity to new realms. Since the digital medium holds raw data and artwork in the

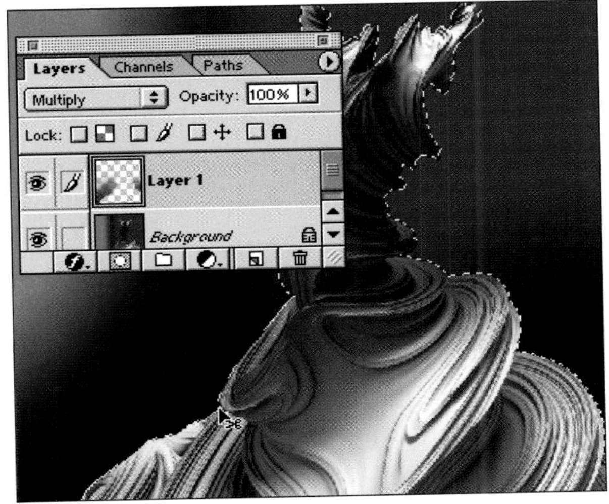

5.8

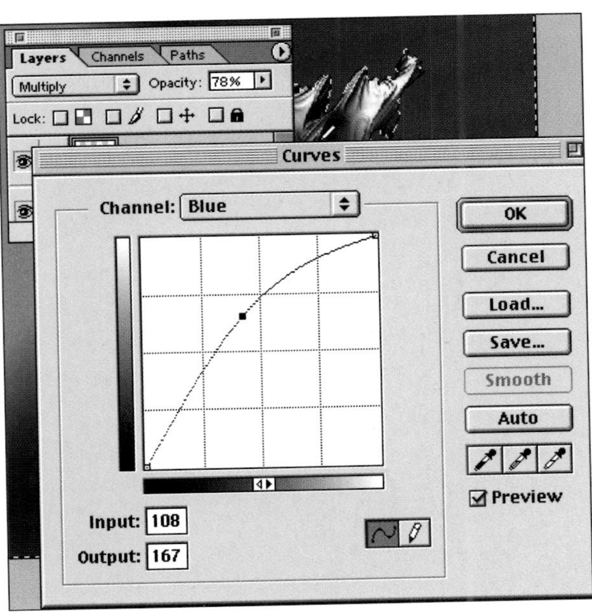

5.9

same format, data can be manipulated, and computation of complex mathematical algorithms can be explored to produce works previously unimaginable.

I've found that the digital realm enables me to concentrate on two aspects of what are in my view, most important in art: "ideas" and ease of manipulation to accomplish the goal of a piece of work. The combined benefit of this is that an idea can be linked to a set of parameters that bring the idea into a visualization. Several ideas can be explored and their parameters blended into a new visualization. Manipulating the elements of a composition, juxtaposing objects, and adjusting their scale and relationship are key to the development of an image or model or scene. To me, this is the heart of the creative process, where the artist experiments at progressively higher levels until the goal of realizing the initial idea is achieved.

It is similar to sketching; only the sketch is used as the foundation directly in the final piece. I usually do traditional sketching with pen and paper before starting a work but with a somewhat different goal. I am a firm believer that knowing a direction is crucial prior to heading out into the unknown. However, I tend to break that process early when I see where to go, and start work in 2D and 3D on the computer.

Artists push and bend their medium to the point where they are comfortable with their result. Look at any number of modern artists who forged new definitions of their media. I feel the digital realm is the most flexible of all, allowing for blending of ideas, data, animation, and sound in one environment. Wonderful things happen when you channel an otherwise unassociated medium to drive creation in another. Tools take on new forms. That is my ultimate goal in using the computer as a tool for creation. The digital realm is incredibly flexible at high and low levels of the process.

Advice for Artists Working in the Digital Medium

Don't be intimidated by mathematical code. Find new ways to explore how you can generate, control, and influence an image. It's what a computer is ultimately best at doing.

Push the limits of output devices and work to develop better methods for bringing digital work into the physical realm.

Work in RBG

Never work in CMYK unless you are using the medium of offset lithography or silkscreen as your sole means of output and don't mind the limitations of the colorspace. CMYK is a colorspace for printing, not a true colorspace. RGB is the widest colorspace and can best accommodate the full spectrum of color. It can be separated to CMYK, CcMmYK, and Hexachrome. Don't scan to CMYK on a scanner, unless you are outputting directly to a color printer profiled to match the scan.

Output

I like the recent developments that have occurred in the Epson line of printers, though I first fell in love with the Iris Giclee printers. The Epson line seems to be more affordable, and nearly the same quality as the early Iris prints. The increased color gamut of the CcMmYK printers is really remarkable when used with archival papers specially prepared for inkjet output.

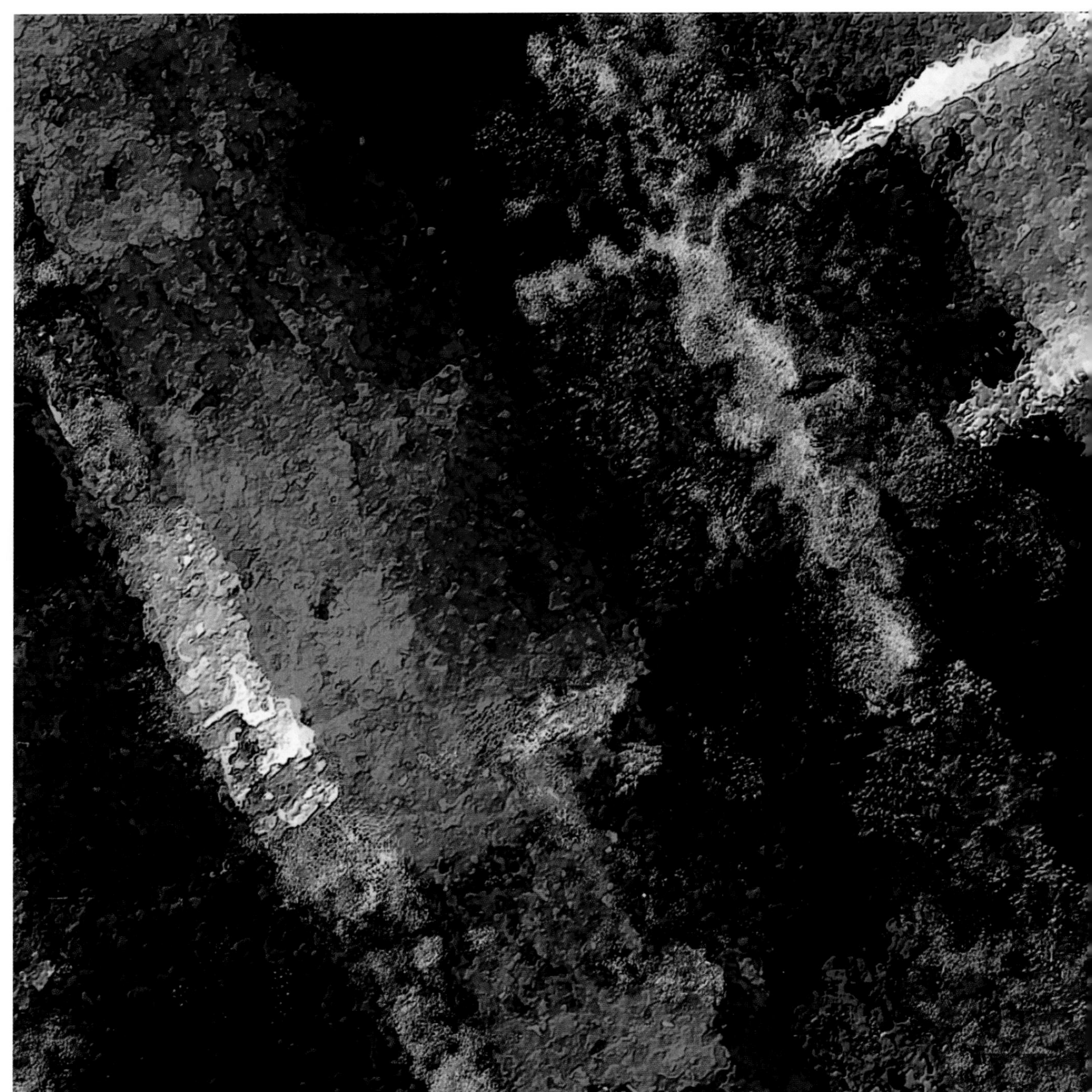

Chapter 6

Hollywood & Vine

by Catherine Elliot

Artist's Statement

My art has always come from a desire to please the eye. I want people to enjoy the beauty of color and texture. I love the process of art, and I have tried to portray dimension and depth in digital art that is drawn from my experience with clay and paper.

The Story Behind the Artwork

The inspiration for *Hollywood & Vine* (6.1) was a piece of Japanese paper that Catherine had made. She didn't scan the paper, but rather used its texture and tonality as a starting point. Catherine, originally a ceramist and traditional abstract artist, is very inspired by textures. She doesn't copy the texture but simply lets it take her where it goes. In this fashion, Catherine is a process artist.

The Creative Process

She started in Painter, using mostly Impasto brushes to create a lot of texture. Each color was painted on a separate layer, allowing her as much leeway to change things around as possible.

After the piece was composed in Painter, Catherine brought it into Photoshop where she played with several filters, such as the Spatter, Rough Pastels, Watercolor, and Dry Brush filters, applying them to various layers. Although Photoshop's "artistic" filters are not as organic or "real" as Painter's brushes, when

◀6.1

used over layers that are painted in Painter, they can add wonderful effects. Catherine also used a paintbrush set to the Dissolve blending mode to paint the yellow areas. Layers themselves were set to different blending modes. Catherine played a lot with the opacity of the various layers.

Hollywood & Vine took about 40 hours to complete.

Technique: Creating and Applying a Seamless Pattern (Photoshop)

This technique describes how Catherine generated a seamless pattern and then applied it to layers in her composition.

1. **Create a 1-inch square new file in Photoshop at the resolution of the final piece.**
2. **Use various brushes and painting tools in both Painter and Photoshop to paint an abstract pattern.**
3. **Choose Filter→Other→Offset.**
4. **Set the offset to 50% of the horizontal and vertical size of the document, with the Wrap Around option checked (6.2).**

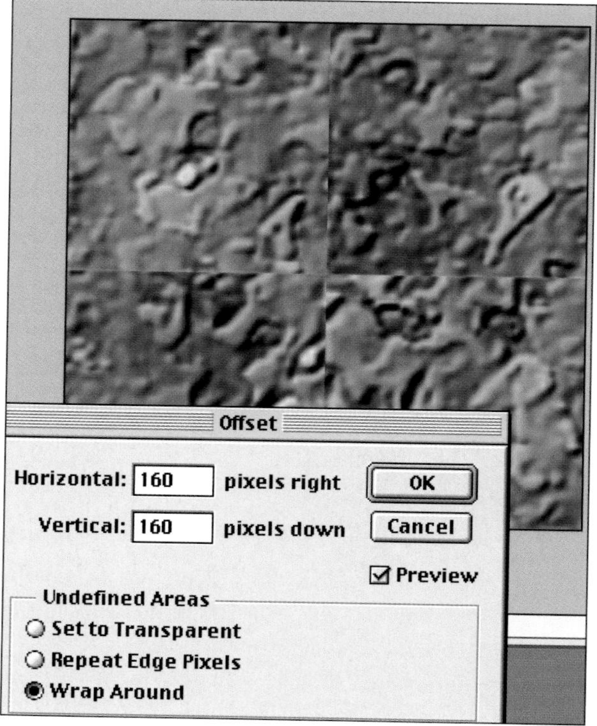

6.2

Notice the lines that appear on the image when you do this (6.3).

dS

About the Artist

Biography

Catherine began her art career as a ceramist, making large abstract wall pieces, and had several shows. However, shipping ceramic art to shows around the country wasn't cost effective, so she changed her medium to handmade paper. Catherine has always loved the process of art, and she found that with paper she could achieve much of the tactile quality of clay without the cost of weight and breakage. She also painted, using both oils and acrylics, and originally thought she would use the computer as a "sketch pad" for developing ideas before transferring them to canvas. She soon realized that the computer was simply another tool, or brush, she could use to create artwork from beginning to end. For the last nine years, she has been using her Wacom pen like a brush, and has printed directly from the computer. Catherine's digital art has won several awards, including the Strathmore Greeting Card Award, and Seybold Digital Art Contests in San Francisco 2001, and New York, 2002.

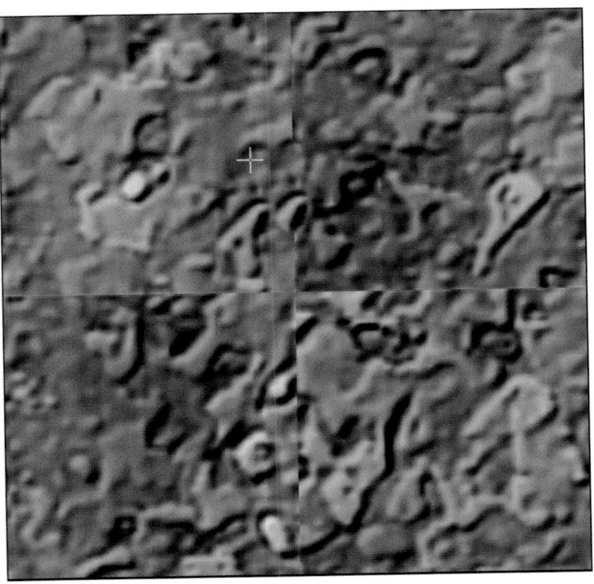

● 6.3

5. **Choose the Clone Stamp tool (also known as the Rubber Stamp tool).**
6. **By setting the clone source point within the document (Option/Alt-click), clone out the lines created by the Offset filter.**

   The pattern now appears to flow seamlessly (6.4).

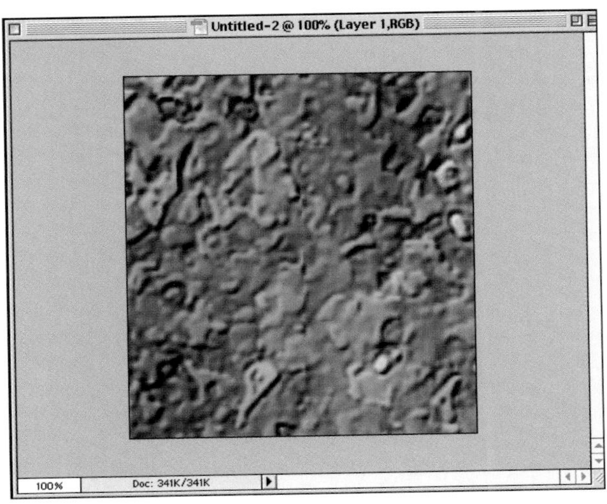

● 6.4

7. **Choose Edit→Define Pattern and then name the pattern (6.5).**

Influences

Georgia O'Keeffe and Sam Francis.

Studio

Computer System:
Power Macintosh G4
120GB hard drive
1.5GB RAM

Monitors:
2 x 21 Viewsonic Monitors

Software:
Adobe Photoshop
Procreate Painter
Adobe Illustrator

Tablet:
6 x 8 Wacom Intuos Graphics Tablet

Input Devices:
Epson Perfection 1200 Photo Flatbed

Removable Media:
100MB Zip Drive
1GB Jaz Drive

Archive Media:
16x/10x/40x Que Firewire CDRW drive

Printers:
HP Laserjet 5MP
Epson 1520
Epson 2000P

Contact

Catherine Elliot
Los Angeles, California
`Catherine@cathart.net`
`www.cathart.net`

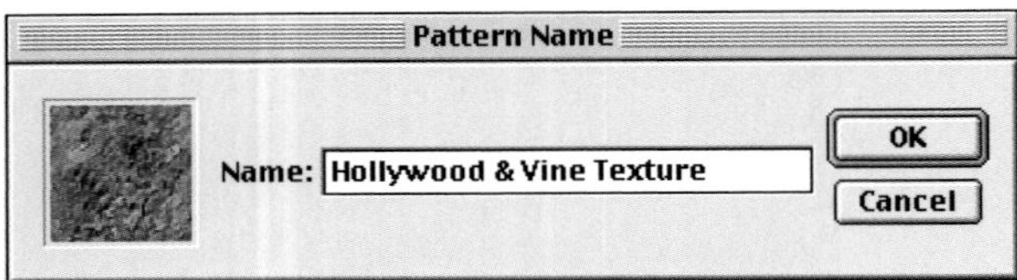

● 6.5

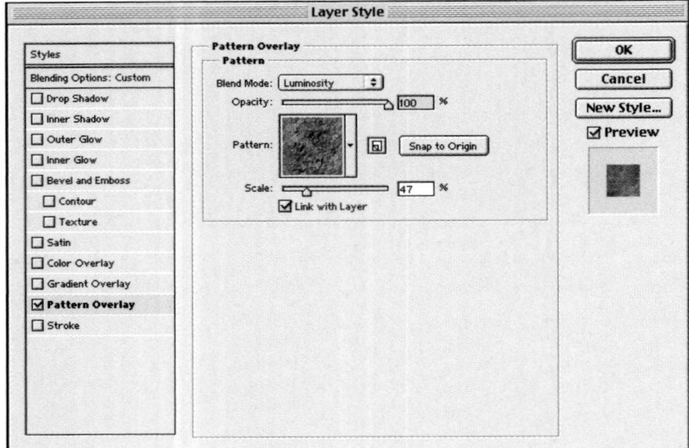

● 6.6

8. **Choose Layer→Layer Style→Pattern Overlay.**
9. **In the Pattern Overlay window (6.6), set the Blend Mode to Luminosity, which maintains the color on the layer. Apply the color to individual layers, using the saved pattern at different scales to create some variance.**

The pattern repeats over the entire layer. As an alternative to this step, you can choose the Pattern Stamp tool and then apply the pattern to various parts of different layers, with the layer Blend Mode set to Luminosity.

Judge's Critique

Seybold Digital Art Contest, New York, 2002

"The painting shows good surface design. There are eroded, splotchy areas.

The use of color is bold. All-in-all, it's interesting in nuance."

– MARK ZIMMER

Artist's Creative Insight and Advice

Why Digital?

I originally intended to use the computer as a convenient sketch pad and an easy way to try out variations prior to transferring the image to a "real" canvas. Then I asked myself why I was doing that — the computer was a valid art medium in itself. Working on a computer gives me the ability to be much more spontaneous than I was able to be with traditional media. It also allows me to take more chances — if it doesn't work, I can just erase it. Of course, I am always challenged by the fact that I worked three dimensionally for so long, using clay and paper. So I try to bring that feeling to my digital art.

The most difficult part of painting on the computer for me is to know when to stop. By using separate layers for each stage of a painting, I can backtrack easily, and often in the end, throw away many layers. In other words, my last step is usually to simplify a painting. This is something I could never do when I worked with natural media. I know that this painting has more of a digital feel than a natural feel, but to me that is simply the character of the digital medium. I don't try to avoid the digital look. After all, an oil painting looks like it was created with oil paints, acrylic paintings look like they were created with acrylics, and a watercolor definitely looks like a watercolor. To me, a digital painting is what it is, and it's just like using another medium. My digital art looks very much like art I have created in other media, at least in terms of style. It's just a different kind of paint.

Abstract Art and Naming

I never start out with a name for a piece. I work this way because, to me, abstract art is a visual experience which develops as I paint. I know when a piece is done, and then I name it. That way, I don't feel constrained by a concept, and I don't feel that a picture has to fit a particular title. I named *Hollywood & Vine* after I had finished it.

Learning Software

I recommend learning to use graphics software as you would learn how to use a certain kind of paint or paper. If you don't know the software, you don't know what is possible. It's like trying to fire a kiln without understanding why you must achieve a certain temperature.

Handling Large Files

I have a lot of RAM on my machine, and two dedicated 4GB scratch disks. That way, I never really need to worry about Photoshop choking on a large image. I do usually get out of Painter before the image gets too large, since Photoshop handles massive files better than Painter does. Sometimes a working image can grow to over a gigabyte, especially if I want the freedom to print it at a large size. I add a different layer for each stage, only occasionally merging them. I do trash layers if they're really not working for me, but I like to give myself the freedom to play.

Color Correction

Because my work is abstract in nature, I am less attached to perfect color than if I were trying to represent something recognizable. I always print out images on my desktop inkjet printer, but allow for a certain latitude in color reproduction. I enjoy this freedom as a change from doing commercial projects. So far, by using accepted methods of printing, I have had good luck in reproducing my images.

DOWNEY
NORWALK
FULLERTON
BELLFLOWER
LAKEWOOD
BUENA PARK
ORANGE
TUSTIN
SANTA ANA
LONG BEACH
COSTA MESA
IRVINE
KEY PLAN:

Chapter 7

Snapping Lines

by Ileana Frómeta Grillo

Artist's Statement

I infuse my artwork with conscious and unconscious symbols culled from my upbringing in the lush beauty of the Caribbean and my experience as a woman. My mission is to create a dialogue by inviting the observer to unite with a piece and discover his or her own personal meaning. I feel I have succeeded when the viewer makes this connection, and we can both claim the piece as our own.

The Story Behind the Artwork

A well-known Southern California writer asked Ileana to illustrate the cover of a book that he had written, titled *Snapping Lines.* He explained that the title referred to a construction term that involved the comparison of an erected building with the original blueprints.

In this work (7.1), Ileana combined images of places and situations described in the book, all built upon a blueprint grid. She envisioned the piece as a metaphor, an invitation to meditate about our current lives, and how the present fits into what we were meant to be. The image didn't make it onto the book's cover; however, it acquired a life of its own. The image reflected Ileana's own life and career changes and symbolized the starting point of her professional life as a digital artist.

◀7.1

The Creative Process

The main image initially came together as a series of loosely drawn sketches. Since *Snapping Lines* was originally conceived as the cover for a book, Ileana incorporated visual elements that reflected the general theme of the story.

Ileana found that the pose of the woman in the yellow dress that she had painted in her picture *Dreaming Venezuelan* would fit into this general theme (7.2). She especially liked the smooth, warm skin tones present in the woman's face (see the technique later in this chapter to learn how Ileana painted the face). She had saved a version of *Dreaming* in Photoshop, with all the elements separated into layers.

Ileana opened a new blank canvas in Painter and transferred the yellow figure onto it, along with a section of the background. Using the soft chalk, she completed the figure's dress and back so that the woman would stand as a whole element in the new picture (7.3).

7.2

dS

About the Artist

Biography

Prior to discovering digital drawing in 1988, Ileana studied traditional media in her native Caracas and California, including drawing, painting, sculpture, and photography. Ileana's first digital project was a children's book, *La Bicicleta de Nubes*, published in 1995. Her work appears in numerous Internet galleries and has been featured in magazine and book publications such as *Design Graphics, Agosto, Digital Output, IDEA,* and *Mastering Digital Printing: The Photographer's and Artist's Guide to High-Quality, Digital Output* (Cincinnati: Muska & Lipman, 2002). In 2000, Ileana's work was selected for the MacworldExpo Digital Art contest, and she attended the Sawdust Art Festival in Laguna Beach, California as a Guest Artist.

7.3

She captured digital photos consistent with the theme of the piece and imported them — masked, cropped, and contrast-enhanced — into the image. Each element became a separate layer that was worked on independently using various Blending modes, Photoshop filters, and adjusting the Hue/Saturation levels (7.4).

One example of how Ileana applied Blending modes was the blueprint image. She wanted it to show

For the flower in the woman's hair, she created blooms of different size and shades. These flowers were grouped together as a nozzle and sprayed onto a selected area to create the final composition. The completed yellow figure was then opened in Photoshop.

7.4

Influences

Early influences are the works of Latin American artists from the Dominican Republic, such as Candido Bidó, and Venezuelan painter Hector Poleo. Both artist's work rely heavily on the use of vivid colors and an interplay between flat and modeled surfaces. Later influences are the works of Gauguin, the Fauve painters, and David Hockney. More recent influences are the works of women artists, such as Nivia Gonzales and Pegger Hopper, both American artists.

Studio

Computer System:
Apple G4, 500 MHz
30GB hard drive
1GB RAM

Monitors:
Apple 15-inch Studio Display
Apple 14-inch Monitor

Software:
Corel Painter
Adobe Photoshop
Genuine Fractals
Corel Knockout

Tablet:
Wacom Intuos 6 x 8

Input:
HP ScanJet 300dpi scanner
Canon S-10 2.2 megapixel digital camera

Removable Media:
Que! Fire 12 x 10 x 32 CD-RW

Contact

Ileana Frómeta Grillo
Laguna Beach, California
`lleana@ileanaspage.com`
`www.ileanaspage.com`

through the front image, without overpowering the whole composition. She duplicated a section of the blueprint layer (selected the area, then chose Layer→Duplicate Layer from the Layers palette pop-up menu), which she had placed as the background (Layer 0).The resulting copy was placed on top of the other layers. Ileana selected the Blending Options from the Layers pop-up menu. In the Blending Options dialog box, she changed the blend mode to Multiply and reduced the opacity to 40%. This changed the copy of the blueprint into a more transparent layer.

For the bird of paradise, she scaled a digital photo, increased the brightness and contrast (Image→Adjust→Brightness and Contrast), and later increased the saturation of individual colors (Image→Adjust→Hue/Saturation). Ileana also used the Watercolor filter (Filter→Artistic→Watercolor) in order to give the bird a more "painterly" look.

Ileana played with the positioning of the different layers until she found an arrangement that she liked. Next, she used the blending and contrast tools to amalgamate the separate layers into a balanced whole. For instance, she decreased the opacity of front layers to let some of the background layers show through, or used the Blending Options sliders to bring some of the underlying colors into the upper layers.

The final composition was flattened (after saving a layered version for future reference). She then reopened the flattened version in Painter. Ileana smoothed some harsher edges with the Simple Water tool, added some highlights with the Airbrush and Chalk brush tools, and painted in some fine details, such as strands of hair.

The original image was 10 inches wide by 9 inches tall at 300 dpi (since it was intended to be the cover of a book). Ileana found that Altamira Genuine Fractals was a helpful tool when she enlarged the image to 16 inches wide by 14 inches tall (a more suitable size for a fine art print). Ileana kept four versions of the image: a layered and a flat version (Photoshop format, at a smaller size), another one in Genuine Fractals STN format (which gives the flexibility to conveniently resize at any time in the future), and the final output version (at 300dpi, Photoshop format).

This project took about three weeks to complete.

Technique 1: Painting a Face (Painter)

This technique describes the way Ileana creates smooth, warm skin tones in her paintings (7.5).

1. **Scan a pencil sketch of a face.**
2. **Open the scanned sketch in Painter.**
3. **Select the Large Chalk variant in the Dry Media brush category of the Brushes palette.**
4. **Set the Method Subcategory to Grainy Soft Cover in the General section of the Brush Controls palette.**
5. **Set the brush size to 12 in the Size section of the Brush Controls palette.**
6. **Set the opacity to 30% in the Controls: Brush palette.**

● 7.5

7. **Apply different colors, using this customized brush, in the face (7.6).**
   Ileana uses a special color set she's developed for skin tones. To pick a color from a color set, you just click on the color square. Alternatively, you can just pick your colors from the Color Picker in the Colors section of the Art Materials palette.
   You can make your own custom color set in Painter for special needs, such as skin color tones or bright saturated printable colors. See the technique later in this chapter and also Ileana's comments on color calibration.

[TIP]

If you think you may want to use these brush settings again in the future, choose Variant→Save Variant in the Brushes palette. Name the custom variant something descriptive, such as "Skin Brush," so that you can identify it in the Dry Media variants list, and then click OK. This saves the settings for this brush for any future times you want to use it.

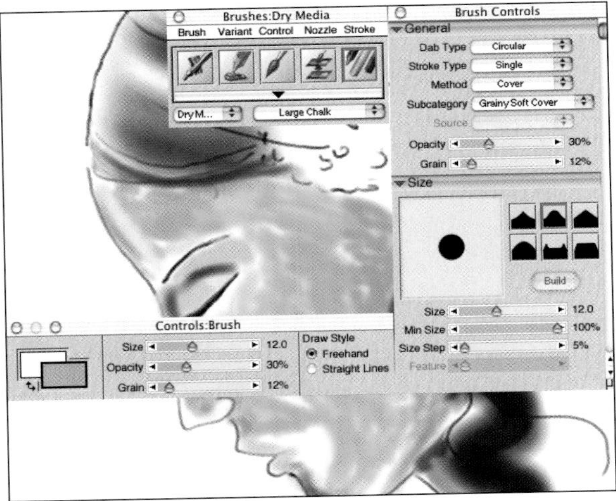

● 7.6

8. **After you fill the face with color, select the Just Add Water variant in the Liquid brush category. Use this brush to smoothly blend and mix the colors to form the final skin color.**

Technique 2: Making Your Own Color Set (Painter)

Color sets allow you to restrict your palette to a particular range of colors, and easily pick those colors just by clicking on the color squares. These colors may be your favorite colors, colors you need to apply with consistency for a particular project, colors you know from experience will print well, or colors that are good for certain jobs, such as skin colors. Ileana makes her own color sets for getting bright, printable colors and achieving good skin tones.

1. **Choose Window→Show Color Set.**
2. **Choose Cmd/Ctrl-O.**
3. **Open an image in Painter that you want to use as a source of color.**
   This source image could be a digital photo of a face for skin tones, or could even be a scan of Ileana's own color set as illustrated in this book.
4. **Open the Color Set section of the Art Materials palette.**
5. **Click the left-hand square button (the icon with an array of vertical and horizontal lines) in the Color Set section and choose Create New Empty Color Set (7.7).**

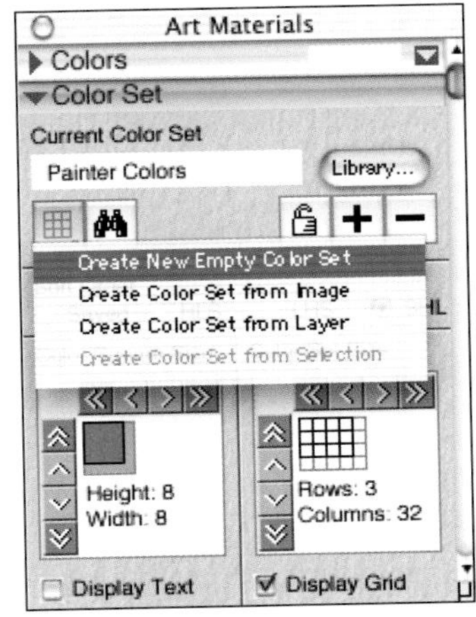

● 7.7

This generates a tiny, almost invisible empty color set. All you can see on your computer screen is a small section of the title bar (7.8).

6. **Select the Dropper tool.**
7. **Click with the Dropper tool on the first color in your scanned image that you want to select.**
8. **Click on the "+" button in the Color Set section.**
   This adds the chosen color to the current color set.
9. **Continue this process until you have saved all the colors you want in your color set.**
10. **When finished click on the Color Set Library button.**
    You see a message asking you "Do you wish to save the changes you've made to the current color set?" (7.9).
11. **Click Save.**
12. **Name the color set.**
13. **Click Save again, saving it in the Color Sets folder in your Painter 7 folder.**
    You now see a dialog box where you can select a color set. Just click Cancel and you'll be back with your newly named custom color set. You see the name in the Color Set section to the left of the library button. You can add to an existing color set at any time.

● 7.8

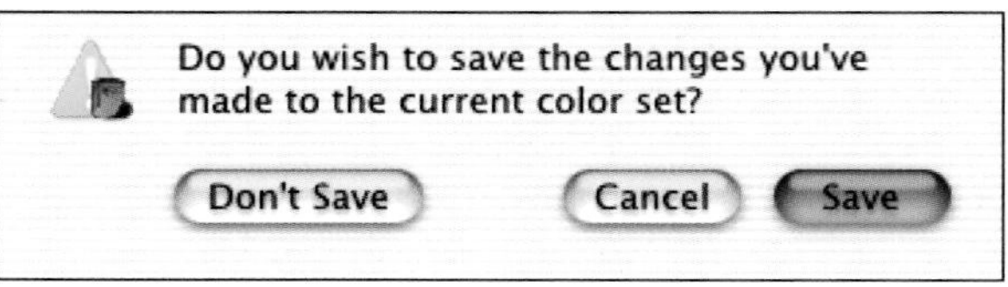

● 7.9

Artist's Creative Insight and Advice

Why Digital?

I love working digitally because of programs like Painter. These programs mirror the steps taken by an artist regarding the way he or she approaches traditional media. Thus, I am able to work intuitively in the same way I would with traditional media. At the same time, the access to a wide variety of art mediums, and the amazing quality of its rendering, allows me to expand my visual vocabulary. I am able to integrate in one picture a variety of mediums, such as watercolor, oil pastel, airbrush, charcoal, ink, and photos, and still make it look good as a whole. This program can be as complex as you want it to be, yet, it is intuitive enough that any fine artist can get started, with some basic computer knowledge, and get involved from the start.

Digital Art and the Art Establishment

Digital imagery, long embraced by the graphic arts, has faced reluctant acceptance in fine art circles. However, as technology progresses and artists become more adept at using this new art form, a revolution is brewing. Digital fine art is creating its own audience around the world, mainly through hundreds of dedicated virtual galleries and personal Web sites. Consequently, digital imagery is no longer dependent on the scrutiny of a particular gallery for its marketing and exposure.

In spite of its often-contested name, the word giclée, describing a digital art print, has become quite popular in gallery circles and with the buying public. The fine art industry is already embracing a giclée market that grows at a rate of about 25% per year and shows no signs of slowing down.

Just as digital art dissolves barriers, it also creates new ones — often by challenging long-held practices of the "traditional" artwork without being able to reach a clear, unanimous decision of what it is all about. The digital medium is multifaceted in its creation as well as its expression. Consequently, it is hard to seek consensus amid this constantly changing technology.

The process of "legitimacy" of the digital arts will have to address important issues such as: the difference between a digital reproduction of traditional art versus work created entirely in the computer; how much credit should be given to the artist in the creation of "computer generated" imagery; the definition of originality versus reproduction of a medium that allows nearly identical iterations from an original source; organizing the variety of digital output, which ranges from video to print; and copyright and authenticity issues that affect both the artist and the buyer.

A digital artist will be able to dispel a great deal of misunderstanding and confusion by becoming aware of the strengths and difficulties inherent in the digital medium. In spite of all of its growing pains, it is a pretty exciting place to be.

Color Calibration

My goal is to create vibrant colors that jump out. My colors are a very important part of my art, and they are frequently identified as an integral part of my artistic style. For this reason, I pay a lot of attention to reproducing the vibrant colors I see on my computer screen in my prints. To achieve this, I create my own calibration color sets in Painter. For instance, I like to use a very deep royal blue. Blues tend to come out with a purple cast in prints. To overcome this, I printed a lot of different blues and sampled the colors that worked best into a custom Painter Color Set specially for picking blues. Likewise, I have developed, through trial and error, a color set for skin colors. I highly recommend taking the time to do this — the results are dramatic.

Chapter 8

Archer

by Li Shen

Artist's Statement

My approach to digital art, and this particular piece, is to create something that has a mixture of the old and new. As someone who believes strongly in traditional media and the artistic process, I wanted to explore the possibilities of merging the digital medium with a traditional aspect of art making. My goal was not to create something that looks like a 15th-century painting done in Photoshop, nor did I want a supersharp, meticulous, computer-rendered image. I wanted something between the two.

The Story Behind the Artwork

Archer (8.1) is the second part of a digital art series that Li started a couple of years ago. Li has always been intrigued by ancient Chinese warriors, and in this series he wanted to bring the gracefulness and savagery of these ancient fighters into the digital realm.

At the time that Shen created *Archer,* he felt the digital art that was out there lacked a certain hands-on feel. It was too sterile; he wanted to bring warmth into the medium. Li wanted texture, free lines, simplicity, and a little dirtiness.

◀8.1

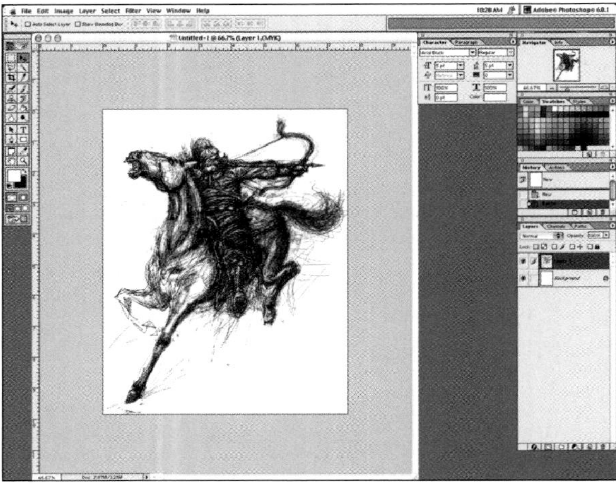

8.2

The Creative Process

When he started this piece, Li still didn't have a tablet, so all of the lines and the figure were drawn directly with a mouse. Later, he scanned in the Chinese text and other materials and manipulated them in Photoshop to give the image a textured look. The creative process entailed mainly drawing lines, layering the lines, and applying different textures. The whole process took approximately 36 hours.

For Li, one of the most important aspects of a piece is its texture. Texture can be very instrumental in giving a mood to a particular work. With *Archer*, he wanted to give a rustic mood with texture. Since the subject is an ancient warrior, he didn't want to make it very shiny and clean. To achieve this dirty

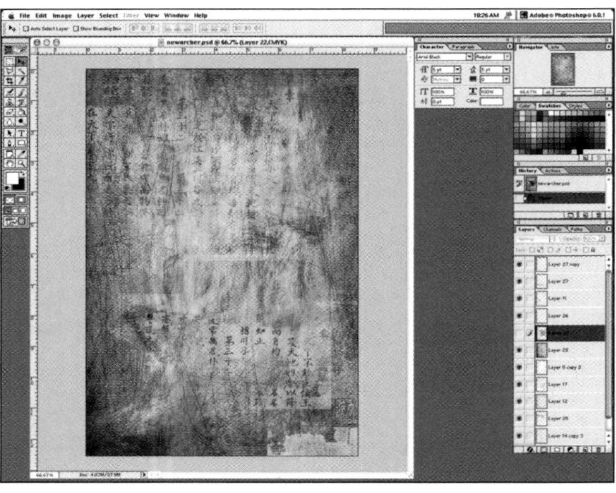

8.3

8.4

About the Artist

Biography

Li was born in Shanghai, China. In 1986, he immigrated to the United States with his parents; he was nine at the time. He's been living in San Francisco for almost 16 years now, and he loves every part of this great city.

Li attended the University of California at Davis and majored in Graphic Design for four years. It was during these years that he got to know the computer and began to use it not just for design but also for illustration.

Li currently works as a graphic designer for a video game publishing company in San Francisco. He continues to draw and create art on the side and hopes that one day he will be able to focus completely on drawing/illustration as a way of making a and rusted texture, he worked with many layers and many different effects.

First, there are the lines, at least three or four layers of lines all together, some white and some black. Some layers with lines are in Overlay mode, and some have their opacity turned down. This gives a sense of dimension to the background (8.2).

The Chinese characters were scanned from a book (8.3).

The green background was achieved by using a solid base green layer with many different textured layers set in a variety of modes such as Overlay, Color Dodge, and Color Burn. These textured layers were old light wave images Li had made with Photoshop blur filters, and oil painting textures and photographs of his that he'd scanned (8.4).

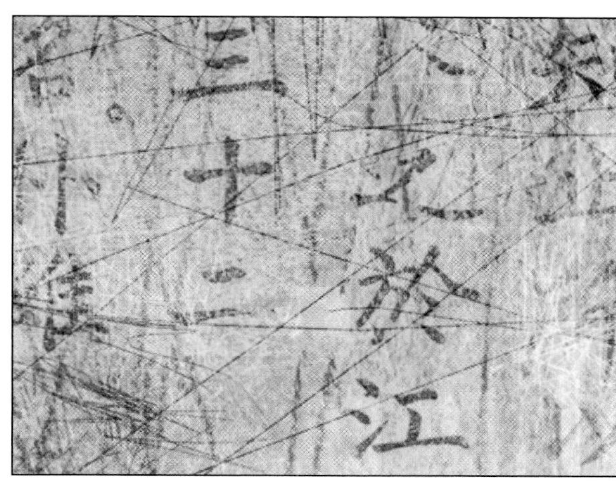

● 8.5

Technique: Applying Texture to Scanned Text (Photoshop)

This technique demonstrates the method Li applied to create the beautiful, tattered, and rustic look to the Chinese text in his piece (8.5).

1. **Scan the Chinese text (or whatever text or image elements you want to use).**

   Li just used a page from a Chinese book (8.6).

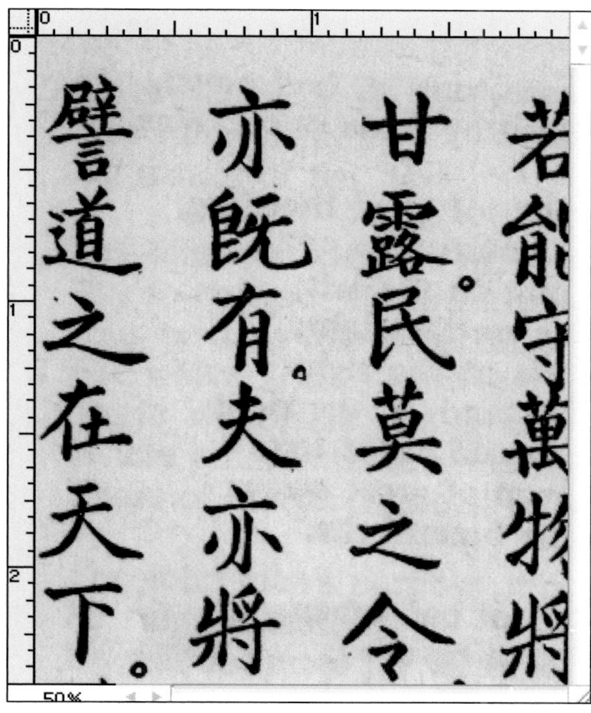

● 8.6

living. His career goal is to become a pre-production conceptual designer for sci-fi movies and video games.

Influences

Derek Lea, Dave McKean, David Ho, and David Carson. Musically, the work of Tool and Dredg. Classically, the visual punning of Rene Magritte and MC Escher.

Studio

Computer System:
Mac G3, 400 MHz
4GB hard drive
128MB RAM

Monitor:
Sony 19-inch

Software:
Adobe Photoshop
Illustrator

Tablet:
Wacom 6 x 8 inches

Printer:
Epson 700

Contact

Li Shen
San Francisco, California
shenlix@hotmail.com
lishen.ucdavis.edu

2. **Open another image that includes an interesting texture you would like to apply to your text (8.7).**
   The texture can be a scanned image or something you created with Photoshop filters.
3. **Choose Duplicate Layer from the Layers palette pop-up menu.**
   You see a Duplicate Layer dialog box with the default layer name Background copy.

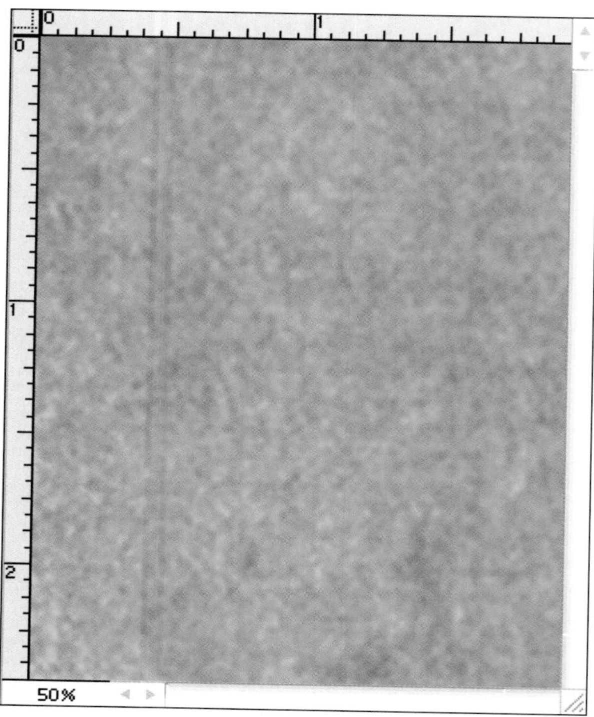

8.7

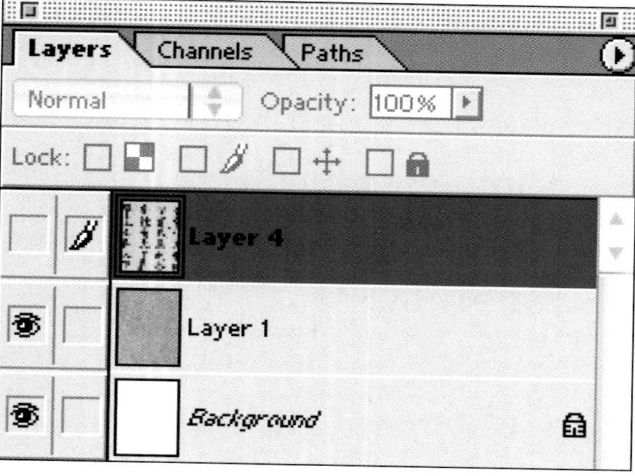

8.8

4. **Click OK.**
5. **Select the background in the Layers palette.**
6. **Choose Cmd/Ctrl-A (Select All command).**
7. **Ensure the background color is white.**
8. **Click the Delete/Backspace key.**
   This makes the background white.
9. **Use the Move tool to drag the scanned text as a layer on top of the texture image layer (the "Background copy" layer).**
   In 8.8, you see the Chinese text layer highlighted and called "Layer 2" and the texture image layer called "Layer 1".
10. **Choose Select→Color Range to open the Color Range dialog box (8.9).**
11. **Drag the Dropper tool over the image (left mouse button pressed down if you're using a mouse) until there are a lot of small, black-and-white dots.**
12. **Click OK.**
    Now you have a selection in the texture layer (Background copy or Layer 1). To observe this, just turn off the eye icon next to the upper layer (Layer 2) in the Layers palette (8.10).
13. **Select the text layer in the Layers palette with the Color Range selection still active.**

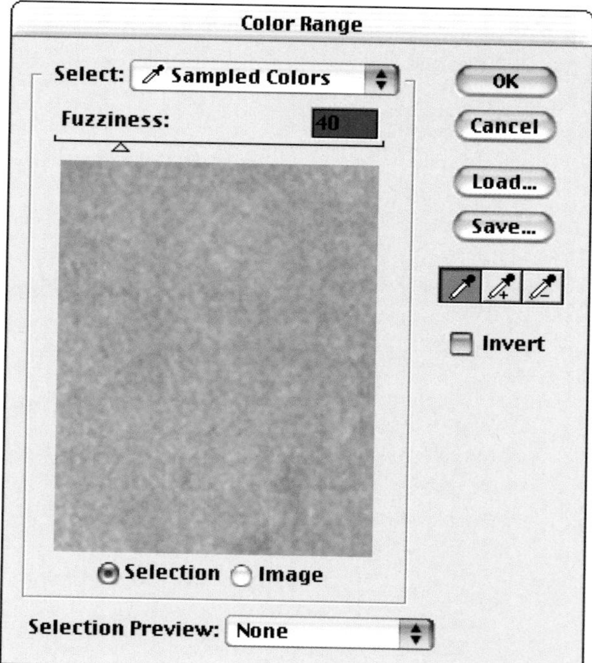

8.9

Make sure you turn on the eye icon next to the uppermost Layer 2. You see the same selection on the top layer (8.11).

14. Choose Edit→Copy.

15. Select New Layer in the Layers palette pop-up menu.
This creates a new (empty) layer.

16. Choose Edit→Paste.
This pastes the selection into the new layer.

17. Turn off the eye icons for Layers 1 and 2.
You now see the textured text with white showing through from the background (8.12).

Artist's Creative Insight and Advice

Why Digital?

I was introduced to the computer as a creative medium in college. Being a graphic design major, we had to learn programs like Photoshop and Illustrator. Because I love to draw and paint, it was just natural that I progress to the computer as another tool for me to create art.

● 8.10

There are many advantages of using the computer to make your art. I like the undo option. You can always go back to a certain stage of the art piece, which makes it easier for me to experiment with different effects and techniques. It's a lot easier to mix colors on a computer. You have the option of zooming and working with single pixels if you choose to on a computer. That kind of control is not really possible with traditional mediums.

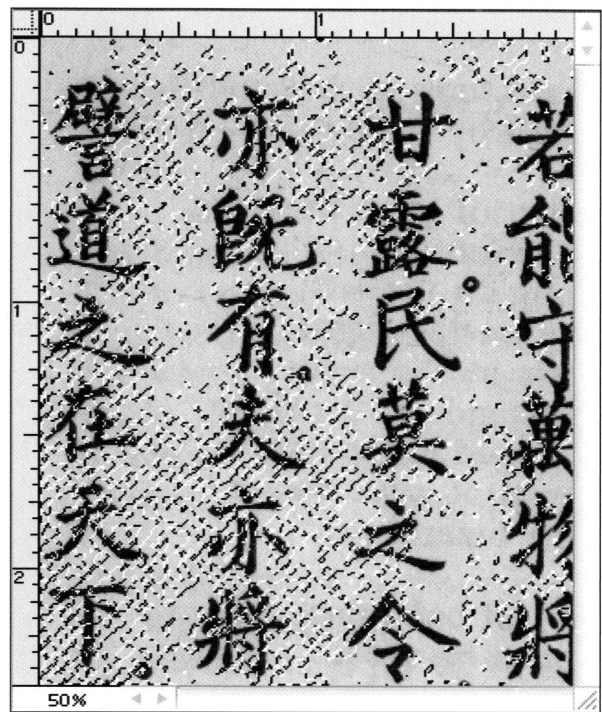

● 8.11

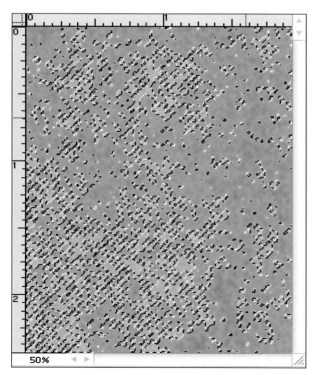

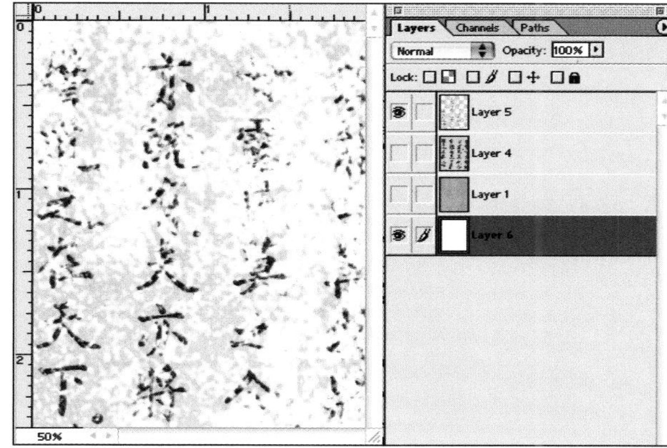

● 8.12

The disadvantage of working with the computer is that I feel, no matter what, an oil painting or a watercolor will always feel more personal and real than a digital image. You can't achieve that texture of the thick oil paint of a Van Gogh with Photoshop. Another disadvantage is missing the feel of a brush or pencil and the sound they make on a canvas or a piece of paper.

Advice for Artists Working in the Digital Medium

Experiment! The best advice I can give to people is to give yourself time to play and experiment with different techniques and effects in your digital art piece. There are so many different combinations of techniques and effects that are available to you in a program like Photoshop. It will take time for you to find your own techniques and style. You have to go into something with the expectation of not really knowing what you will get, and be excited about that. The surprise is the best part.

Use layers! Don't be shy about using a lot of layers. Layers are a great tool to give your piece dimension and textures. Oil painters have been using layers to give life to their paintings for hundreds of years; it shouldn't be any different if you are working on a computer instead of a canvas. I hardly ever use the filters in Photoshop except for the blur effect, but I can't live without the layer opacity tool and the layer effects tools. Experiment with effects like overlay, multiply, color burn, or color dodge. See what these effects do to your layer and how they interact with the other layers. These effects play a huge role in achieving a mood with my digital pieces.

Save your work often! A computer can crash at any time. I've lost many hours of work because the computer crashed and I didn't save.

It's still a very new medium, so you can become a pioneer in this field and do something that no one else has done.

Bert Monroy on Li Shen's *Archer*

"Excellent use of the computer to resemble traditional media. A viewer is hard-pressed to argue the authenticity and antiquity of the art within the time period it seems to have come from."

— Bert Monroy, Digital Art Teacher and Author (www.bertmonroy.com)

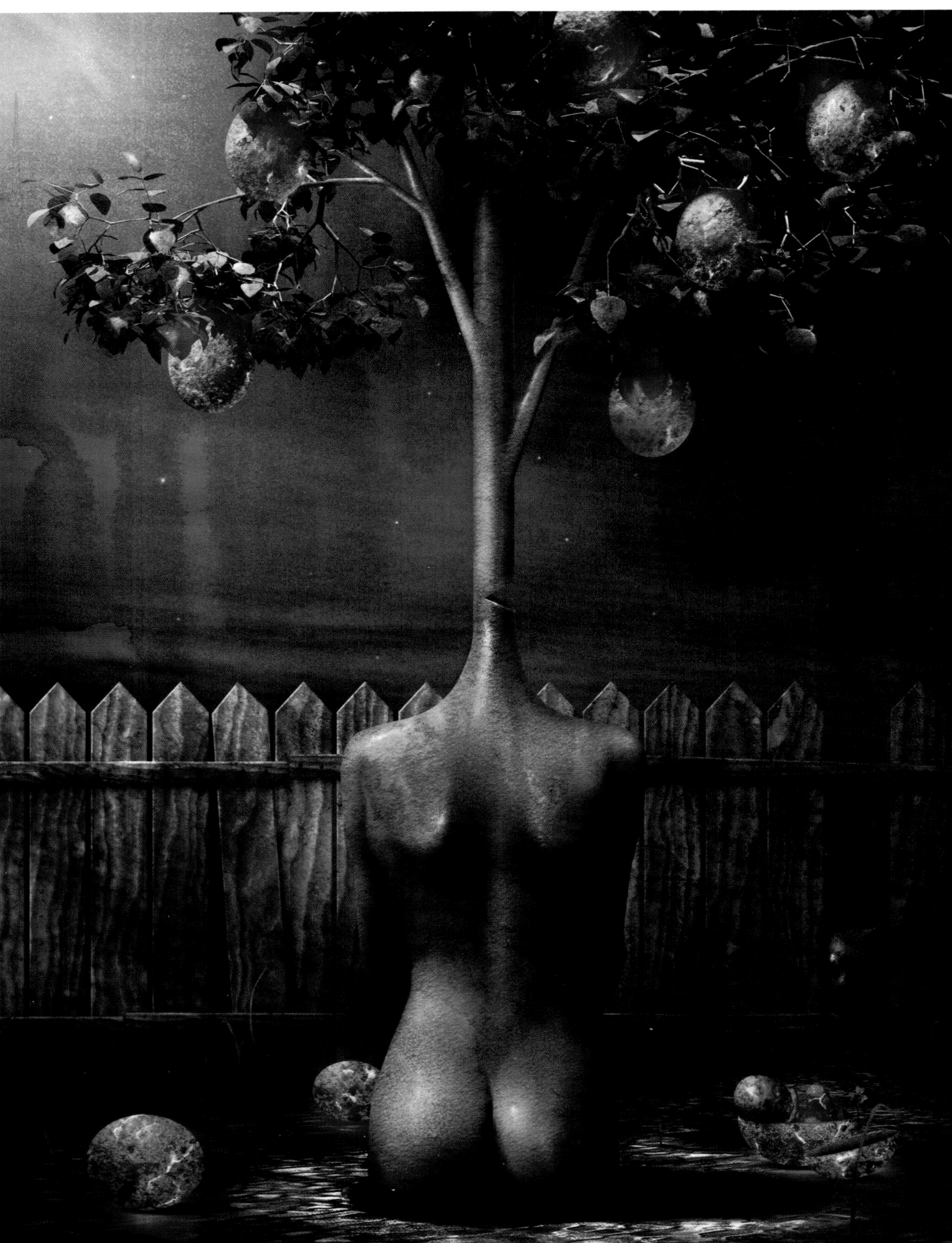

Chapter 9

Contemplations 11: Nature vs. Nurture

by David Ho

Artist's Statement

The power of art lies in its ability to help us feel, think, and imagine. Creating art to generate an impact on the viewer is secondary to me.

I create art for one reason only — to quiet the demons that reside in my soul.

The Story Behind the Artwork

David has always loved manipulating the human form into a more surrealist context. *Nature vs. Nurture* (9.1) signifies the female figure as the ultimate life giver (symbolized by the tree). Her fruits of labor represent her offspring.

The Creative Process

Each of the elements in this image was created separately in different programs and then later brought together in Photoshop. The female figure was created in Poser (9.2). The tree, ground, and eggs were rendered in Bryce. The rest of the elements were created directly in Photoshop.

The entire file was first created in grayscale to save time and hard disk space (the original file size was 8.5 x 11 inches at 300dpi). In grayscale, David could concentrate more on the composition and the play of light and shade, without getting distracted by color (9.3).

Some of the textures in the piece were painted traditionally on watercolor paper. These textures were scanned and then introduced into the image as layers with various modes (such as Overlay or Hard Light).

◀9.1

Once David was satisfied with the piece, he merged some layers (of the less important items) into the background, leaving just the main elements as separate layers. He then converted the whole file from grayscale into RGB mode. Each remaining layer was then separately colorized.

Once he had colorized the layers, David created a new layer over the whole image, set in Overlay mode, and sprayed brown to give a "grungier" feel to the image. As a final touch, to create highlights in the piece, David added one more new layer set to Color Dodge mode. He painted white to give a more glistening feel to the image; he smeared the white on this layer to give a more painterly effect.

● 9.2

● 9.3

About the Artist

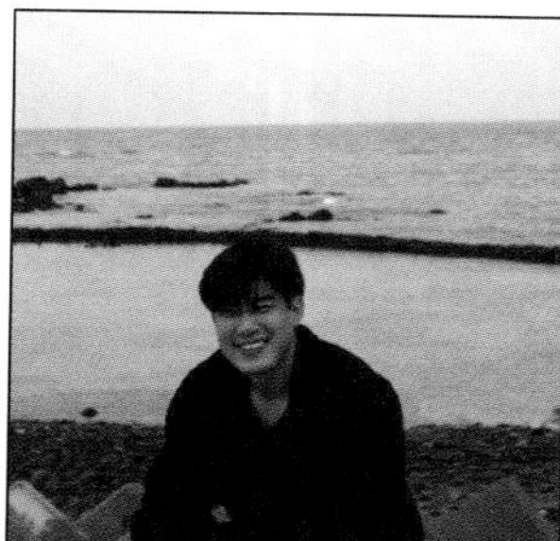

Biography

David has a Bachelors of Art in Sociology from UC Berkeley and a Bachelors of Art in Art History with a minor in Fine Arts from San Jose State University.

David has been creating digital work for the past ten years. His works have been accepted into numerous competitions, including those of the Society of Illustrators, the San Francisco Society of Illustrators, Step-by Step Graphics Illustration, the Macworld Expo, and Seybold Digital Gallery. David has also been featured in many publications, including *EFX Art and Design, Computer Arts,* and *Digital Photo User.*

David's clients have included The Chicago Tribune, Ziff Davis, Interscope Records, Sony Music, and the National Rifle Association. He recently published an artbook entitled *Shadow Maker: the Digital Art of David Ho,* available at `www.davidho.com`.

Technique: Creating a Realistic Glow on a Layer (Photoshop)

This technique illustrates how to generate a very real-looking glow around an object, as David succeeded in doing in this image with the glowing egg-shaped objects. David also tells you how to make the texture that appears on these objects.

1. **Open the artwork image, into which you want to place the glowing object, in Photoshop.**
2. **Open an image of the object, on which you want to create a realistic glow, also in Photoshop.**
3. **Using the Move tool, click in the image of the object and drag the Move tool over the artwork image.**
   This places a copy of the object as a layer over the artwork (9.4).
4. **Import the scanned texture of an actual rock into Photoshop.**
5. **Choose Select→Select All on the scanned texture image.**
6. **Choose Edit→Copy.**
7. **Make the artwork image active.**
8. **Select the object layer by clicking on the layer in the Layers palette.**
9. **Choose Edit→Paste Into.**
   This pastes the rock texture on top of the object as a layer with the same boundaries as the object (9.5).
10. **Set this new layer to Hard Light mode in the Layers palette.**
11. **Choose Image→Adjust→Hue/Saturation.**

● 9.4

● 9.5

Influences

Odd Nerdrum, traditional Norwegian oil painter (`www.nerdrum.com`); HR Giger, creator of the alien in the movie *Alien* (`www.hrgiger.com`); Michael Whelan, fantasy artist (`www.michaelwhelan.com`); Michael Parkes; Dave McKean, digital illustrator who uses Photoshop; and John Jude Palencar, traditional artist.

Studio

Computer System:
Macintosh G4, 500 MHz
80GB hard drive

Monitors:
Mitsubishi Diamond Pro 2040u
22-inch CRT Monitor

Software:
Adobe Photoshop
Illustrator
Poser
Bryce

Tablet:
Wacom tablet

Input Devices:
Nikon Scantouch flatbed scanner

Removable Media:
Iomega Zip

Archive Media:
CDRW

Printers:
Epson 1200

Contact

David Ho
Fremont, California
`ho@davidho.com`
`www.davidho.com`

12. Keep the channel set to Master in the Hue/ Saturation window, and move the Hue slider to the left until you see an orange hue in your rock texture layer.

13. Click OK.

14. Create a new layer (Layers pop-up menu) and set it to Color Dodge in the Layers palette.

15. Use the Airbrush tool to spray random areas with white.

This creates the effect of streaks of lights emerging from the egg.

16. Use the Smudge tool, set to 85% pressure, to pull the paint into streaks, creating a painterly effect.

17. Choose New Layer on the Layers palette pop-up menu.

18. Set the new layer to Screen mode.

19. Use the Airbrush tool to spray the egg, which makes it glow more.

The airbrush setting chosen from the Brush pop-up menu can be seen in (9.6).

20. Choose New Layer on the Layers palette pop-up menu.

21. Reposition this new layer to be behind the object by dragging the layer down below the object layer in the Layers palette.

22. Set the new layer to Hard Light mode with an Opacity of around 50%.

● 9.6

23. Spray an orange hue with the Airbrush tool into this layer.

This creates the effect of the reflection of light on the ground, which adds a finishing touch to the realistic glow.

Judge's Critique

Seybold Digital Gallery, 2002, 2nd place

"David's work has always been a favorite of mine for the strength and uniqueness of his vision. He draws us into his dark world that is executed with a skill that borders on photographic. The somber use of color and texture heightens this eerie vision that is David's unusual take on a mythological creature."

— DIANE FENSTER, Digital Artist

(www.dianefenster.com)

Artist's Creative Insight and Advice

Why Digital?

The digital medium is a wonderful, powerful tool, but it is no substitute for a traditional fine art training that teaches you to see how light falls and how to realistically depict the play of light on an object.

Advice for Artists

I believe that a real artist should have his or her own style and voice. I've seen too many digital artworks out there that always look like a generic Poser piece or a generic Bryce artwork or a Photoshop piece filled with KPT filters. I think artists should try to find their own inner vision, and that the software should serve as a means to get to that destination, not as an end in itself.

Color Management

Color management has always been a big problem for artists because what you see on the screen may not always come out the same when it's printed. I've purchased the Pantone Color Spyder color calibrator, and I find it very helpful. Every time I finish an artwork, I always output a 3M Rainbow proof to double check the colors. This ensures my color consistency with offset CMYK printing.

Chapter 10

A Place in the Sun

by Wendy Morris

Artist's Statement

I draw personal experiences into my artwork. In a sense, they are whimsical vignettes. A sense of humor is essential in my approach to art and life.

Although I deal with joy and disappointment in my drawings, they are always optimistic. Hopefully, the end result will influence people and make them smile.

The Story Behind the Artwork

The message Wendy wanted to express when making *A Place in the Sun* (10.1) was that "when you encounter difficulties, approach them with patience, kindness, and an open heart. The love within you will bring light into any situation."

This piece started as a black-and-white line drawing of an angel bringing light to a home she was visiting. Wendy had taken a scan of this drawing with her to use at a computer art demonstration that she was participating in at the San Francisco Museum of Modern Art. (The demonstration was promoting Macworld San Francisco 2000.) She was invited, with other Macworld Expo Digital Art Contest winners, to create artwork to show the event attendees some of the basics of digital art.

At first, she made the figure an angel, but then she decided to make her a woman with gray in her hair to denote wisdom. The dog urinating in the grass provided a darker sense of humor. That night, she finished the version of the image at the event but had no way to save it. When she returned from San Francisco, she reworked the piece and subsequently entered it into the Macworld Expo Digital Art Contest, where it was chosen as a finalist.

◀ 10.1

The Creative Process

Wendy began this piece by hand drawing on cotton paper. Using a Rapidograph pen, she completed the outline of her image. She scanned the pen-and-ink image using Photoshop and generated a black-and-white (grayscale) digitized version. She scanned the image at a high enough resolution to produce a large format image (17 x 12 inches at 300 dpi). This is a versatile image size since it serves as a master image that can subsequently be reduced and resaved at various smaller sizes and resolutions to suit different uses.

Before adding color to the scan, Wendy magnified the image and carefully checked for broken lines, filling in where necessary with the Pencil tool. She saved a copy of this black-and-white file to keep as a safety net she could refer to later. She saved another copy of the black-and-white image to work on and add color to.

Wendy filled in the white regions of the image with various colors and textures by first selecting the regions using the Magic Wand and then applying Airbrush brushes. By adjusting the tool settings, she reproduced the look and feel of her traditional marker, pastel, and oil pastel drawings.

When she sent several images to her New York artist representative, they posted her digital images on their Web site labeled as traditionally-rendered art. She had to convince them they were digitally generated and not finished art scanned into the computer!

Technique #1: Colorizing a Scanned Pen-and-Ink Drawing (Photoshop)

This technique illustrates the ease of using the Photoshop Magic Wand selection tool to transform a black-and-white line drawing into a colorized image.

1. **Create a black-and-white line drawing on paper using traditional pen and ink.**
2. **Scan the drawing in Photoshop at 300 dpi.**

[TIP]

This resolution ensures that your final image will have a sufficiently high resolution to produce high-quality fine art prints.

3. **Open the scanned black-and-white drawing in Photoshop in RGB mode (10.2).**
4. **Click on the Photoshop Magnifier tool in the Tools palette.**
5. **Correct any broken lines using the Paintbrush tool.** Visually inspect the lines to make sure that they are solid, unbroken, continuous contours that completely enclose regions of white. Where you come across an incomplete line, use the Paintbrush tool with black to make the lines solid. The result is a clean, digitized, black-and-white line drawing.
6. **Make sure the image mode is RGB (choose Image→Mode→RGB Color).**
7. **Click on the Magic Wand tool in the Tools palette.**

dS.

About the Artist

Biography

Wendy Morris has a BA in Fine Arts, honors graduate in Art History, from the University of Pittsburgh, and she teaches art to developmentally disabled adults in San Diego. She is an award-winning computer artist with a successful career in illustration. Wendy is a three-time Macworld Expo digital art contest winner and has an Artville CD that includes her stock images. Her work has been widely published internationally in books and magazines. Her most recent show includes "2001 Facing Faces" at the Museo de Arte del Inba at Ciudad Juarz, Mexico.

Influences

John Kane, Paul Klee, and Ernest H. Shepard.

8. In the Magic Wand properties menu bar, type in 100 in the Magic Wand tolerance window.
9. Hold the Shift key down and click with the Magic Wand tool once in each of the flat white areas you want filled with a particular color.
10. Select the desired fill color for the selected region.
11. Click the Paint Bucket tool in the Tools palette.
12. Adjust the Paint Bucket tolerance to 60 in the Paint Bucket properties menu bar.
13. Click with the Fill Bucket tool in the selected regions to fill them with color (10.3).

● 10.2

● 10.3

Studio

Computer System:
Macintosh Power PC 7600/120

Monitors:
Apple Display Cinema 22-inch flat screen

Software:
Adobe Photoshop
Painter

Tablet:
Wacom tablet

Input Devices:
Umax scanner

Removable Media:
Iomega Zip

Archive Media:
Lacie CD-ROM burner

Printers:
Epson Stylus Printer 600

Contact

Wendy Morris
Alpine, California
wendydraw@aol.com
www.wendydraw.com

14. **Keeping the selections active, refine and texturize the flat regions of color using the Airbrush tool.** Start with a large brush size, working in large areas, and work towards a small brush size in smaller areas.

Technique #2: Adding an Image Layer with Drop Shadow (Photoshop)

This technique describes how to add an image element as a layer in the main image and then create a skewed drop shadow. Wendy used this technique to add the dog to her composition.

1. **Draw the image that you want to add to your composition.**

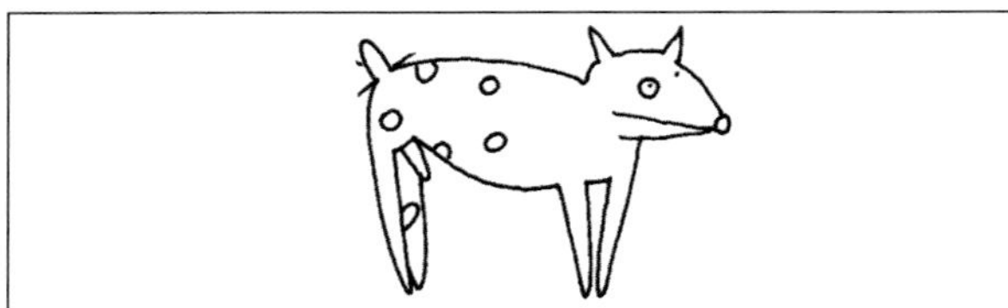

● 10.4

● 10.5

[TIP]

To help you get the proportion of this new image correct, place your drawing paper over the original composition, and then draw over a light table.

2. **Scan the new drawing at 300 dpi, which opens in Photoshop (10.4).**
3. **Use the Magnifier to check the new image for broken or incomplete lines.**
   Where any lines are broken, use the Paint Brush tool to fill the gaps.
4. **Select the Magic Wand tool.**
5. **Click outside the drawn image with the Magic Wand tool.**
6. **Choose Select→Invert.**
   Inverting the selection selects the drawn image (the Magic Wand selection is everything outside the drawn image).
7. **Choose Edit→Copy.**
8. **Select the original composition and paste the new image onto the main image by choosing Edit→Paste (10.5).**
9. **Move the new image into the desired position with the Move tool.**
   Use the arrow keys to "nudge" the image pixel by pixel into its final place.
10. **Save the image as a Photoshop file.**
11. **With the new layer active (highlighted in the Layer palette), choose Duplicate Layer from the Layers menu.**
    A window appears with the name of the duplicate layer. Click OK to complete the process of making the duplicate layer.
12. **In the Layer palette, select the lower of the two layers by clicking on the layer.**
13. **Select black in the color Swatch.**
14. **Fill the lower layer with black by choosing Edit→Fill.**
    To see the black lower layer, click once on the "eye" visibility symbol next to the upper layer in the Layer palette. This makes the upper layer invisible and reveals the black lower layer beneath (10.6).
15. **With the lower black-filled layer active, choose Filter→Blur→Gaussian Blur.**
    This blurring effect turns the lower layer into a fuzzy soft-edged shadow.
16. **Adjust the Gaussian Blur setting until you have the desired soft edge to the shadow. Click OK.**
17. **Choose Edit→Transform→Distort.**

A bounding box with control points appears around the blurred new image. Drag on the top two corner control points to elongate and skew the black layer into a shadow.

18. **When satisfied with the shadow, hit the Return/Enter key.**
19. **In the Layers palette, reduce the black layer opacity from 100% to 65%.**

[TIP]

For added realism you could apply a layer mask and run a gradient through it to fade the shadow at the edges. However, Wendy didn't do that for this image.

20. **Click on the visibility box on the left of the upper layer in the Layers palette.**
    This brings back the visibility "eye" symbol and the upper layer reappears on top of the shadow (10.7).
21. **Colorize the upper layer using the same techniques as described in Technique #1.**

Judge's Critique

Macworld Expo Digital Art Contest, 2000

"I liked Wendy's strong sense of line to illustrate whimsical characters populating a world of their own. The somber color palette juxtaposes the lightheartedness of the drawing, producing a mysterious tension."

— JOHN DERRY, Principle Author Painter, Digital Artist (`www.fractal.com`)

Artist's Creative Insights and Advice

Developing a Style

While it is fun to experiment with different programs, various tools, and styles of art, I believe it is imperative that you develop a personal style, one that expresses your inner feelings and is identifiable by art directors and the public.

10.6

10.7

Being True to Yourself

Most art directors say they love my work, then they ask me to change it. There is a balancing act between the whimsical nature of my art and those who ask me to make it more appealing for business, advertising needs. I have found a middle ground by not changing the style or spirit of my art yet addressing the needs of my clients. A case in point is a client who needed illustrations for a promotional campaign. They ended up using an angel theme. I drew angels lifting weights and women meditating and "being one with a rock." The assignment turned out to be a lot of fun.

Another challenge concerns people's misconceptions about computer art. They seem to think that the computer does all the work. Such prejudices become an opportunity to educate and demonstrate how the computer is just one more tool for an artist to master.

Believe in yourself. Believe in your art, and always listen to your intuition and inner guidance. Once, while deciding whether to take a trip to San Francisco for a computer art event, I actually heard a voice say, "Go! You don't know who you might meet there." That very evening, at an art and jazz party hosted by Fractal Design, I introduced myself to a man lingering over my artwork that was on display. He turned out to be the Vice President of a company called Artville that represents artists and sells "stock" digital artwork. As a direct result, I was licensed for their new stock illustration company. To this day, I still am involved with them and that opportunity has given me worldwide recognition.

Chapter 11

boy/girl/boy/girl

by Susan LeVan

Artist's Statement

My personal work spins out on its own, more or less unconsciously. I'll begin with a figure, human or animal, and just start to paint. The work goes where it will. I rarely think, "This guy needs a hat." I just put down the next stroke. For me, this is the pleasure of it — the adventure of not really knowing where we're going.

As a child of modern, abstract art, I am most interested in color, line, texture, and the formal elements of an image. The figures are there to hang "paint" on, and a picture's meaning is embedded in the visual language of form.

I love to make art. When it isn't making me crazy, it makes me happy. This has been true since I was a little girl.

The Story Behind the Artwork

Boy/girl/boy/girl (11.1) is a personal piece, the first piece of art Susan created after she moved out to Indianola, Washington, from Boston, Massachusetts. As with most of her art, this piece was not pre-planned but simply grew organically as Susan played with paint on the canvas. She let things come and develop in their own way.

The Creative Process

Susan's working techniques in the digital medium are the same techniques she used as a traditional artist. You can see this illustrated in this piece. Susan used direct, additive strokes and pasted on bits of this and that, continually building up layers and then flattening the image in Painter 6.

As a starting place, Susan used a customized color palette she has built up over several years of using Painter (see the section "Color Calibration" later in this chapter). She applied an assortment of her favorite basic brushes from the Painter 6 brush library. These included the Square Chalk, Basic Crayons, and Artist Pastel Chalk variants from the Dry Media brush category; the 2B Pencil variant from the Pencils category; the Simple Water variant from the Water Color brush category; and the Scratchboard Tool variant in the Pens category. Susan also used a custom library of her favorite paper textures.

◀ 11.1

The following series of figures shows the development of the image at various stages. The first stage (11.2) shows the left female figure roughly mapped out and the right-hand figure outlined in black on a separate layer. Susan then filled in some blocks of color and texture behind the black lines and altered the color of some of the lines (11.3).

In the next stage (11.4), more of the background is filled in and more attention is paid to changing the color of the line work of the left-hand figure. Then, the build-up of colorization and texturization is continued (11.5). In the final stage (11.6), the left-hand figure is transformed.

● 11.3

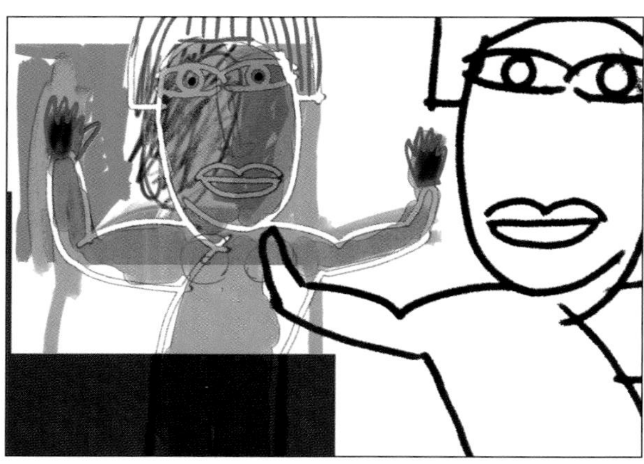

● 11.2

● 11.4

dS.

About the Artist

Biography

Susan has an MFA in Printmaking from Cranbrook Academy of Art and a BA in Anthropology from the University of Michigan. She has also studied at the California College of Arts and Crafts, and Massachusetts College of Art. She began her career as a mixed-media fine artist with an interest in illustration. In 1993, Ernest Barbee and Susan founded LeVan/Barbee, a digital art and design studio in Boston.

Susan was the Yosemite National Park Artist-In-Residence (1992), and her work has been displayed widely, including solo shows in Boston galleries in 1987, 1990, and 1992. Digital honors include work in major illustration annuals, including *Communication Arts, HOW,* and *Print;* inclusion in books such as *PainterWOW!* (Cher Threinen-Pendarvis) and *Painter* (Hiroshi Yoshii); articles about the studio in *EFX Art&Design, Newsweek,* and *MacUser;* and in digital art exhibitions, including Macworld, New York Digital Salon, Seybold, and Siggraph.

● 11.5

Technique: Filling In and Painting Behind Lines (Painter)

This technique shows one of the ways that Susan uses a simple line to create an interesting effect in her paintings.

1. **Open a blank white canvas in Painter.**
2. **Select Load Library from the bottom of the Brush Category pop-up menu (in the lower left of the Brushes palette).**
3. **Select the Ver 6 library in the Brushes folder in the Painter 7 application folder.**
4. **Select the Basic Crayons brush variant in the Dry Media brush category.**
5. **Ensure black is selected in the Colors section of the Art Materials palette.**
6. **Draw a black line drawing (11.7).**

● 11.6

● 11.7

Influences

Matisse, Picasso, Primitive Art, Medieval religious icons and paintings, jazz, popular culture, poetry, Buddhism, and the natural world.

Studio

Computer System:
Power Mac G4, 400 MHz
10GB hard drive
768MB RAM

Monitors:
Hitachi SuperScan 811 21-inch

Software:
Procreate Painter
Adobe Photoshop

Archive Media:
Iomega Predator CD-RW drive

Tablet:
Wacom Intuos 9 x 12

Input Devices:
Epson Perfection 1200 Photo scanner

Printers:
Epson Stylus Photo 1270 printer

Contact

Susan LeVan, LeVan/Barbee Studio
Indianola, Washington
lvbwa@earthlink.net
www.bruckandmoss.com

7. With the Eyedropper tool, click in the white background.
8. Choose Select→Auto Select.
9. Choose Using: Current Color and check the Invert box in the Auto Select dialog box (11.8).
10. Hold down the Option/Alt key and choose Select→Float.

[NOTE]

This floats the selection to a layer ("Layer 1") while leaving a copy behind on the background canvas. In Figure 11.9 the layer is slightly displaced so that you can see the layer and the copy left in the background.

11.8

11. Double click on the Layer 1 name in the Layers section of the Objects palette and rename it "original line."
12. Close the "eye" icon of the original line layer in Layers section.
13. Click on the canvas in the Layers section.
14. Choose the Magic Wand and select the interior of the line on the canvas.
15. Select Delete/Backspace to clear the interior of the line, making it an empty, or hollowed-out, line (11.10).
16. Choose Select→Auto Select.
17. Choose Using: Current Color and check the Invert box in the Auto Select window.
18. Hold down the Option/Alt key and choose Select→Float.
19. Double click on the new layer in the Layers section and rename it "hollow line."
20. Make sure the Preserve Transparency box is checked in the Layers section.
21. Click on the original line layer in the Layers section to select it.
22. Click on the eye of the original line layer in the Layers section to open it and make the original line layer visible beneath the hollow line layer.
23. Choose Effects→Fill (Cmd/Ctrl-F).
24. Select Fill With:Weave in the Fill dialog box (11.11).
25. Choose the Composite Method: Gel in the Layers section for the hollow line layer.
26. Paint on the canvas underneath these layers using the Square Chalk variant in Dry Media category (11.12), the 2B Pencil variant in the Pencils

11.9

11.10

category, and the Simple Water variant from the Water Color category.

[NOTE]

This last variant creates a Water Color layer above the other layers. You can always rearrange the ordering of the layers. You can apply this process with many variations, using colors and patterns instead of weaves. You can also follow this technique, then drop all the layers into the background canvas and start building up a fresh set of layers and paint. In this way, you build up a rich, textured painting.

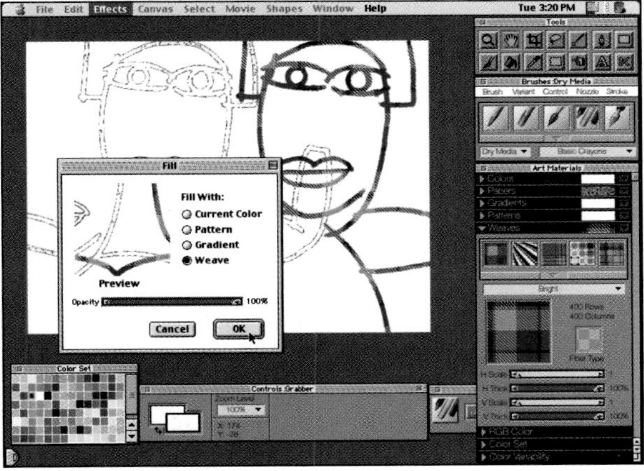

● 11.11

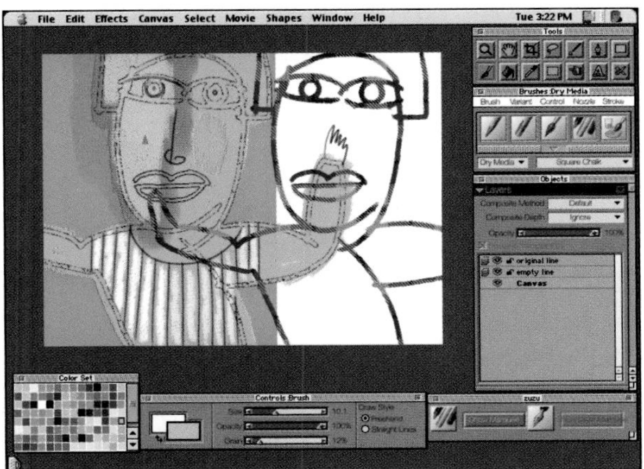

● 11.12

Artist's Creative Insight and Advice

Why Digital?

I became a digital artist only because my partner, Ernest Barbee, insisted that digital art was the wave of the future, and that our studio needed to be computer based. Having become a digital artist, I found working digitally takes a lot of risk out of art making. Work can be saved at any point, and a variety of paths explored without loss. This encourages risk taking.

There is a kind of synergy between artist and computer. The computer process takes you places conceptually that you would not come up with on your own. All these combine to greatly increase the opportunities for serendipity.

Advice for Artists Working in the Digital Medium

There is a danger that technique will overwhelm art. This happens in traditional mediums as well, but there are so many tricks and effects and gee-gaws in graphic software that there is an even greater likelihood that the image will get lost in technique. It is also very easy to over-work an image. Digital work can have a mechanical, slick, superficial feel. This is not a problem if it is deliberate, but can spoil the work if the artist is not aesthetically confident.

Color Calibration

I suggest that artists working in Painter create a custom palette of RGB colors. Take the colors into Photoshop and convert them to CMYK. (Or start in Photoshop with CMYK safe colors, and take them back into Painter.) Either way, have a printed proof made by a good commercial pre-press service bureau so that you can be sure of what to expect.

I started with a color set based on the main eight or ten colors I used in traditional acrylic and oils. I printed these colors out in pre-press and threw away, or altered, the colors that didn't translate well from RGB to CMYK. I now know how the colors are going to shift. This gives me predictability, consistency, and control. As a commercial artist, I sometimes have very little control over who prints a piece, and therefore it is important for me to have a fool-proof palette which is difficult to print badly. I use many bright, saturated colors that sometimes shift when they're printed, but I know how they'll shift, and this usually prevents total disasters.

Chapter 12

Trae

by Christine Auda

Artist's Statement

I explore the off-beat side of life to create colorful, modern, and unusual images with a twist. Each image may convey a bold or subtle message depending on the eye of the viewer.

I allow my subconscious to play out the scene on the computer instead of meticulously planning ahead.

The Story Behind the Artwork

Trae (12.1) emerged after Christine's mother's death. She believes the image expresses the depth of grief felt during that time. It wasn't until the image was complete that she truly identified with the various layers of the artwork.

This strong image depicts the strength, courage, pain, inner healing, and growth that she felt during her grieving process.

The Creative Process

Christine opened a new 9-x-6-inch canvas at 300 ppi (2700 pixels high by 1800 pixels wide) in Painter Classic and sketched the outline using a Pen tool. She then filled in the image using a round brush from the Brush palette. After that, she went back and defined Trae's features with the Pen tool. Once she defined the features of the image in Painter, she opened the image in Photoshop and adjusted the brightness and contrast.

◀ 12.1

Christine created depth by using her custom-made brushes and overlaying them at about 30% opacity in various areas. She also created luminosity by spontaneously adding curves in RGB mode. Months later, she completed the image by masking off the perimeter of the piece in black using a brush tool in Painter.

Trae took about ten hours to complete. Christine knew the piece was finished when she masked off the face of the image in black.

Technique: Customizing a Brush to Create Depth and Luminosity (Photoshop)

This technique shows the way that Christine adapts the brush options in Photoshop to create a sense of depth and luminosity in her paintings, as illustrated in *Trae.*

Another example where she applied this technique is her painting *Sandhill Crane*, which you can see here at an early stage (12.2) with flat background and muted feathers. Compare that early stage with the final stage (12.3), after she added texture to the background and depth and luminosity to the crane.

Photoshop allows you to capture and define custom brush shapes from samples of your own paintings. Auda's use of such custom brushes imbues her work with a deep sense of personal connection.

1. **Open a drawing (or photograph) in Grayscale mode in Photoshop that you want to use to sample for the custom brush.**
2. **Select the Lasso tool.**

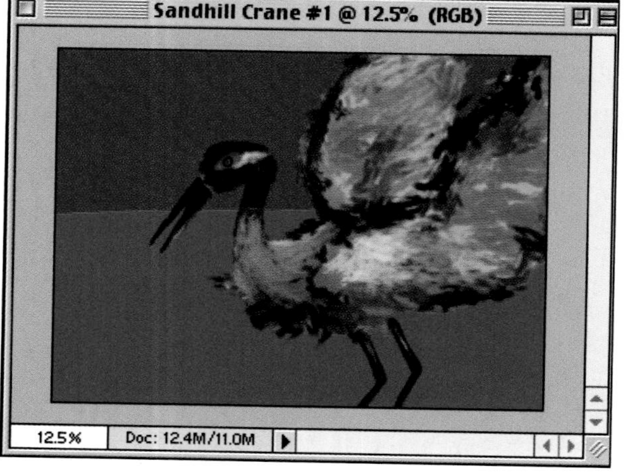

● 12.2

● 12.3

About the Artist

Biography

Christine began her art career as a jewelry designer in 1988. In the 1990s, she sold her jewelry to shops and galleries across the United States. In 1999 she crossed over to digital art, which she is passionate about. She began selling mixed media handmade cards, which included digital renderings, to both galleries and private customers. Soon she felt the need to create larger images, which culminated in being chosen as one of 30 winners in the Macworld Conference and Expo 2001 Digital Art Contest. Since then, some of her work has been exhibited in galleries in the United States.

Influences

Christine cites God and spirituality as her first influences. She doesn't think she would be a balanced artist without a sense of being connected to God or a higher being. She's been impacted by some of the masters, such as Picasso and Kandinsky, and also by Peter Max and present-day artists, such as Jimmy Winans, Nancy Egol Nikkal, and Tommy Vision.

3. **Use the Lasso tool to select a portion of your image for sampling as a custom brush (12.4).**
4. **Select the regular Paintbrush tool.**
5. **Double-click on the brush preview icon to access the Brush pop-up menu.**
6. **From the Brush pop-up menu, select Define Brush (12.5).**
   This creates a custom brush whose shape is defined by the sample of the image you selected.

[NOTE]

The precise details for creating a custom brush may differ according to which version of Photoshop you use.

7. **Open a preliminary painting that you want to add depth and luminosity to.**
   This preliminary painting could have been generated in another program, such as Painter, or created traditionally outside the computer and then scanned in.
8. **Click on the preview icon of your newly created custom brush to access the Brush Options dialog box.**

12.4

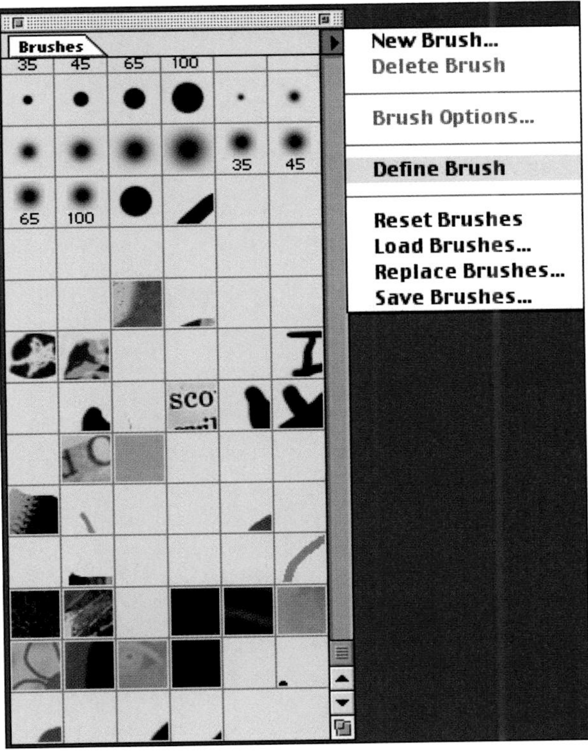

12.5

She is very influenced by people and the full spectrum of human emotion.

Being a nature lover, she is also influenced by animals, especially cats, dogs, and birds.

Studio

Computer System:
Mac G4, 867 MHz
120GB hard drive
640MB RAM

Monitors:
Mitsubishi Diamond Pro 920, 19 inches

Software:
Adobe Photoshop
Procreate Painter

Removable Media:
Zip 250

Archive Media:
CD-RW

Tablet:
Wacom 6 x 8

Input Devices:
Cannon flatbed scanner
Nikkon Coolpix 775 digital camera

Printers:
Epson Stylus Photo 2000P
Epson Stylus Photo 870

Contact

Christine Auda
Hawthorne, New Jersey
chrisandjim@earthlink.net
www.artcrawl.com

9. **Set the spacing at 125% (12.6).**
10. **Choose Mode: Overlay in the Paintbrush Options palette.**
11. **Set the paintbrush opacity level to about 30% in the Paintbrush Options palette (12.7).**
12. **Pick a light color, such as off-white, and paint randomly over the image, allowing for areas of luminosity and depth to occur.**
13. **Choose Image→Adjust→Curves.**
14. **Experiment with adjusting the curves until you are satisfied with the result (12.8).**

[TIP]

Christine found that a gentle S-curve for the RGB adjustment worked well in making the colors more saturated and brighter. It helped the whole painting "pop out" more.

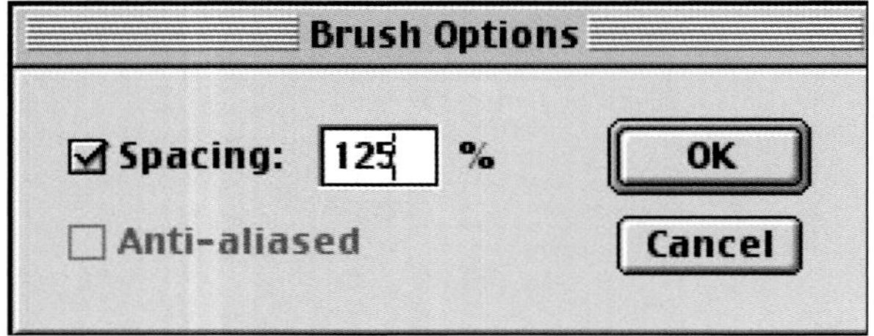

● 12.6

● 12.7

Artist's Creative Insight and Advice

Why Digital?

No other painting or illustration medium has the immediacy of digital. It is also the most forgiving artistic medium, allowing unlimited variations on artistic inspiration. It's not messy, and, for some, that is a plus.

I find one disadvantage when working digitally is the difficulty of working large-scale. I yearn to create monster-size wall hangings, but find I am hindered in the digital environment because of monitor size limitations and printing costs. At times, I find I compromise the tactile component of working in traditional media. I sometimes miss that element but feel the advantages of working digitally outweigh this disadvantage.

Digital art can look organic if that's the look you're after! This was a pleasant surprise to me when I first began creating digital art. I've actually had a friend look at some of my work and say — "Are you sure this was done on a computer? It looks like a "real" painting!" I took that as a compliment since that was the look I was after.

Advice for Artists Working in the Digital Medium

Be spontaneous! Be a big kid and play. Continually experiment. Never let the software intimidate you. Break any self-imposed rules or limitations.

Make friends with your software. By that, I mean take time to get to know its nuances. If you do, there will be some happy surprises in store for you.

Output

I still find color consistency between screen and print somewhat of a mystery. Sometimes, I play around with color-synch options. Otherwise, I usually am

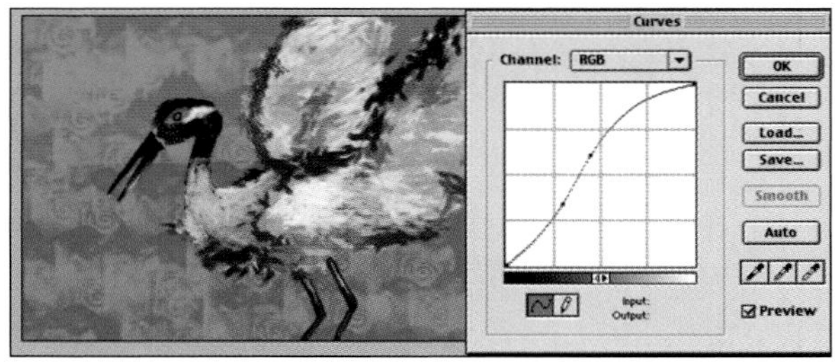

● 12.8

satisfied with the output since my work tends to be spontaneous anyway.

Presently my favorite output is Epson Water Color Paper — Radiant White printed using the Epson 2000P Printer. I find the slight texture of the paper lends an organic feel to the print. My finished work is printed using the Epson 2000P because of its archival rating of about 100 years according to The Wilhelm Imaging Research, Inc.

Occasionally, I incorporate non-digital media into my work, such as watercolor paints, acrylics, collage papers, variegated leaf, and pen and ink. I think I may do more of this in the future, but for now, I'm having too much fun in the pure digital world.

Chapter 13

Window with Chair

by Richard Bornemann

Artist's Statement

My work is driven by a balance between pure imagination and observations of light and color. I am captivated by the light softly flowing out of a window onto a snowy roof on a winter's night, or the subtle blue tint spilling through a skylight at sundown. These images motivate me to create new works that communicate this sensitivity to others.

I begin by creating elemental architectural spaces, and then fill them with brilliant light and color. In keeping with the stark simplicity of the compositions, all ornament and decoration have been eliminated. Each image includes a solitary scale-giving object: a chair, a staircase, or a doorway, for example. These not only give the piece a relative size and scale, but they also draw in the viewer as a participant, as an actor to a stage.

The Story Behind the Artwork

Window with Chair (13.1), like most of Richard's pieces, began as a mental image late at night in a dark, quiet room. Focusing on the image in his mind, Richard manipulated it by adding color, changing proportions, and adding and removing elements. When he was satisfied with the resulting mental image, he memorized it. Shortly thereafter, he began sketching it with software on his computer.

Richard's primary motivation was simply to coax the mental image into physical form, where it could be viewed and shared with others. Another was to communicate the joy of radiant light and color filling the architectural space.

Pat Watson on Richard Bornemann's *Window with Chair*

"Pictorially, Bornemann uses powerful but simple metaphors. A vacant chair, oversized empty walls, an open window, and a long stretch of sunlight on a bare floor combine to create a very poetic and austere meditation on a number of feelings — possibly arrival, anticipation, loneliness, or loss. The improbably low perspective amplifies the sense of scale and distance, making the distorted perspective that much more dramatic. The use of gradients gives an unmistakable digital flavor to the overall effort, and the dramatic use of color contrast heightens the tension, giving the very static depiction of chair and room a vibrancy that provides added emotional impact.

— Pat Watson, Digital Art Teacher, California State, Monterey Bay (www.csumb.edu)

◀ 13.1

The Creative Process

From the image he created in his mind and memorized, Richard began to rough-out and create the walls and chair in Strata 3DPro (13.2).

In this first stage, he modeled the shape and form of the space (13.3) and the chair (13.4). The chair design is based on a ladder back, Shaker style, which Richard selected for its simplicity.

Because the space depicted is exceedingly simple and spare, every compositional element is critical to the overall effect of the piece. The thickness of the wall, the sizing and exact placement of the window, the angle of view, the lighting and color scheme, and the cropping of the image were all studied. Proofs were run of multiple variations on these and other elements. Richard sometimes brought 9 or 10 studies of the same object up on his screen to evaluate and select the most successful variation.

The most critical element in *Window with Chair* is the scale of the chair itself. Richard wanted to create an interior space that was scaled in a dramatic fashion, avoiding an unremarkable room with an eight-foot ceiling. He studied this by scaling the chair multiple times (13.5), each time creating a different effect.

As the chair was reduced in size, the room appeared larger and larger. The window was scaled to a grand proportion to match the room. He moved the window up high in the wall, adding to the mystery of the piece. This process resulted in a composition of familiar objects, expressed in unfamiliar ways.

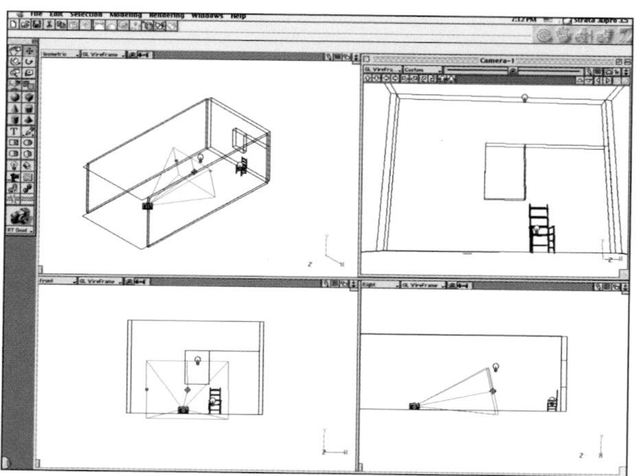

● 13.2

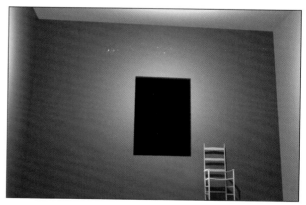

● 13.3

About the Artist

Biography

Richard is a graduate of the University of Maryland School of Architecture (1978), and he has worked designing (and building) large buildings in Washington, D.C. In 1983, he started The Architectural Art, Inc., a studio of artists who crafted architectural illustrations for real estate developers. He left this company to work as a digital fine artist in 2000. This change was prompted by one of those rare flashes of insight that gave him the idea for a whole body of work.

Richard's digital work has been recognized in the 2000 and 2001 Macworld and the 2001 Seybold art contests, and has been exhibited at the Rocky Mountain Digital Arts Gallery, Denver, Colorado, and Peck Gallery, Providence, Rhode Island. Richard has also worked in traditional media, including oils and graphite.

Influences

Light and color in the real world.

13.4

13.5

13.6

After he resolved the basic concept of the piece, he exported the file, as a 3D model, into the program Lightscape. He selected final colors, refined the viewpoint, and rendered the piece (which created a bitmapped file) using a raydiosity algorithm, a mathematical formula that calculates the illumination on a surface caused by reflected light from nearby objects. As an example, raydiosity occurs if you place a brightly colored object in a well illuminated space, and move it up against a white wall (13.6). You will notice the color from the object bounce on to the adjacent white wall.

This image had many obvious flaws, which were artifacts of the raydiosity "solution" generated by the model. It served, however, as raw material for the final piece.

The color, shading, and tinting needed to be redone by hand throughout the image. To do so, he imported the file into Photoshop. He then generated channels for all the major elements. This piece had 14 channels (for example, channels for the window opening,

Studio

Computer System:
Macintosh G4, 400 MHz
10GB hard drive
448MB RAM

Monitors:
Optiquest 19-inch
KDS flat-screen 15-inch

Software:
Adobe Photoshop
Strata 3DPro
Amapi
VitualPC
Lightscape
PresenterActive

Removable Media:
Zip drive

Archive Media:
CD

Printers:
Epson 1280

Contact

Richard Bornemann
Acton, Massachusetts
pixelist@erols.com
www.richardbornemann.com

window head, window sill, chair, ceiling, floor, pool of light on floor, left wall, and so). He then adjusted each channel.

The dark shadow bands where the walls join the ceiling were reworked within the respective wall channel. The window was filled with a gradient representing the brilliant sky. One by one, each of the channels was changed, proofed, and refined.

The last step was to crop the image. Richard first created a low resolution snapshot of the piece and tested several different cropping solutions before settling on the final one.

This piece took 74 hours to create — a complex and intuitive process that involved 37 different proofs that were used to modify and refine the image.

Technique: Casting a Delicate Shadow (Photoshop)

This is the Photoshop technique Richard used to create the shadow of the chair on the wall.

1. **Open a bitmapped image in Photoshop.**
2. **Select the Magic Wand tool.**
3. **Set the Magic Wand tolerance to 22 in the tool options menu.**
4. **Click on the object in your image to which you want to add a delicate shadow.**

   Richard applied this method to the chair in his composition.
5. **Choose Select→Similar in the Select pop-up menu.**

[TIP]

By holding down the Shift or Option/Alt keys while clicking with the Magic Wand, you can add to or subtract from a selection.

6. **Choose Select→Save Selection.**
7. **Name the selection something descriptive, such as chair (13.7).**
8. **Create a new layer by selecting New Layer in the Layers palette pop-up menu.**
9. **Name the new layer "Chair Shadow" or another appropriate name.**

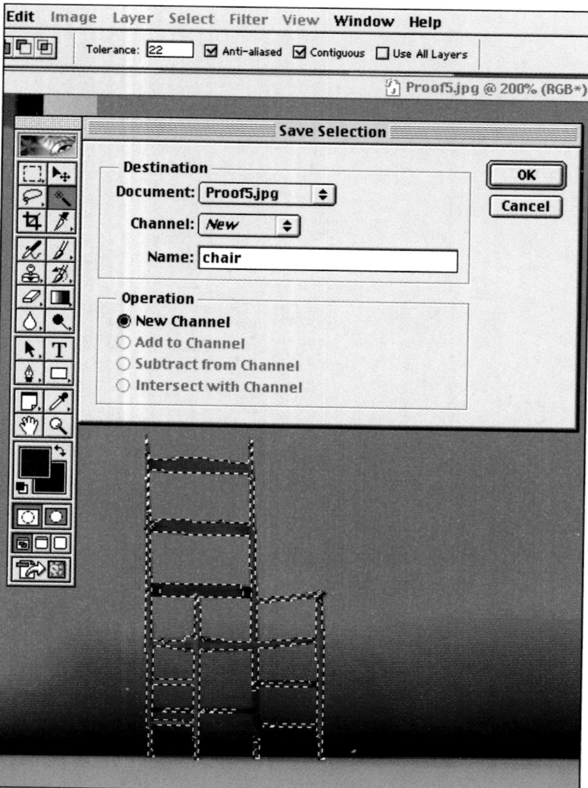

13.7

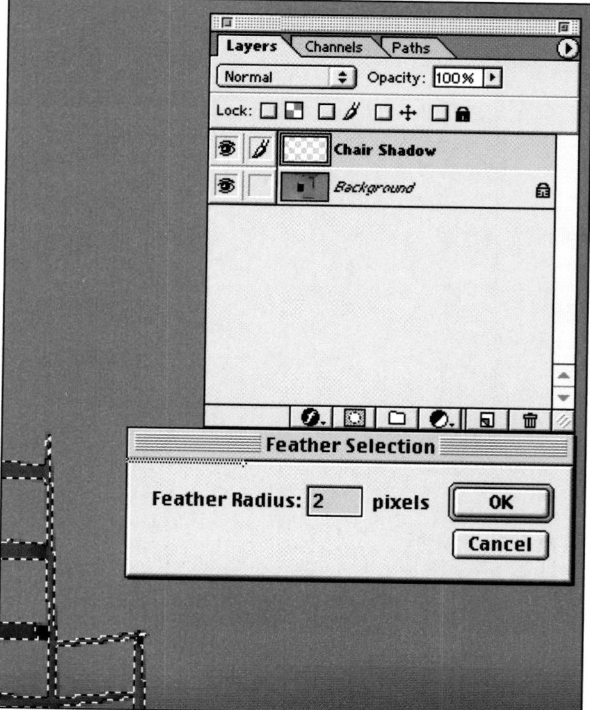

13.8

10. **Choose Select→Feather.**
11. **Set the feather to 2 pixels in the Feather Selection dialog box (13.8).**
12. **Choose the Eyedropper tool.**
13. **Click on a region of dark tone in your image.**
    This color, picked using the Eyedropper, becomes the foreground color and will be used as a fill color for the shadow. In the case of *Window with Chair,* the color at the base of the wall behind the chair was sampled.

[TIP]

The advantage of sampling a dark color from within the image, rather than just picking a dark gray from the color picker, is that the shadow blends and harmonizes much better with the rest of the image.

14. **Choose Option/Alt-Delete/Backspace to fill the selection with the current foreground color (picked using the Eyedropper in the previous step).**
15. **Choose Select→Deselect (Command/Ctrl-D) to deselect the selection.**
16. **Choose Filter→Blur→Gaussian Blur.**
17. **Set the radius to 2 pixels in the Gaussian Blur window (13.9).**
18. **Use the Move tool to place the shadow to the left of your object (13.10).**
19. **Select the Polygonal Lasso tool.**
20. **Make a selection around the part of the shadow that protrudes into the floor (click Return/Enter to close the polygonal selection).**
21. **Choose Select→Load Selection.**
22. **Select the object selection in the Load Selection dialog box.**
23. **Choose Add to Selection in the Load Selection dialog box (13.11) and click OK.**
24. **Click Delete/Backspace.**
    This clears the shadow from where it overlaps the chair, making the shadow appear to be behind the chair.
25. **Adjust the layer opacity to 55% (13.12).**

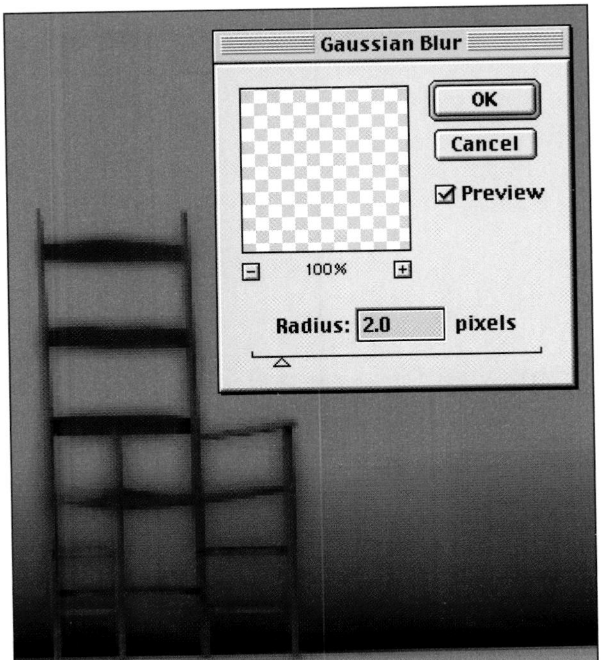

● 13.9

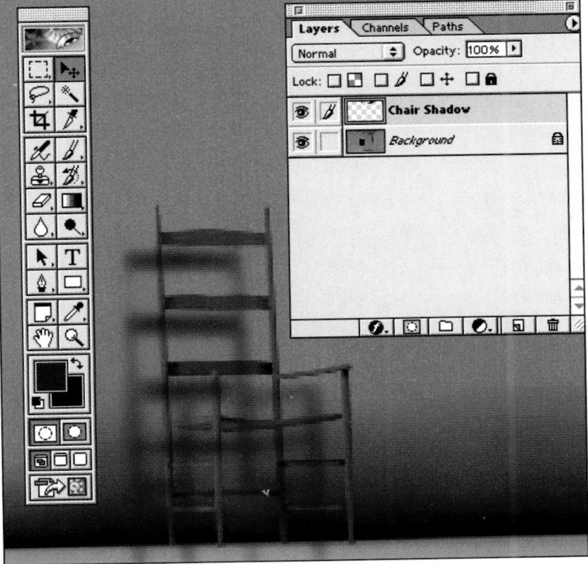

● 13.10

Artist's Creative Insight and Advice

Why Digital?

Digital has many advantages for the type of images that I create. It would be difficult or impossible to achieve the subtle gradients of color and radiant lighting effects with any other media. Additionally, working digitally changes the process of creating a piece from one that is less accidental to one that is more deliberative. Traditional media has the inherent quality of being fixed as the brush hits the canvas. A stroke or a color choice that is less than optimal nonetheless becomes part of the final work. Although there is a joy that comes from the immediacy of creating art in this fashion, there is a resultant diminishment in control.

In the digital medium, you have the opportunity to change and refine a work as it progresses. Layers, multiple undos, and the History palette in Photoshop all give the artist unprecedented control over the image that he or she is creating.

Advice for Artists Working in the Digital Medium

Think of the digital medium as just another tool to use to create your work. Study as much as possible the work and techniques of others. Become an expert in the software and medium of your choice.

Enter competitions, call galleries, show and share your work with others. It is incredibly validating when others become enthusiastic about your work.

Color Calibration

There are both advantages and disadvantages in the final output used by digital artists. One advantage is that the work can be printed multiple times, and thereby sold to more than one collector. A disadvantage is the challenge that comes from converting the screen RGB image to the printed CMYK image, with the inevitable loss in color gamut. By working with an excellent printer that specializes in fine art giclée printing, I have found that this disadvantage can be overcome.

If you are printing out your work, find an excellent printer. Your printmaker will become an integral part of your process. I deliver my files to the printer in RGB, and we review them on screen to note any potential problems with gamut, banding, or other printing issues.

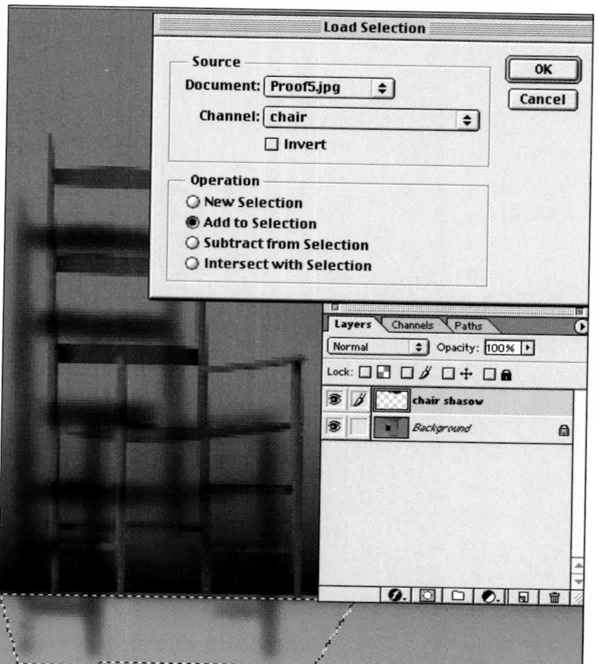

● 13.11

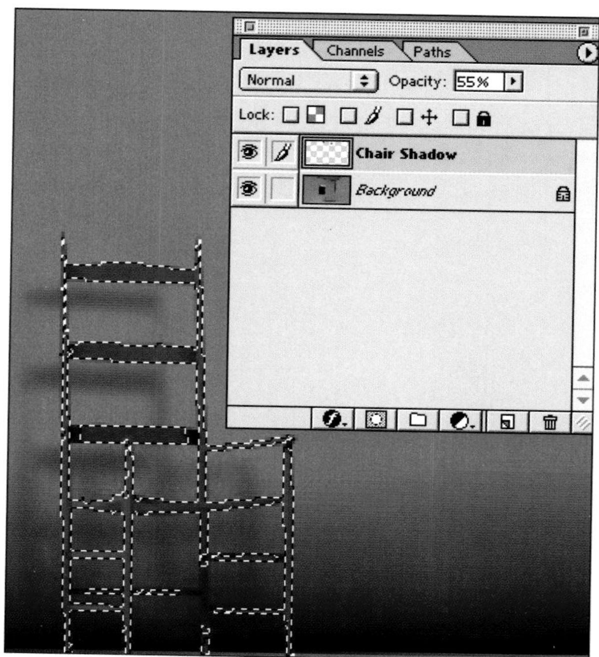

● 13.12

Chapter 14

Lantern Street, Autumn

by Aleksander "aljen" Jensko

Artist's Statement

A computer is just a tool like any other — a powerful and fine one, of course, but whatever you make out of it, it's up to you.

It's not the computer that dominates my life; it's art.

The Story Behind the Artwork

Lantern Street, Autumn (14.1) came into being as a personal work, involving no deadlines or contracts. The old town it shows has some similarities to Aleksander's hometown of Lübeck, Germany.

He sketched the perspective from scratch in Painter one day. Some time later, his wife asked why the image hadn't been worked on in a while, which prompted him to sit down and do the final touches and varnish, also in Painter.

The Creative Process

Aleksander works spontaneously and from scratch. In this image, he used a variety of brushes in Painter, including the following: the Scratchboard Tool variant in the Pens category for the scratchy line work; the Large Chalk and Charcoal variants in the Dry Media category; and the Colored Pencil variant in the Pencils category.

The Chalks, Charcoal, and Pencils were used for sketching and refining the lines. Charcoal was used for fill and washed using the Just Add Water brush in the Liquid category. Some Watercolor Brush was also applied. Last but not least, Aleksander took his beloved Oil Pencil variant, among others, to paint the sky. The Oil Pencil variant is located in the Graphic Design 1 brush category that you find on the Painter CD 2.

◀ 14.1

In the "work in progress" shown here (14.2), you can still see the original rough sketch. Aleksander had just begun applying colors; there is still no sky, which was painted in later.

The original image was created rather small, so Aleksander enlarged it in Painter by approximately 200%. This resulted in a washed look. He then cloned the entire (enlarged) image and worked on the clone applying a lot of paper textures and original luminance to re-create the sharpness. He used a lot of different Paper Textures while overlaying the paint to give it this "Painter-unique-rough-structured" look (14.3). (See the technique later in this chapter.) The total process took about 10 to 12 hours.

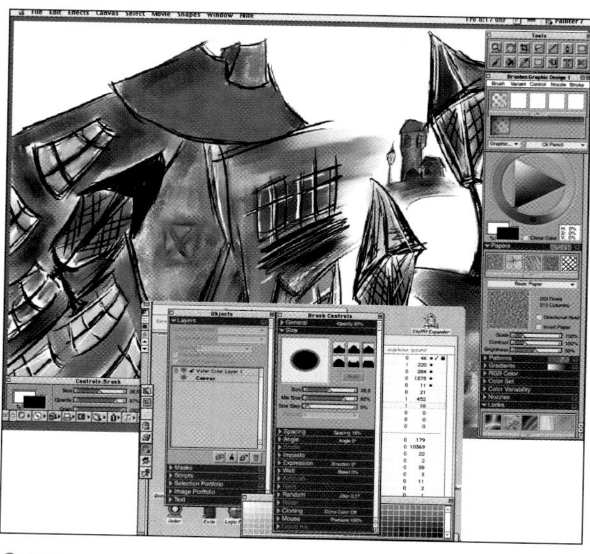

● 14.2

Technique: Creating a "Painter-Unique-Rough-Structured" Look (Painter)

In this technique, you see how Aleksander applies paper and original luminance to create the unusual look you find in *Lantern Street, Autumn*.

1. **Open an image in Painter.**
   This image could be an original painting created from scratch in Painter, or a scanned drawing, or a digital photo.
2. **Choose Canvas→Resize.**
3. **Uncheck the Constrain File Size check box.**
4. **Double the Width setting (in pixels).**
   Doing so automatically doubles the Height setting too.

● 14.3

About the Artist

Biography

Aleksander started with conventional photography at the age of 15. He learned the darkroom process and created collage with scissors, glue, darkroom witchcraft, and slide-sandwich techniques. Looking for the limits of traditional photography, he was also active as a freelance writer and journalist in the '80s; he published two books of short stories with his own illustrations.

Aleksander showed drawings and watercolors at several local exhibitions in Germany and did audio/video performances with slide shows and live electronic music.

About 1993, he noticed that a Macintosh computer could help him start over where conventional techniques stop. Using Photoshop, and later Painter, he's been developing his own worlds.

Influences

French Surrealism, German Expressionism, some Romantic stuff. Mid-80s rock, post-punk, and new wave music. Sound artists like Autechre, Orbital, Roni Size, and David Holmes. Photographers like Ralph Gibson and Eva Rubinstein. Early movies of the 1920s. Artists like Paul Wenger,

[TIP]

If you want to make additional enlargements, do so in several steps, repeating the whole technique described previously. Otherwise, you get an unsharp, blurred image due to the pixel interpolation.

5. **Choose File→Clone.**
   This generates a 100% identical copy of your image.
6. **Choose Cmd/Ctrl-M to mount your clone copy.**
7. **Working on the clone copy, choose Effects→Surface Control→Apply Surface Texture.**
8. **Set the Using menu to Original Luminance. Set the Reflection to about 14%. Drag the Amount slider to the left (14.4) and click OK.**
9. **Use Apply Surface Texture again the same way, but this time with the Using menu set to Paper (14.5).**
   Look for papers in your Papers library (Art Materials palette) which best match your needs. There are many extra papers on the Painter CD-ROM and even more on the Internet. You can also make your own textures. Inverting the original paper structure helps sometimes, too.
10. **Choose File→Save As. Save and rename the clone copy image.**
11. **Wash and smear over the clone copy using brush variants from the Liquid category.**
    Don't worry if details are rendered unrecognizable. Just play.

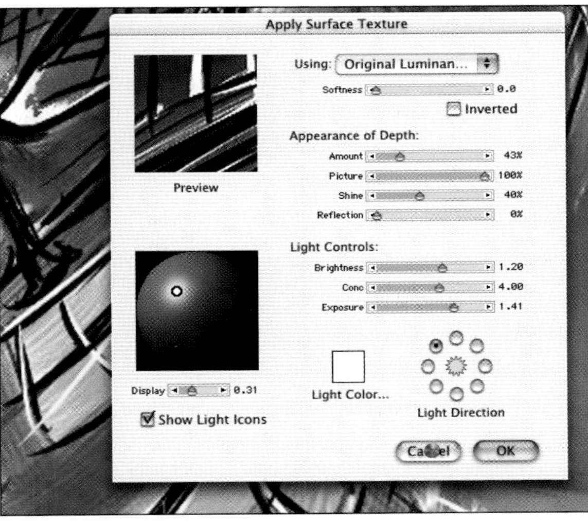

● 14.4

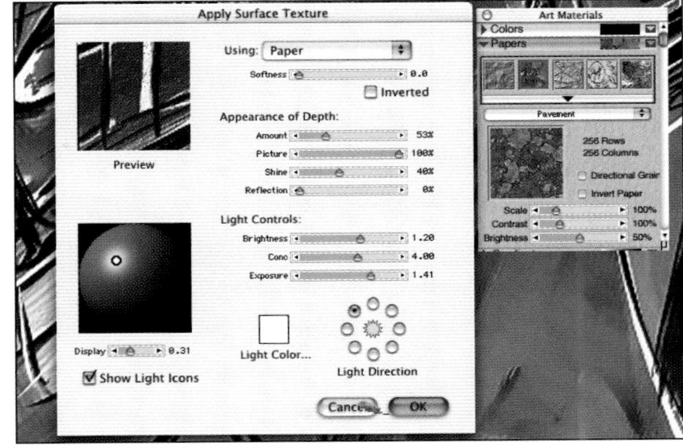

● 14.5

Fritz Lang, Peter Lorre, Boris Karloff. Painters like Max Ernst, Paul Delvaux, and Joan Miró.

Studio

Computer System:
PowerMac G3, 300 Mhz
60GB hard drive
576MB RAM
PowerBook "Pismo" G3
576MB RAM

Monitors:
ELSA Ecomo 19-inch
Old Apple 13-inch

Software:
Adobe Photoshop
Adobe Illustrator
Painter
Linocolor Elite
Bryce
Poser
Flash
Thorsten Lemke GraphicConverter
Apple QuickTime VR Authoring Studio

Tablet:
Wacom Intuos ADB
Wacom Grafire graphite USB

Input Devices:
Nikon Coolscan III
Linoscan 1200
Nikon Coolpix 950
Olympus E10 digital cameras, Manfrotto QTVR Head

Printers:
Epson Stylus Photo 1270
HP 970Cxi

Contact

Aleksander "aljen" Jensko
Lübeck, Germany
aljen@mac.com
www.aljen.de

12. **Select the original image.**
    You can select the filename at the bottom of the Windows pop-up menu.
13. **Choose Cmd/Ctrl-C.**
    This copies the original image to the scratch disk.
14. **Select the clone copy image.**
15. **Hold down the space bar and click once.**
    This centers the canvas in your screen (and ensures any pasted image is centered).
16. **Choose Cmd/Ctrl-V.**
    This pastes the original image over your clone copy.
17. **Go to the Layers section of the Objects palette and experiment with different Composite Methods (14.6).**
    There is no general advice here, because there are no two identical images. The layers interact with each other in a sometimes quite unpredictable way. In this way, you can achieve a sharp, structured look while the details remain recognizable.

[TIP]

You can also put the painted layer on the top of what you pasted, by choosing Cmd/Ctrl-A to select all and then holding down the Option/Alt key while you choose Select→Float. Then try out the Multiply, Screen, and Magic Combine Composite Methods. Watch your image change.

Artist's Creative Insight and Advice

Why Digital?

The digital techniques are definitely here; you can't ignore them. The industry gives me another medium, another tool, which takes over where the conventional techniques stop. Computers by themselves do number crunching. It is the artist who turns the computer into a digital art medium.

With digital imaging, the standards of quality were redefined. Think of tasks like posterizing — or just inverting — a photograph. It used to be a two-night job to make a poster-like enlargement using the conventional darkroom toolbox, and this in black-and-white. Now you can get a poster effect within seconds, and nobody will be impressed. So you have to get more out of it. The same applies for collages: glue, scissors, and retouching have been replaced with layers and layer masks, great clone tools, and so on.

All this didn't make the artist's life any easier, of course. It didn't make the traditional techniques any worse, either. The digital media is just another tool, like Cinemascope or TV. Cinemascope didn't replace the traditional theatre, and TV didn't kill the cinema. My early Super 8 movies were short and without sound. Today, you can shoot one-hour movies with a pocket size DV camcorder. So what? There are also filters that make videos look like Super 8.

This whole discussion brings electronic music to mind. In the '80s, everybody believed the future would be digital and programmable; but try to buy an old, used Minimoog or a TB303 today. Virtual-analogue synthesizers, like Virus or Clavia Nord, are being built in order to get analog sound out of digital circuits. It's just crazy — I love it!

Some advantages of digital techniques are obvious: undo, copy, and paste, for example. Last summer, I was in Norway, beyond the Polar Circle. I had my PowerBook with me, along with a digital camera and a small, funny Wacom Grafire. It was great to sit at the seashore, load a (just taken!) photo from the camera, and paint over it. It was great to shoot a QTVR panorama from the top of the mountain and to show it later that evening to other people. It was great to make music on rainy days — everything I needed was on my backpack-compatible, foldable computer.

There are also other advantages: You can feel free to play around with different tools and techniques without wasting valuable materials. Taking photos in

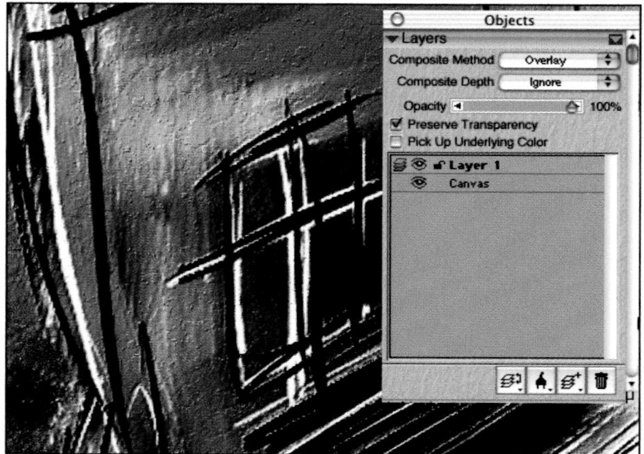

● 14.6

the subway at night? Or on the highway without looking through the finder? If the pictures are worthless, you simply delete them. This is good for your wallet, and also for the environment — no excess chemistry, no material waste.

You can also try some techniques you probably wouldn't otherwise try in traditional media. Painter gives me the freedom to do so, at least virtually.

Disadvantages? Okay, the virtual "chemistry" doesn't smell, and your clothes won't get dirty from the digital paint. A part of the sensitive, sensual experience goes away if you work digital.

The major disadvantage, however, seems to be the social one. At least here in Germany, you aren't a "real" artist if you work digitally. This is a little bit contradictory in a country where the music genre of techno was born, but it's true.

Everyone has a computer today. I mean, a powerful computer, capable of doing things that were only in the domain of huge workstations several years ago. Everybody can get a copy of Photoshop, Painter, FreeHand, whatever. The rule of thumb seems to be, "Okay, nicely done, but I could do the same if I only would . . . " People believe that computers can take them by the hand and do everything they want with just a mouse click. I do hope that people wake up from this dream sooner or later. Nobody believes in the omnipotence of the atom energy today, but hey, in the 60s, everybody did. So watch out for things to come.

Advice for Artists Working in the Digital Medium

Don't get fooled by the computer. It's just another tool. Get a Mac, a fine and easy tool.

Don't let yourself be fooled by the folks telling you that digital isn't a serious art medium. The same was said about photography 150 years ago. Have fun. Love your work. Believe in your dreams. Breathe your visions. It's as easy as that.

The equipment myth is just another fairy tale. Of course, you can work much faster if you have a brand new computer, but hey, that one will also be old in a couple of months. Currently, I am working with a three-year-old, blue-and-white Macintosh. It *could* be faster, for sure, but I can still use it and work efficiently and with lots of fun.

No computer, no program will do the job. You will (or you will not).

Color Calibration

I use QuickTime with Heidelberg profiles. I have no problems using inkjet printers or offset print.

Cher Threinen-Pendarvis on Jensko's *Lantern Street, Autumn*

"*Lantern Street* evokes a dream-like quality and a strong sense of place. The whimsical spiraling leaves and dark clouds tell us that a storm may be approaching. The village is drawn with lively black charcoal lines and painted in rich somber colors. Is this a signal for an end to summer and the beginning of a new season?"

— Cher Threinen-Pendarvis, Author, Teacher, Digital Artist (`www.pendarvis-studios.com`)

Chapter 15

Sister of the Bride

by Zsuzsanna V. Szegedi

Artist's Statement

Brushstroke, color, and contrast comprise my language. Although *Sister of the Bride* is digital, it conveys my desire to make a personal connection with the viewer because it still contains the motions of my hand.

I love nature but also am amazed by technology, which motivates my exploration of both traditional and digital art, while emphasizing nature in its techno-modern context.

The Story Behind the Artwork

Zsuzsanna's inspiration sometimes comes unintentionally. She usually works best from observation and always uses models in her art.

This image was created specifically as an entry for the Seybold Seminars Digital Art Contest. After hours of sitting in front of the computer and trying to find inspiration to be creative, she decided to take a break and take a shower. Afterwards, with a towel on her head, she looked into the mirror and said, "I've got to figure out something." At that very moment, Zsuzsanna says, the idea of the *Sister of the Bride* was born. She began sketching. Her concentration on her reflection then turned into inspiration for an image. That image became the *Sister of the Bride* (15.1).

This piece's title was inspired by the sister of the bride in the movie *Like Water for Chocolate* by Alfonso Arau (one of Zsuzsanna's favorite movies). In that movie, the sister uses cooking to express her feelings about her true love marrying her sister, and those feelings, in turn, are passed onto those who eat the food.

She chose colors that brought out her feelings. Zsuzsanna says she really enjoys the process of playing with colors that accentuate opposites; this is the reason she uses high hues as well as deep darks for contrast.

◀ 15.1

The Creative Process

This image started as a hand-drawn portrait (15.2) that was scanned and colorized in Photoshop.

For a basic framework, Zsuzsanna created a pencil drawing on 8.5-by-11-inch paper. Since she built the rest of the image on top of this line drawing, she made sure to have enough detail and room for smooth color surfaces and further development.

● 15.2

She scanned this pencil drawing at 900 dpi. She scanned at this high resolution with an eye to a final output of 23 inches by 30 inches from an HP5000 printer. This printer requires a 300 dpi file for the optimum quality. Therefore, since the original 8.5-by-11-inch sketch was three times smaller than the final output, she had to scan the sketch at three times the desired output resolution (see the section on output later in this chapter).

After scanning the sketch, Zsuzsanna used Photoshop to apply color to the image. She worked with many layers, each with different opacity and layer blending mode settings (15.3). For every major change, she used a new layer so that she could move or alter its content independently throughout the entire process. Zsuzsanna used these layers to emphasize surface differences with different brushes and brush tool settings on the different layers. This approach gave her a lot of flexibility. It also resulted in a large, 120MB, multi-layered Photoshop file, in spite of careful layer management that included merging layers.

● 15.3

About the Artist

Biography

Zsuzsanna studied both the fine arts and the digital arts in Hungary at Janus Pannonius University, Pecs, and at Eszterhazy Karoly College, Eger. The traditional techniques she learned there gave her the foundation for continuing an education in digital media.

Her first encounter with computer graphics was in 1997 when she moved to the United States. Zsuzsanna graduated with a BFA in Fine Art and Communication Design, at the Massachusetts College of Art in Boston. Her work in both digital and traditional media has been recognized by a number of organizations, including the Society of Illustrators of Los Angeles, for excellence in traditional media, and in digital work at the Macworld Conference and Expo and Seybold Seminars Digital Art Contests in the student awards.

Her work has been exhibited at major shows and galleries in Los Angeles, San Francisco, New York, and Boston. She now works as a graphic designer and illustrator in Boston, in addition to pursuing a career in fine art painting.

Influences

Zsuzsanna is influenced by music, motion, color, and light. Her strong attachment to

Using customized paintbrush tools, Zsuzsanna created a watercolor quality in her image. She used the Color Burn layer blend mode to colorize lines, emphasize details and set in contrast with cooler colors. (See the technique later in this chapter for more information on the Color Burn effect.)

Here you can see some snapshots of how the image progressed (15.4). You can read more about these different phases in the following section.

Technique: From Line Art to Digital Watercolor (Photoshop)

This technique shares Zsuzsanna's approach to taking a hand-drawn line art sketch and transforming it into a beautiful digital watercolor painting.

1. **Scan a pencil drawing at 300 ppi into Photoshop as a CMYK file.**

   A sketch on letter-size paper (8.5 by 11 inches) works well. For more information regarding resolution and color mode, see the section on output later in this chapter.
2. **Select New Layer from the Layers pop-up menu.**

   This adds a new layer to your background copy.
3. **Select the Paintbrush tool. In the Paintbrush toolbox options select a soft round brush with size 45.**
4. **Click on the Brush Preview to access the Brush Options pop-up window. In the Brush Options window adjust the brush shape from circular to smooth oval.**
5. **Click on the Brush Dynamics icon (located on the far-right end of the brush options palette). In the Brush Dynamics pop-up window, set the Size to Fade with 100 steps (15.5). Leave the Opacity and Color settings to their defaults (Off).**
6. **With this customized paintbrush, loosely paint over the lines with various colors.**

15.4

15.5

the techniques of the old impressionist masters, and influences from Monet, van Gogh, Degas, and Sargent, has led her to explore and create her own distinct color palette and style. The artist she most admires and respects is Hungarian-born Gyorgy Kepes (who was the Founder and Director of the Center for Advanced Visual Studies at MIT).

Studio

Computer System:
PC, 400 MHz
8GB hard drive
256MB RAM

Monitors:
17-inch Princeton Graphics

Software:
Adobe Photoshop
Adobe Illustrator
Macromedia Flash
Macromedia Dreamweaver
Macromedia Freehand
ACDsee

Archive Media:
HP CD Writer

Tablet:
Tabletworks Creation Station 6 x 9

Input Devices:
Scanner
Toshiba digital camera

Printers:
HP 722C Deskjet

Contact

Zsuzsanna V. Szegedi
Boston, Massachusetts
zsuzsi@zsuzsanna.com
www.zsuzsanna.com

[TIP]

As you paint, follow the form of your subject with your brush strokes. This builds up a sense of form and harmony in the picture.

7. **Change the Layer Blend mode from Normal to Color Burn.**
   This not only colorizes the lines but also emphasizes the details with a burnt effect.
8. **Select New Layer from the Layers pop-up menu.**
9. **Set the opacity of the new layer to be 45% to 50%.**
10. **On this layer color the blank areas of a portion of your image where you want to add color with a soft, smooth effect (such as the face, in the case of Zsuzsanna's picture) (15.6).**
    Zsuzsanna used the soft oval custom Paintbrush with low opacity for the face. This soft brush allowed her to capture the smoothness and softness of the skin.

[TIP]

Use a bigger brush size for setting the main planes of your subject's form, such as for the cheek bones, forehead, and jawline in a portrait. Use small brushes for details, such as eyes, nose, and mouth. Try vivid, bolder, brighter colors to draw attention to specific regions of your image, such as the eyes.

11. **Select New Layer from the Layers pop-up menu.**
12. **Check the Wet Edges setting in the Paintbrush toolbox options, opacity set at 75%, and Brush Dynamics Size set to Fade at 200 steps.**

● 15.6

13. **Apply this modified Paintbrush on the new layer where you want to have a watercolor effect.**
    Zsuzsanna used this custom Paintbrush for the clothing in her image (15.7 and 15.8). The brush gave a watercolor effect that suited the folds of the clothing. Look for parts of your image where the watercolor effect can help convey the feel of your subject.
14. **Select New Layer from the Layers pop-up menu.**
15. **Set the Layer Blend mode to Overlay.**
    Overlay Blend mode adds a touch of darker tone to the image. Thus this layer can be used to bring out contrast and establish the darkest regions.
16. **Add dark paint loosely with a large brush in the areas of your image where you want to bring out major contrast and emphasize the darker tones (15.9).**
17. **Select New Layer from the Layers pop-up menu.**
18. **Set the Layer Blend mode to Screen.**

● 15.7

19. **Use light colors to bring out highlights in your image.**
20. **Choose Flatten Image from the Layers palette pop-up menu.**
    Choose File→Save As and save your multi-layered file as a Photoshop document before flattening it. That way, you preserve your layers and maintain the ability to go back and edit your image later.
21. **Use the Smudge tool to combine the original line drawing with the painted details.**
    Now that the image is flat, you can smear and blend together the brush work you painted on the separate layers with the original lines of your scanned line drawing (which was on the background layer). This allows you to create a softer, more organic look in your picture. Zsuzsanna applied the Smudge tool to the background of her image, outside the central subject (the face), to make it blurrier and thus appear to recede into the distance.
22. **Save your image as a TIFF or JPEG file for final output (TIFF for print, JPEG for the Web).**

Artist's Creative Insight and Advice

Why Digital?

There is no undo setting in traditional art and no mess in digital art. (Though I must admit I miss the mess in digital art!)

Advice for Artists Working in the Digital Medium

Instead of separating digital art from traditional art, try to enrich the digital medium with organic thoughts.

Work with what you have. Don't try to make an excuse of waiting for the latest technology. You'll never catch up!

Just because there is an endless number of tools and settings, it doesn't mean that you have to use them all

● 15.8

● 15.9

to create an artwork. Piling it up isn't art. You're the artist — don't let the machine do everything for you.

Output

First of all, calibrate your monitor at the start of every blank canvas and never believe your screen display.

CMYK (Cyan Magenta Yellow Black) is the Color mode that most printing devices use and that ensures the most accurate consistency between what you see on the screen and what you see on your final print. I recommend working with CMYK throughout your creative process in Photoshop since that avoids the disappointment and frustration of color changes that occur when you change back and forth between RGB (Red Green Blue) and CMYK. RGB has many bright, saturated colors that don't exist in the CMYK color space. When you convert from RGB to CMYK, your image tends to become duller and your blues and yellows can shift noticeably.

The optimum resolution for most printing devices is 300 dpi. Therefore, if you plan to print your artwork, you need at least 300 ppi file resolution at the final output size for professional output. Scan your sketch at 300 ppi if you want to keep the size the same. If you want the final artwork to be printed twice as big as your sketch (for example, you start with a 8.5-by-11-inch sketch and want to end up with a 17-by-22-inch print), scan it in two times 300 ppi, which is 600 ppi. In this case, you then need to covert your scanned image from 8.5 by 11 inch at 600 ppi to 17 inch by 22 inch at 300 ppi. To do this, choose Image➔Image Size in Photoshop. In the Image Size property window check Constrain Proportions, which keeps the image proportions constant; and uncheck Resample Image, which keeps the total file size (total number of pixels in the image) the same. Type in 300 in the resolution window, and the size changes automatically from 8.5 by 11 inches to 17 by 22 inches.

Always print proof after proof. Never use low-quality paper. Even if it looks white, you'll need the purest white paper for the richest color.

If you are creating art specifically for the Web, much lower resolutions (75 to 150 ppi) are acceptable since your final output resolution is screen resolution (typically 72 ppi for the Macintosh and 96 ppi for the PC).

Leslie Hunt on Szegedi's *Sister of the Bride*

"Here's a dead-on illustration of ambiguous emotions, from the riveting eyes, to the nuance of shadows and light, to the striking contrast of the cool tones against fiery colors. A very effective work."

— Leslie Hunt, Features Editor, *PEI* and *Professional Photographer* (www.peimag.com)

563
563

Chapter 16

Missing Link

by Mark Bloom

Artist's Statement

One of the great advantages of building 3D models is the opportunity to play with reality. So long as the final image looks good, I don't mind cheating just a little.

The Story Behind the Artwork

The image of the train engine was inspired by the photography of O. Winston Link. Link recorded the last years of the great American steam railroads in stunning black-and-white photographs. Mark wanted the challenge of building a digital model of one of these engines just because it seemed so intimidating. He knew nothing about the mechanics of train engines, so he began by finding as many pictures (most taken by Winston Link) to use as a reference point.

Shortly before Mark entered the image (16.1) in the Macworld Expo Digital Art contest, Winston Link died, and so the title, *Missing Link,* was intended as a private tribute to the inspiration behind this image.

The Creative Process

Mark's initial task was to build the 3D model of the train, followed by a 3D model of the environment around the train. He wanted a dramatic, close-up view of the engine, and he knew he wanted to see steam in the final image. The model needed a significant amount of detail, including building a lot of pipes, plates, and rivets. The inclusion of a lot of steam also meant a dramatic increase in the rendering time to produce the final, complete image.

◀ 16.1

3D models themselves are, in their most basic form, skeletons built out of so-called *wireframes*. You can see an example here (16.2) showing the complexity of the wireframe model for the train and its environment.

16.2

Mark chose the wheels as a starting point, and, using his photographic references, he methodically began constructing the train. He quickly found that the more nuts and bolts (literally) he included, the better the model looked, and the better the model looked, the more inspired he got. It took about a week to finish the train itself. He wanted the train to be enveloped in clouds of steam, and this only happens if the engine isn't moving, which led to the addition of the station.

You can see in the untextured renderings the progression of the building process as first the wheels are created (16.3), then the wheel housing (16.4), and finally the whole engine (16.5).

After Mark finished the model, he needed to work on making the surface of the train look more realistic by generating a bump map and adding textures; the untextured engine looked like a model (16.6).

16.3

16.4

dS

About the Artist

Biography

In 1982, after a two-year Art and Photography course in London, Mark began working as a commercial illustrator and storyboard artist. He moved to New York in 1988, continuing work as an illustrator and storyboard artist. In the early 1990s, Mark got his first computer, a Macintosh Quadra 800, and began experimenting with digital art and 3D modeling. By 2000 the technology had advanced sufficiently to finally enable Mark to create 3D models and artwork within the tight deadlines of the commercial world.

In 2001 Mark placed as a Macworld Expo digital art finalist.

Influences

Tin robots, film noir, Stanley Kubrick, Ken Adam, German Expressionism, Art Deco, Marvin Gaye, video games, classic Disney, the Fleischer brothers, Frank Sinatra, Fritz Lang, and *The Cabinet of Dr. Caligari*.

[NOTE]

A *BUMP MAP* is a black-and-white image imported into a 3D program; the different values of gray in the image are applied to a texture and interpreted as variations in height to give the illusion of depth, or bumps. Black is the lowest point and white the highest point. The same black-and-white image mapped onto a lattice or terrain creates a real bump, and, by adding subtle imperfections into the grayscale image, you can create objects that don't look obviously 3D (16.7).

An equally important aspect of creating scenes in 3D, as in any art form, is composition. Mark frequently spends a significant amount of time on composition alone. He began this project with the idea of the train emerging from a tunnel, but he found the inclusion of the natural elements, such as rocks, trees, and plants, detracted from the main point of focus, the train itself. By placing the train in the station surrounded by steam, he ended up hiding much of the work he put into building the model but felt the train belonged there.

16.6

16.5

16.7

Studio

Computer System:
Mac G4 dual, 500 MHz
40GB hard drive
1GB RAM

Mac Titanium Powerbook, 667 MHz
30GB hard drive
1GB RAM

Monitor:
Apple 22-inch Cinema Display

Removable Media:
Zip drive
CD-RW/DVD-RW

Software:
Bryce
Adobe Photoshop

Tablet:
Wacom 12-inch

Input Devices:
AGFA Duoscan

Printers:
Epson

Contact

Mark Bloom
New York, New York
markb@thebigrobot.com
www.thebigrobot.com

As part of the process of experimenting with different compositional possibilities, Mark created small test images that were rendered without texture (16.8–16.10). This speeded up the rendering times so that he could efficiently experiment with camera placement and composition. At this point, the unique advantage of creating in 3D came into play. Mark could look at the model from any angle and select the one that he felt worked the best. In a traditional 2D illustration, the composition has to be determined beforehand, and once a composition is chosen, it has to be adhered to. Mark enjoyed the liberating experience of finding new images from a single model. Also at this time, the effort he put into building a complete 3D model paid off.

When building a realistic scene in 3D, as opposed to an imaginary scene, the project is finished when it looks real. This project took about 100 hours to complete.

16.8

16.9

Technique: Achieving a Realistic "Used" Look in 3D (Photoshop, Bryce)

When creating 3D art, Mark tries to avoid making everything look too perfect. The following technique shows how to create an object with that realistic "used" look; this involves creating a bump map image in Photoshop for use in Bryce.

1. **Create a new grayscale image (512 pixels high by 512 pixels wide at 72dpi) with the background color set to black.**
2. **Using the Lasso, Marquee, and Pen tools, draw some shapes, each on its own layer.**

[TIP]

Keeping elements on separate layers allows you later to adjust the brightness of individual layers (by choosing Image→Adjust→Brightness/Contrast) to enhance the depth of the image.

3. **Fill each shape with a different value of gray, remembering that the lighter the gray, the higher the elevation (16.11).**
4. **Continue adding more shapes, placing each shape on its own layer.**
5. **Feather (choose Select→Feather) or blur (Filter→Blur→Gaussian Blur) some of the outlines to create smoother transitions between the dark and light areas (16.12).**
6. **Select one layer.**

   It doesn't matter which layer you start with. However, bear in mind that layers on top obscure layers below.
7. **Check the Preserve Transparency box in the Layers palette.**

16.10

[NOTE]

The Preserve Transparency is off by default.

8. **Choose Filter→Noise→Add Noise→Amount →20.**
9. **Choose Filter→Blur→Gaussian Blur→Radius→4.**
   By experimenting with different amounts of noise and blur, you can alter the "bumpiness" of the surface (16.13).
10. **Uncheck the Preserve Transparency box in the Layers palette.**
11. **Use the Eraser tool, with a small-sized brush, to roughen some of the straight lines.**
12. **Repeat this procedure (steps 6 to 11) for the other layers.**

[NOTE]

It may not be necessary or desirable to add noise and/or blur to every element in the image. This depends on the desired end result.

This results in a grayscale layered image (16.14).

13. **Choose File→Save As and save the layered image as a Photoshop format file.**
    You can keep this file for possible future editing and adjustments.

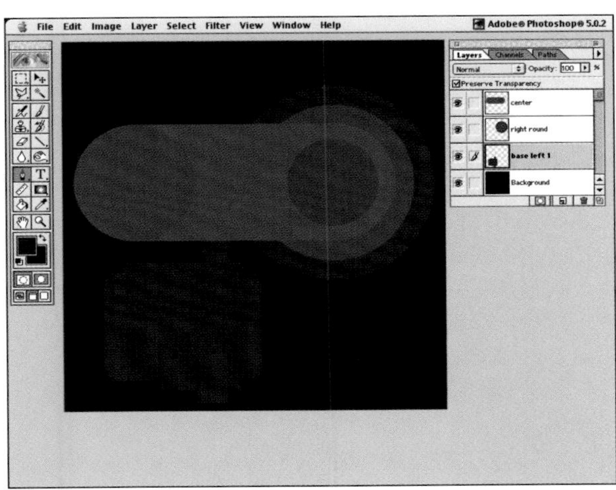

16.11

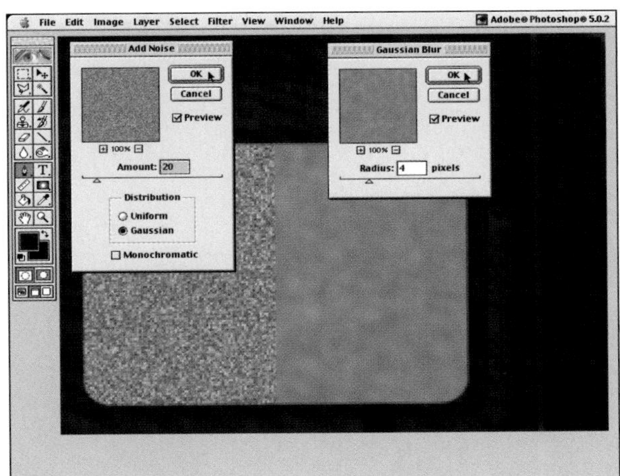

16.13

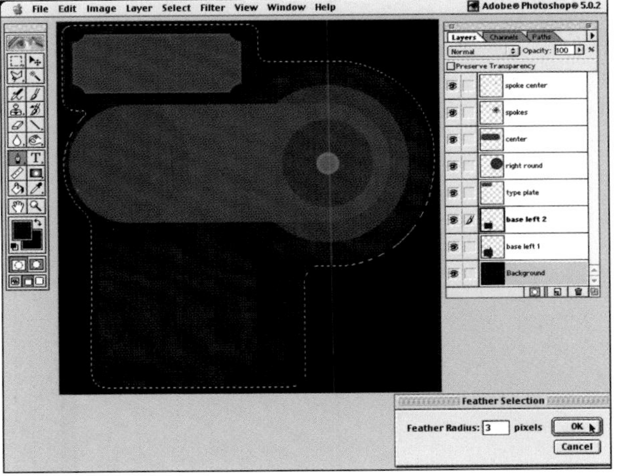

16.12

16.14

14. **Choose Layers→Flatten Image.**

    This flattens all the layers into the background.
15. **Choose File→Save As and save the layered image as a Pict format file.**
16. **Import the grayscale image into Bryce (16.15).**
17. **Apply the imported grayscale image to a lattice or terrain object in Bryce (16.16).**
18. **Complete the object texturing and incorporate it into a scene (16.17).**

Object texturing is a complex subject on its own. The details for this operation, and which texture you would use, depend entirely on the image/object you were building. The application process for applying textures varies from program to program.

In the case of the *Missing Link* image, Mark used a simple gray concrete-looking texture (with its own slight bump). There is a second texture applied to the pipes and handles and a third (brass) texture applied to the handle. A single overhead light source was used to create strong shadows and illustrate the bump.

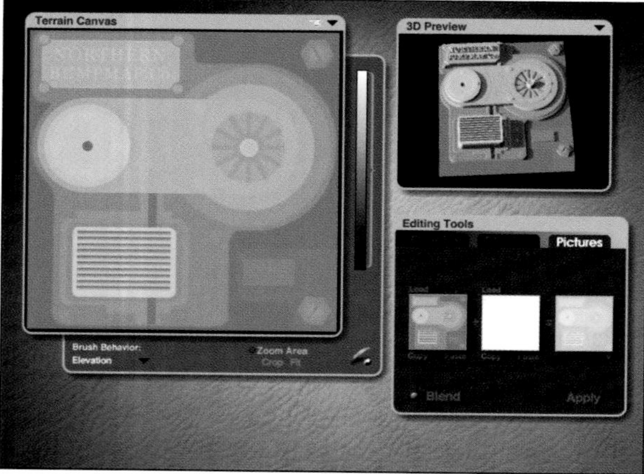

● 16.15

● 16.16

● 16.17

Artist's Creative Insight and Advice

Why Digital?

I truly love drawing with a pencil on a piece of paper. The first thing I tried to do with my first computer was simulate the feeling of a pencil drawing. With a copy of Painter and a tablet by my side, I spent many, many hours trying to simulate what seemed to be a very simple procedure: recreating the beauty of a line. I could get a textured paper and a grainy pencil, but everything seemed too perfect. And I missed the portability of my familiar pencil and paper. I kept asking myself why I was trying to use a $3000 desk-bound machine to replicate what I could achieve with a $1 pencil any time and place I chose. I gave up.

And then along came a little program called Bryce. Designed as a 3D landscape creator, this seemed like a fun tool to experiment with. I could create 3D models and view them from any angle! Something I couldn't do with my pencil.

It seemed as though Bryce had been designed to appeal to people, like myself, who were new to the world of 3D. The interface was unconventional and promoted experimentation, with its "touchy-feely" buttons, single-view window, and ease of use. Most importantly, the renders Bryce produced looked like no other 3D images I had seen, certainly not from a program costing $150. It was this beautiful rendering that kept me interested in the program. I had found a digital tool that could create images I was unable to produce using traditional artistic tools.

Thus began my transition from the $1, pen-and-pencil, conventional art world into the $3,000, upgrade-your-computer-every-other-year, digital world.

Artwork that only really exists when the electricity is turned on can create an interesting mental tug of war between frustration and fascination. The frustration comes from working within the limitations of a program whose parameters have been established by the software developers. The fascination comes in exploring the boundaries of a program and then using that program in new, unexplored ways. The realm of digital art can offer an almost infinite number of possibilities for manipulating one single object, scene, or world that the artist creates. Of course, an indecisive artist can become overwhelmed by the possibilities.

Advice for Artists Working in the Digital Medium

In the field of 3D art, I find it is not enough to simply create good models. This is what the computer and software does very well. Exactly how they do it is a complete mystery to me, and that becomes part of the magic of digital art. Equally, and possibly more important, is the ability to light and compose a scene. This is a skill that comes entirely from the artist.

Traditional artistic skills are equally applicable and important in the digital world.

I try to create scenes that are not obviously 3D. Almost nothing in life is completely perfect, and yet, most 3D art has that perfect look. Everything is too straight, too shiny, and too neat. With careful texturing of models and interesting lighting and composition, you can build imperfect 3D models. Adding the subtlest kinks and bumps and dirt to 3D models and textures, even though they may never be seen, changes an image from a "push the button and let the computer do the work" image, into a powerful means of personal expression.

Ciro Marchetti 200

Chapter 17

Contemplating the System

by Ciro Marchetti

Artist's Statement

The freedom to experiment with color, intensity, position, and size is an integral part of my creative process. I have a basic feel of what I'm aiming for from the onset. I'm nevertheless constantly surprised at the difference in mood or emphasis an image takes on as I preview alternative colors, very often settling on combinations far different to those I had originally intended.

The Story Behind the Artwork

Contemplating the System (17.1) is the outcome of a vacation Ciro took in the spring of 2001. He had returned from Europe with some additions to his collection of old brass instruments, such as compasses and marine sextants, which he had picked up from Portobello market in his home town of London. Along with these acquisitions were a number of photos he'd taken of Venice and its numerous carnival masks. Ciro found that these underlying elements symbolized so many opposing concepts: logic, science, and the future versus art, magic, and tradition. In *Contemplating the System,* Ciro captures a moment when these contradictory worlds are brought together.

In the image, the mechanical physics of the astronomical viewing machine contrast the magical levitation of the jester character. The jester's costume is comical, but his expression is serious and pensive. You could interpret that he's not merely observing, but contemplating the significance of the machine and the logical science it represents, a concept completely opposed to his world. But, in Ciro's own words, "to contemplate is to think, to consider, and possibly to conclude. . . . He may be a court jester, but not a fool."

◀ 17.1

The Creative Process

Apart from the very fine line work of the dragonfly wings, background trees, and a preliminary sketch of the jester, which were simple line drawings Ciro had prepared and scanned in, the rest of the image was produced directly within Photoshop.

All the shapes, from the leaves of ivy and stone columns, to the jester's arms and legs, were prepared laboriously using the Pen tool and then converted to selections and saved as masks. Even at this early stage, Ciro often deviated from his original line drawing if he felt an angle or curve could be improved. Once the masks were loaded, Ciro individually filled those selections, initially with sold colors, and then continued developing form and volume via freestyle application of the Airbrush tool. Since he had used an airbrush in his pre-digital days, the process of spraying (albeit virtually) through a mask was familiar territory. At various stages, Ciro adjusted the hue and saturation of parts of the image, trying multiple options before settling on a final combination. The jester's costume was a case in point.

Ciro deliberately broke up the surface of the images by applying selected dark or light texture via a series of custom-prepared alpha channels. This is particularly noticeable on the stone surface of the columns. He sometimes achieved these textures by applying a lighting-effects filter through those same alpha channels.

The mechanical machines are constructed from Ciro's virtual spare parts shop, where he has prepared numerous cogs of varying size and style, along with springs, flywheels, rivets, and rods. Each piece was separated into various component parts that were spread over various layers, ready to be selected and pasted into his final document.

Ciro had an approximate idea of the look and shape of the machine he wanted to construct, but the actual process was completely arbitrary and intuitive. He continually rearranged the relative positions and size of the elements until he achieved an arrangement that not only had an interesting composition but also conveyed a reasonably convincing mechanical structure.

To enhance the overall mood of the scene, he used the glow of the astronomical machine as the principal source of light. Then, applying the airbrush in Color Dodge mode, he added corresponding highlights to areas such as the columns.

Contemplating the System took approximately 50 hours to complete.

dS

About the Artist

Biography

Ciro graduated from Croydon College of Art and Design, London. His career has covered working both in Europe and the Americas. In the early '80s, along with a partner, he co-founded Graform, an international graphic design group. While working out of their Caracas office, Ciro was involved with the Venezuelan National Design Institute, where he gave lectures on art direction. He also presented various seminars on visual identity and branding to corporations such as IBM, American Express, and 3M.

In 1992 Ciro moved to Miami to open Graform's U.S. office. Since then, he has continued to balance his time between corporate design projects, illustration work, and teaching. He is currently a part-time instructor at the Fort Lauderdale Art Institute, giving classes on digital imagery.

Ciro is now devoting more time to his personal illustration work, which has been rewarded in the last few years, winning the Macworld Digital Art competition in 2000 with a work called *Evening Commute*. He also received the 2002 Grand Prize award in the same competition for *Contemplating*

Technique: Creating Translucent Wings (Photoshop)

Part of the credibility of the dragon flies, and contributing to their importance in Ciro's composition, is the fact that the background can be seen through the transparency of their wings. To control the degree of that transparency and limit it only to the wings, not the body, Ciro used the following procedure. You can apply this technique in any situation where you want to create a translucent membrane in a composition.

1. **Open an image in Photoshop that contains an element or subject, such as Ciro's dragonfly, that is made of parts, each of which is a separate layer.**

   One part, which we refer to as the wing, corresponds to the surface that you want to make translucent. This wing is made up of two layers, one which contains black lines on a white background, the linear structural detail, the wing line layer, and the other which contains a solid fill with color, the wing color layer (17.2).

2. **Select the wing color layer in the Layers palette.**
3. **Choose the Airbrush tool.**
4. **Select a suitable shadow color and airbrush in dark tones into the shadow areas of the wing.**
5. **Select a suitable highlight color and airbrush in light tones into the highlight areas of the wing (17.3).**
6. **Select the wing line layer in the Layers palette.**

● 17.2

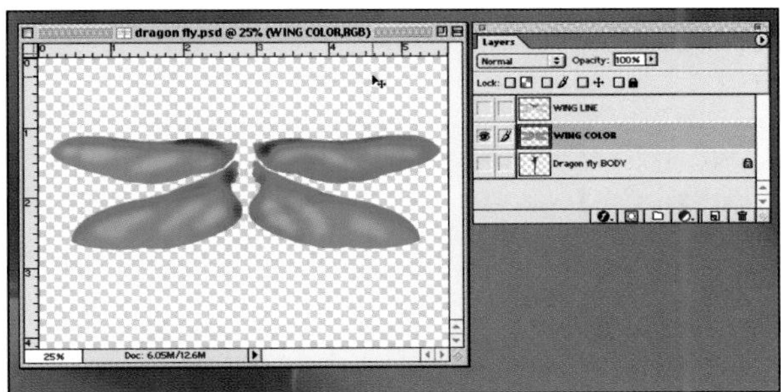

● 17.3

the System. This piece also won two National Association of Photoshop Professionals GURU awards in Tampa Florida 2001, for Artistic Category and Best of Show.

Influences

Many sources, but primarily the surrealistic imagery of Michael Parkes, the whimsical worlds of James Christiansen and the late Arthur Rackham, and the mechanical, textured compositions of Chichoni.

Studio

Computer System:
Macintosh Power PC G4
20GB hard drive
576MB RAM

Monitor:
Apple 17-inch flat-screen display
Mitsubishi Diamond Pro 900u

Software:
Adobe Photoshop

Tablet:
Wacom tablets (various sizes)

Input Devices:
Microtek Scanner

Removable Media:
La Cie 40GB external hard drive

Printers:
Epson 1520, 3000, and 2000P (with archival inks)

Contact

Ciro Marchetti
Miami Lakes, Florida
cirom@bellsouth.net
www.graform.com

7. **Change the Layer mode of the wing line layer from Normal to Multiply (17.4).**
   This has the effect of maintaining the visibility of the black line work in the layer while making the white transparent.
8. **Select all the layers in the Layers palette that correspond to the image element you want to introduce to your main composition.**
9. **Click in the column immediately to the left of these selected layers.**
   A link icon appears in the column indicating that these layers are now linked (17.5).
10. **Open your main artwork image, into which you want to add the image element with its soon-to-be translucent membrane.**
11. **Choose the Move tool and drag the linked layers into the main image.**
    Since they are linked, the layers maintain their relationship to each other, including the visual transparency of the Multiply Color mode. By keeping the layers of the image element linked (not the background) it can be scaled, moved, or rotated within the composition.
12. **Select the wing color layer.**
13. **Change the Layer mode in the Layers palette for the wing color layer from Normal to Screen.**
14. **Reduce the opacity for the wing color layer by adjusting the opacity slider in the Layers palette from 100% to about 80% (17.6).**
    By adjusting the color mode and opacity levels of the wing color layer, various degrees of tone and transparency can be achieved.

[NOTE]

The settings listed in these steps are arbitrary. In Ciro's main illustration, different settings were used for each dragonfly.

Judge's Critique

Macworld 2001 Digital Art Contest, Best of Show

"I like Ciro's approach to image creation: a style reminiscent of the traditional airbrush artist. Each image element is individually handcrafted with a hyper-real level of detail. All of the final elements are composed into a fanciful storybook-like scene inviting the viewer's interpretation. As a result, I found myself examining this image for quite some time."

— JOHN DERRY, Principal Author Painter, Digital Artist
(www.fractal.com)

● 17.4

Artist's Creative Insight and Advice

Why Digital?

Having been an illustrator since the pre-digital era, I can't underestimate the benefits that technology has brought to my particular working style. If there is one word that symbolizes the significance and the influence it represents, not only to the production process, but also the creative one, that word must

● 17.5

● 17.6

surely be UNDO. Anyone familiar with using traditional physical stencils, masking film, and temperamental airbrushes, for example, should pay regular homage to the digital altar.

The Flip Side

You can rely too much on the software's capacity, especially in terms of image manipulation and special effects. Taken to an extreme, the process might become one of importing scanned images, repeated application of filtered effects, and violà! — art.

This isn't intended as a criticism, for indeed it may well be art, but for me, I'm consciously avoiding a process that can be reduced to a number of key strokes. To this end, I probably under-use the digital possibilities. For example, in my corporate work, I regularly do use third-party filters, whereas in my personal illustrations, I very deliberately avoid them. Many of the textured effects, lighting, and water reflections that are common themes in my illustrations could arguably be produced more accurately, and certainly faster, using any number of specialized applications. But the whole point for me is the hands-on involvement of creating my own masks through which I build up those textures, or creating my own displacement maps to distort reflected water, modifying and tweaking along the way, as opposed to merely pressing a "render" button.

Printing Technology

Another significant development in digital art must surely be the hardware advances of color printing, in my case a number of ink jet printers. The quality and resolution that is now achievable is nothing short of phenomenal.

There is now a growing interest in limited-edition reproduction of digital art using archival inks and high-quality output such as giclée prints on watercolor paper. However, this system isn't particularly suited to my work, which tends to lose a significant degree of color intensity when reproduced on such a matte surface. I've maintained far more of the original vibrancy when outputting from my Epson printers onto semi-gloss coated stock, also using archival inks.

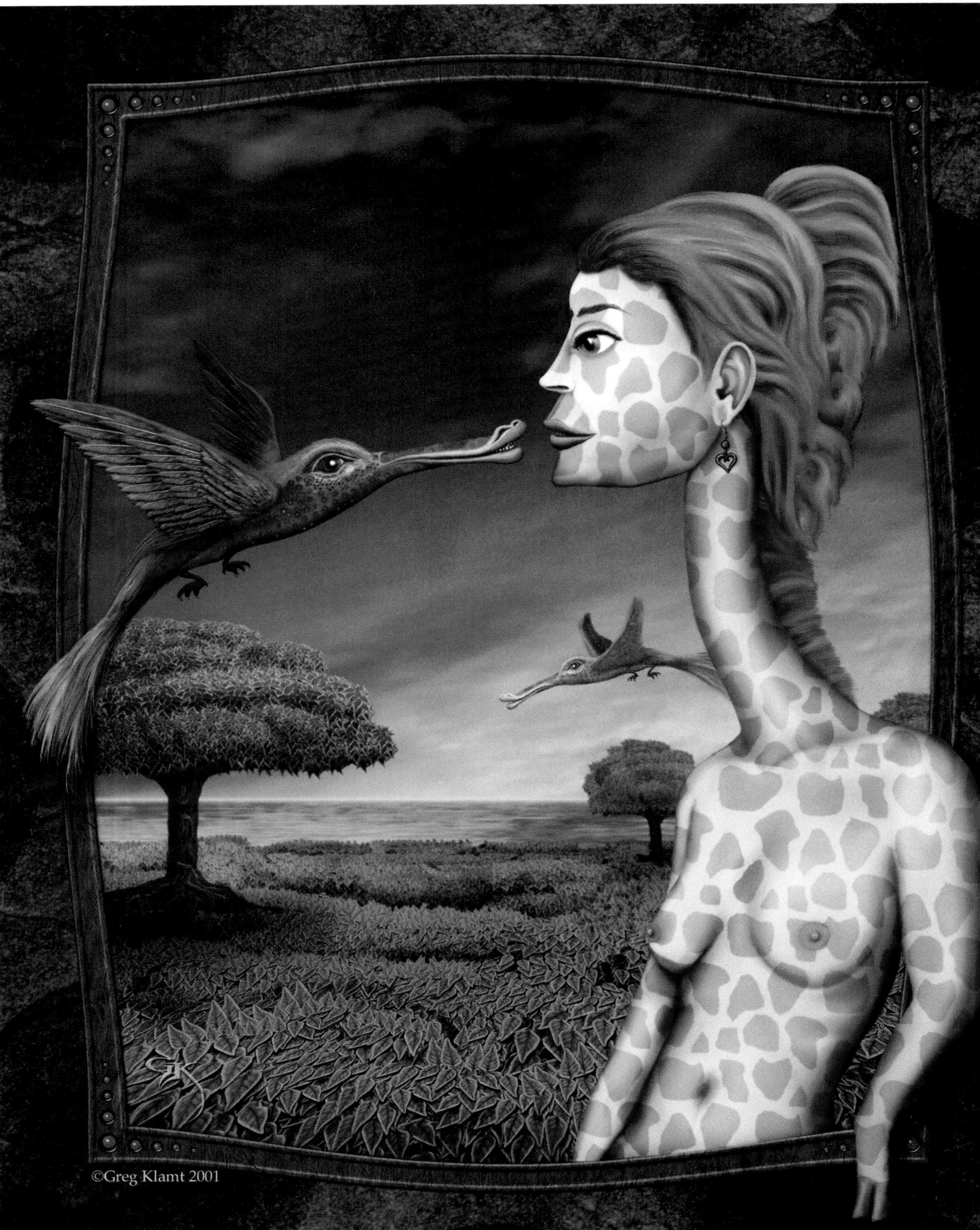

Chapter 18

A Forbidden Love

by Greg Klamt

Artist's Statement

My art illuminates the twilight of consciousness that dwells between so-called reality and the fantastic realms of our dreams. I seek to create possible moments in improbable worlds.

The Story Behind the Artwork

A Forbidden Love (18.1) was inspired by Greg's drawing of the woman's face. This was the first strong element that he scanned and added as a layer in his working file in Photoshop. He then found, scanned, and added a body drawing that worked well in the composition. Gradually, the image developed from there.

Greg didn't have an original intent or goal, but just let the creative process flow on its own, drawing upon his extensive collection of existing paintings and photographs to add elements and textures. Greg worked on this piece in an intuitive way, evolving organically from the original pencil drawings. *A Forbidden Love* reflects Greg's fascination with form and texture — both natural and man-made.

Towards the end of the process, Greg added a bird in the foreground and then decided to add another bird in background. This second bird came to represent the jealous wife or would-be lover. Thus emerged the title of the piece, *A Forbidden Love.* As Greg puts it, the image is "an examination of jealousy and intolerance as a by-product of inter-species dating."

◀ 18.1

● 18.2

The Creative Process

This image began as a pencil drawing of the woman's face. After scanning the original pencil drawing into Photoshop, Greg used the Smudge, Airbrush, and Dodge and Burn tools to paint, shape, highlight, and texturize the face and hair (18.2).

The woman's torso was from a separate life drawing in charcoal that was also scanned and worked on in Photoshop (18.3) until it reached a similar state as the face. The two files were then composited. They didn't quite fit, so the woman's neck grew to adapt (18.4).

The stretching of the neck suggested a giraffe to Greg, so he painted giraffe spots on a separate layer, linked that layer to the underlying body, neck,

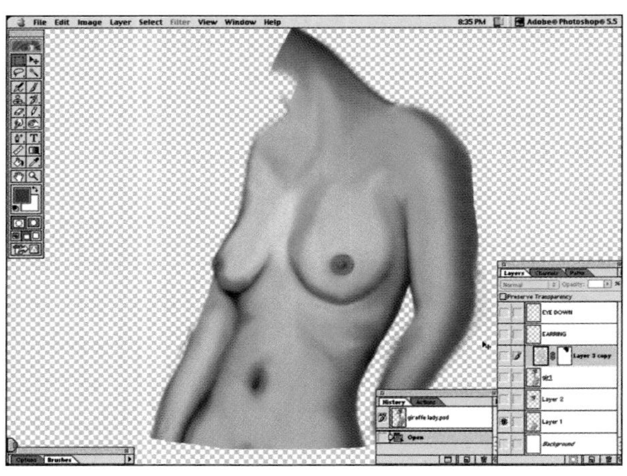

● 18.3

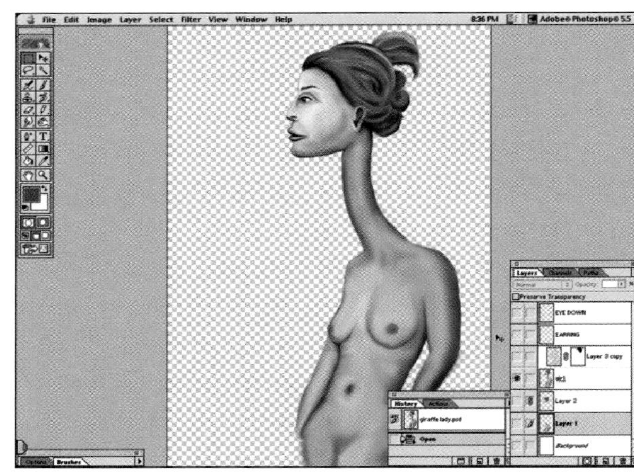

● 18.4

About the Artist

Biography

Greg has a BA from the University of California, San Diego. His digital art experience since 1982 has been interwoven between commercial and fine art applications. His background in traditional media includes drawing, painting, mixed media, film animation, photography, and printmaking (including screen printing, etching, collography, and linoleum block).

Greg has worked in the fields of graphic design and art direction since 1981. He is also a recording artist, and co-owner and Art Director at Spotted Peccary Music, an independent Ambient/New Age label in San Diego County, California.

His work has been featured in *Photoshop 6 WOW* (Peachpit Press) and on the cover of *Inside Dreamweaver 4* (New Riders Publications). His awards include first place in Digital Art for 1999, 2000, and 2001 in the Southern California Exposition.

Greg's art embodies an air of mystery, a reverence for nature, a sense of humor, and a strong appreciation of the absurd. Greg integrates a variety of traditional art and face layers, and overlaid it using Multiply mode (18.5).

Greg used little photography in the image; a couple of rock texture photographs were scanned and layered with other textures in the border area. He used few filters and no stock photos. Greg prefers to create unique textures (based on his own painted or photographed textures) and to apply creative layering and more basic Photoshop functions, rather than use third-party effects and filters.

The bird was completely drawn from imagination in Photoshop. The wings were created by drawing one feather initially, then duplicating it and modifying it in size, detail, and color (18.6). He repeated this process several times. Once the bird was complete, he duplicated the layer, made modifications, and resized it as the smaller bird in the background (18.7).

● 18.6

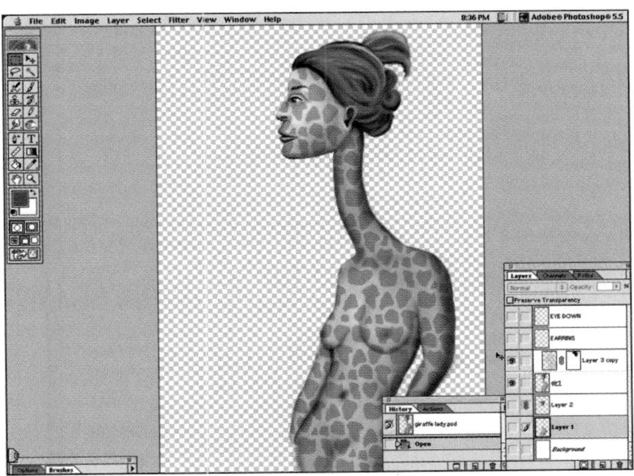

● 18.5

● 18.7

media – photography, paintings, drawings, and other resources – with computer technology in a style he calls Techno-Organic Surrealism. His goal is to bring an organic, natural, and integrated feel to his art through a broad range of resources and influences.

Influences

Heironymous Bosch, M.C. Escher, Salvador Dalí, Patrick Woodroffe, Charles Bragg, Michael Parkes, Jacek Yerka, and Mother Nature.

Studio

Computer System:
Macintosh G3, 333 MHz
60GB hard drive
512MB RAM

Monitors:
Sony Multiscan 17sf

Software:
Adobe Photoshop
Macromedia Freehand

Removable Media:
Iomega Zip

Archive Media:
CD-R

Tablet:
WACOM Art Z

Input Devices:
Epson Expression 1600

Contact

Greg Klamt
Oceanside, California
greg@gregklamt.com
www.gregklamt.com

● 18.8

The sky was a composite of many skies. Greg kept layering them with each other to create new cloudscapes (18.8) (see the technique described later in this chapter).

The water was created in a similar fashion — multilayering textures, applying perspective, and adjusting color. Greg started the trees by painting one leaf and then cloning it (18.9). These cloned leaves were then rotated. Greg merged a few of them into a small bunch and cloned that bunch. He then merged that bunch with other bunches. This process of cloning and merging was repeated to create entire trees of foliage (18.10). Greg applied this same process to creating ground leaves (18.11).

By cloning separate layers and resizing, Greg created the depth of the leaves as they go back into the distance (18.12). The tree trunk was put together using the

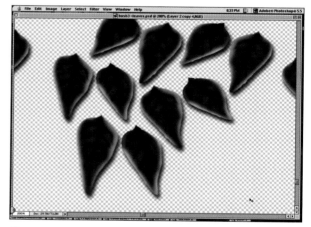

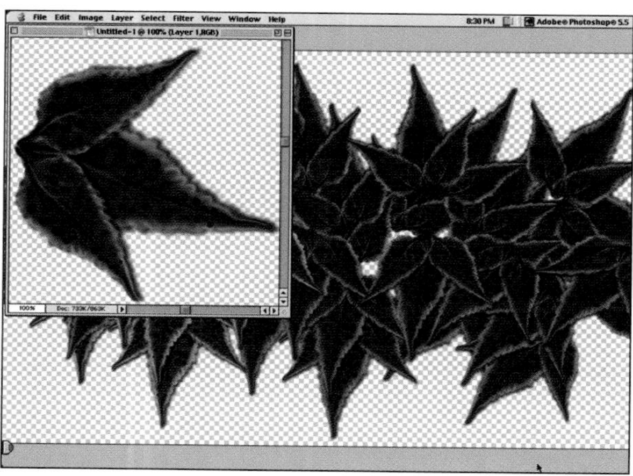

● 18.9

● 18.11

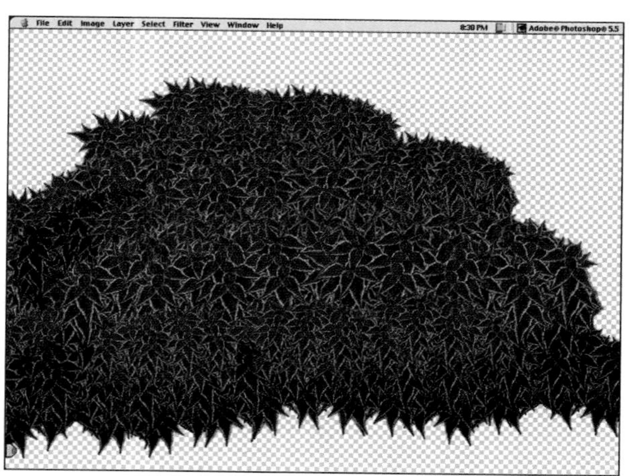

● 18.10

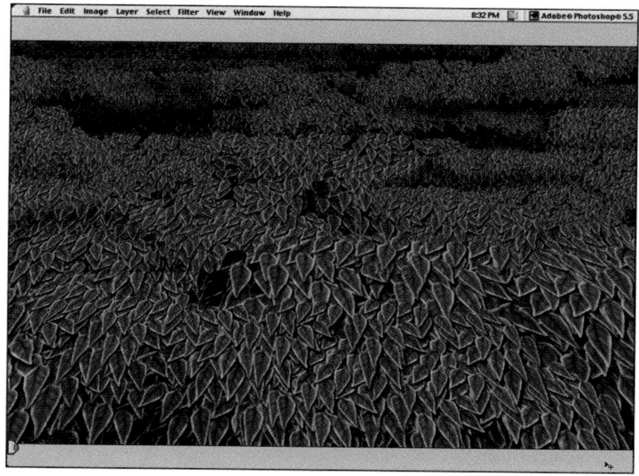

● 18.12

Airbrush and Smudge tools in another illustration and reused with modifications in this image. Greg applied the same technique for the bushes on the ground.

The piece took about 150 hours to complete.

Technique: Creating Realistic Clouds (Photoshop)

Greg created an original, realistic cloudscape by applying the Difference Clouds filter and using the Transform tool to create perspective. This technique describes the creation of a single image, which can be combined with other cloud image layers, or even with photographs of clouds, to create a very realistic sky — or even a surreal one.

1. **Create a new image, in RGB color mode, in Photoshop. Image size and resolution should be appropriate for the final image in which the sky will be used.**
2. **Set foreground and background colors to the default black and white (or choose any two colors if you feel more experimental).**
3. **Choose Filter→Render→Difference Clouds.**
   Doing so generates a cloud form (18.13).
4. **Select the entire image.**
5. **Select the Transform tool.**
6. **While holding down Ctrl-Alt-Shift (Windows) or Command-Option-Shift (Mac), drag one of the top corner transform handles to the side to create perspective on the clouds (18.14).**
7. **Press Enter (Windows), Return (Mac OS).**
   This completes the combined transform and crop operations (18.15).
8. **Duplicate the layer and Transform again to create a different cloudscape layer.**
   This gives you a different cloud texture that will be combined with your original to create different clouds.

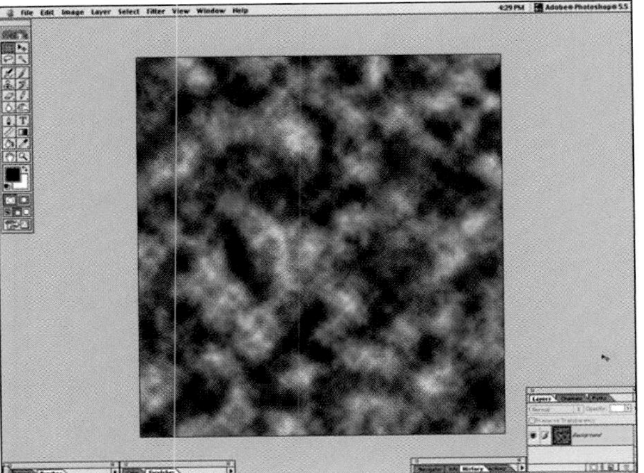

18.13

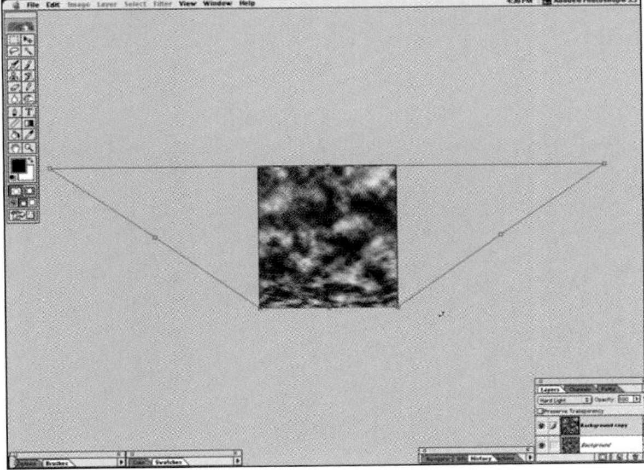

18.14

18.15

18.16

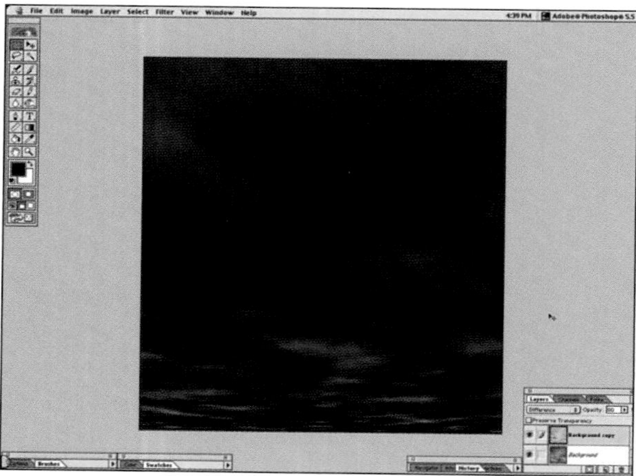

18.17

Experiment with the interplay between color, transparency and overlay modes. Choose Image➔Adjust➔Hue/Saturation or Image➔Adjust➔Curves. Experiment with the settings in the Hue/Saturation or Curves to change the color of each of the layers. Change the transparency value of the top layer to try different effects. Change the overlay mode for the layer to Difference or Hard Light to get entirely new effects.

When Greg applies this technique he just plays with the sliders and curves and sees what happens. He continues playing until he finds a result he likes. You can see some examples of how he used Image/Adjust/Hue/Saturation to change color in 18.16.

A second layer was duplicated and further perspective was applied. The layer was then changed to Difference mode, and set at 80% transparency. The same image with the top layer at 50% transparency is shown in 18.17. An Adjustment layer was added using curves to modify the entire image color (18.18).

He did the same as with the first layer using curves to add red and blue and remove green from that layer (18.19).

As you create these different colorations, you can duplicate the variations, transform them, and bring them into the original file as separate layers and use transparency and modes to those layers as well.

Repeat this process with different color combinations and perspectives to build up a realistic multilayered cloudscape in your working image.

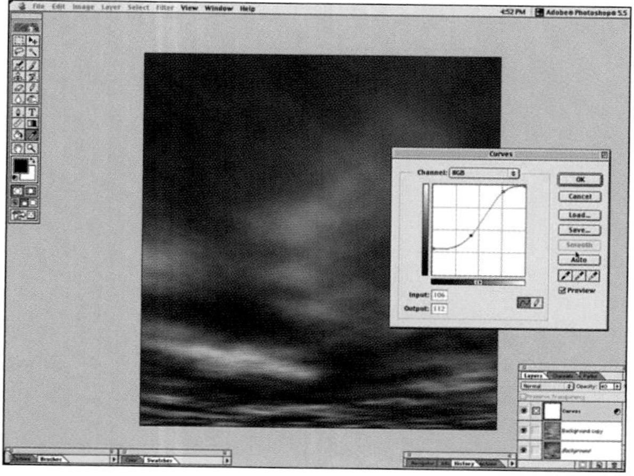

18.18

18.19

Artist's Creative Insight and Advice

Why Digital?

Though I still occasionally work in traditional media, most of what I do ends up in the digital realm due to the control and creative freedom it offers, the ability to integrate media, and my comfort level in the medium. Computer technology has reached a point where making art is quick and fluid enough that I can be completely immersed in the moment, where all else fades away. At least when not fighting technical problems, I am no longer wrapped up in the medium, in cleaning up paint or breathing fumes. It's more creative than traditional media because I can capture an idea quicker or experiment with it more easily when inspiration hits.

The possible permutations and combinations are amazing. I have the ability to save and reuse elements and take them in a variety of different directions. I can take a character or source element and extend its life into several different worlds.

On the Acceptance of Digital Art

It took many years for photography to be accepted as fine art in the art world, and digital art is still young. People require time and education to accept and understand new forms of expression.

There seems to be a public perception that digital art is not fine art — that the computer does the work. It is sad that people turn up their noses or walk away when they hear that art is digitally created, because they think that the artist did not really create it, or they cheated. In some cases this is, at least partially, true. Anyone with a computer can now run a few filters or generate a fractal and swish it around with a liquid-effects brush and make a somewhat original image with beautiful colors. With the low cost of inkjet printers, they can output them and put them on their walls and call them art. All this can be done in minutes. Anyone can also snap a photograph with a camera. That does not necessarily make good art.

I believe good digital art — as with all art — requires the understanding of form, color, composition, and concept. Most importantly, I believe it requires the unique expression of the individual. Something that only that individual artist could or would do. Quality photo-compositing requires good photos to begin with (and shouldn't be done from someone else's stock photos). Filters don't create original art without an original method of working them. Software effects aren't usually expressive of the artist's voice or intent. When the software is more prevalent than the voice of the artist, it may be visually appealing, but its artistic value is questionable. Eventually, as our eyes adjust to the artform, it will be easier to recognize art that expresses a unique vision rather than accidents that are more the work of software designers. I still like a lot of the effects but do not use them much unless buried in imagery that is more of me than the filter.

The public sees fractals, uninventive filter abuse, or basic 3D landscapes and thinks "I have seen that before" or "I could do that with my computer." When those of us who spend dozens or hundreds of hours bringing our souls into an image are associated with this concept of digital art, it dilutes our work.

My hope is that the art world — galleries, publications, collectors, and the general public — will learn to focus on quality digital art. In that way, my hope is that our work is seen as art — not just as "digital art."

Advice for Artists Working in the Digital Medium

Don't fall back on filters or software to make the art. The point in making art is that it is your expression, not that of software programmers. Work to find your own voice and make art rather than just making digital art that looks like that of anyone else using the same effects or applications. Learn traditional techniques that teach you to understand and control form and composition.

Output

I output through various Ateliers (fine art printers) on watercolor paper, and sometimes on canvas. While I have output some prints on glossy photo paper, I prefer the fine art look of the more traditional substrates. It depends on the image, though, as to what size and surface looks best. Some images are best small, others as full sheets. Some with sharper detail, and some with a softer look. Sometimes I work the images with paint, pens, and other media after printing. You have to be careful about the water-soluble nature of the giclée inks. This may require some experimentation.

Chapter 19

Royal's Flat

by David Grzybowski

Artist's Statement

I love the freedom of digital. The freedom to experiment. The feeling that no matter what you do, if something isn't going in the direction you like, you can always back up a couple of steps and change course.

The Story Behind the Artwork

Royal's Flat (19.1) is a scene from a graphic novel David is working on called *The Dark Veil*. The story takes place during the late '30s and follows a detective as he investigates the strange goings-on at the state asylum. The character lives and works out of a studio flat above an all-night diner.

The Creative Process

Since the scene is of an apartment from the late 1930's, David began with some research at the local library, antique shops, and online auction sites (like eBay, a great place to buy photographic reference materials). After he finished his research, he began with a floor plan, deciding on the dimensions of the flat, then designing and arranging what furniture would populate the scene. He then created the objects in Lightwave Modeler and textured them using combinations of scanned, photographed, or painted textures. The map on the wall, for example, was scanned from an actual 1937 street map.

To lessen test rendering times while adjusting the lighting, David modeled simple primitives of each of the main objects (the desk, table, chair, and so on) and brought those into Lightwave Layout where they were arranged on the stage according to his floor plan. (See the technique later in this chapter.) Once he was satisfied with the camera angles and lighting setup, he replaced the primitive objects with their detailed counterparts and did the final renders. (For

◀19.1

those who aren't familiar with 3D work, Figure 19.2 shows the basic components of a 3D model.)

The piece took approximately 160 hours, which includes planning, research, modeling, texturing, layout, and lighting.

Technique: Setting Up a 3D Scene for Lighting (Lightwave)

This technique describes an efficient way to set up a 3D scene for lighting. Render times for 3D images can take an enormous amount of time; this technique helps keep the render times down as you experiment with lighting your scene.

1. **Create a box with the dimensions of one of the completed objects in your scene (19.3). Save the box as a separate object with a descriptive name, such as chair_box.**

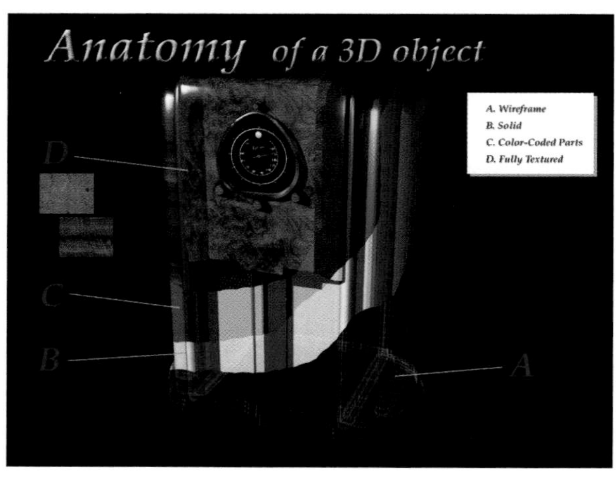

19.2

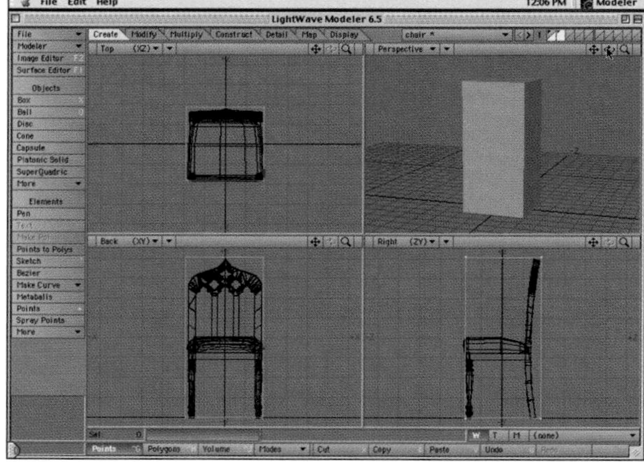

19.3

About the Artist

Biography

David Grzybowski is a self-taught 3D illustrator with a background in traditional art. Although he began his career as a computer programmer, which eventually led to co-owning a company that created software for the printing industry, he later returned to his love of art and became increasingly active in computer graphics.

Currently, he's working on two books: a graphic novel, *The Dark Veil* (the source of *Royal's Flat*), and a children's book entitled *Hats To Where*, both available in 2003. *Royal's Flat* was displayed at the Macworld Expo in 2001 and 2002. David lives and renders in Wisconsin with his wife Marjie and their eight-year-old daughter Megan.

Influences

Norman Rockwell, N.C. Wyeth, Paul Lehr, Frank Frazetta, Alex Ross, Mike Mignola, H.R. Giger, Wayne Barlowe, Edward Hopper, and Zdzislaw Beksinski.

Create boxes for all major objects in your scene.

2. **In your scene, set your 'stage' using one (key) light set at 100% (19.4).**

[TIP]

David likes starting with a point light when doing a room scene to get a better overall feel for what the specific lighting needs will be. Since point lights are used for creating sources of light that emit in all directions, like a lamp or candle, he generally places the point in the area of the objects that represent light sources, such as lamp or candle.

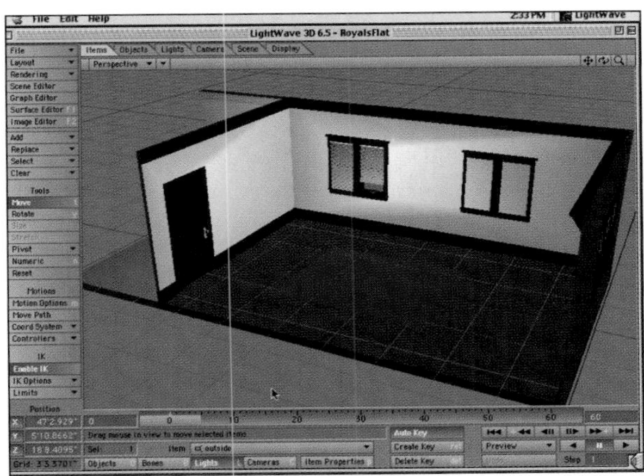

19.4

3. **Start loading in the box objects you created (19.5).**
4. **Position the box objects in the scene where their completed counterparts will be (19.6).**

19.5

19.6

Studio

Computer System:
Mac 8500 pumped up with a G4 400
40GB hard drive
1GB RAM

Monitors:
NEC P750 17 monitor

Software:
Adobe Photoshop
Painter
Poser
Bryce
Freehand
Fontographer
Lightwave 6.5

Tablet:
6 x 8-inch Wacom Intuos graphics tablet

Input Devices:
Umax Astra 3400 scanner

Removable Media:
100MB Zip Drive

Archive Media:
Yamaha CDRW
CRW4416SX

Printers:
Epson Stylus 800 printer

Contact

David Grzybowski
Franklin, Wisconsin
davegriz@dmg3d.com
www.dmg3d.com

5. **Populate your scene with whatever lights you feel you need (19.7).**
   Do renders along the way to check brightness, shadows, falloff, and so on until the scene is lit to your liking.
6. **Replace each box object with its completed counterpart (19.8).**

[NOTE]

If your application has a Replace With Object File feature like Lightwave, the task is even easier; the completed object is placed in the exact position as the box it was replacing.

Judge's Critique

Macworld Expo, 2001

"To me, Dave's work is a marriage of the sculptor's hand with the photographer's eye. The result is a photo-realistic scene bathed in dramatic lighting. I particularly noticed the absence of a human presence, which further instills the scene with a sense of foreboding."

— JOHN DERRY, Principle Author Painter, Digital Artist (www.fractal.com)

Artist's Creative Insights and Advice

Why Digital?

For me the question "Why digital?" is summed up by the term "Multiple undos." The fact that you can save your piece at various stages, too, and potentially end up with multiple variations to choose from. The disadvantage to all this freedom, for me, is knowing when to stop — when to call it complete.

I think whether or not you're proficient in traditional skills, you can do extraordinary things in the digital medium as long as you have good ideas and can plan your project well.

Why 3D?

My interest in 3D artwork really took hold with the computer games Myst, Gadget, The Journeyman Project, and Sinkha. The more I saw of that type of art, the more I felt THAT is what I wanted to do.

Inspiration from Movies

Movies are a major influence for me, especially SciFi and Horror (*Bladerunner, Dark City, Star Wars, Stargate, Alien, The Thing, City Of Lost Children,* and *12 Monkeys* to name a few). You can get a great feel for composition and lighting watching movies, especially some of the old *noir* films. Sometimes I'll watch a favorite DVD, sketchbook in hand, and pause it at a great shot and analyze it in a sketch.

Planning and Research

I feel the planning and research stages are the most crucial in the development of a 3D illustration, more so when striving for realism. Sometimes I spend a week or more sketching out ideas and researching my subject matter. Many traditional artists, such as Norman Rockwell and Alex Ross, have made use of live models and photographs to aid in illustrating realism. If you're painting a picture of a flower, it takes much of the guesswork out of the task if you have the flower right in front of you. The same is true for building a digital scene. The more you can draw from real life, the more realistic your piece can be.

● 19.7

● 19.8

staudesign©

Chapter 20

A Few of My Favorite Things

by Suzanne Staud

Artist's Statement

My approach is fearless when creating an illustration or graphic design. Creating fine art, on the other hand, intimidates me at times because it is so personal. My illustration is usually the "feel good" side of my psyche. My dark side comes out in the fine art.

I see my life as a huge design project, a collage if you will.

I make mistakes, live with them for a time, then find the needed changes.

The Story Behind the Artwork

The idea for *A Few of My Favorite Things* (20.1) came from Suzanne's desire to share with her clients, for Christmas, a bit of herself through the little things that she has collected, for her home, during treasure hunts (estate sales). She bought insulated coffee tumblers, at a local coffee shop, that allowed her to insert her own art. With her art inserted, these tumblers, the type you place in your car cup-holder that keep your coffee warm while you drive to work, made personal and practical gifts for her clients.

She has depicted in this piece her vision of a world these little things, the ones she collected, may inhabit. She has placed herself in the boat of this illustration, floating up stream against the tide.

Suzanne is influenced by self-taught folk artists (such as Art Brut) and art from different cultures. You can see this in the way she fills the canvas entirely, and the unrealistic way elements in the image are juxtaposed and positioned. She uses colors that complement each other in just the right intensity, so that outlining the art in black is unnecessary. Suzanne says, "I want the viewer to enter my mind and world . . . a pictorial stream of consciousness." The Art-Brut approach she adopts is usually thought of as fine art rather than graphic design, even though the imagery has a graphic, hard-edged feel to it. This piece shows how she drew from varied sources for her inspiration.

The Creative Process

Suzanne started off by taking some photos of her environment at home and using a few of her existing original library of illustrations, including the woman in the boat, the pillars, the pelican, some leaves and

◀ 20.1

flora, the dog in the sky, the moon, the jewels, a few trees, clouds, birds, and a lady bug.

She illustrated, for example, a row of ducks (20.2) that appear floating on the sea next to the boat in the artwork. Another photo shows the toy (20.3) that inspired the monkey in the lower center of the artwork. The cat, elephant, angel, and the fabric fish were also photographed from life (20.4).

Suzanne purchased art-insertable, insulated drink containers from her local Starbucks. They came with paper inserts that she used as a template for the artwork. Working with a pencil on one of these templates, she planned her illustration, deciding what elements she wanted to include and what source images to use. Having selected these source photos, Suzanne completed the rough pencil sketch on the paper template that was the appropriate shape to be inserted into the coffee container (20.5).

● 20.2

She scanned this sketch into the computer as a Tiff file at 72 ppi and placed it in Freehand (20.6).

When first opened in Freehand, the sketch was placed as a black scanned image, which was too dark

● 20.3

About the Artist

Biography

Suzanne went to school expecting to be the next Picasso, taking only fine art courses (and typing, which her father suggested so that she would have something to fall back on!). From 1973 to 1991, she worked in store display, various print shops, a corrugated container plant, and, finally, a design studio where she began with a t-square and drafting table only to be forced into using a computer.

She learned graphic design by looking through Print Annuals and design-winning stationery promos. Over the years, she has won numerous awards (including in the prestigious Seventh Annual RSVP Competition) for her fine art and graphic design, and her artwork has been published in various annuals and magazines (including being featured on the cover of the January 2000 *Step-By-Step Graphics* magazine). She has used the computer for over 12 years and is loving it.

to trace. She picked light-gray in the Color Mixer to render the rough sketch as a light-gray image (20.7) so that it was as colorless and transparent as possible, almost not there — just visible enough to act as a

20.4

20.6

20.5

20.7

Influences

Matisse, Chagal, Eastern Indian patterns, Renaissance colors, Folk/Primitive Art, garage sale finds, nature, and her religion.

Studio

Computer System:
Apple Macintosh G4
Two 20GB hard drives
384MB RAM

Monitors:
21-inch CRT

Software:
Macromedia Freehand

Removable Media:
CD-ROM
CD-RW
DVD
Compact flash card

Archive Media:
CD-RW

Tablet:
Wacom Tablet

Input Devices:
Umax-Astra 600S

Printers:
Epson Stylus Photo 870
Hewlett Packard Laserjet 2100M

Contact

Suzanne Staud
Modesto, California
staudesign@aol.com
www.staudesign.com

guide. This allowed her to refer to the sketch while building up the rest of the artwork on one layer in the Freehand image.

She then checked the Transparent check box for the rough sketch (referred to as a Grayscale TIFF within Freehand). This allowed her to see through the layer onto the background canvas below. Thus she could trace over, or under, the rough sketch.

Her next step was to start creating a palette of colors using the Color Options box (where she could select Pantone Colors, Process Colors, Special Metallic Inks, and so on) and by making her own colors with the Color Mixer (20.8). She used the Color and Fill tools in Freehand to paint on the canvas behind the gray translucent sketch. Here (20.9) you can see the gray rough sketch line work superimposed over the colored layers in the background.

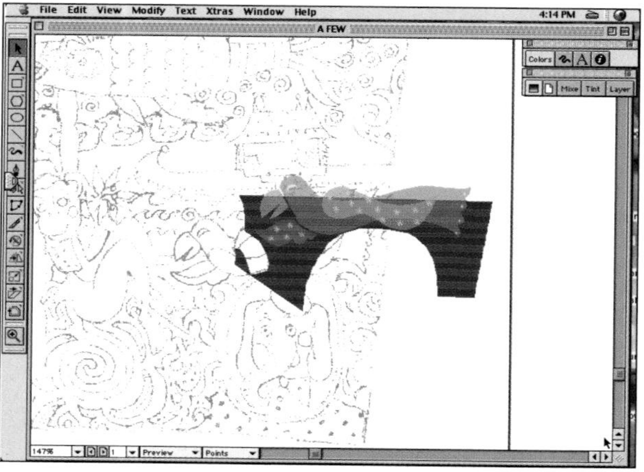

● 20.8

[TIP]

Suzanne sometimes made the sketch white and sent it to the back so that she could see the work in the stage it was in. She then turned the sketch back to gray and continued to trace over the rough sketch.

Suzanne has collected textures for years and has built up a large texture library. She imported some of her own textures and patterns, in addition to her source photos, for use in this image. (Importing imagery into an image is done with simple copy and paste. Suzanne always uses the keyboard shortcuts Cmd/Ctrl-C for copy and Cmd/Ctrl-V for paste.)

If she needed to resize a source image or texture, she chose Modify→Transform→Scale and resized the imported illustration to suit her artwork image size. She used the rough sketch as a reference to correctly scale, position, and orient the imported illustrations. She could also use the rescaling and orientation tools in the Tools palette. She held down the Shift key while she clicked and dragged with the rescaling tool to keep the aspect ratio (height to width) constant.

She used the Auto Trace tool and auto trace on some of her chosen textures to make the textures into line art. To understand auto tracing in Freehand, imagine you had scanned a leopard print. Auto tracing allows you to outline each spot so that each spot can become an independent object with a different color or even a different shape. You can take out a spot and add a flower instead, for instance. You can then alter and modify each element by itself.

In Suzanne's piece, you can see examples where she's applied auto tracing in the monkey's vest, all the

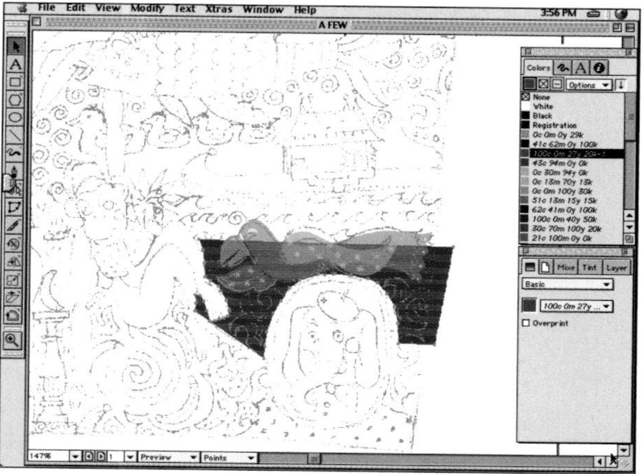

● 20.9

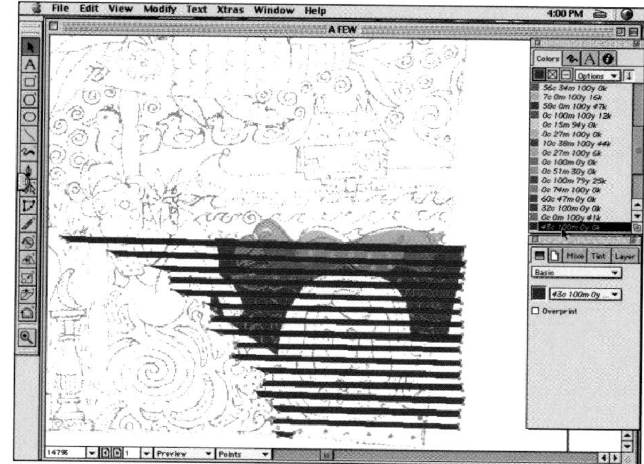

● 20.10

flora, the fabric below the monkey, the spots on the mountains, and the stars in the sky.

The purple parallel bars (20.10) were all created separately to give a more hand-done look to the image. After creating the blue shape with the Pen tool, Suzanne pasted the bars into the shape (20.11).

She then drew the transparent bird character with the Pen tool and filled the shape with an orange color from her palette, then made it transparent by using the Lens/Transparent tool in the Fill box. Notice how the transparency gives the background color a new pinkish tinge instead of the purple and turquoise around it. Even the waves behind take on a different hue.

She then drew the wings by using the same process, but making this lens/transparency a different color, yellow orange. The other wing is a deep orange red but still transparent. She felt it gave more sense of motion in the transparent mode.

The next step was to make the little asterisk pattern with the Line tool. She colored it pale golden and put it behind the transparent wing of the bird.

The eye of the bird is transparent as well; it was made simply by creating two circles with the Ellipse tool and overlapping them, then going up to Modify, then to Combine, then to Punch. This gave her a quick half moon shape for the eye. She then filled the half moon shape with transparent white and removed the line (20.12 to 20.15).

After building up her image, adding color layers, and importing illustrations, source images, textures and patterns, Suzanne added some final touches using the veiled/transparent effect in selected regions of

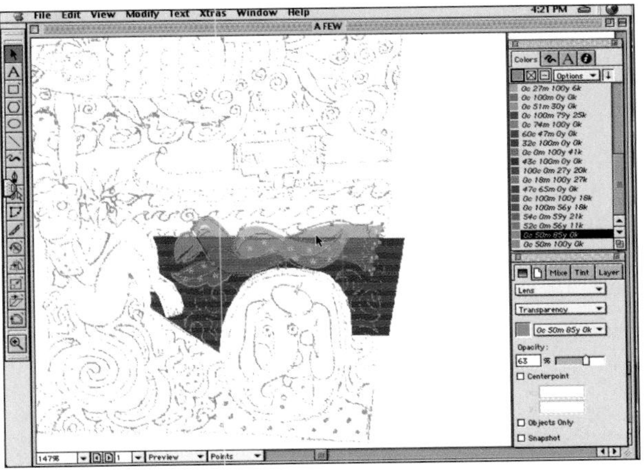

● 20.11

● 20.13

● 20.12

● 20.14

the image, such as over her image in the boat. The details for this technique are described in the technique section of this chapter.

She estimates that she spent about six to eight hours creating this image.

Technique: Making a Veiled/Transparent Effect (Freehand)

This technique shows you how Suzanne created a veiled/transparent effect in her artwork using Freehand.

1. **Open a file in Freehand that contains a light gray rough sketch of the design you want to work on.**
2. **Use either the Freehand tool or the Pen tool to describe shapes that you want to fill with color for the design.**

   These shapes are drawn based on the light gray line drawing.
3. **Add color to the shapes with Fill Inspector.**

   The Fill Inspector allows you to blend colors, make them transparent, make gradients from them, and smudge them together.

[TIP]

Sometimes it's fun to use a famous work of art to generate your color palette. If you are creating your own custom color palette, do so now using the Color Tool and options.

An example of how the Fill Inspector was used to fill with a gradient, a fading or blending between two or more colors, can be seen here (20.16) in a leaves segment of Suzanne's design. After this stage she clipped the leaves design to be visible just within a path she defined with the Pen tool (20.17).

4. **Choose Modify→Fill.**
5. **In the Fill palette, select the Lens tool option from the top drop-down menu and the Transparency tool from the bottom drop-down menu.**

   The lens combined with the transparency option results in a veiled/transparent look. Notice that there are varying degrees of opacity. You can go with a very slight transparency of color, or you can make it nearly opaque. You can layer color on color to create new colors you may not have even thought of.

20.15

20.16

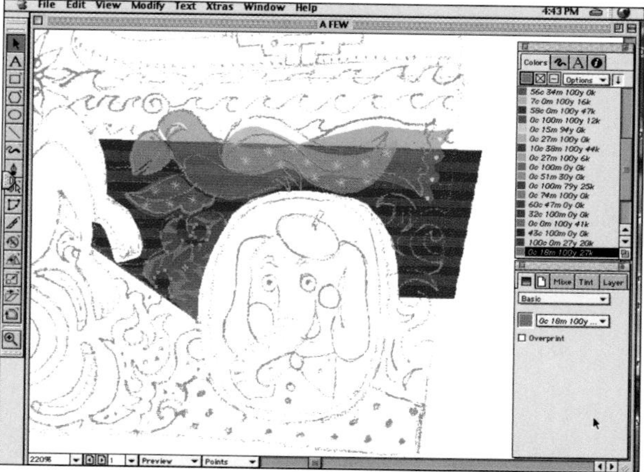

20.17

[NOTE]

You can paste a veiled/transparent effect (using the Lens Fill option as described previously) inside an object. An example of where Suzanne pasted this effect is in the bird and wings under the floating boat. She used white transparency over her image in the boat for the veiled/transparent effect. You can see the before and after of the veiled/transparent effect in the illustrations here (20.18 and 20.19).

Artist's Creative Insight and Advice

Why Digital?

I like the digital medium because it is so immediate and versatile. Currently I generally create graphic design on the computer and create fine art in traditional media. I find my graphic design effects my fine art and vice versa. My experience creating imagery on the computer leads me to ask myself whether I should I learn Painter and whether creating fine art with Painter will be the same as the actual hands-on process of creating fine art.

I can feel a merging of my graphic design and fine art worlds coming along within the digital medium. The search for the perfect collage material is the same as the search for the perfect flower in a digital illustration. For now, I am comfortable keeping the two worlds separate. However, someday they will overlap or perhaps merge. I am continually evolving, so I look forward to great things to come.

Advice for Artists Working in the Digital Medium

Be bold and daring. Make mistakes and learn from them. I've learned to walk away from the illustration for a time, then come back and take a second look.

I always start with the colors I like or need to use (per client instructions), then I convert them for printing properly. I love the Lens tool in Freehand — it makes it possible to layer colors to create other unexpected colors. The Gradient and Blending tools are also fun, along with the Union tool under Modify (combine) at the top of the screen. It's wonderful working within the computer to do illustration and design — the choices are endless.

Read the manual (something I never do — I'm too restless).

Output

Glossy color copies and Megachromes are my favorite types of output. The service bureau that does my printing uses an Epson ink jet printer for match print proofs.

● 20.18

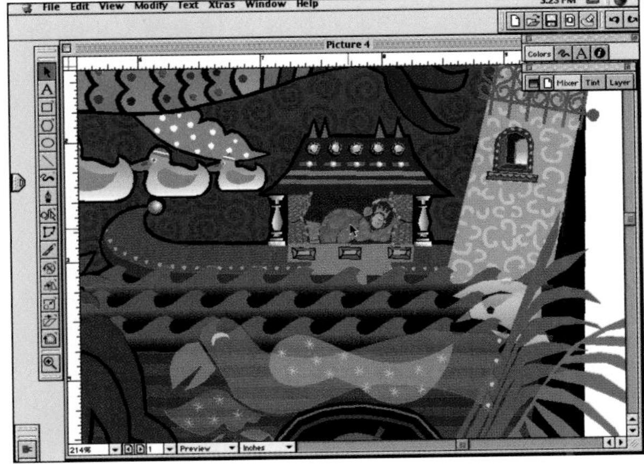

● 20.19

Chapter 21

Bark Twain

by Chet Phillips

Artist's Statement

My artwork has influences from popular culture and surrealism with a large dose of humor thrown in. Incongruities in life and stories that may have many meanings also intrigue me. Exploring these areas with my artwork is a constant source of inspiration. As usual, no electrons are harmed in the creation of my work.

The Story Behind the Artwork

With all the various projects and clients Chet works with on a daily basis, somehow he finds himself eventually gravitating to the myriad interpretations of cat and dog personalities.

Bark Twain (21.1) was the second in a series of promotional pieces that portrayed famous authors as dogs or cats. Among them were Edgar Allan Pug, Jane Pawsten, Jack Russell Kerouac, and Sir Arthur Canine Doyle, to name a few. Mark Twain proved to be a perfect subject with a face and character not unlike a feisty, hairy-faced Cairn terrier.

◀ 21.1

The Creative Process

Chet started *Bark Twain* by making a pencil sketch on paper. He scanned this sketch (21.2) at 300 ppi and opened it in Painter.

In Painter, he created a clone of the image, selected all, and deleted the cloned image information. After that, he turned on the tracing paper feature in Painter to access a ghosted image (21.3) of the original sketch, which he used for visual reference.

21.2

He filled in selected areas with black and used the Scratchboard tool to carve away with white strokes. Next, he selected the entire black-and-white image and floated it to a layer. After he floated the image to a layer, he chose the Gel Composite Method for the layer. This makes the white areas transparent while the black areas remain opaque.

He used the Digital Airbrush and Scratchboard tool brush variants to apply feathered color and colored line work to the background. As a final step, the layer was dropped and the flattened image was saved in Photoshop format for print and Web use.

The image took about four hours including sketch time. The piece was unofficially finished after Chet felt that he had captured the spirit of Mark Twain's expression in the dog's face and pose.

21.3

dS

About the Artist

Biography

With a BFA in Painting and Drawing, Chet has worked as a commercial illustrator for many years, the first 21 with traditional tools. His work has been created exclusively with Painter since 1992.

He has been the recipient of numerous Best of Show, Gold, and Silver Awards from the Dallas Society of Illustrators juried shows, and his Painter work has been included in numerous traveling shows for Fractal Design, MetaCreations, and Macworld Conference and Expo. His commercial clients include American Airlines, Frito Lay, the *Dallas Morning News*, JCPenney, and Warner Brothers.

Influences

The importance of art in Chet's life came to him when he discovered a sharpener built into the back of a crayon box.

Technique: Creating a Colorful Scratchboard Image (Painter)

This technique takes you through the exact steps that Chet followed to create his colorful and lively image that emulates the look and feel of a traditional scratchboard drawing.

1. **Make a pencil sketch on paper.**
2. **Scan the sketch at 300 ppi and save it as an RGB Tiff file.**
3. **Open the scanned sketch in Painter.**
4. **Choose File→Clone.**
   This creates a clone copy, or duplicate, of the original image.
5. **Choose Select→All (Ctrl/Cmd-A).**
6. **Click the Backspace/Delete key.**
   This clears the clone image so that all you see is a white canvas.
7. **Choose Canvas→Tracing Paper (Ctrl/Cmd-T).**
   Tracing paper superposes a 50% opacity image of the original source image with a 50% opacity image of whatever is on your clone copy canvas. The keyboard shortcut Ctrl/Cmd-T toggles the Tracing Paper on and off.

[TIP]

Regularly turn Tracing Paper off so that you can see what your image really looks like.

8. **Use the Lasso tool to make a selection around portions of the image you want to fill with black line work, using the ghosted image of the original sketch for visual reference.**

[TIP]

If there is more than one contiguous area you want to fill with black line work, then hold down the Shift key as you make additional selections; these are added to the total selection without loosing your previous selections.

9. **Ensure black is selected in the Colors section of the Art Materials palette and is showing in the Primary Color rectangle (the forward of the two overlapping rectangles).**
10. **Click in the selection with the Fill Bucket tool (21.4).**
    This fills the selected areas with solid black. Tracing Paper is turned on, so you can see

● 21.4

He is influenced by the work of Edgar Degas, Rene Magritte, and Henri de Toulouse-Lautrec.

Studio

Computer System:
Mac G4, 350 MHz
10GB hard drive
192MB RAM

Monitors:
19-inch Sony G400

Software:
Procreate Painter
Adobe Photoshop
Adobe Illustrator

Removable Media:
Iomega Zip100

Archive Media:
Que CD-RW

Tablet:
Wacom Intuos 6 x 8

Input Devices:
CanoScan flatbed scanner

Printers:
Epson 2180

Contact

Chet Phillips
Dallas, Texas
chet@airmail.net
www.chetart.com

the original sketch as reference. The black fill appears gray until you turn Tracing Paper off, at which time the black fill turns to solid black.

11. **Choose Select→Deselect.**

    This is a precautionary measure to ensure you don't accidentally float a selected region prematurely.

12. **Pick white in the color picker.**

13. **Use the Scratchboard tool brush variant, located in the Pens category of the Brushes palette, to carve away at the black areas with white strokes.**

14. **When you finish carving away the black areas, and you complete the line work, choose Select→All (Ctrl/Cmd-A).**

15. **Choose Select→Float.**

    This floats the entire black-and-white image into a layer, leaving behind a white background canvas. You can see this layer listed as Layer 1 in the Layers section of the Objects palette. If Tracing Paper is still on, turn it off at this stage; you don't need it any more.

● 21.5

16. **With the new layer highlighted in the layers list, choose the Gel Composite Method for this layer (21.5).**

    This makes the white areas transparent while the black areas remain opaque. You can now see through the white areas to the white background canvas.

17. **Click on the background canvas in the layers list (named "canvas" and situated below Layer 1) so the canvas is highlighted.**

18. **Use the Digital Airbrush variant in the Airbrush category to apply soft-feathered color to the background canvas (21.6).**

19. **Use the Scratchboard tool variant in the Pens category to apply flat color line work to the background canvas (21.7).**

    The color work you add to the background canvas shows through the transparent regions in the layer (which used to be white until the Composite Method was changed to Gel).

    If you click on the small eye icon next to Layer 1 in the Layers list, you can turn off the visibility of the layer, and you can see the actual marks you are making on the background canvas beneath the black-and-white layer. Here is an example from an early stage of Chet's picture (21.8).

20. **When you are satisfied with your final image, select Drop from the Layers pop-up menu (or the left-hand Button pop-up menu on the bottom of the Layers section).**

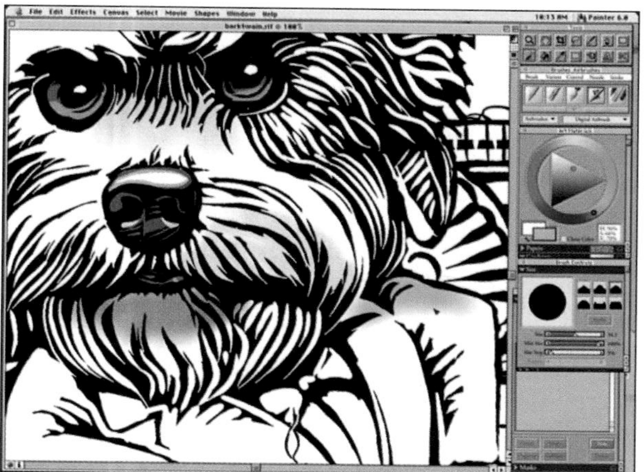

● 21.6

● 21.7

This flattens the image. Choose File→Save As before you drop the layer and save the file, with the layer, as a Riff file; this allows you to go back and edit the image later. It also allows you to retrieve the black-and-white line art (which is on its own layer) at any time.

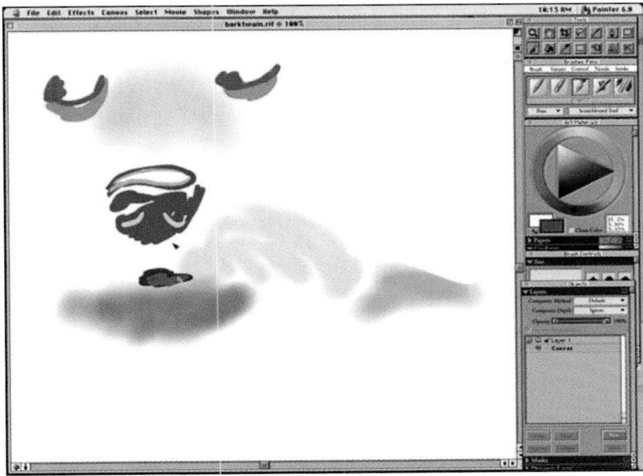

● 21.8

21. Choose File→Save As and save the flattened image in Photoshop or Tiff format for print and Web use.

Artist's Creative Insight and Advice

Why Digital?

To me, working digitally offers speed and versatility without sacrificing quality.

Advice for Artists Working in the Digital Medium

Start with a solid footing of traditional tools and techniques.

Printing and Color Consistency

If you use a service bureau or digital printer, stay with one and work out a system of color consistency.

I really like the Lysonic coated papers and inks when using Iris watercolor prints. In the case of my artwork, it keeps the inks from soaking in and maintains color brilliancy.

Chapter 22

Visage

by Ned Meneses

Artist's Statement

As an artist, you are constantly learning how too see. Whether it means to hold on or let go of a particular idea, to challenge a notion, or to simply explore, it belies a constant state of motion. Being in motion means becoming aware of the senses that you need to heighten, and dissuade.

The Story Behind the Artwork

As an artist, Ned is watchful of science. "Technology advances so fast, and we need to know and understand what effect it has on us," he explains. "Further, technology has also changed the way science probes into the human mind, revealing the idea of post-human existence. I wanted to develop this work to portray this idea in a way that infuses optimism . . . a conscious, harmonious expansion of our mind."

The Creative Process

The primary elements for *Visage* (22.1) came from two separate pieces that Ned created last year. These pieces were, in themselves, a combination of illustrations that were retouched by digital airbrushing.

First, he experimented with the possible ways in which these images could come together. The two images were scanned in. Then the robot was superimposed on the other so it could be moved around and placed carefully.

Then, he strategically erased and reworked the combined image, also cutting and pasting a couple of sections to have different transparencies. After combining the works, he did some highlighting and

◀ 22.1

detailing before uniting all of the image pieces in one layer. Finally, a border was added, similar to the one described in technique later in this chapter. You can see a breakdown of some of the stages in 22.2.

Time is relative in his creative process. Meneses feels his work is finished when it resonates a certain way. He describes this resonance as visually acquiring a state of higher or lower entropy: a higher entropy projects a certain charged energy, and a lower entropy projects a stable, mostly elemental and grounded state.

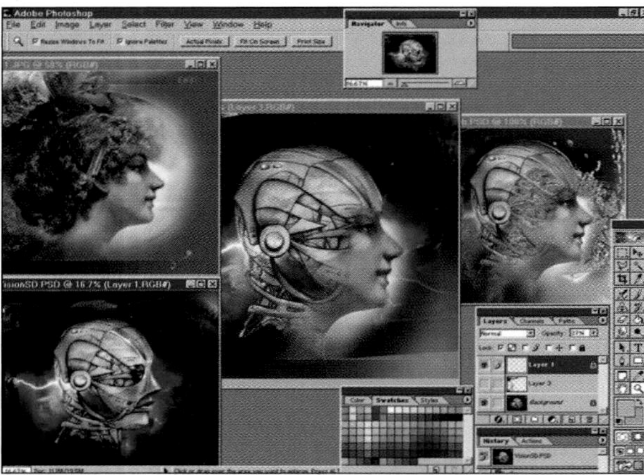

● 22.2

Technique: Creating a Soft, Glowing Border (Photoshop)

Borders can add depth and richness to a work. They can help create an atmosphere and evoke a feeling. As such, adding a border to your work requires both thoughtfulness and spontaneity.

This technique shares the way Ned created the soft, glowing border you see in *Visage*, a border that sets the atmosphere for the piece and draws the viewer into the composition.

1. **In Photoshop, go to the Layers palette and select Duplicate Layer from the pop-up menu.**
2. **Select Duplicate Layer again, creating a third identical layer.**
3. **Click Select Background Color in the toolbar (the lower of the two overlapping color squares).**
4. **Pick a color from the color picker corresponding to the color you'd like to fill the border region with.** Pick a color that would work well as a matte for the image.
5. **Choose Image→Canvas Size, click the center square in the canvas size box to add the new pixels evenly around the original image, and increase the canvas size by 3 inches on each side.** You end up adding a total of 6 inches to the height and width.

About the Artist

Biography

Ned Meneses received a Bachelor of Arts degree in Art from the University of the Incarnate Word in San Antonio, Texas. He has worked as a freelance illustrator and taught high school computer graphics. Recently, his work was accepted for the Seybold 2002 NY and SIGGRAPH 2002 digital art galleries. Since his arrival from Bolivia when he was young, art has always been a part of his life, including sketching, working with clay, watercolor, and acrylics.

Influences

Technology has been a great influence on Ned. He is also fascinated by a source of its expression in physics and mathematics. Inspiration for him comes mainly from beauty, especially beauty in nature: lightning in a rainstorm, dusk in the mountains, and that of many fascinating, courageous thinkers out there. There is also a spiritual influence that he finds not at his side, but at his center.

6. **Select the second layer in the Layers palette so it is highlighted.**
7. **Choose Filter→Blur→Motion Blur. Move the slider to preview the blur distance and angles.**

[TIP]

Try these setting degrees: 50 for the distance, 58 pixels.

8. **Select the Background Layer in the Layers palette so it is highlighted.**
9. **Choose Filter→Blur→Motion Blur. Move the slider to preview blur distance and angles.**

   Try these settings: 53 for the distance, 69 pixels (22.3).

[NOTE]

The exact motion blur settings are not critical. Experiment and see what works well with your image. The important point here is to make the motion blur in the background layer different from the motion blur in the second layer.

10. **Select the Feathered Eraser and use it to strategically soften edges on the top layer.**

    You may want to generate another duplicate layer that remains hidden and untouched. This is useful as a safety backup should you want to return any of the layers to the original image at a later date.

[TIP]

Try something wild, such as Filter→Render→Lighting Effects→Spotlight on the background combined with setting the layer mode on the second layer to Difference and applying an oblique transformation (Edit→Transform→Distort) also to the second layer.

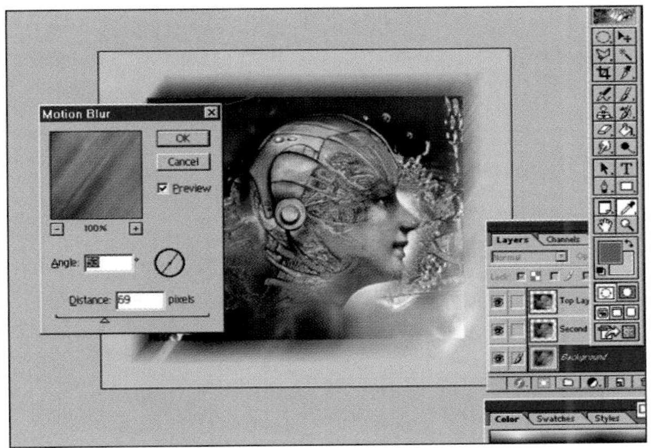

● 22.3

Studio

Computer System:
PENTIUM III

Monitor:
Maxtech

Software:
Adobe Photoshop
Adobe Illustrator
Lightwave
Strata 3D

Archive Media:
CD

Input Devices:
Logitech scanner

Printers:
Epson Stylus 1520
HP Deskjet

Contact

Ned Meneses
Converse, Texas
Nedscape7@yahoo.com
www.absolutearts.com/portfolios/n/nedscape/

Artist's Creative Insight and Advice

Why Digital?

Digital art offers a way of expression that has few limits — that is why it feels so much like art. It has no size unless you want it to; it is less connected to time, and, it can capture the process. The transitory aspect of digital art gives it part of its appeal for me.

I have found the line between my own digital and traditional art becoming blurred to the point that I often think of them as the same thing. An image is a little more real when it is an object in print rather than a collection of points of light. A 5- by 6-foot giclée is not seen the same as a scrolling image on screen. Zooming in and out gives a slight sense dimension, and gives a perspective like no other. All vision is an illusion anyway.

Long ago, I remember thinking of some ideas that I thought I would never try, like color field experiments of varied styles and even some mathematical abstractions. I had started the sketches, but deep inside I knew they would just take too long this way, so they were put aside for a while. Since then, I have entered the world of digital art; now I casually attempt works in many scales, stylized portraits, and do some of those things I thought I would never see. I find myself more ambitious — looking for the things not yet seen, this time knowing that the time will come for those things.

Advice for Artists Working in the Digital Medium

Strive for a rhythm; find it. Sometimes it is about the road, other times it is about the destination, and sometimes it is about you. Practice your craft to make it as effortless as possible, just as anything that you want to do well. When you do not have to think about the technical aspects, you can just go for a particular feel and inspiration comes.

Even if you are comfortable with the way in which you handle your medium, be constantly aware of the ways that other artists work. Learn from others. What you create has part of you in it. By looking at others' works, you see something meaningful of them that is outside of yourself. Go to art openings. To be an artist, you have the privilege and license to create and ask the questions that you would like to answer.

Output

Every image should be handled individually — from inception to reproduction. There are some images that look much better in print than on the screen, others are just the opposite. Some colors just do not print well. For all these nuances, it is important to proof and to know the characteristics of the printer you will be using for the final output — archival giclée is very important.

Charmaine Conui on Meneses' *Visage*

"This image combines many elements: The real and the futuristic, traditional illustration and computer-rendered elements, painterly style and computer filters. You can see the levels of blending and overlays. The subject matter has an almost religious feel to it. Maybe a premonition of things to come . . . artificial intelligence taking over humanity."

— Charmaine Conui, Art Director, Seybold Seminars (`www.seyboldseminars.com`)

Chapter 23

Vertical 8

by Toru Kosaka

Artist's Statement

My work is inspired by various industrial materials that I deform to create the finished work. The volume of the main object creates a dramatic space as a whole.

The Story Behind the Artwork

In *Vertical 8* (23.1), Toru wanted to express an engine's mechanical charm and beauty. Toru started drawing it 3D from the beginning since he already had a completed image in his mind. Although this object was only part of the carburetor and muffler, he tried to express the realistic atmosphere in which an engine was about to start.

The Creative Process

"I must admit, no special technique was used for this work," explained Toru. He combines simply formed 3D objects to create a photo-realistic illusion of a complex mechanical structure, in this case an engine.

Anders F Ronnblom on Toru Kosaka

"Toru Kosaka was nominated for the Digital Hall Of Fame Award 1999 with his entry *Vertical 8*. By utilizing 3D software, Toru Kosaka models and paints with digital lights to achieve a remarkable sense of photorealism."

— Anders F Ronnblom, Editor in Chief, EFX Art & Design (www.macartdesign.matchbox.se)

◀23.1

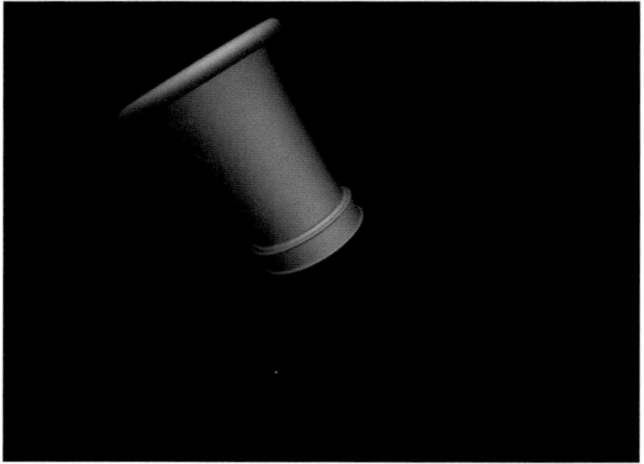

23.2

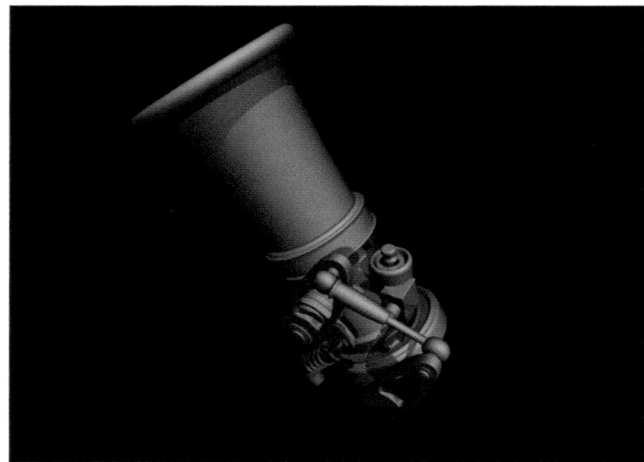

23.4

23.3

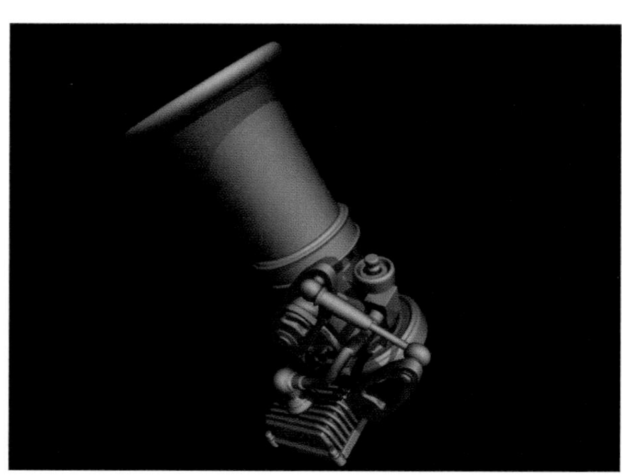

23.5

About the Artist

Biography

Born in Nagoya, Japan, in 1965, digital designer Toru Kosaka uses mechanical elements as inspiration in his artwork. In 1998, Kosaka participated in the 3D Festival Digital Hall of Fame held in Sweden. The following year, he won an award in the same festival. The artist also had his work broadcasted on Swedish National Television in 2000. Recently, Kosaka had his work featured in Walt Disney Company and Isaac V. Kerlow's The Art of 3D Computer Animation and Imaging.

Influences

Though there is no one person who influenced Toru's style, his father, an architect and interior planner, was a big influence on him regarding his overall aesthetic sense of things.

Studio

Computer System:
Power Mac G4, 800 MHz
120GB hard drive
1.5GB RAM

In the following images (23.2 through 23.5), you can see the way Toru built up a complex structure by putting together simple basic forms and components, almost as if he was constructing a piece of machinery from a kit.

In this first stage (23.2), you see a simple gray cylindrical form with basic lighting and perspective.

The next stages (23.3 through 23.5) show more complicated components being added. You can now see cast shadows.

Here (23.6) you can see the same structure from a slightly different angle and with an additional component added.

This structure was then duplicated four times (23.7) to create half of the V8 engine that forms the subject of this artwork.

Here (23.8) you can see several sections of the structure being displayed as "wire frames" within Toru's 3D software (ExpressionTools' Shade). The wire frame display mode, which resembles an engineer's schematic or technical drawing, is the most

● 23.7

● 23.6

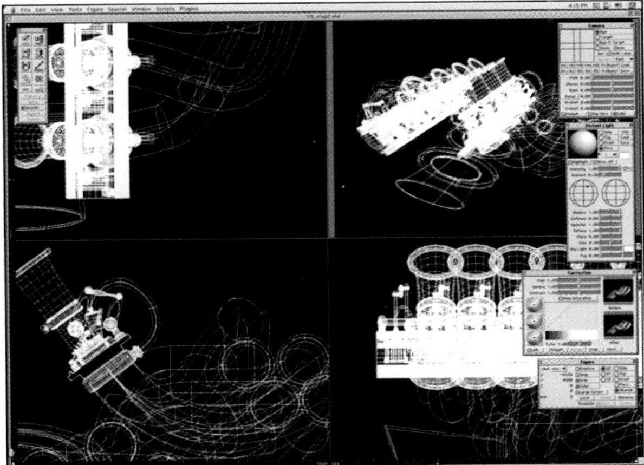

● 23.8

Monitors:
21- and 15-inch Dual CRT

Software:
Adobe Photoshop
Illustrator
ExpressionTools' Shade
Robert McNeel & Associates' Rhinoceros

Removable Media:
CD-ROM

Tablet:
Wacom i-1820 18 x 24

Printers:
Pictrography 3000

Contact

Toru Kosaka
Tokyo, Japan
kosaka@creat.cc
www.linkclub.or.jp/~eggman/

efficient way to work on the structural aspects of the design since the file sizes are small and the rendering times short.

One of the powerful aspects of constructing objects in a 3D program is the ability to control perspective and lighting. Here (23.9 and 23.10) you can see part of the structure viewed from two different angles.

After carefully and methodically constructing the entire engine structure, Toru then worked on the surface characteristics. He gave the surfaces a metallic finish.

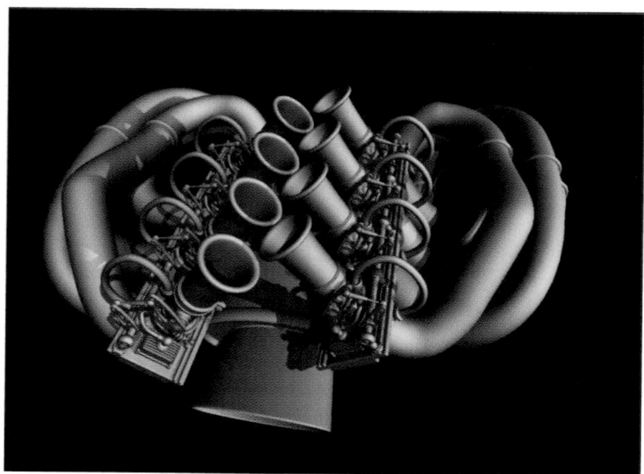

● 23.9

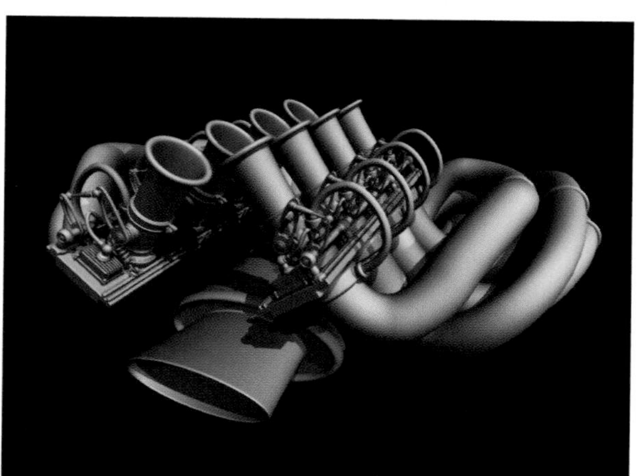

● 23.10

Technique: Creating the Illusion of Light and Shadow on Rounded Surfaces

This technique explains Toru's use of light, shadow, and reflection to make his rounded surfaces look realistic. This is not a step-by-step instruction for a specific piece of software; the principles described here can be applied in any software, whether 3D or 2D.

1. **Add light delicately to the parts of the rounded surface that would protrude the most and catch the highlight from the ambient light.**
2. **Exaggerate the contrast between the highlighted areas and the shadow areas. Delicately airbrush in the shaded side of the surfaces and any shadow areas cast.**
3. **Finally, add a low opacity spherical reflection of the surroundings on the surface (23.11).**

   This gives the impression of a rounded metallic surface reflecting the environment.

Artist's Creative Insight and Advice

Why Digital?

There is no end unless you stop drawing.

Advice for Artists Working in the Digital Medium

Do not depend on your software.

Output

I like to use Seat Type Reversal Film and Pictrography (Fuji Photo Film Co., Ltd) since they give color that's very close to what I see on my monitor.

● 23.11

Chapter 24

Chloe

by Robert Corwin

Artist's Statement

My digital compositions resemble very expressive paintings in their color and evolutionary process. Human connection with the pixel makes computer art more vibrant and less computer-generated. In my work, human imperfections are emphasized to the degree that it strengthens the texture of the piece and the uniqueness of the electronic field.

I want to strike the viewer's consciousness with emotionally direct imagery. Like any expressionistic painter, my inner afflictions are released onto the pictorial plane in a spontaneous and vigorous manner. I create unnatural settings that conjure up altered states of dementia. Opposition between man and computer, brush versus pixel, emotions versus logic, and global versus personal comprise the visual elements of my distorted scenarios.

The Story Behind the Artwork

With *Chloe* (24.1), Robert wanted to transform a beautiful image into a painting. He started with a photograph of someone he loved and thought was beautiful. With this base image, he began to abstract the human form. His process uses computer technology while following an Abstract-Expressionist way of making art — very fast and instinctual, in the tradition of artists like Jackson Pollock.

The Creative Process

With the realistic image of a nude woman open in Painter, Robert applied the Water Rake brush variant. With many varied strokes, in a painterly manner, he transformed the image. As he painted, Robert changed the brush size and his brush strokes. He thus created a completely altered image.

He repeated this process many times, producing several different versions of the transformed image. Robert brought all these separate images into Photoshop and combined them into a single multi-layered image (where each version formed a separate layer). In *Chloe,* he had about 10 layers of the abstract nude. Robert then experimented with different blend modes, filters, and color adjustments for the different layers. Finally, Robert selectively brushed away unwanted brush-work from different layers (painting on the layer mask). In this way, a new image emerged out of the chaos.

◀24.1

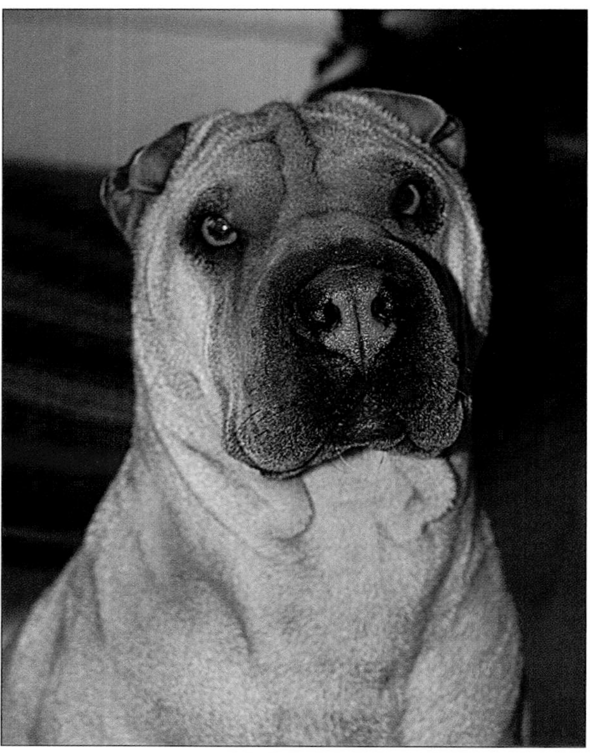

● 24.2

Technique: Abstract-Expressionist Transformation of a Photograph (Painter and Photoshop)

In this technique, you follow the three-fold process Robert used to create *Chloe.* First you create a series of transformations of your source image in Painter; second, you make a multi-layered image out of these versions and experiment with layer modes, filters, and color adjustments in Photoshop; and finally, you flatten the image and make some final adjustments in Painter.

The examples shown here to illustrate the technique are based on an image of Robert's dog Lilly.

1. **Open your source image in Painter (24.2).**
2. **Choose File→Clone.**

[T I P]

This makes a copy of the source image. It's a good habit to only paint on copies of the original image, not directly on the original source image because you ensure that you preserve your source image for future reference.

3. **Choose Window→Screen Mode Toggle (Cmd/Ctrl-M) to mount your image.**
4. **Choose Load Library from the very bottom of the left-hand Brush Category pop-up menu in the Brushes palette.**
5. **Select the brush library called Ver 5, located in the Brushes folder in the Painter 7 application folder on your computer hard drive. Click Load.**

About the Artist

Biography

Robert, who graduated with a Masters of Fine Arts from Bradley University, Peoria, Illinois, is a freelance digital artist whose work has been widely exhibited and published. He is a Puffin Foundation Grant recipient, was awarded an Honorable Mention in the 2000 Second Annual Richard Nagler Photography Competition, and won the Best of Show Award from Central Arts Collective "Free at Last" Exhibition in 1997.

Influences

The Abstract Expressionists (1950s) and the Surrealists (1920s).

This brush library contains the default brush library that originally appeared in Painter 5.

6. **Select the Water brush category (left-hand pop-up menu in the Brushes palette).**
7. **Select the Water Rake brush variant (right-hand pop-up menu in the Brushes palette).**
8. **Use the Water Rake brush to distort and alter the image (24.3).**
9. **Choose File→Save As.**
10. **Name this version and save it as a TIFF file.**
11. **Click Save.**
12. **Select the original source image.**

[TIP]

You can select its name from the bottom of the Windows menu.

● 24.3

Karen Sperling on Corwin's *Chloe*

"When viewing *Chloe*, as with most good abstract art, you don't look for meaning – the experience is more visceral than that. Your eye travels up, down, and around the image on a visual roller coaster. What looks at first glance like a cacophony of line and color is ultimately a harmonic symphony of composition and form. Move my eyes, move me."

– Karen Sperling, Editor/Publisher, Artistry Painter tutorials and classes (`www.artistrymag.com`)

Studio

Computer System:
G4, 867 MHz
80MB hard drive
1.2GB RAM

Removable Media:
10GB Firewire

Monitors:
20- and 15-inch

Software:
Adobe Photoshop
Painter

Tablet:
18-x-12-inch Wacom tablet

Input Devices:
Olympus E-10

Contact

Robert Corwin
Chicago, Illinois
`corwin@telocity.com`
`homepage.mac.com/fusionspace/`
`www.911gallery.org/`

13. **Repeat steps 2 through 11 until you have generated ten different versions of the original image, each saved with a different version number.**
    24.4, 24.5, and 24.6 show different ways that Robert alerted his original source image of Lilly. The possibilities are, of course, endless.
14. **Open all the different versions of your altered source image in Photoshop.**
15. **Choose one of the altered images.**
16. **Select Cmd/Ctrl-A to select all.**
17. **Choose Cmd/Ctrl-C to copy.**
18. **Select another altered image.**
19. **Choose Cmd/Ctrl-V to paste the first image as a layer centered over the second image.**
    Continue copying and pasting with the other images until you have built up a multi-layered image.
20. **Go through each layer in turn and experiment with layer modes, filters, and color adjustments (24.7).**
    As an example, Robert might typically first choose Image➔Adjust➔Curves and create an "s" line in the Curves dialog box. He might then change the layer blending mode in the Layers palette from Normal to, say, Overlay.
21. **Select each layer in turn, click on the Layer mask icon in the Layers palette, and use the Brush tool with black to selectively brush away portions of some layers.**
    Deciding which parts of a layer to brush away is the unconscious part of art making. Robert generally tries to stick with the form of the original figure in the way he brushes away imagery — he wants any changes he makes to support the basic composition. He doesn't want to get to so abstract that the original image gets completely lost.
22. **Save the image in PSD file format to preserve the layers.**
23. **Select Flatten Image from the Layers pop-up menu.**
24. **Resave the image with a different name.**
25. **Open the flattened image in Painter and continue working on it with the Water Rake brush variant (24.8).**

● 24.4

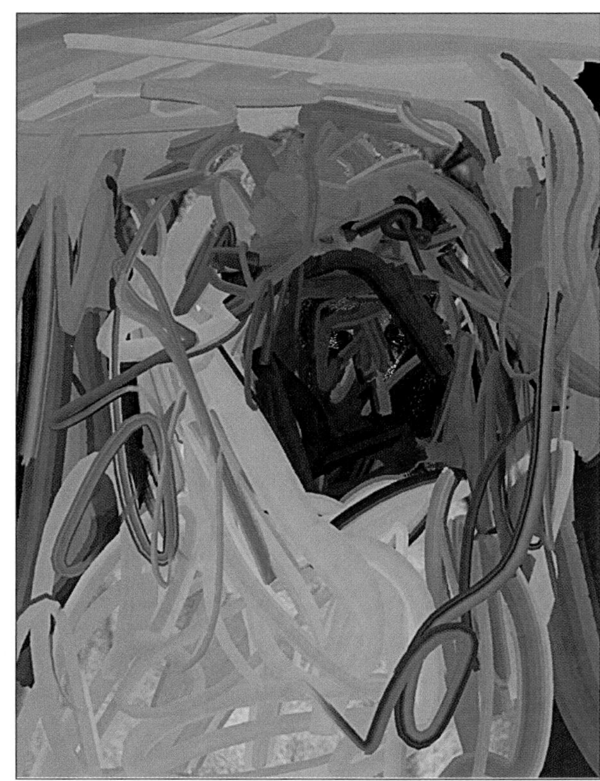

● 24.5

You can continue generating versions in Painter and using the versions to construct multi-layered images in Photoshop. This is an intuitive, creative process and there is no set formula. Each picture suggests its own path.

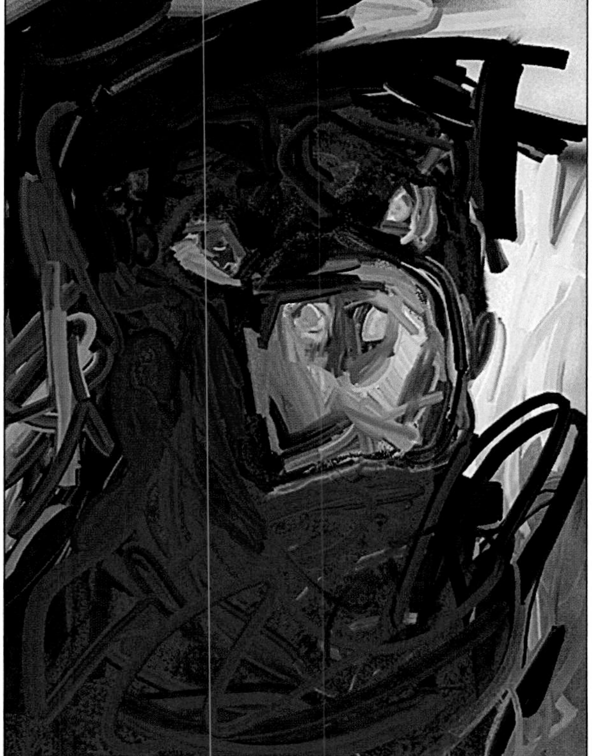

● 24.6

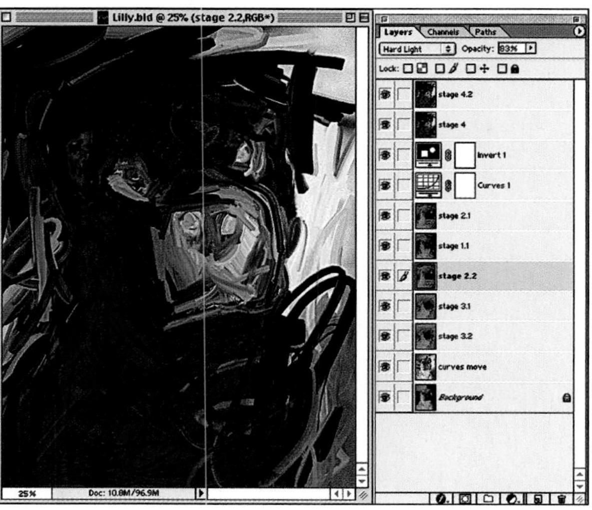

● 24.7

Artist's Creative Insight and Advice

Why Digital?

With my background in traditional art (painting and drawing), I thought I would bring a different look to photography. Plus, I think most digital works are unemotional and have no connection to human experience. I want to bring in my emotions and subconscious to harnessing technology for art making.

Advice for Artists Working in the Digital Medium

Learn art (traditional) skills; it is our language to communicate with others. Computers only go so far — they don't make good art, artists do.

Learn the programs, and with your art skills, you will stop thinking how to do something; you will just do the artistic effect. Using filters doesn't make you an artist.

● 24.8

Chapter 25

Apple Series: Beth

by Pamela Wells

Artist's Statement

The purpose of my life is to paint a compelling message. This message is about feminine archetypes of transformation, which I believe are of immediate importance in helping contemporary men and women understand how to become the individuals they are meant to be.

I also love animals and hope that we will all find a way to live with nature in harmony. What motivates me personally, and as an artist with a message, is being in contact with and talking about the infinite. I believe this is the most important question of our lives.

The Story Behind the Artwork

Apple Series: Beth (25.1) is part of a series of paintings dedicated to nurturing and understanding the feminine energy within each person and the world. The central reclining figure represents a goddess archetype. The tree symbolizes the Tree of Life. The snake, one of the most ancient and powerful symbols in mythology, represents the combining of the masculine and feminine, and a rebirthing into wholeness and harmony.

The Creative Process

Pamela began this piece by researching and taking photos while working on the composition in her head and on paper. You can see here the source image of the model (25.2) and a composite of low resolution photos of a tree (25.3). She then scanned the photos into Photoshop and made a rough collage to be used as a visual reference for her work in Painter. She saved the file as a TIFF and imported it into Painter.

◀25.1

● 25.2

● 25.3

In Painter, she made a clone of the reference image. She deleted the contents of the clone and then turned on Tracing Paper. She used a pressure-sensitive Wacom tablet and stylus to draw a detailed black-and-white line sketch with the Pencil tool in the clone image.

Then, Pamela painted in color on the black-and-white pencil sketch, starting with the background and working her way to the foreground (25.4). Pamela modeled the forms and figures, also working from the background, such as the sky and clouds, to the foreground, leaving the foremost elements to last. She applied layers of color with the Soft Charcoal tool, using a light pressure on the stylus. To blend areas, she applied very subtle shades of color over existing color (see the technique later in this chapter).

● 25.4

About the Artist

Biography

After completing a business degree and a major in marketing at George Washington University, Pamela worked for a publishing company in Maryland and then as a Communications Supervisor for a non-profit corporation in Washington, D.C. During that time, she supplemented her skills with art-related courses at the Corcoran School of Art.

Pamela began to experiment with desktop publishing software around 1988. After three years of working for others, she moved to California, where she opened her own design studio. For 12 years, she has been a successful designer, illustrator, and fine artist. Her artwork is sold in fine art and commercial markets. She has won several awards in both design and fine art and has been featured in the *Painter 6.0 Wow!* book.

Her primary fine art interest is in the human figure and how it relates to the compositional elements of a piece. Psychoanalyst Carl Jung once said, "The spiritual adventure of our time is the exposure of human consciousness to the undefined and indefinable." This is the spiritual adventure Pamela embodies when she paints. She deals with archetypes.

Though Pamela uses photographs for building reference compositions, her final work is completely painted by hand with the stylus. For *Apple Series: Beth,* Pamela spent approximately 54 hours, including the time for the photo shoots and painting. She knew the painting was finished when she could sit back and say to herself, "Mmm."

Technique: Creating Realistic Skin Tones (Painter)

The major part of Pamela's painting involves shading with pixels. The following technique shows how Pamela achieves hand-painted and realistic skin tones using digital shading.

[NOTE]

This technique takes some practice to master, but over time, it will be a rewarding addition to your creative process. In practice Pamela makes use of skin color sets she has made, based on colors picked from classic paintings. In the following description, to keep things simple for you to follow, the skin colors are picked from the original reference photo. Picking colors from a scanned, fine art painting offers greater richness and warmth in the color palette.

1. **Open the original reference image in Painter.**
   Pamela creates her photo-composites in Photoshop.
2. **Choose File→Clone.**
   This creates an identical copy of the original reference image.
3. **Position the original reference file and the clone copy side by side, with the clone image active.**
   In this way, you can continually use the reference file as a visual source while painting on the clone image.
4. **Choose Select→All (Ctrl/Command-A) to select all in the clone image.**
5. **Press the Backspace/Delete key to clear the clone canvas to white.**
6. **Choose Canvas→Tracing Paper (Ctrl/Command-T) to turn the Tracing Paper feature on.**
   This shows the clone source image (in this case the reference image) at 50% opacity in the clone image so that it can be used for tracing.
7. **Select the 2B Pencil variant in the Pencils category of the Brushes palette.**
8. **Choose black in the Color Picker.**
   You find the Color Picker in the Colors section of the Art Materials palette.
9. **Use the pressure-sensitive Wacom tablet and stylus to draw a detailed black-and-white line sketch in the clone image based on the reference image as seen through the tracing paper.**
10. **Choose File→Save As, rename your clone image, and save as a TIFF file.**
11. **Choose Canvas→Tracing Paper (Ctrl/Command-T) to turn tracing paper off.**
12. **Select the Dropper tool.**

Creating art for her is like placing dream imagery from the unconscious mind onto canvas. George Bernard Shaw said, "We use a mirror to see our faces, we use art to see our soul." Pamela sees her art in that light, as a means for the viewer to see his soul. She honors what the viewer sees in her paintings as unique to their psyche. She believes there are many ways for the viewer to explain or "see" the imagery.

Influences

Rubens, Michelangelo, Maxfield Parrish, J.W. Waterhouse, Dante Gabriel Rossetti, and Sir Lawrence Alma-Tadema.

Studio

Computer System:
Mac G3
6GB hard drive
192MB RAM

Monitors:
20-inch Viewsonic Monitor

Software:
Quark Xpress
Adobe Illustrator
Adobe Photoshop
MetaCreations Painter
Pagemaker

Tablet:
Wacom Tablet UD-1212, 16 x 16.5 inches

Removable Media:
Zip
CDRW

Input:
HP Scanjet IIcx
IXLA Digital Camera

Printers:
HP Deskjet 870C
Apple LaserWriter 12/640

Contact

Pamela Wells
Cardiff, California
Tangawells@aol.com
www.artmagic.net

13. **Click on a skin tone in the original photo composite (reference image).**
14. **Modify the color slightly, if desired, by moving the cursors in the Color Picker to suit the coloring you'd like to use in your painting.**

[TIP]

Pamela finds that adding a little yellow or red adds to the "aged" look of her paintings.

15. **Click the close button on the top-left corner of the current Color Set.**
16. **Choose Create New Empty Color Set (25.5) from the Color Set pop-up menu in the Color Set section of the Art Materials palette.**
    A tiny, barely noticeable, palette title bar appears on your desktop.
17. **Click the "+" button in the Color Set palette.**
    This adds the selected color to your new color set.
18. **Repeat this process, picking colors from the source photo and adding them to your new color set (25.6) until you build up a wide range of skin tones to choose from.**

[TIP]

To save and name this custom color set for future use, close the color set, click on the Color Set Library button, click Save, and name the color set (Skin Colors, for example). To retrieve the color set, click again on the Color Set Library button and locate the saved library.

19. **Choose the Fill Bucket tool (Paint Bucket).**
    Make sure the Controls: Paint Bucket palette has the setting What to Fill: Image and Fill With: Current Color.
20. **Select a base skin color by clicking on a square in the skin color set you have created.**
    This color will be the foundation or background color you fill your skin regions with. You can choose either the most common color or the lightest color. The purpose of filling in large regions with the Fill Bucket, rather than painting them in, is to save time.
21. **Click in the face region with the Fill Bucket (25.7) where you wish to fill with skin tone.**
    The area fills with the current color.

[TIP]

If the fill extends beyond the face region and spreads too far, choose Edit→Undo (Ctrl/Command-Z) to undo the fill. Reduce the Tolerance setting in the Controls: Paint Bucket palette down to about 10. Then try the fill again. You can also go over the contour line work to ensure a continuous line completely encloses the region you are trying to fill.

● 25.5

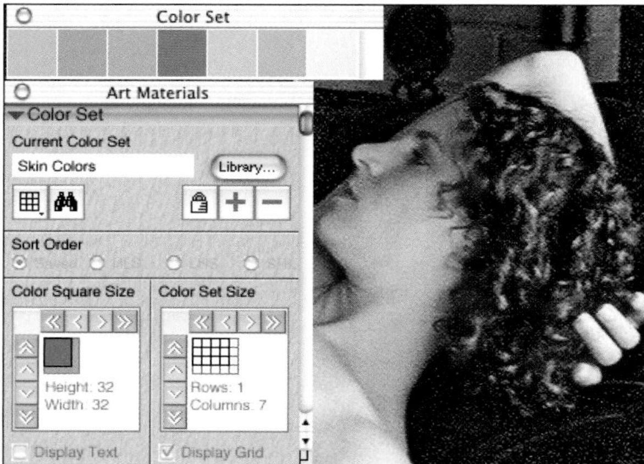

● 25.6

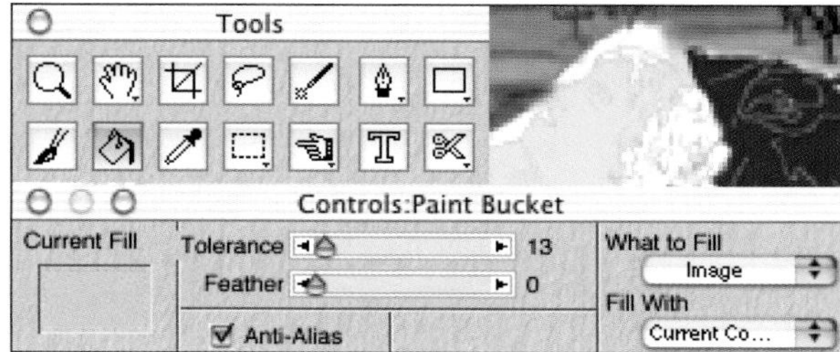

● 25.7

[TIP]

Pamela starts at the face of the figure and works down from there. She begins with the face since it is a key area, the life of the painting. By starting here, Pamela soon gets a sense of whether her chosen skin tones are working.

22. **Select the Soft Charcoal variant in the Dry Media brush category, or any other paint tool in Painter that sprays on the pixels like a traditional airbrush.**
23. **Pick another color from your skin tone color set.**
24. **Press softly with your stylus on your digital tablet and lightly spray the pixels over the background color, referring to the original photo-composite for visual reference.**

    Continue this process, blending the colors by building up colors over the top of the background skin color.

Artist's Creative Insight and Advice

Why Digital?

Digital is faster than painting with traditional oil paints, which would otherwise be my medium of choice. Painting digitally, I don't have to remix or rematch paint; I can "undo" indefinitely and quickly; and the composition phase of the process (in Photoshop) is quicker to put together than projecting the images from a projector onto canvas and hand tracing them or using a manual grid system.

Advice for Artists Working in the Digital Medium

Take basic drawing and painting courses. Get your technical/anatomical drawing skills mastered. Practice, practice, and more practice! Follow your intuition and heart throughout your creative process. Do what you love. Listen to your "own music."

There is a misperception by many that digital fine art is not "real" art. Because we are pioneers in this field, it is important that we overcome this historical trend of shortsighted thinking. Keep putting your work out in the fine art markets despite the confusion and reluctance to support this new form of visionary art.

Serve your community as a role model and a mentor by sharing your creative process with art buyers and students. Reproduce your work with archival inks and papers to build trust and confidence with investment art buyers. Invest in yourself and your process.

Output

Find a competent and experienced third-party vendor to output the highest quality archival prints. A good print bureau will provide you with ICC profiles and will walk you through the install and color correction process so that you are both speaking the same color language. If they don't give you an ICC profile, go somewhere else. Don't let your printer make *you* responsible for the color results! Output and color correction is a team effort.

I prefer Rolland printers, with the final imagery output on canvas. My work is rather large and very detailed, so I am looking to see the detail in the final output. Canvas tends to "pop" the imagery more than watercolor papers, which tend to soak-in and spread the inks out, creating a softer look.

I UV coat all my finished work and sometimes work over them with an acrylic gel or a crackle varnish.

Chapter 26

Art in Wartime

by Stephan L. Campbell

Artist's Statement

My best work is either completely unplanned or the result of an image in my head that I can't rid myself of in any other way but to make it into art. I sometimes assign myself a number of sketchbook pages to fill within some time period, moving on to a new one before the temptation to finish the piece sets in, sometimes drawing a number of empty frames, and then going back and filling them in.

The Story Behind the Artwork

Steve created the original painting, depicting a figure playing the saxophone against a colorful background, while working as a demo artist at the Seybold 2001 Digital Art Gallery in San Francisco, just a few weeks after the 9/11 attacks. Steve wanted to create a piece that expressed how the artist, in this case represented by the musician, continues to create art and beauty in spite of world events, in spite of economic dips and rises, in spite of governments, terrorists, elected officials, and what ever else falls out of the sky.

Steve worked on a small file of 800 pixels by 600 pixels, in Corel Painter 7, so that he could work quickly in the tradeshow demo environment. Steve was inspired to continue working on the piece after the show.

As the war in Afghanistan began to take shape, Steve's feeling of being besieged on all fronts expressed itself by placing the musician, playing his sax in defiance, beneath a rain of bombs.

Eventually, *Art in Wartime* (26.1) took shape.

◀ 26.1

The Creative Process

Steve saved the original painting (26.2) as a RIFF file, the native format of Painter. He then resaved a version as a Photoshop file so he could continue working with it in Photoshop and Studio Artist (on both Mac and PC).

Back in his home studio, Steve opened the image in Synthetik Studio Artist on his Mac and resized it to 200%. Studio Artist is a Macintosh-only image transformation program. It is based on the way a musical synthesizer works. You set up a series of filter and brush parameters and then apply them, using your original image as a source image, to create a completely new modified image.

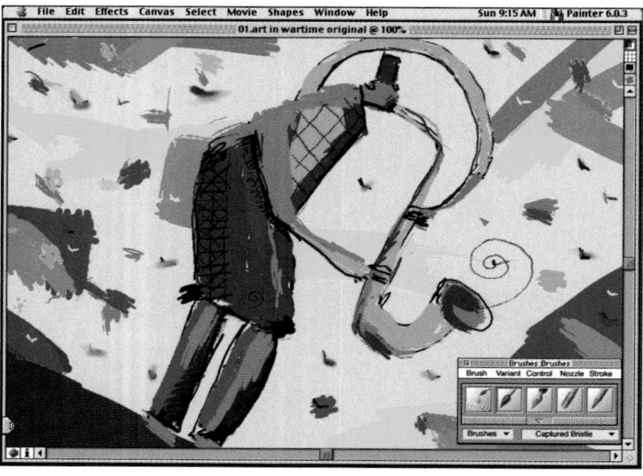

● 26.2

Studio Artist incorporates optical recognition techniques like those used by the human eye. When an image is "repainted" in Studio Artist, there is a lot more going on than the usual color point–sampling that occurs when cloning an image in Photoshop or Painter. Studio Artist recognizes line and shape as well as color. It automatically "repaints" the image using the currently chosen paint Patch, a saved "recipe" that incorporates the nature of the brush, as well as a background texture (similar to a Brush Look in Painter). The texture, rather than being a simple luminance map as in Painter, is generated mathematically on the fly underneath the brush in Studio Artist and can be image-wide and non-tiling.

After opening his original painting in Studio Artist, Steve chose an existing paint Patch, which he modified slightly in Studio Artist's Paint Synthesizer module. He then clicked the Action button, which automatically painted a new canvas based on the information in the source image, the original artwork.

Steve tried out several different modified Patches, one run on top of another on the same image, for a cumulative effect. The result has a rich and organic, textured and patterned feel that otherwise would have taken a great deal of time to do by hand. Submitting an image to this process also has an unplanned aspect to it, allowing you to be surprised at what the software has done with your original artwork. Steve simply experimented with each Patch, in each case choosing a result that he found pleasing.

About the Artist

Biography

Steve's earliest memories are of drawing and painting, which he pursued compulsively through grade school and college in Kansas City, Missouri. While working at a magazine devoted to early Apple computers, the first Mac was set up in the art department; his real job suddenly became problematic.

Since acquiring his first Macintosh computer, Steve has been creating digital work. His art has won several awards, including Grand Prize in the first annual Macworld Digital Art Competition, and First Place Prize, Fine Arts Division, in the first MicroPublishing/3M Digital Art Competition. He has been included in many touring galleries and publications (such as the Painter WOW! Book series, authored by Cher Pendarvis).

Influences

Art Brut, The Beatles, Miles Davis, The Meters, Zoot Sims, The Grateful Dead, Tool videos, Jan Vermeer, Jose Guadalupe Posada, Willem deKooning, Max Ernst, Carlos Almaraz (and everything else that comes out of Mexico), the Quay Brothers, the Coe Sisters, Basil Wolverton, Will Eisner, and bad-but-colorful packaging art.

The Studio Artist modified image was opened in Photoshop. Steve placed the musician into a separate layer from the background using the Lasso tool and then used the Quick Mask to touch up the edges. Having the musician on a separate layer allowed him to reduce the brightness and saturation of the background so that the musician stood out.

Steve then took the image over to the PC and added more detail with Painter 6 running under Windows NT (26.3). In Painter, he used the tools (which resemble traditional Natural Media brush characteristics), to touch up, refine and in some cases, bring out the texture and detail introduced by Studio Artist. He also added detail to the image, like the stripes on the figure's pants, the rainbow on the musician's bowed left arm, details on his face, and so forth.

The prototype bomb (26.4), on which all the bombs raining down on the figure were based, was created in Ray Dream Studio on the PC.

The rendered bomb image was pasted multiple times into multiple layers, allowing individual control of the scaling, transparency, and blending mode for each bomb, to create the feeling of depth.

The imagery developed from here. He created a city in the background using Painter vectors, or Shapes, which were then grouped; he also altered the transparency to make it look as if the city was distant on the horizon. Painter's Image Hose was used with a Fern nozzle (from the Garden Hose 2 collection) to create the patch of greenery that the sax player is

● 26.3

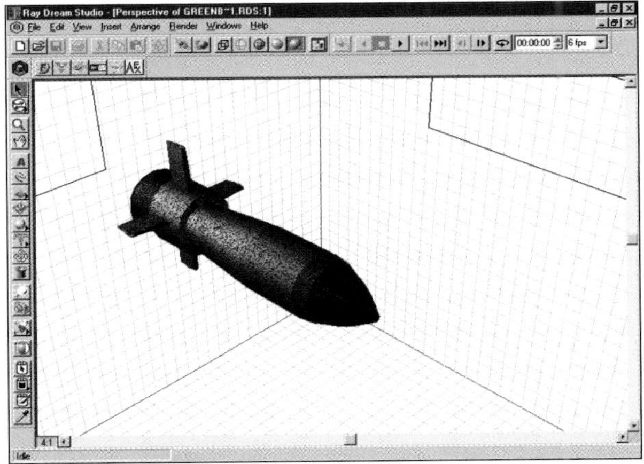

● 26.4

Studio

Computer System:

Macintosh 8500, 400MHz G3 processor adapter
144MB RAM
2GB internal SCSI drive
4GB external drive
Intergraph Windows NT Workstation
Dual 333MHz Pentium II processors
256MB RAM
9GB internal Ultra-SCSI hard drive

Monitors:

17-inch ViewSonic
19-inch Intergraph multi-syncGraphics

Software:

Adobe Photoshop
Illustrator
Corel Painter
Synthetik Studio Artist
Ray Dream Studio
Bryce
Ulead Web Razor Pro
CorelDRAW (and Paint)

Removable Media:

100 & 250MB Zip external drives
2 CD drives
Creative 12X CD burner

Archive Media:

CDs
APS DAT drive

Tablet:

Wacom ArtZ 8-inch
Wacom Intuos 12-inch

Input Devices:

Visioneer PaperPort 6100 scanner

Printers:

Epson Stylus Photo 6
Epson Stylus Color 860

Contact

Stephan L. Campbell
campbell12@mindspring.com
http://campbell12.home.mindspring.com

protecting from the bombs between his feet. The main figure was finished with the Pencil and Just Add Water tools.

The image was finally flattened and repainted again in Studio Artist to get a slightly more splattered paint look.

The whole process took three to four days. At a certain point, he simply felt it was finished, and he stopped working.

Technique: Creating a Rich, Organic, and Textured Version Based on an Original Image (Studio Artist)

This technique shares Steve's approach to using Studio Artist (a Macintosh-only painting program) to create a modified version of his original painting. The modified version has a richer, more organic, and more textured look than his original painting.

1. **Open Studio Artist.**
   A standard dialog box appears asking you to select an image file to act as a source image.
2. **Select the source image (your painting) you want to work with.**
3. **Click OK.**
   A Set Canvas Size dialog box appear that allows you to specify the working canvas size.
4. **Choose a canvas size larger than the original source image (26.5).**
   Steve changed his canvas specifications from 800 x 600 pixels at 72 dpi to 1600 x 1200 pixels at 300 dpi.

[NOTE]

The actual source image isn't modified in any way. The image canvas, which is a blank document linked to the source image, will be your final saved image. In other words, the image canvas is created larger than the source image. The repainting, based on the original color information from the source image, is automatically generated at the higher resolution and overall size of the image canvas.

5. **Click OK in the Set Canvas Size dialog box.**
   After you do this, the cursor spins for a short period of time while Studio Artist examines your source image. Then, the main Studio Artist Canvas window appears showing a white canvas containing, by default, one layer (Layer 1). You don't have to do anything specific, besides defining a source image, to generate that first layer.
6. **Choose Image from the Source Image Options for Layer 1.**
   You see the source image in the Layer 1. In other words, Steve set up the first layer of his document to contain a straight copy of the source image at the new size.
7. **Choose Canvas→Layer Commands→New Canvas Layer from the top menu.**
   This creates a second, blank layer (Layer 2), in which you "repaint" your source image using Studio Artist's tools.
8. **Choose Image from the source image options for Layer 2.**
   Studio Artist opens, by default, with the Paint Patch Presets.
9. **Experiment, "repainting" in the canvas Layer 2 with different Paint Patch Categories and Patches.**

[NOTE]

It is difficult to give a specific recipe of Patches or Patch categories to choose for your image, since they will have very different effects depending on what your source image looks like. Painting in Studio Artist is not like painting in Photoshop or Painter since you are actually applying a brush to your canvas by hand. It is more like customizing a special filter or effect and then applying that to the image and seeing what happens. There is a lot of serendipity rather than a preset method.

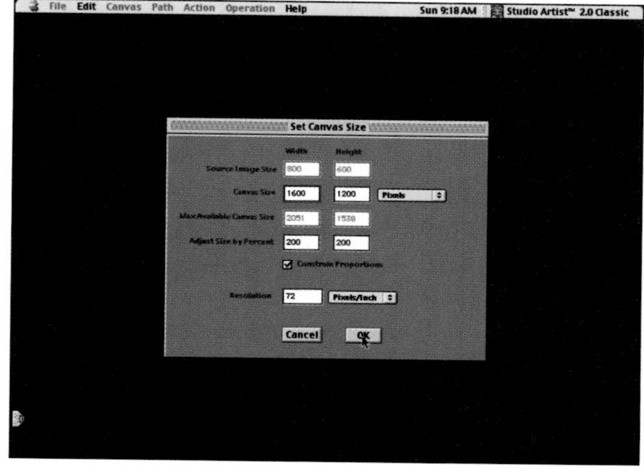

● 26.5

10. **Choose Canvas→Layer Window.**
11. **Choose View→All Layers.**
12. **Select Layer 2 in the Layers window by clicking on the Layer 2 check box.**

[TIP]

You can see the layer number in the layer pop-up menu located on your screen just above the canvas (separate to the Layers window).

13. **Experiment with different composite modes from the pop-up menu next to the layer name in the Layers window (26.6).**
    The Composite modes in Studio Artist are like Blending modes in Photoshop or Composite methods in Painter in so far as they determine the way an image on a layer interacts with imagery contained in layers below the chosen layer. The Composite modes in Studio Artist determine how the first layer (Layer 1), which contains a copy of the original source image, is composited, or blended, with the repainted layer (Layer 2).
    Some Composite modes in Studio Artist have similar effects to certain Blending modes in Photoshop or Composite methods in Painter. For instance, the Min Composite mode in Studio Artist essentially acts like the Darker Layer Blending mode in Photoshop — it allows pixels darker than the background image to blend in while masking off those that are lighter. Steve used the Min Composite mode in Studio Artist for merging two sets of pixels (from layers 1 and 2), emerging with a result that was better than each layer individually. There are other Composite modes in Studio Artist that have no equivalent in either Photoshop or Painter. It is worth playing with these and exploring the way they can alter your imagery.
    In experimenting with the Composite modes in Studio Artist, Steve strove to have the base layer (Layer 1 with the copy of the original image) blend with, and come through, the second layer (Layer 2 with the repainted image). In this way he was able to hold onto the basic look of the original image while creating an interesting, rich, organic, and textured version of it.
14. **Choose Save As regularly and name each version with a different name, especially when you reach a stage of the image you like.**
    You may find you can't exactly repeat a stage in the development of your image in Studio Artist unless you save versions as you go. For versatility and quality, save the images as Photoshop format. In Steve's case, he saved 5 or 6 files as he was working on this piece. He ended up picking his favorite version to continue working with in Painter and Photoshop (26.7).

Artist's Creative Insight and Advice

Why Digital?

I *do* like working digitally because I don't end up with "medium" all over my hands; I *don't* like working

● 26.6

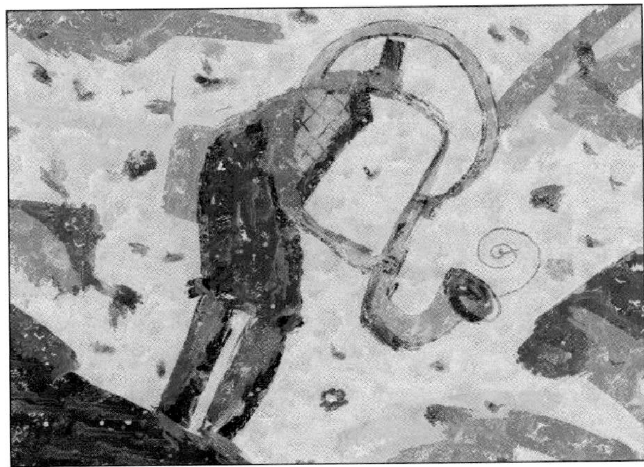

● 26.7

digitally because I don't end up with "medium" all over my hands. Working digitally is more convenient in most respects and allows effects that would be very difficult, if not impossible, to create using real world media — although working in the real world provides a more satisfying tactile sensation. I keep my real world 'digits' in both, as much as I can, working to a large extent from scanned pencil sketches. *Art in Wartime,* however, was conceived and created entirely on the computer.

Advice for Artists Working in the Digital Medium

Reality First. Learn how to do the real task with your real hands, as nearly as is possible, before allowing yourself to be deluded into thinking that the computer is making anything easy for you. Everything looks good on a computer screen — including your firstborn's diapers and Taco Bell TV spots — *especially* your own work. Digital art is as much hard work and acquired sensibility as any other art.

Printing Issues

I like Epson printers a lot. The output, particularly that of a six-color process on Epson's matte paper, is rich and robust. I'm partial to matte papers; shiny papers always seem more appropriate for photography, for some reason. Giclée prints on high quality rag paper are wonderful — but are very expensive for an artist without a trust fund to produce in number.

Unfortunately, I'm far deeper in image creation than output, which is an imbalance I want to rectify in the near future. I'm very interested in learning about large-format printing and how digital printing is starting to work with more tactilely interesting papers.

Leslie Hunt on Campbell's *Art in Warmtime*

"The artist's musician in this case functions as both interpreter and mitigator. As long as there are artists to reconfigure the chaos, there's hope, as evidenced in the rainbow, an ancient symbol of cosmic promise."

— Leslie Hunt, Features Editor, *PEI* and *Professional Photographer* (`www.peimag.com`)

Part 2

Photography

Each piece of artwork in this part of the book has a basis in photography. You can not only see the finished product of each artist's process, but also learn how the artist finessed each image into a polished artistic statement.

Chapter 27

First Aid Tin

by Michael Garson

Artist's Statement

I really like inspiring a sense of mystery and wonder. I like to give people clues — enough to make them ask questions, but not enough to solve the riddle.

The Story Behind the Artwork

Michael found an old band-aid tin and accidentally burnt it with an artist friend's welding torch. This made the texture inside the tin very interesting and something he wanted to use in the creation of art.

He eventually got the idea to create a post-apocalyptic Mad Max-type of spy device. "I wanted people to think it looked like it did something important," he says, "but not be able to figure out exactly what." To collect source materials for this project, Michael went garbage-picking and junk-yarding for odd objects. He took some of the objects he found, started scanning them, and then composed them into this piece. (Sometimes he had to put a black or white cloth over the objects on the scanner for the appropriate shading and background.) He enjoys hearing the mistaken perception that the *First Aid Tin* (27.1) was physically assembled.

The Creative Process

After scanning in the found objects he needed for source material, as well as making a scan of the original burnt First Aid Tin, Michael worked out his over-all composition in a sketch. Then he started with a low resolution, 72 ppi rough draft in Photoshop. By starting with a small file at low resolution, he gave himself the freedom to try anything and not worry about waiting for filters and other tools to work.

◀ 27.1

He then cut out the individual objects with the Lasso tool and made a channel, or layer mask, with which he could control the transparency of different regions of the individual objects in the composition by painting onto the layer mask. (He doesn't like clipping paths because they don't give enough control.)

At times, he zoomed in and edited pixel by pixel. Once he had an object cut-out, he would duplicate the layer several times and start trying a combination of layer blending modes and transparency levels on the layers. This let the background textures and color come through to the object in front. For example, he tried Hard Light at 100% on one layer, and Hard Light at 50% on another, or Darken 20% on the next, sometimes adding a color layer to one of the individual layers. He had up to ten copies of the same layer piled on top of each other to get the correct effect. This is how he achieved the dark muted oranges, reds, and browns in this image.

He relied heavily on applying the Filter➔Blur➔Gaussian Blur and Filter➔Sharpen➔Unsharp Mask filters. Intermittently, when the file got too big for his computer to handle, or the dozens of layers got confusing, he saved the file, renamed it, and flattened some layers to reduce the document size.

Michael spent about a 100 hours on this piece.

Technique: Achieving a Dramatic Corrosive Effect (Photoshop)

Michael spends a lot of time introducing imperfections into his images so that they have an earthy, organic look. He wants to avoid having his images look too clean and too digital. To achieve this he follows a painstaking process of building up and altering layers.

The procedure described here is simply an example of one pathway that Michael followed intuitively to build up a base image from which the rest of his piece began to take shape. There are no hard and fast rules. Use these steps as a guide to give you ideas to try out on your own images.

1. **Scan your main object (in Michael's case, the burnt tin) at 300 ppi into an RGB file in Photoshop (27.2).**

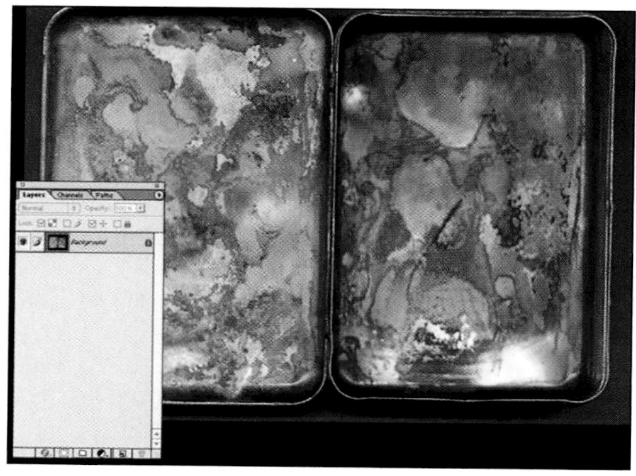

● 27.2

About the Artist

Biography

Michael Garson has been creating digital art for eight years. He was awarded a Bachelor of Science degree in Theology from Valley Forge Christian College, Philadelphia. His work has been honored at a number of shows including the Purple Door Arts and Music Festival, Lancaster, Pennsylvania, Best of Show, 1998; Cornerstone Music and Arts Festival, Peoria, Illinois, Best of Show, 1999; and Seybold Digital Art Gallery, San Francisco, Best of Show, 2001.

Influences

Garson finds old dilapidated buildings, like those in Philadelphia where he lived, a source of inspiration. Also inspiring are junkyards, flea markets, electrical devices of the 20s and 50s, or a piece of trash on the street.

Influential artists include Rauschenburg, Warhol, Gaudi's Cathedral in Barcelona, and ancient iconography. He also enjoys creating to the music of Tom Waits.

2. **Choose Duplicate Layer from the Layers pop-up menu (or keyboard shortcut Cmd/Ctrl-J).**
   This makes a new layer called Background copy, which is a duplicate of the original background image. This safeguards the original image in case you want to go back to it at any point.
3. **With the Background copy layer highlighted in the Layers palette, use the Lasso tool with anti-aliasing to cut out your chosen object from its surroundings.**

[TIP]

You could also use the Extract tool or Pen tool, both of which offer accuracy and editability.

4. **Click on the Backspace (Windows) or Delete (Macintosh) key to make a hole in the Background copy layer where the object was.**
5. **Choose Select→Inverse.**
   This selects the surroundings.
6. **Make sure white is in the foreground.**
7. **Choose Edit→Fill.**
   This fills the Background copy layer with white, leaving the object showing through the hole in the center.
8. **Choose Layer Properties from the Layers palette pop-up menu.**
9. **Rename the Background copy layer "White Layer" (27.3).**

[TIP]

When creating a complex multi-layered file, as in this example, you should methodically rename all your layers as you generate them. That way, you can easily identify what each layer is and avoid wasting time searching through the layers.

10. **Open scans of objects and miscellaneous textures that you like.**
11. **Use the Move tool to place the first texture as a texture layer on top of the main object image.**

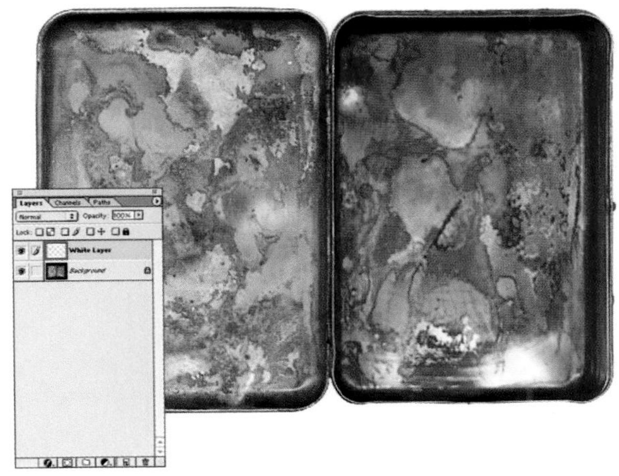

● 27.3

Studio

Computer System:
Power Computing Mac Clone
G3, 400 MHz upgrade
6 and 4GB SCSI internal drives
512MB RAM

Monitors:
17-inch Sony
15-inch second monitor (for the Tool pallets)

Software:
Adobe Photoshop
Painter

Removable Media:
640MB magneto-optical drive
CD-R burner

Tablet:
Wacom Intuit 9 x 12

Input Devices:
Microtek Scanmaker E6 (it's old but works)

Printers:
Epson Color Printer

Other Tools:
Propane torch to age object
Boxes of miscellaneous found objects.

Contact

Michael Garson
Venice, California
michael@garson.net
www.garson.net

12. **Put the first texture layer in Overlay layer mode at 100% opacity.**
    This was the Jesus layer in Michael's case (27.4).
13. **Choose Duplicate Layer from the Layers pop-up menu.**
14. **Set the duplicate layer to Overlay mode at 40% opacity (27.5).**
15. **Introduce the next layer, using a scan of an element that you want to superimpose over the inside of your main object.**
    In Michael's case, he chose the circuit board. You can rearrange the ordering of your layers just by dragging them up and down in the Layers palette.

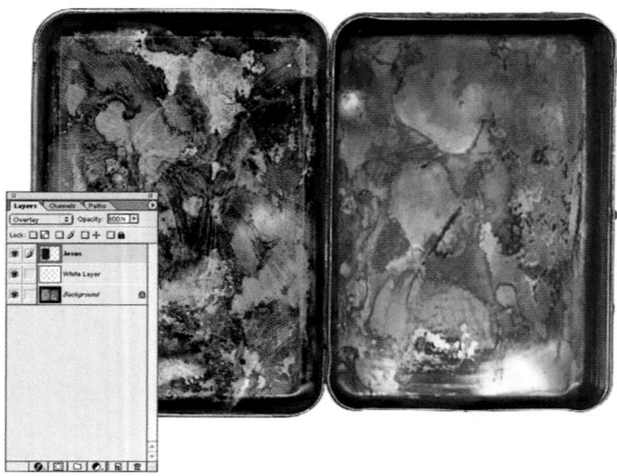

27.4

16. **Use the Lasso tool to cut out the inner dimensions of your object (for example, the inside of the tin).**
17. **Choose Select→Feather and feather the edges of the selection by a few (2 or 3) pixels.**
18. **Choose Select→Inverse.**
19. **Click on your Backspace or Delete key.**
    This deletes the part of the texture layer, in this case, the circuit board, that is not within the underlying main object (the tin).
20. **Apply this texture layer in Hard Light mode at 90% opacity (27.6).**
21. **Choose Select→Inverse.**
    This makes the selection visible.
22. **Select New Layer from the Layers pop-up menu.**
23. **Double-click on the Foreground color and choose a color in the color picker.**
24. **Choose Edit→Fill.**
    This fills the new layer with a color.
25. **Click on the Load Selection icon (second from left) in the bottom of the Layers palette.**
    This loads the selection that you just feathered and applies this mask to the new layer of solid color, giving the color the same shape as the selection.
26. **Apply this new layer in Hard Light mode at 50% opacity (27.7).**
27. **Select the original background layer with your original object.**
28. **Choose Duplicate Layer.**

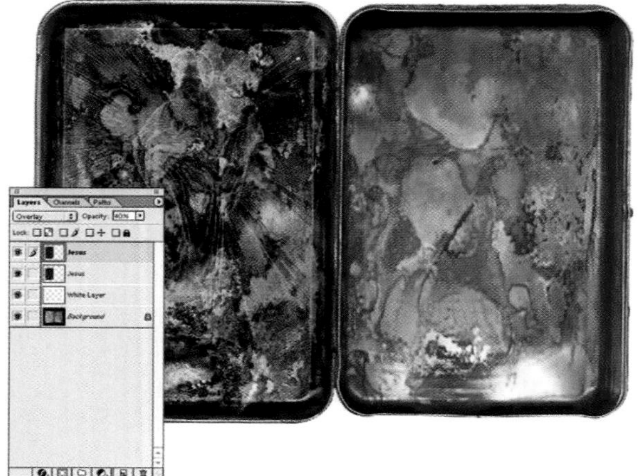

27.5

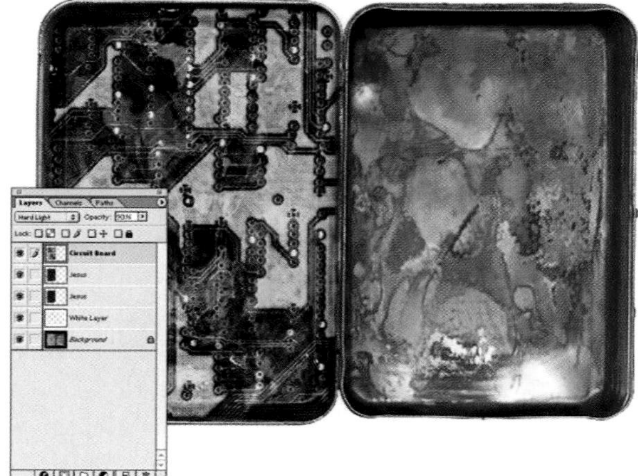

27.6

29. **Drag the Duplicate Layer up to the top of all the layers.**
30. **Apply the Duplicate Layer of the original object in Color Burn mode at 40% opacity (27.8).**
31. **Introduce a new texture layer that has some organic brush stroke work on it.**

    In Michael's case, he scanned some computer chips, brought the scan into Painter, and used a cloning technique to transform the scanned chips into some brownish orange brushstrokes.
32. **Apply this new textured layer in Hard Light mode at 100% opacity (27.9).**
33. **Make the next layer a scan, duplicated into rows with the background deleted.**
34. **Apply this layer in Hard Light mode at 100% opacity (27.10).**
35. **Add a final texture layer.**

    Michael duplicated the same chip many times into hard rows and applied this layer onto the bottom left section of his image.

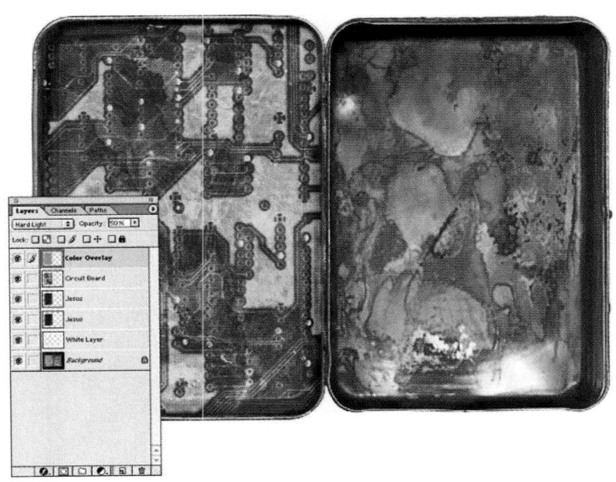

 27.7

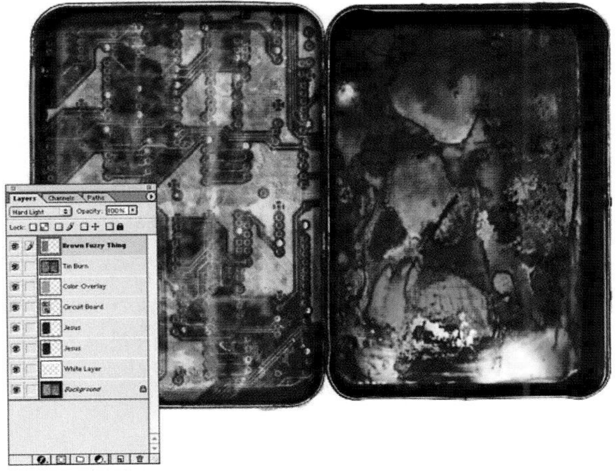

27.9

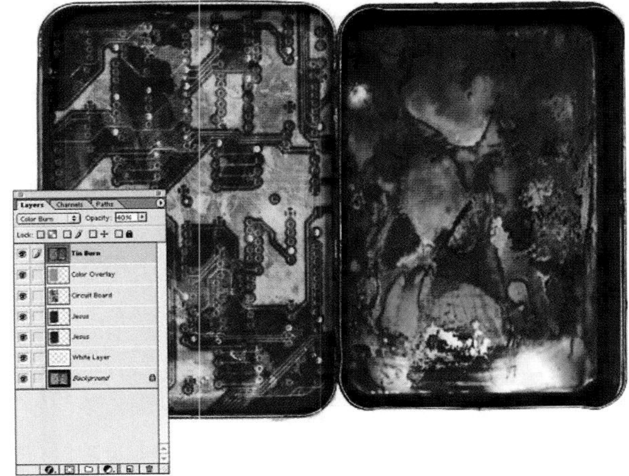

27.8

27.10

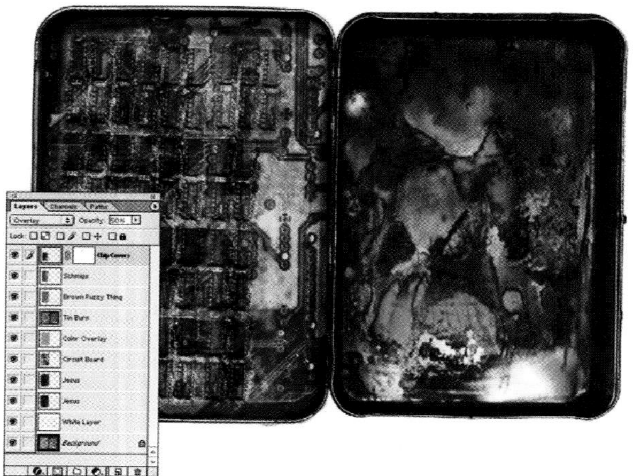

● 27.11

36. Apply this final textured layer in Overlay mode at 50% opacity (27.11).

Rick Smolan on Garson's *First Aid Tin*

"The image works on many levels. The colors are inviting, and there is a calm smoothness to the image that is very tranquil. The tranquillity is unusual given the harsh edges of the tin, and my reaction was the opposite of what I expected to feel when I first saw the subject matter. I was also attracted to the shapes and then pleasantly surprised by how the old-time tool was connected to the modern LED with both of them looking faded and used, like antiques. This is an image I'd enjoy having on my wall to look at every time I walk by."

– Rick Smolan, Digital Photographer, Founder, Against All Odds Productions (`www.againstallodds.com`)

Artist's Creative Insight and Advice

Why Digital?

Without the computer, I perhaps would never have gotten very involved with art. I didn't like to draw very much. I had played with art before, but the traditional methods (as a kid) were not so much fun.

I bought a computer to be a writer and found it more fun to design and play with the art programs. I started to pick up odd objects, scan them into the computer, and manipulate them in Photoshop. I learned about photomontage and began combining the images into photo-illustrations. Now I have progressed to making my own frames and boxes out of found objects to display the prints of my digital work.

At some point, I will progress to non-digital art. I find the computer is a liberating tool that opened the door to my creativity, but it can't do everything I want it to. It lacks the spontaneity of the physical world.

Advice for Artists Working in the Digital Medium

Digital art starts out with solid colors, smooth curves, and perfect angles. In order to make something look realistic, it needs some imperfections. It takes a lot of work to put imperfection into a digital image, and I spend a large percentage of the process working in (not out) the imperfections. Sometimes I spend a couple of hours retouching a scan on the computer only to realize that I could have just modified the physical object and re-scanned it into the computer in a few minutes.

Always save steps so that you can go back; the History palette (in Photoshop) doesn't always help. I might make five or six giant files, throughout the process. Sometimes after flattening layers and moving on, you need to revert to see what you did before, or a new process you're trying doesn't always work and you have to go back a step or two.

On Finishing Work

I am never quite sure when a piece is finished. Sometimes I get frustrated and leave it for a few days or even weeks, before finishing it. Other times I have left a half finished piece alone to realize later that it actually was already finished.

Output

For prints, I prefer Iris Gilcee. I prefer the limited color spectrum that Iris produces because it complements the tones in my artwork. I prefer a textured watercolor paper because it gives my prints a painterly feel, and prints are supposed to last about 75 years or so before fading.

Mystery that is,
anything.
we feel then,
through the same gate?
you're
and have
Is what I
not flawed
but complete

Chapter 28

The Great Mystery

by Negar Nahidian

Artist's Statement

The Great Mystery (28.1) is a self-portrait about my thoughts and beliefs on life and death. I used black-and-white images to keep the artwork simple and was able to portray good and evil, life and death, the positive and the negative.

I use Middle Eastern motifs and poetry in my work. I like the use of borders within borders, something that's consistent in all of my artworks. Since this image was intended for digital printmaking, contrast played an important role.

The Story Behind the Artwork

This project was created for a graduate printmaking class at George Mason University, Fairfax, Virginia. The theme was self-portraiture, so the work had to be personal.

Persian motifs and Negar's Persian culture play an important role in her artwork. She is drawn to the appearance of handmade prints, such as intaglio, relief, collographs, and monoprints. Professor Jane Leonard introduced Negar to photo-digital printmaking, where she could get the best of both worlds, digital and traditional printmaking.

In *The Great Mystery,* she wanted to create a piece that was about life and death, her Persian culture and background, and her favorite poet, Rumi, a Persian Sufi mystic.

◀ 28.1

The Creative Process

The first part of the project involved creating the artwork on the computer. The resulting digital file was used to generate a photo-lithographic plate. This plate produced the hand-printed final image.

The initial digital process first involved collecting and preparing two photographic self-portraits, one with her eyes open (28.2), representing life, and one with her eyes closed (28.3), representing death. Negar collaborated with her brother, Navid, who took the photographs using a Canon Elan2e.

Besides the two images of herself, Negar also prepared other source images for use in this collage. These other source images included writing from her journal (lower-right corner), which she scanned and then inverted; a Persian bird motif (lower-left corner), which she drew with the Pen tool in Macromedia Freehand; a tree bark texture (background) from a textures CD; and the text of a translation of a poem by Rumi (upper-half of the

● 28.2

● 28.3

About the Artist

Biography

Negar Nahidian graduated with a BA in Art Studio from George Mason University (GMU), Fairfax, Virginia, in 1997. After receiving her BA, she entered GMU's MFA program in Digital Arts. She invested in a Macintosh computer and programs and started creating projects that later became portfolio pieces. She also took four semesters of printmaking in which monoprints and collograph plates were created and multi-color works were printed by hand.

Negar also worked in Washington, D.C., as a graphic designer for six months and in a small design studio in Virginia for three years. She is currently a freelance designer, working from her home studio and teaching Digital Arts as an adjunct faculty at GMU. She is also working on her thesis paper and exhibition, and she plans to graduate in 2003.

image), which she originally enlarged from a book using a photocopier, then tore the edges, and scanned. All the source images were scanned at 300 ppi to ensure sufficient data was collected for a high quality print.

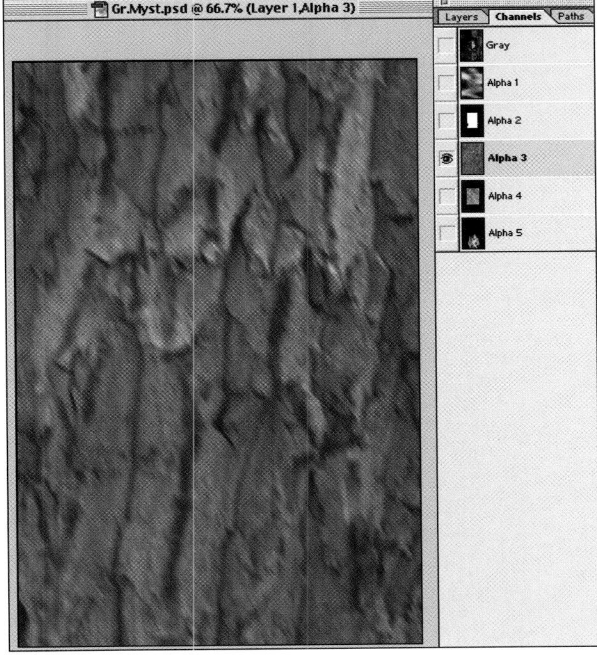

● 28.4

Negar created a new file in Photoshop (the "working document"), 8 x 12 inches at 300 ppi. The image was in Grayscale color mode to keep the file size manageable. (If Negar had created this image in full color with CMYK color mode, she'd have bigger file sizes and would have needed to create four different plates instead of one, which leads to registration issues.) More important to Negar than the convenience of working in grayscale was the artistic importance of keeping the image as a simple and stark black-and-white image.

Negar opened the tree bark background texture in Photoshop. She selected all and copied and pasted the bark texture into the alpha channel in her working document (28.4).

She filled the background layer of her working document with black. With the background layer selected, she held the Cmd/Ctrl key and clicked on the alpha channel icon, which loaded the alpha channel into the background layer as a selection. After turning off the marching ants, she adjusted the Brightness/Contrast, Curves, Levels, and Hue/Saturation in the selected region, also inverting the selection to add contrast. At this stage, the bark texture became visible in the background. After deselecting, she blurred the whole background layer. She then used the Marquee tool to select half the layer and change the brightness and contrast in that half, making the right side lighter and the left side darker (fitting in with the life and death theme).

Influences

Negar subscribes to art magazines such as *Communication Arts*, *Print*, and *How*. She finds the articles helpful in developing and discovering her own style, and for keeping up with new trends and techniques.

She has also been influenced by artists such as Roy Lichtenstein, Kandinsky, Braque, Paul Rand, and Steven Heller.

Studio

Computer System:
iMac 500
23GB hard drive
256MB RAM

Software:
Adobe Photoshop
Macromedia Freehand
Adobe Illustrator
Procreate Painter
Macromedia Flash
Macromedia Dreamweaver

Removable Media:
Zip drive

Archive Media:
Que Fire CD-RW

Input Devices:
Umax 1100 Scanner

Printers:
HP Deskjet 1220C

Contact

Negar Nahidian
Haymarket, Virginia
nnah@aol.com
www.n2dezign.com

In a new alpha channel, she used the Lighting Effect Pencil tool to create harsh white lines, and then added motion blur. She then used the Air Brush tool to add big dabs of white paint, which she also blurred (28.5).

She applied this channel as a selection in the background player to add further texture to the bark. You can see the resulting background layer shown here (28.6). Next, she added Persian motifs in the lower-left corner using Soft Light layer mode at 30% opacity (28.7).

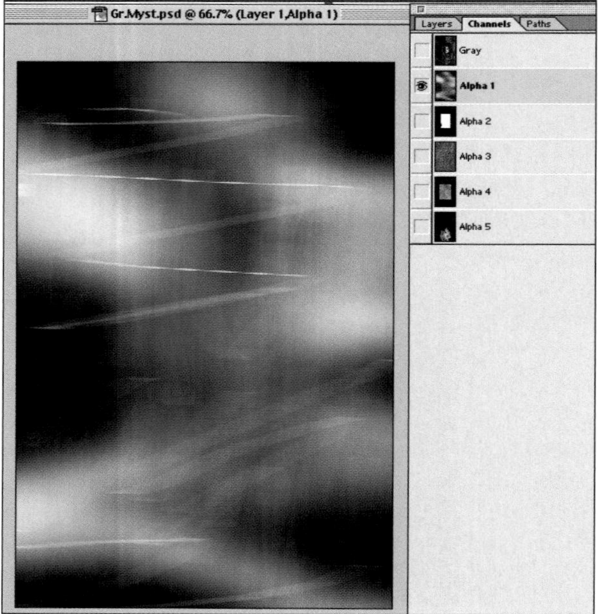

● 28.5

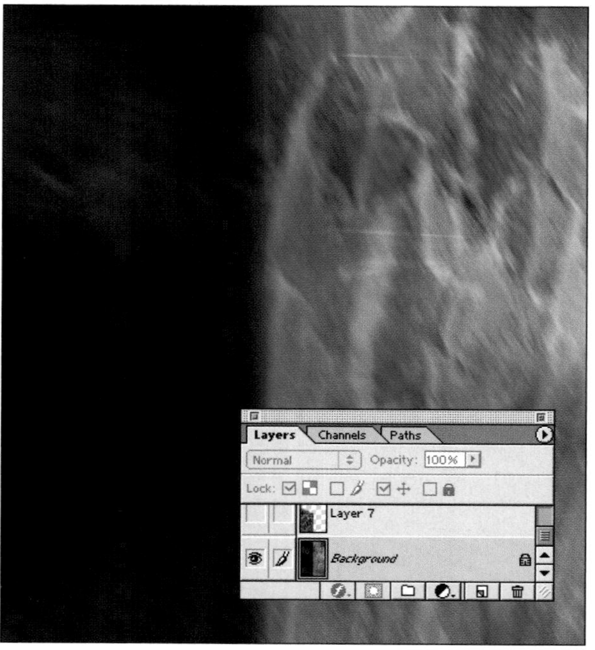

● 28.6

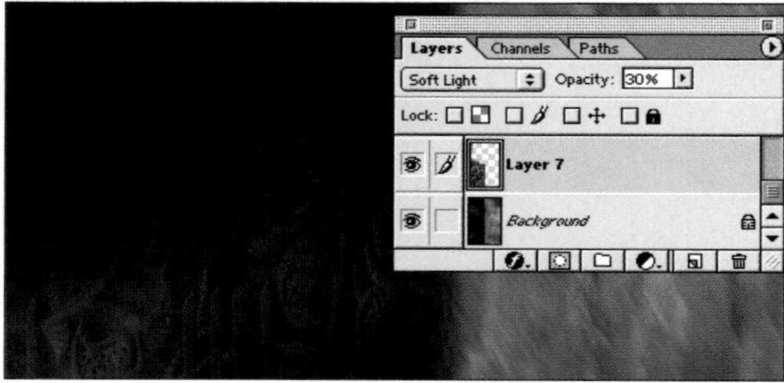

● 28.7

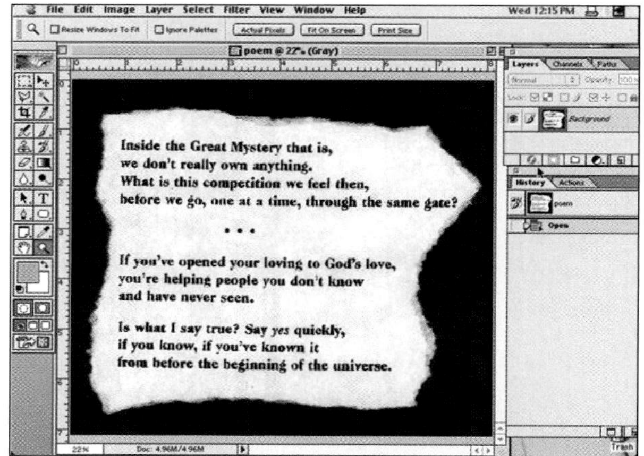

● 28.8

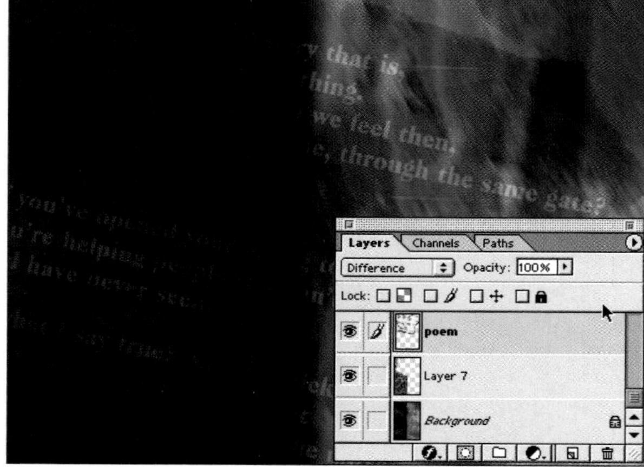

● 28.9

Negar photocopied a translation of a poem by Rumi, blew it up by 300% (on the photocopier), and tore the edges. She then glued the poem onto black paper, scanned it (28.8), and placed it in a new layer in the top-right corner using Difference layer mode at 100% opacity (28.9). She continued adding layers and adjusting the layer modes and opacities (28.10 and 28.11).

The next step was to create the jagged border within a border in the central part of the image. She went to the Channels palette and created a new channel, filling the channel with black. She then drew an irregular, jagged, organic shape using the Freehand Lasso tool, filled the selection with white, and then deselected the channel (28.12). She applied Filter→ Stylize→Diffuse two or three times, followed by Filter→ Blur→Guassian to soften the edge.

Next, she created a new layer, loaded the jagged edge channel as a selection in the new layer, and filled the selection with a subtle black to dark gray vertical gradient. She also used the Dodge and Burn tools to create a burned look for the edges. She clicked on the left most icon ("f" for filter) in the bottom of the Layers palette and selected the Outer Glow filter. She set the Outer Glow spread to be 42 and left all the other settings as default. Finally, a jagged-edged layer with an outer glow and drop shadow (28.13) emerged.

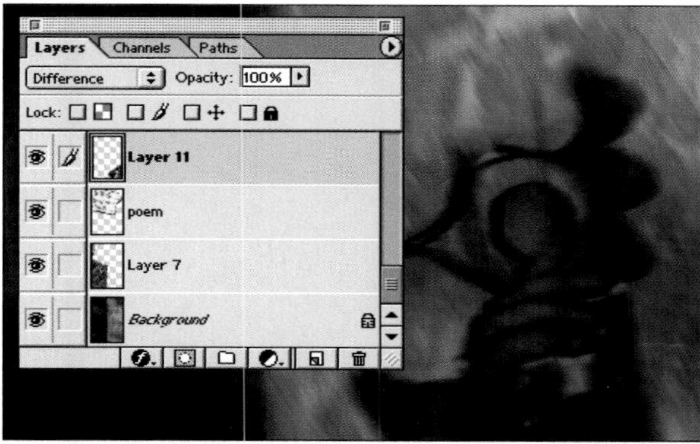

● 28.10

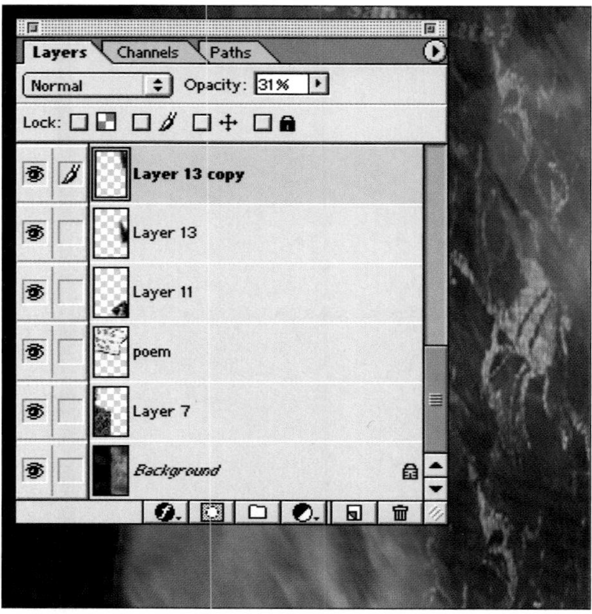

● 28.11

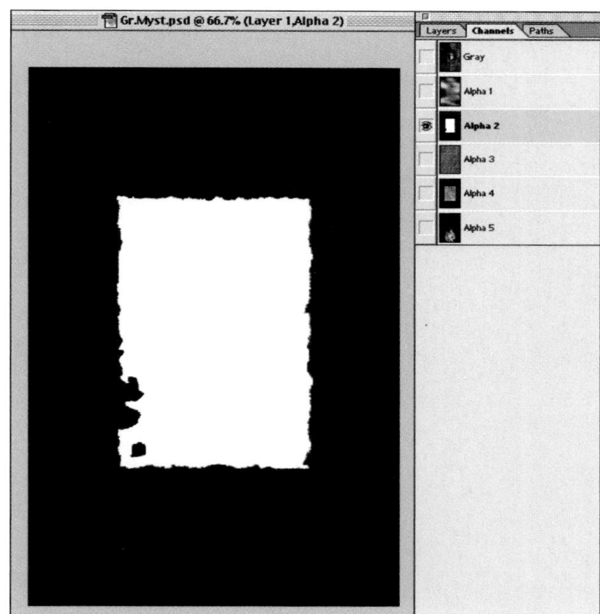

● 28.12

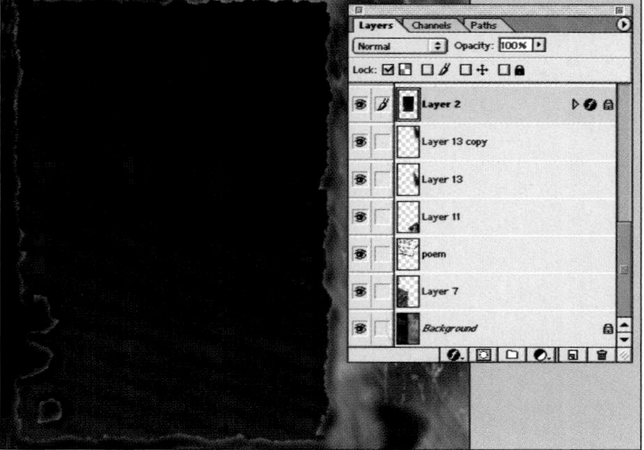

● 28.13

She worked in the center region, adding more of the bark texture with a defined split down the center (28.14), which she would use to divide her life and death sides. Then she added her face with her eyes open, at a slightly reduced opacity of 91%, on the right side of the center dividing line (28.15).

As mentioned earlier, Negar created the Persian bird (dove) motif using the Pen tool in Macromedia Freehand. She saved the file as an EPS file and opened it in Photoshop. The bird appeared in the file as a black motif against a white background. It was on a separate layer, and she simply dragged the bird motif layer from the Layers palette directly into the working document. She then duplicated this layer, making one version with Hard Light layer mode, and adjusting the opacities of different layers. She also applied Filter→Blur→Motion Blur to blur the dove images (28.16).

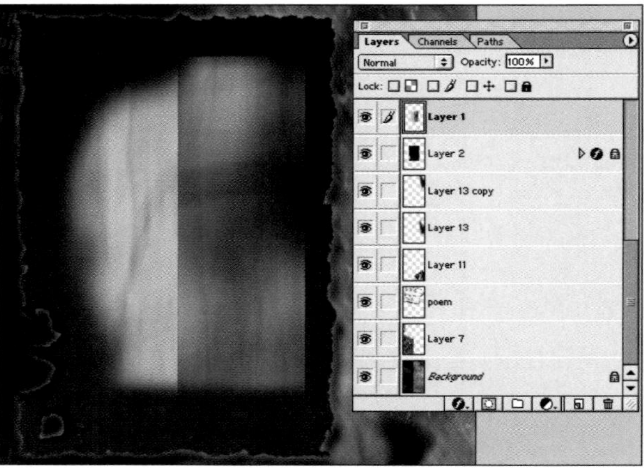

● 28.14

● 28.15

She added the inverted scan of her journal writing using Exclusion layer mode in the lower-right corner of the image (28.17).

Finally, Negar added the photo with her eyes closed on the left side of the image (28.18). She used Difference layer mode to give a more ominous "negative" effect.

Negar wanted her final print to be about 11 x 17 inches. Without adding any extra pixels to her digital image, she could achieve this by printing at about 211 dots per inch. She knew the black-and-white contrast would be very critical to the success of her final print; the contrast would translate to a clear, crisp printed image once she had gone through the photo-lithographic plate process. To get the contrast

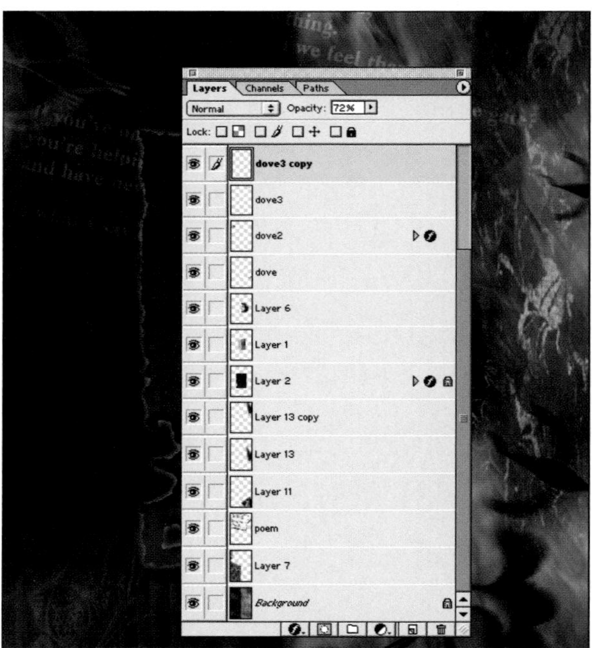

● 28.16

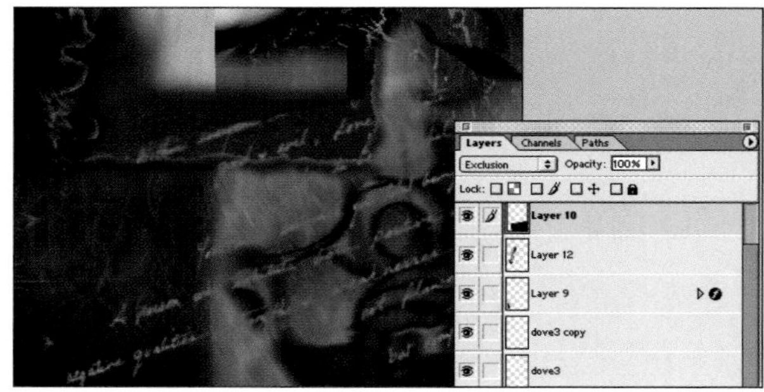

● 28.17

right, she conducted a series of full-size ink jet print proofs of her image using her HP Deskjet 1220C. These tests allowed her to go back to her digital image and make adjustments to fine-tune and enhance the image contrast.

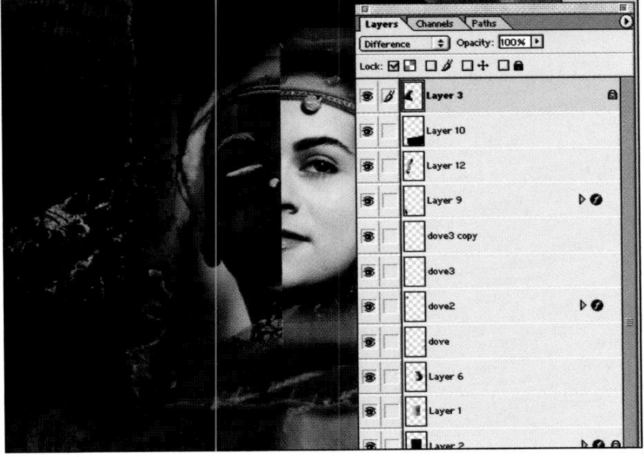

28.18

When she was satisfied, she made a full-size print on transparent plastic film (28.19), similar to the transparency film used for overhead projectors.

This transparent film was then secured tightly over a photo-lithographic plate that was coated in a resist that was sensitive to ultra-violet (UV) light. This plate was placed in a special piece of equipment that exposed the plate to UV light. A reddish acidic chemical was then gently rubbed over the exposed plate (while wearing gloves!) and then washed away. Where the plate was exposed to UV, the resist was etched away by the acidic chemical.

After the UV-exposed resist had been etched away, a dab of black printing ink was put on a brayer roller. The roller was gently and evenly rolled a couple of times onto the etched plate, leaving its ink in the regions of the plate where the resist had been removed (28.20).

28.19

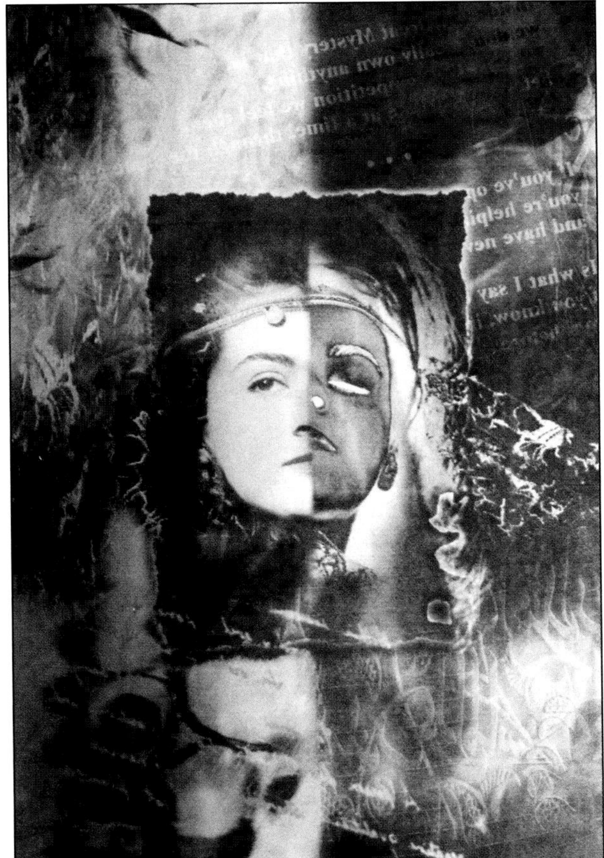

28.20

The regions on the plate where the resist was etched away are the regions where the brayer roller leaves printing ink. This ink ends up being transferred to the final printed image.

Several tests had to be conducted to get the right exposure of UV. Too little exposure would result in too little of the resist being removed, and thus the final image would end up too light. Too much exposure would result in too much of the resist being removed, making the final image too dark.

Note that the plate appears back to front (left and right are inverted, as if looking in a mirror). The image would be reflected once more in the final part of the printing process, which brought the image back to the same orientation it had when it was originally created on the computer.

The final step was to soak the paper for the finished print. The paper was allowed to almost dry. The inked etched plate was then put on an etching press and the slightly moist paper was run through the press.

Negar made several prints of this image and experimented with different techniques. In one case she applied colored inks to a clear, hard Perspex sheet, using the transparency print laying beneath the Perspex as a visual reference for painting and a means for registering the painted Perspex plate precisely over one of her prints. She then pressed the Perpsex plate against the print and transferred the hand painted ink from the Perspex to the print (28.21).

The digital process for *The Great Mystery* took between 20 and 30 hours; the printing process took another 5 to 10 hours or so, including the preparation

● 28.21

● 28.22

and proofing of the digital image and the trial runs to get the UV exposure right.

Technique: Applying Textures with Versatility and Control (Photoshop)

Negar applies textures in a way that gives her an immense amount of flexibility and control over how the texture appears. By making use of alpha channels, she can apply the same texture to many layers, each time in a different way.

This technique shares the basic principles of her approach as applied to a grayscale image. The technique also works on RGB or CMYK images.

1. **Select an image that you want to use as a source for a texture.**
   Good sources for textures can be scanning found materials and objects, or using digital photographs of surfaces you come across in the environment. The example used here is the bark texture that Negar placed in the background of her artwork.
2. **If your texture image is RGB, change the color mode to Grayscale (Image→Mode→Grayscale) (28.22).**
3. **Choose Image→Adjust→Levels.**

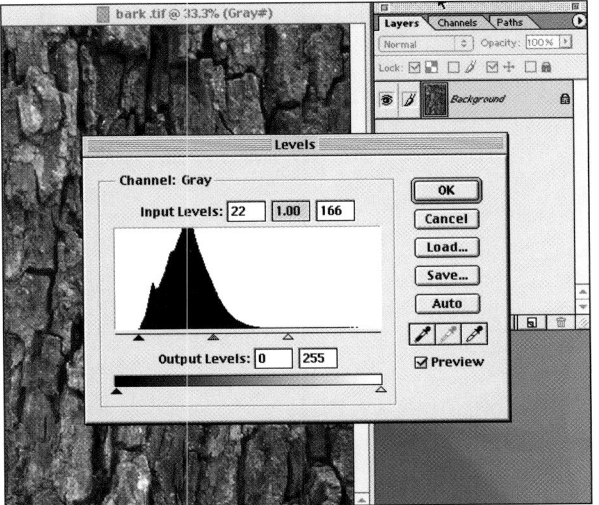

● 28.23

   Adjust the black-and-white point cursors in the Levels window to optimize the contrast in the texture image (28.23).
4. **Open your Grayscale working image, the one where you are going to apply the texture, in Photoshop.**
   Your working document should be saved as a Photoshop format document (.psd) since you will want to be able to preserve it with all the layers and alpha channels. The working image could be a new empty document or an image you are already working on. The background layer of your working document should either be filled with black or have an image that you want to superimpose the texture on. For this example the working document is a new document with no layers other than the Background layer, which is filled with black. To fill your background layer with black, choose black as the foreground color and then choose Edit→Fill using Contents Use: Foreground Color.
5. **Choose Image→Image Size and note the pixel size of your working image.**
6. **Choose Cancel.**
   Don't change the image size of your working image. The purpose of opening the Image Size window is just to confirm the pixel size of your image.
7. **Select the texture image and choose Image→Image Size.**
   Note the pixel size of your texture image.
8. **If necessary, choose Image→Image Size, check Resample Image, and adjust the pixel size of your texture to cover the entire working image.**
   Leave the Constrain Proportions option checked since the idea isn't to distort the texture, but just to make sure it's big enough to cover the entire working image.
9. **Choose Select→All (Cmd/Ctrl-A).**
   The whole texture image is now selected.
10. **Choose Edit→Copy (Cmd/Ctrl-C).**
11. **Select the working image document and open the Channels palette.**
    If your Grayscale document is new, you see one channel called Gray.

12. Choose Edit→Paste (Cmd/Ctrl-V).

This pastes the texture image into the alpha channel called Gray and simultaneously pastes the texture image in as a layer.

If you have a document with existing modified alpha channels, you can always just generate a new alpha channel by choosing New Channel from the Channels pop-up menu located in the top right corner of the Channels palette.

13. Choose Duplicate Channel from the Channels pop-up menu.

This generates a new alpha channel with the default name "Gray copy." This duplicate channel contains the pasted texture.

14. In the Duplicate Channel window rename the duplicate channel with a name that indicates the texture type and that it is an alpha channel (28.24).

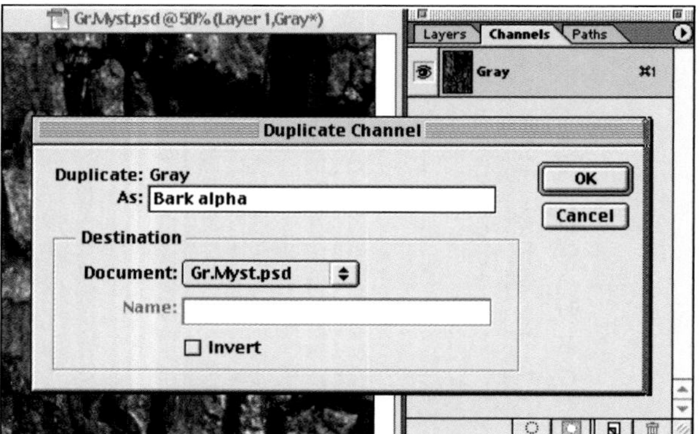

● 28.24

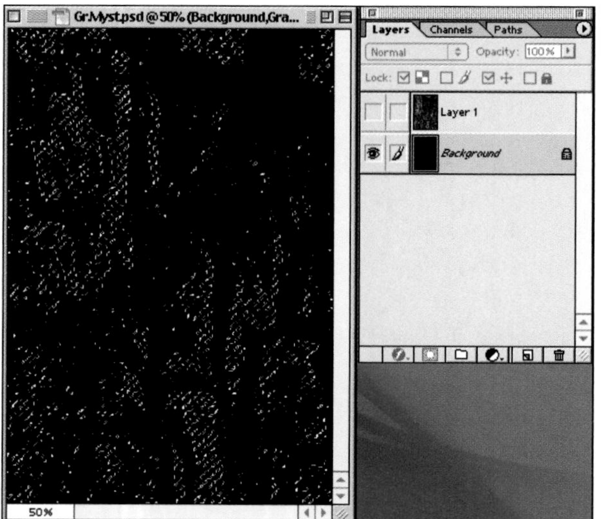

● 28.25

[TIP]

Renaming alpha channels helps you keep track of things as you build up more complex images with multiple alpha channels. In this case the renamed duplicate channel was called "Bark alpha."

15. Open the Layers palette and turn off the "eye" icon for the texture layer you pasted in.

16. Select the Background layer.

17. In the Channels palette select the renamed alpha channel.

18. Click on the Load Selection icon at the bottom of the Channels palette (the circular dashed icon all the way to the left).

This loads the highlighted alpha channel as a selection in the current layer.

19. Return to the Layers palette where you can see the marching ants indicating where the selection is (28.25).

20. Soften the selection slightly by choosing Select→Feather and setting the feather to be 2 or 3 pixels.

21. Choose View→Show→Selection Edges so there is no check by Selection Edges.

This turns off the marching ants while leaving the selection active.

22. Choose Image→Adjust→Brightness/Contrast (28.26).

Adjust the sliders so that you see the texture appear in the background.

Try other adjustments, such as Levels or Curves, and alter the layers based on the texture alpha channel selection. Also try inverting the selection and making further adjustments to enhance the contrast. If you have an RGB image you can also adjust the Hue/Saturation sliders.

Artist's Creative Insight and Advice

Why Digital?

It's important for an artist to realize that the computer is just another medium, a tool.

The first step is knowing the design basics, color, balance, and contrast. I always ask my students to sketch their ideas along with notes and make these basics a major part of their grade.

With Photoshop, the creative possibilities are endless. I like to use alpha channels to create my own textures.

Printmaking gave me insight into how printing was done in the old days, and gave me the chance to work with both digital and traditional techniques. I like to mix digital and traditional techniques. For example, I enjoy creating a digital image on the computer and using a traditional press, inking techniques, and different papers to print out the digital artwork.

Advice for Artists Working in the Digital Medium

Sketch out the idea first; write down what you want to accomplish and your thoughts. It's okay if your concept changes during the process.

Output

I always ask my students to use the info bar and look at their CMYK values, especially if working on different stations to complete the project. Don't look just at monitors.

I make sure to color-correct my images, using the Pantone and the Agfa process color guide, so that there are no surprises when the job is printed.

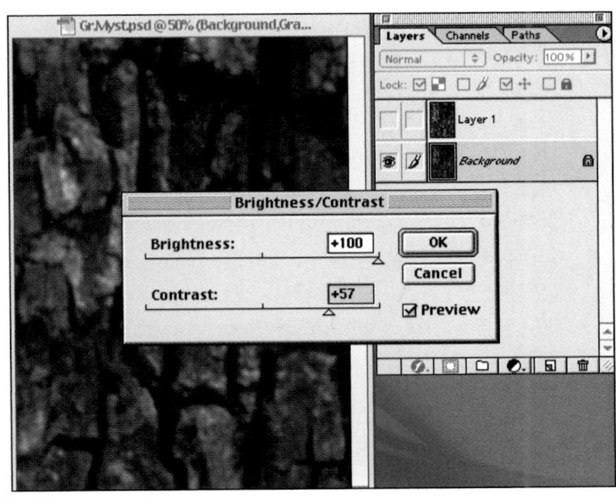

● 28.26

Chapter 29

On the Boulevard

by Richard Swiatlowski

Artist's Statement

I create art that shows my view and feelings about the world. It is my way of communicating. My creative process is an intellectual pursuit based on imagination, not on rules.

I keep a journal. When an idea comes to me, I put it down on paper and then try to develop it into an image. The ideas for images come from everywhere, internally and externally.

The Story Behind the Artwork

The story for this artwork started with a trip Richard took to Boston. He photographed several images that day and put them together. He wanted to show how everyone is oblivious to everyone else — the couple on the bench, the boy reading the newspaper, and the people dining, all engrossed in their own worlds even though they occupy the same space.

On the Boulevard (29.1) provides an example of Richard's way of seeing the world. His artwork is his life, conscious and subconscious, put into visual images.

◀ 29.1

The Creative Process

Richard started by scanning the photographs into Photoshop. His original source photographs included a scene with people dining under sun umbrellas (29.2), a woman sitting on a bench with a sculpture of a man (29.3), and a man reading a map (29.4).

● 29.2

Richard took the background image with the people dining under the umbrellas and pasted it into a canvas 7.5 inches high by 10 inches wide at 300dpi. He used the Photoshop Pen tool to crudely cut out the woman on the bench and the man reading the map from the other source photos. He didn't worry about getting exact edges and borders with his selections since he knew he would end up painting over everything. He then pasted the selected parts of the images over the background image in a multi-layered composite collage.

He adjusted the scale of the image layers within the collage composite by selecting the individual layers one at a time in the Layers palette, and then, for each layer separately, choosing Edit→Transform→Scale. Control handles then appear in the corners and middle of each side of the selected layer. By dragging the corner control handles, Richard adjusted the scale and aspect ratio (height-to-width ratio) of the layers

● 29.3

● 29.4

About the Artist

Biography

Richard is a self-taught artist whose work is characterized by brilliant colors and bold brush strokes. He creates images using his photography, drawings, paintings, and digital manipulations. He has received numerous awards, including the Grand Prize award for Popular Photography for his *New York Minute*, selected from over 60,000 entries. He has also won two first-place awards in the Ritz Camera Annual Contest and the Directors Award from the Cambridge Art Association.

Influences

Henri Matisse, Susan Rothenberg, Frank Auerbach, Richard Diebenkorn, Paul Gaugin, and life experiences.

Studio

Computer System:
PowerMac G4, 450 Dual Processor
30GB hard drive
1GB RAM

to suit his composition. By hitting the Return/Enter key, the transformation was rendered.

He continued the process of distorting each layer by choosing Filter→Distort→Spherize and choosing Mode: Vertical Only in the Spherize dialog box (29.5).

The result (29.6) was figures that looked thin and elongated compared with the original source photos.

At this stage, he selected Image→Adjust→Hue/Saturation and increased the saturation (moving the saturation slider to the right) for different layers, which made the colors in the image "pop out" more. The last adjustment to the layers was Image→Adjust→Levels, where Richard adjusted the contrast. Richard adjusted the saturation and contrast until he felt the image looked right; he likes a highly saturated image for its richness and boldness.

Richard composed the picture and flattened it in Photoshop. He then opened a copy of the image in Painter and began painting. He saved the resulting file as a Photoshop format file, for future editing, and then flattened the image and saved a flat version as a TIFF file to work on in Painter. He closed Photoshop and opened Painter, where he opened the flattened composite file.

[NOTE]

You can open either Photoshop or TIFF files in Painter. In this case, Richard only wanted to paint on the flattened TIFF image.

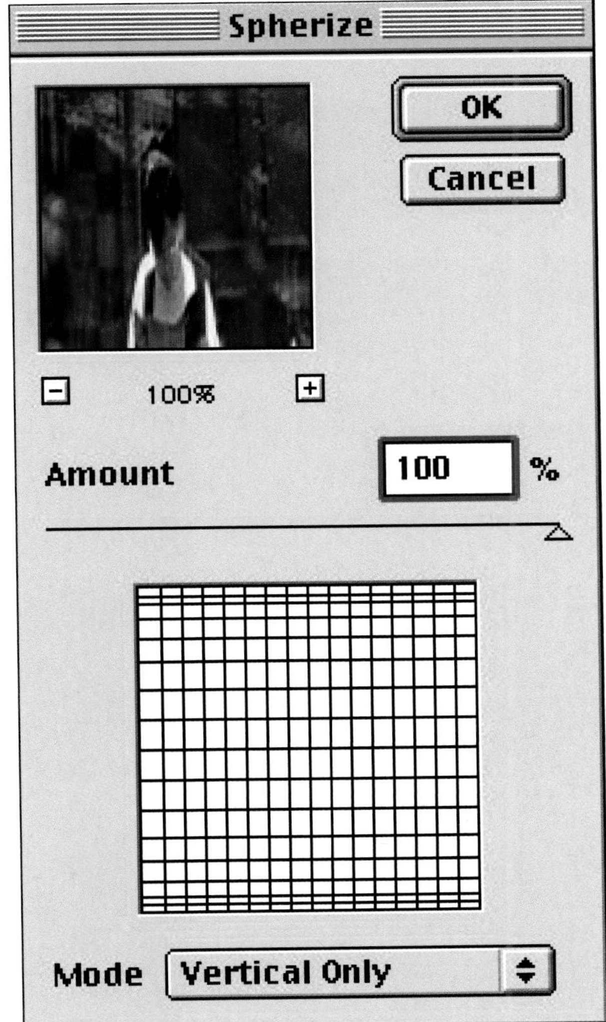

● 29.5

Monitors:
21-inch Viewsonic
17-inch Sony

Software:
Adobe Photoshop
Painter

Tablet:
Wacom Intuos 6 x 8

Input:
Nikon Coolscan II scanner
Canon 35mm EOS
Canon G1 digital camera

Printers:
Epson 2000P

Contact

Richard Swiatlowski
Wilbraham, Massachusetts
Photo.javanet@rcn.com
www.mindsisland.com

In Painter, Richard continued to work on the piece, painting in the elements he needed, such as the leg on the left and the extra people in the background (29.7). In Painter, Richard used the Oil Pastel variant in the Dry Media brush category with different paper textures (see the technique later in this chapter) and brush sizes and pressure to block in areas of color for composition and balance. He began rough and worked towards details at the end.

Richard continued painting over the image until the entire picture was covered in paint, completely obscuring the original photographic elements. This piece took about 20 hours to paint.

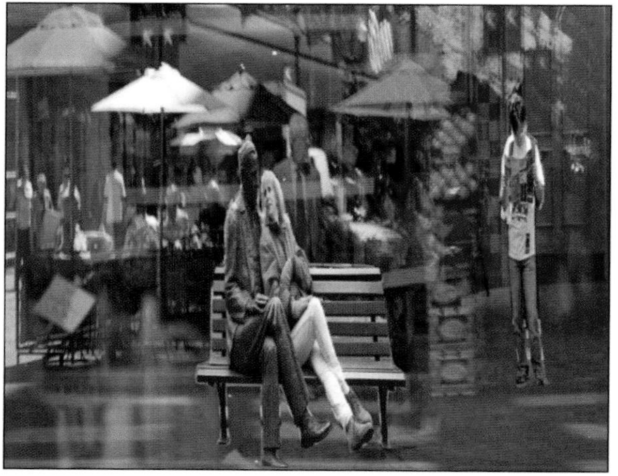

● 29.6

● 29.7

Technique: Using Inverse Paper Texture to Build Up Depth and Richness (Painter)

This technique shows the way Richard transforms a photo collage into a painting by building up many layers of textured paint for a rich, painterly result.

1. **Open a photo collage in Painter.**
2. **Choose File→Clone.**

   This makes a flattened copy of the original picture.

[TIP]

Working on a clone copy, rather than the original image, leaves you the flexibility to return to the original image at any point by using a Cloner brush. You should try to paint on a flat file, rather than a layered file, so that you can blend across from one photo to another with your brush strokes.

3. **Select the Oil Pastel brush variant in the Dry Media brush category of the Brushes palette (29.8).**
4. **Select a color in the Colors section of the Art Materials palette.**
5. **Select a paper texture you like, such as Dry Cracks, from the Papers section of the Art Materials palette (29.9).**
6. **Alter the size of your brush in the Sizes section of the Brush Controls palette to suit the scale of the features you are painting.**
7. **Paint over a section of the image.**
8. **In the Papers palette, invert the paper texture (29.10).**

[NOTE]

Inverting the paper texture essentially reverses the tooth of the paper. It's a very powerful way to create

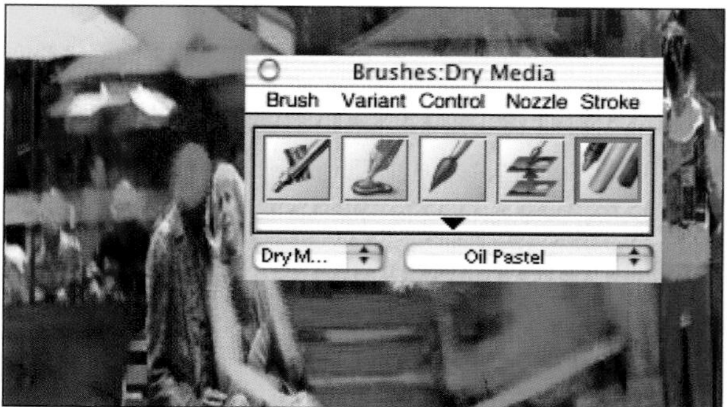

● 29.8

beautiful color-mixing effects where you juxtapose varying colors in close proximity by painting into the positive and negative regions of a texture.

In his image Richard not only inverted the paper texture but also adjusted the scale and contrast of the paper (by adjusting the scale and contrast sliders in the Papers section). He also changed the pastel hues as he altered the paper characteristics. This enhanced the aesthetic quality of the final image.

9. **Change color either using the Color Picker, or by using the Eye-Dropper tool within the image, or by checking the clone color box in the Colors section.**
10. **Continue painting over the same area with the inverted texture.**
11. **Repeat this process, changing paper texture, brush size, and color, building up several layers of paint all over the image.**

Artist's Creative Insight and Advice

Why Digital?

Digital allows me a lot of creative possibilities. It lets me combine my love of photography, painting, and drawing.

Unfortunately, digital art is where photography was at the turn of the last century. It's not widely accepted as fine art. The digital platform is just a different tool at the disposal of the artist. Great art is great no matter how it was created.

Advice for Artists Working in the Digital Medium

My advice holds true for any medium. It is something I once read: you can't sit around and wait for inspiration. In order to keep producing, you have to get in there and work, even if you don't have an idea in your head.

On Output

You have to realize there are compromises between your screen and your printers. I want permanence, so I use pigmented inks and archival paper. My favorite output is with Epson archival inks and matte paper. My images are painterly, and this combination works for me. Many people see my prints and think they are (traditional) paintings. I sometimes apply a matte protective finish and paint with traditional oils directly on the prints.

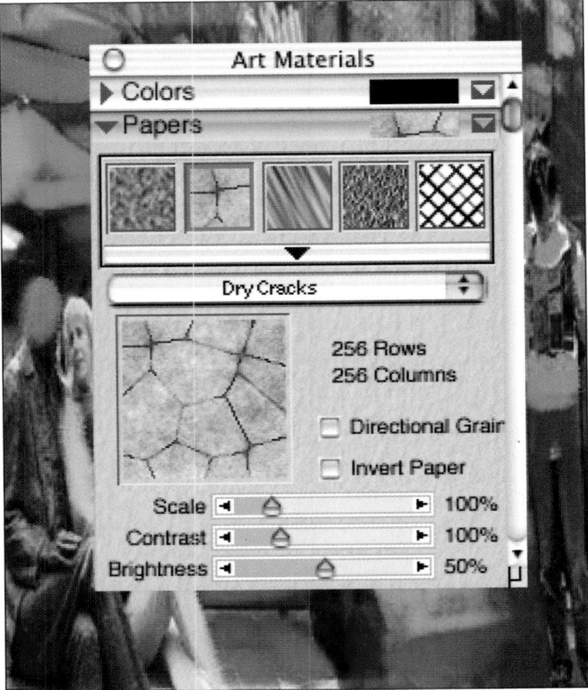

● 29.9

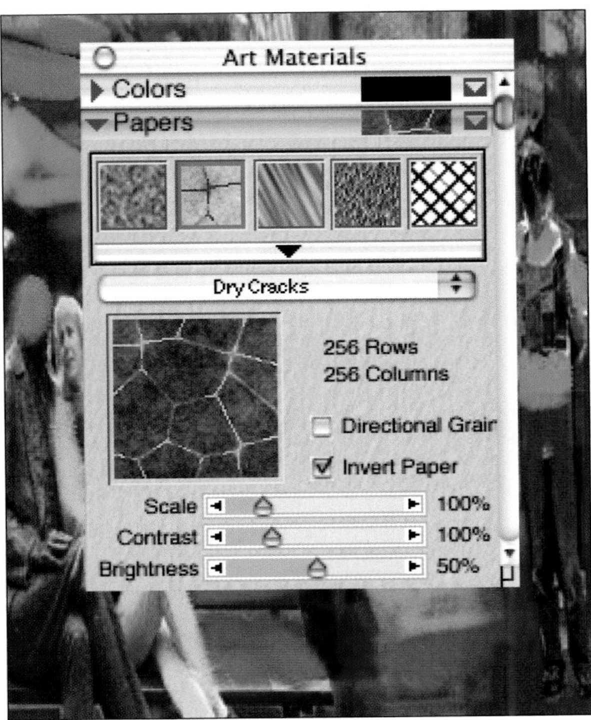

● 29.10

Chapter 30

Spring Poppies

by Elizabeth Carmel

Artist's Statement

I strive to create images that spark an emotional connection with people, that leave something for the viewer to interpret. I consider my images to be a synthesis of photography and imagination.

The Story Behind the Artwork

Elizabeth took a picture of an old rusty truck in a meadow a few years ago in the Sierra foothills of California. She loved how the truck looked in the evening light against a green spring meadow with the poppies blooming. She thought the picture would work well with the Photoshop painting techniques she had been developing. Elizabeth scanned in the slide and created one of her best-selling images, *Spring Poppies* (30.1).

The Creative Process

Elizabeth scanned the slide using a Nikon 4000 ED scanner; she made two separate scans. For the first scan, she exposed for the meadow and the lit part of the truck (30.2).

For the second scan, she exposed for the shadow detail in the truck, since it was just a black area in the first scan with no shadow detail. In order to get the shadow detail from the original slide, Elizabeth had to do a severe curves adjustment in the scanning software, just focusing on trying to get whatever detail there was available in the shadow area of the truck. This caused the color to turn a strange grey (30.3).

● 30.2

◀ 30.1

30.3

30.4

She subsequently adjusted the colors to match the rest of the truck by choosing Image→Adjust→ Curves in Photoshop.

30.5

She compiled the two scans on separate layers in Photoshop. She then created another layer with the foreground poppies, which were from another scanned slide of a nearby poppy field (30.4).

After she compiled the image, Elizabeth used a combination of dry brush, paint daubs, and watercolor filters to give the image more of a painted look (30.5).

About the Artist

Biography

Elizabeth Carmel has spent years photographing the diverse landscapes of the Western United States, and she has pioneered a unique style that combines digital art, traditional fine art techniques, and photography. Her interest in digital photography as an art form was sparked by a digital photography workshop with Stephen Johnson in 2001. She learned the craft of Photoshop through numerous classes and workshops, and she credits the San Francisco Seybold 2001 training seminars with taking her knowledge a quantum leap forward.

Through her technique of Photo Impressionism, Elizabeth creates images that merge both reality and artistic interpretation. Her prints combine dramatic photography, vivid colors, and impressionistic effects to create a new, captivating vision of the American landscape.

Elizabeth Carmel's photography has been selected for display at the Seybold Galleries in San Francisco and New York, the Yosemite Renaissance Fine Art Show in Yosemite, and numerous juried fine art shows throughout the United States. Her limited-edition fine art prints are giclée printed using Epson 9500 archival inks on

She then worked with adjusting the curves to bring out the colors of the image and with adjusting Hue/Saturation to give the colors snap.

The sky was created with a gradient fill and Color layer blending mode. The poppies were pasted as a separate layer. Elizabeth used the Perspective tool to make the poppies look like a natural part of the foreground, receding into the distance.

Technique: Creating a Painted Effect on a Photograph (Photoshop)

Try this technique when you want to give your photographs a rich, textured, painterly effect.

1. **Open a scanned photo in Photoshop.**

[NOTE]

For a final print size of 20 x 30 inches, aim to have a source image that is 9 x 12 inches at 250 dpi.

2. **Choose Layers→New Adjustment Layer→Curves and adjust the RGB Curve to perfect the overall exposure and color in the photo (30.6).**
   Make the colors of the image vivid, but not overdone. Correct any color cast in the photo by adjusting the individual R, G, and B curves. Where adjustment is needed to specific areas in the image, select those regions and apply Adjustment layers to those selections. If necessary, compile different exposures of the same scan or digital image into one photo that is perfectly exposed for highlight and shadow detail.

[TIP]

Be sure to feather the edges of the selections or you will have a "patchwork" looking image.

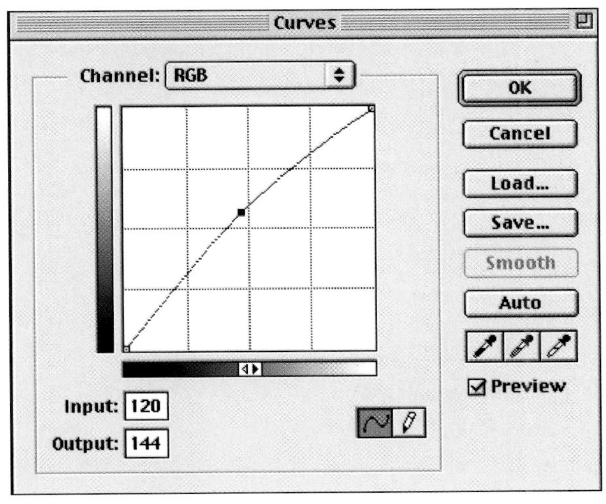

● 30.6

Epson textured fine art paper. She sells her fine art prints from her home-based gallery located in the mountain town of Truckee, California, and through numerous galleries throughout the West.

Influences

Galen Rowell and other leading color landscape photographers, including Steven Johnson's digital landscape photography and the work of John Paul Camponigro.

Studio

Computer System:

Macintosh G4 Dual Processor, 800 MHz

Monitors:

21-inch Apple Cinema Display

Software:

Adobe Photoshop

Tablet:

Wacom Intuous 9 x 12

Input Devices:

Nikon D1x Digital SLR
Nikon Coolpix 995 digital camera
Nikon 4000 ED slide scanner
EPSON 1600 flatbed scanner

Removable Media:

Iomega Peerless 20GB Removable Drives

Printers:

Epson 9500 and 1270

Contact

Elizabeth Carmel
Truckee, California
liz@sierraimageworks.com
www.sierraimageworks.com

3. **Choose Layers→New Adjustment Layer→Hue/Saturation and adjust the Master Saturation slider slightly to the right to increase saturation (30.7).**
   Doing so helps make the colors pop out.
4. **Choose Layers→New Layer from the Layers palette pop-up menu.**
5. **Choose Layers→Merge Visible while holding down the Command and Option keys (Ctrl+Alt on Windows).**
   This compiles everything in a single master layer without deleting the Adjustment layers below it.
6. **Use the Clone tool to remove distracting features, or to add in features you want more of, such as flowers.**

[TIP]

Keep the completed base photo as a background layer. This allows non-destructive editing at a later date. Before applying irreversible filters, protect the compiled photo layer by duplicating it.

7. **Choose Layer→Duplicate Layer in the Layers pop-up menu to duplicate the compiled master layer.**
   It can be useful to rename the new layer the "painting layer" so you can see at a glance in the Layers palette what it is.
8. **Choose Filter→Artistic→Dry Brush and set the Brush Size small (1 to 3), the Brush Detail high (8 to 10), and the Texture to the minimum of 1 (30.8).**
9. **Choose Filter→Artistic→Paint Daubs and set the Brush Size to between 3 and 5 and the Sharpness to between 2 and 4. The Brush Type should be Simple (30.9).**
   This filter is useful for getting smooth highlights in the subject. Don't set the sharpness too high or it may pixelate the image and make it look too digital.
10. **Repeat the Dry Brush/Paint Daubs filter iteration until the image has a more impressionistic look.**
   Experiment with adjusting the brush size each time you apply the filters.
11. **Select those areas where there are highlights or bright areas that need more contrast and definition.**
12. **Choose Filter→Artistic→Watercolor and set the Brush Detail high and the Shadow Intensity and Texture to 0. Apply to the selected areas that need more contrast and definition.**

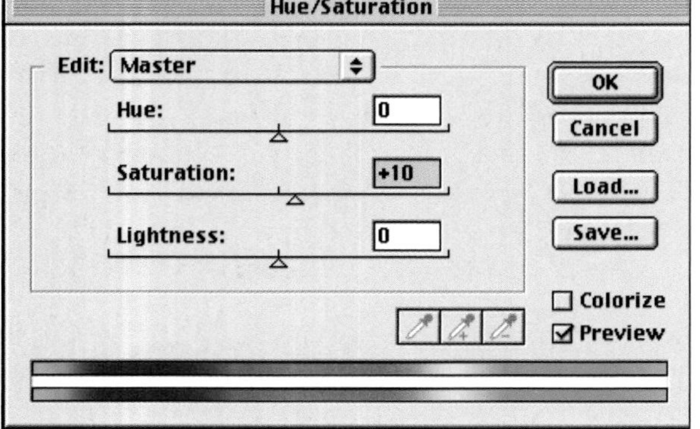

● 30.7

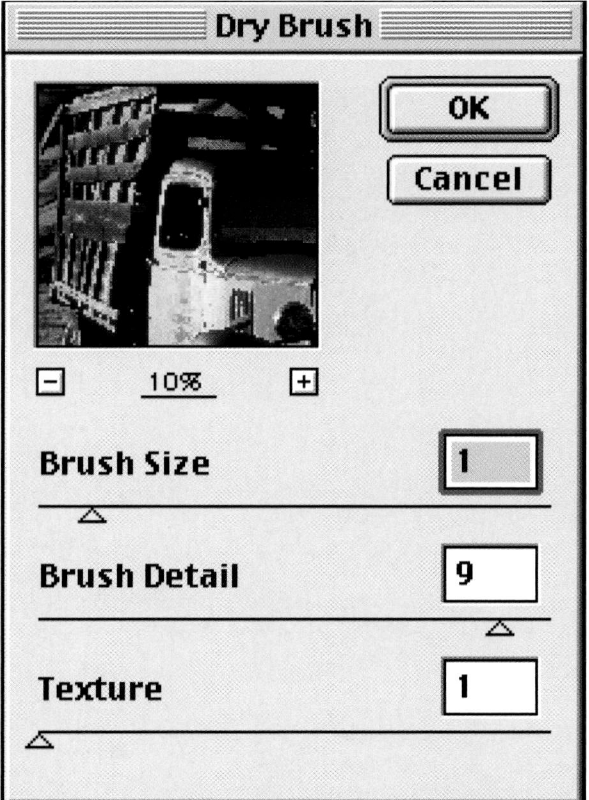

● 30.8

[NOTE]

If you're using this technique on pictures with people, use the History Brush on faces. Faces can only handle about one dry brush filter before they take on a strange texture. Landscape images can handle many iterations, although trees and fine foliage many only sustain one iteration.

Use History Brush Snapshots if you want to preserve a stage of the work you may want to return to.

13. **After you're happy with the painted look of the painted layer, use the Curves and Hue/Saturation Adjustment layers on top of that to make sure the colors are vivid and the contrast is pleasing.**
    Applying the repeated filter effects alters the colors.
14. **Experiment with layer blending modes to further enhance the image and make it pop.**
    The Color blending mode works well since it allows underlying features to show through. A washed-out image can benefit from a Soft Light or Multiply Blending mode on top of the painted layer.
15. **Resize the image to suit the final print size.**
16. **Flatten the image by choosing Image→Flatten.**
17. **Apply one or two final Dry Brush filters on the enlarged image to "depixelate" the edges and make everything look smooth.**
    Remember to use the small brush size and maximum detail settings.
18. **Make small test prints to create final tweaks before printing the large final version that you can sign and number.**

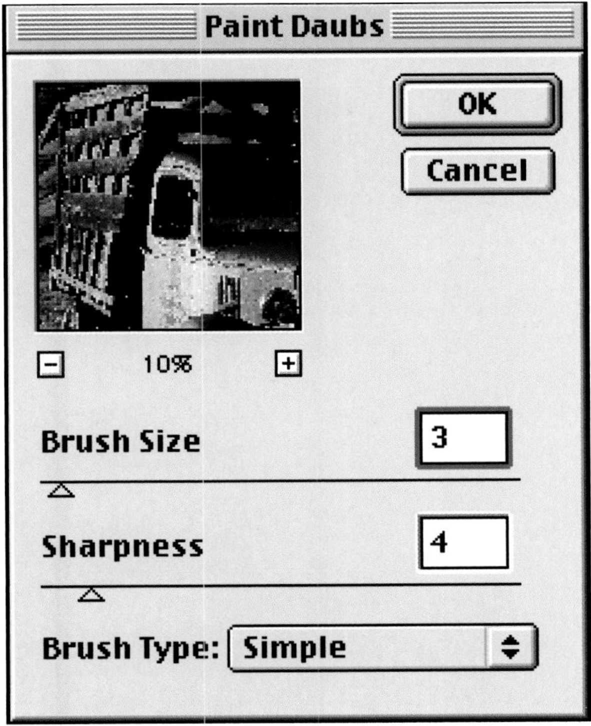

● 30.9

Judge's Critique

Seybold 2002 Digital Art Contest, New York

"I like the mixture of traditional photography, color manipulation, and the artistic application of the tools. Even the sky seems to have been modified to make it look a bit more colorful."

— MARK ZIMMER, Co-Founder, Fractal Design (www.fractal.com)

Artist's Creative Insight and Advice

Why Digital?

Digital art is the wave of the future. The digital medium gives me the flexibility I need to manipulate and enhance color, to create a painted fine art effect, and to enlarge images to the 30-inch size I like to display and sell. It would be impossible to create my images in a traditional darkroom.

Galen Rowell's philosophy about creating work with instantaneous emotional impact led me to explore combining digital art and photography, so that I could produce landscape prints that people would want to purchase and hang on their walls.

I have great admiration of artists who use natural media and pure talent to produce landscape paintings; however, a number of these artists are critical of my work because they see it as trying to "cheat" and encroach on the fine art painting market. I am very up front about how I create my images, and don't try to hide the fact that they are digital, although it's amazing how many people think they are paintings! I think that photography is a well accepted fine art form, and that, if anything, my "photo-impressionism" is a step beyond what a traditional photographer does in terms of creating an artistic image. I think my work sparks an interesting and useful discussion in the fine art community. I just want to create images of the natural world that people find worthy of buying and putting in their homes and offices.

Since my images are large with huge file sizes, computing technology is only now able to handle these images. Having a digital SLR is wonderful; I would hate to be scanning in slides all the time and having to get film processed. I once heard of a photographer who spent 40 hours creating a Photoshop mask. If I ever do this, I hope my husband signs me up for psychotherapy.

I have had success with working faster and trying to be less exacting and more fluid and creative. Color is the one component of my work that I really try to perfect, and that requires a lot of experimentation.

Positive Imagery

I try to create positive images, ones that aren't full of morbid, depressing images and strange things. Maybe some digital artists could try creating a few pleasing images that add a little joy to the world. I really like the pig with butterfly wings created by Maggie Taylor.

Printing, Proofing, and Color Management

The Epson 9500 printer is critical to my work because it produces archival quality prints with lovely colors. The soft proof feature in Photoshop is also critical to my work, since I often need to do a final tweak of colors and contrast to make the final print appear how I would like on the Epson 9500. The most important color management task for me is to get accurate screen matching with the printer. I have been pleased with how well the LCD cinema display can reproduce what the Epson will print. I use the Colorcal calibration software for the LCD monitor. The frustration with CRTs is their short life span — I am a big believer that LCD displays are great for the kind of work I do, and their accuracy is much better for subtle colors and detailed work.

Chapter 31

Fragile

by Bruce R. Bennett

Artist's Statement

I see the world as a giant thrift shop: amidst the junk you sometimes find treasures. I like incorporating these bits of cast-off personal history in my work, evoking connections and associations between seemingly unconnected elements via the combination of archaic and modern imaging techniques.

The Story Behind the Artwork

When Bruce was younger, he used to like to surround himself with new things. As he matured, though, he found himself drawn more and more to antiques, to objects with character, with history, with flaws. "Perhaps this represents a recognition of the fact that all things, ourselves included, are decaying," he conjectures, "or just acceptance that perfection is not necessarily the same thing as beauty."

Bruce created this image while thinking about his family history and the aging process. He lives in the house in which his grandfather used to live and work. His grandfather, who was a carpenter trained in Germany, left behind many wonderful artifacts of his craft, which Bruce has incorporated into different aspects of his own work.

In the garage attic, Bruce found an old, yellowed, moth-eaten label with the word "Fragile" on a steamer trunk — the very luggage that Bruce's grandfather had used when he immigrated to the United States in 1925. The label fell off into Bruce's hand when he moved the trunk. It was so thin and delicate that he couldn't believe it was somehow still holding together after so many years in the intense Florida heat and humidity. The label had such great texture and visual appeal — as well as personal significance — that he immediately knew he wanted to create a piece around it.

The way the resulting illustration evolved from this point was not typical for Bruce. Rather than carefully planning, sketching, plotting, and refining an idea, as he usually does, he assembled the image gradually, in a very stream-of-consciousness manner, hoping more to evoke a mood than to drive home a specific message. When he found other objects and imagery that resonated for him in juxtaposition to his original image of the label, he added these and created a computer collage which became *Fragile* (31.1).

◀31.1

Since his grandfather was a craftsman who worked with his hands, Bruce decided it was important to incorporate some very hands-on techniques in creating the final image. One example of such a hands-on technique was his use of the Polaroid transfer technique. This process removed some sharpness from the image and added texture. Because no two transfers ever turn out alike, it added the personal touch he was seeking.

The Creative Process

Bruce placed the delicate, yellowed, moth-eaten label on top of a cigar box with an old dominoes piece next to it. The cigar box added an interesting wooden texture in the background. He photographed this as his first source image (31.2).

Then he photographed a page from a turn-of-the-century reading primer used by his grandmother (31.3). He scanned both of these images into Photoshop, cropped, and composited them (31.4). Then made a slide of the resulting digital image.

Next, Bruce made a Polaroid print of the slide image on Polaroid 679 film, using a Vivitar Instant Slide Printer.

Polaroid 669 and 679 film have different characteristics. Type 669 film is what Polaroid recommends for transfers. Bruce has discovered, through experimentation, that type 679 works for transfers too, although

● 31.2

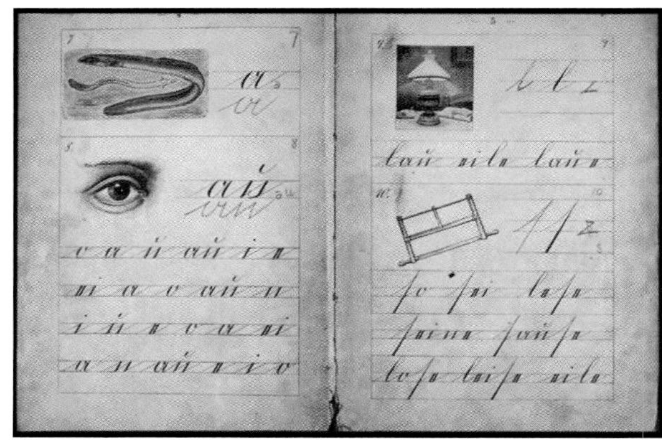

● 31.3

dS

About the Artist

Biography

Bruce has been showing his traditional and alternative process photography since the early '90s. He started using the computer to create collages in 1996, when he first learned Adobe Photoshop. In addition to making photographs, he always liked to sketch, draw, and paint (mostly charcoal, pastel, and watercolor) and uses the computer as a powerful tool to combine his favorite media. He currently works as a photojournalist for a metropolitan daily newspaper (circulation 200,000).

Bruce continues to shoot with toy cameras and exhibits his alternative process photography and digital art. His digital work has been recognized, among others, by Adobe in its Me, My Idea Design Challenge, *Publish* magazine, the Dimensional Illustrators Annual Awards Show, the Macworld Conference and Expo Digital Art Gallery, Seybold Seminars Digital Art Gallery, and the Southern Short Course in News Photography.

it leaves a strong residual yellow cast in the transferred image. This color cast makes it less suitable for images that require faithful color rendition. For this particular image, though, Bruce thought that the unique characteristics of 679 would add to the image's "aged" appearance.

Peeling apart the film's positive/negative sandwich before it had been allowed to fully develop, he pressed the negative side into a piece of dampened watercolor paper using a brayer roller. This process transferred the dyes from the negative onto the watercolor paper. Peeling off the negative quickly created interesting tears and irregularities in the image left on the watercolor paper. Finally, after letting the dyes dry, he scanned the image back into Photoshop on a flatbed scanner.

● 31.4

Since he had used type 679 film to make the transfer instead of type 669, the entire image had acquired a pronounced yellow cast in the transfer process, including an area (the domino) that he wanted to remain white. To restore the domino's white color, he selected the domino with the Lasso tool in Photoshop and decreased its saturation by choosing Image→Adjust→Hue/Saturation and moving the saturation slider to the left.

Bruce completed the image in bits and pieces over the span of about a week. This was a fun illustration for Bruce, "one that I created more with instinct than with my intellect. . . . I didn't agonize about symbolism or endlessly tweak tiny details." Accordingly, the amount of time invested (about three to four hours) was significantly less than what he would typically spend.

Technique: Using the Polaroid Dye Transfer Process to Make a Digital Image Look Old and Weathered (Photoshop)

This technique shows how Bruce took a collage image out of the computer, modified it through the Polaroid dye transfer process, and then brought the result back into the computer for final adjustments. To do this technique, you need Polaroid 669 film

Influences

Photographically, Bruce has been inspired by Keith Carter, Anna Tomczak, and Jerry Uelsmann. He also loves the creative blend of pop culture references and fine art influences in the digital illustration work of Matt Mahurin.

Studio

Computer System:
Apple iMac G4, 700 MHz
40GB hard drive
768MB RAM

Monitors:
15-inch active-matrix flat panel display

Software:
Adobe Photoshop

Removable Media:
CD-ROM
CD-RW
DVD
Compact flash card

Archive Media:
CD-ROM

Input Devices:
Kodak Professional Scanner RFS 2035
Sharp JX-610 flatbed scanner
Canon EOS 1-N
Mamiya C330Pro
Rolleiflex
Holga

Printers:
Kodak Professional 8670 PS Thermal Printer

Contact

Bruce R. Bennett
Lake Worth, Florida
brubenn@aol.com
www.travel.to/bennett

31.5

(which gives better results than type 679 film), a brayer roller, and a Vivitar Instant Slide Printer (31.5).

1. **Open two scanned images in Adobe Photoshop.**
   In Bruce's case for the image featured in this chapter, the film was scanned on a Kodak RFS 2035 scanner at maximum resolution, with normal sharpening, using the generic profile for negative film.
2. **Use the Move tool to pull one image into a new layer on top of the second image.**
   Bruce pulled the reading primer "eye" and text into a new layer on top of the image of the label.
3. **In the Layers palette, adjust the new layer from Normal to Overlay blend mode.**
4. **Choose Edit→Transform→Scale and resize the top layer to suit the scale of the background image.**
5. **Reduce the opacity of the top layer in the Layers palette.**

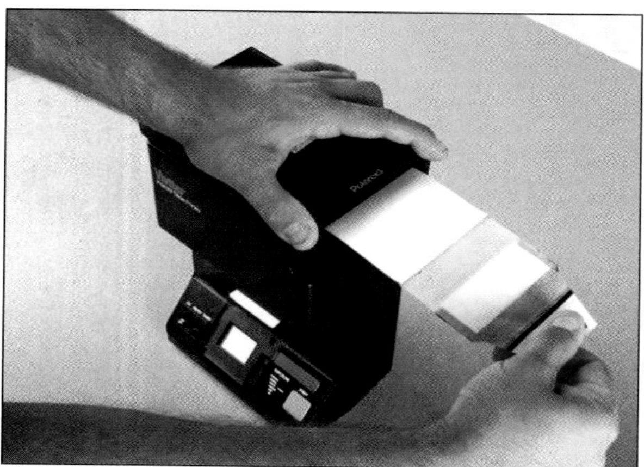

31.6

31.8

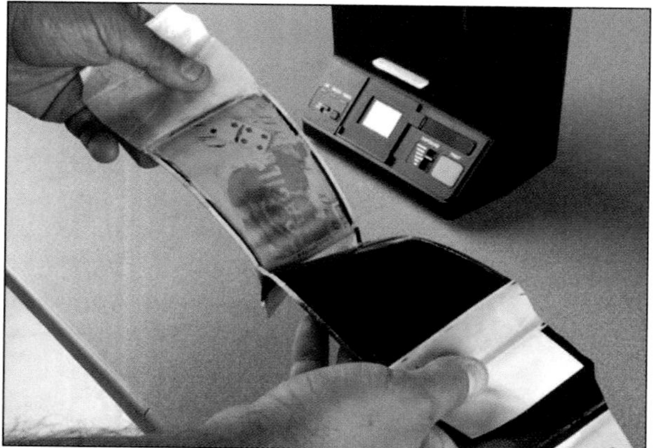
31.7

31.9

6. **Choose Flatten Image from the Layers pop-up menu.**
7. **Save as a Targa file for slide output.**
8. **Insert the slide into a Vivitar Instant Slide Printer.**
9. **Make an exposure on Polaroid 669 film.**
10. **Remove the exposed film from the slide printer (31.6).**
11. **Peel apart the Polaroid film after 10 seconds (31.7).**
12. **Place the negative face down on damp watercolor paper.**
13. **Use a brayer roller to apply even pressure to the back of the negative for two to three minutes (31.8).**
14. **Peel the negative off the watercolor paper (31.9).**

[TIP]

The faster you peel, the more irregular the transfer may be.

15. **After drying, scan the dye transfer image back into Photoshop for final digital manipulation of the image.**

Artist's Creative Insight and Advice

Why Digital?

Working digitally offers up an endless world of possibilities . . . and pitfalls. With endless freedom comes the temptation of using cool-looking effects and filters just because they are cool. I try hard to not be seduced by flashy effects for their own sake. Sometimes, I miss the hands-on nature of pre-digital work. However, using Photoshop frees me up creatively to use techniques I once would have had to labor over endlessly in the darkroom. It is a trade-off; the computer doesn't replace traditional methods and media entirely — it supplements them.

Every artist uses the tools that best fit his or her vision. The computer is just another tool in a very large toolbox. Ultimately, it doesn't matter what tool you use, just what you do with it.

Advice for Artists Working in the Digital Medium

Take the time to play with your software and get to know it. Make sure that you have a concept firmly in mind and that any software techniques you use support that concept: nothing is more distracting than the egregious use of filters or special effects for their own sake.

By all means, do not be afraid to experiment and try things that you've been told not to do. After all, rules are made to be broken. Just remember to stay on-message.

Output

I've been very fortunate with color: I've never had many issues with consistency between screen and print output. Ever since my Epson inkjet broke down, I've been using an online photo printing service almost exclusively for my images. Ofoto.com does a great job with photographic prints: colors have matched my screen almost perfectly every time, and the service can print up to 20 x 30 inches at very reasonable prices.

Chet Helms on Bennett's *Fragile*

"This very sophisticated example of digital compositing echoes and embellishes the tradition in Western art known as trompe l'oeil. Originating in Greek times and reaching its zenith in late nineteenth-century America and Europe, trompe l'oeil attempts to deceive the eye into believing that the image is the object.

Trompe l'oeil has over time developed its own iconography, which is unique to the genre. This work exhibits many of those hallmarks – for example, the seemingly random ordering of still objects (harder than it looks), the precise depiction of wear and tear and the ravages of time, common objects such as hand-addressed letters and postage stamps or currency, and the poignant appeal to nostalgia.

This artist has deceived our eyes twice. Our eyes are asked to accept this image as a trompe l'oeil painting whereas it is in fact a digital composition miming a trompe."

– Chet Helms, Digital Photographer and Art Gallery Owner, Founder, Family Dog Productions

JEFFERSON VALLEY
CARS • MOVING SU
RS • TRUCKS • TR
14 EAST M
FERSON V

Chapter 32

Mort Mechanique

by Howard Berdach

Artist's Statement

We all live within our own heads and personal experiences. Art, and visual art especially, offers the artist the opportunity to share this inner world with all who reside outside the "zone." Essentially, to me, art is all about emotional exchange and transfer. My idea is to create imagery that, either through literal content, or through the more ethereal qualities of form, textures, and colors, effects a particular response in the viewer. Usually my goal is to uplift or enlighten the spirit of the receiver.

The Story Behind the Artwork

Mort Mechanique (32.1) is an artwork born out of serendipity, an unexpected combination of chance and skill. The image arose out of factors that Howard had decided upon, or thought of, initially. Then, the work materialized through an improvisational process.

The process started one day when, while reading the Sunday *New York Times,* Howard discovered an ad announcing an upcoming auction of antiques. The ad indicated that there would be a huge quantity of eclectic material, including carousel horses from Coney Island amusement rides, a fortune-telling gypsy arcade machine, antique pinball machines, games of chance, dolls, stuffed animals, scientific instruments, country home implements, antique cars, and more. Howard decided that he would go to the sale preview, not to buy anything, but rather to photograph objects with the hope of using the photographs as source material for future art compositions.

When he arrived at the auction, Howard discovered that the sale was being held by an elderly couple who had been collecting material for a lifetime. There were three large outdoor tents filled with these objects,

◀ 32.1

displayed somewhat haphazardly on tables, on the floor, and hanging from the tent poles. Howard photographed whatever he found interesting and left the rolls of film sitting on a shelf to await development.

When Howard eventually got the uncut negatives developed (uncut to avoid film workers from cutting negative frames by mistake), he discovered some nicely exposed and sharply focused frames. He scanned these frames at 600dpi on his Umax scanner, and thus began the image-building session that was the start of *Mort Mechanique.*

Starting with a picture of an engineering sextant, he added acid colorization to the straight image by way of KPT and Photoshop manipulation. When he had an interesting color effect, he chose another auction item, (this time, the head of an actual human skeleton) and added to the colorized sextant background. He continued adding auction item elements one after the other, spending careful time controlling the layer adjustments and placements of the elements within the composition. He subsequently spent many hours tweaking colors and experimenting with level and hue saturation variations.

By the end of the initial session, which lasted about three hours, most of the image elements had been set, and a story arose out of the improvised collection of image elements. Howard titled the piece *Mort Mechanique* as a play on words; *Morte Mechanique* means "mechanical death" in French. The mannequin and various technical instruments in the image suggest mechanical qualities, and the skull imagery, of course, suggests death. In French, the word for death would be written *morte* with an "e"; Howard's *Mort* (with no "e") was his way of giving a name to the unnamed soul behind the laughing skeleton, and the skeleton at repose in his Civil War era wicker coffin. *Mort Mechanique* symbolizes all who live, subject to the harsh forces in life.

Howard saved many experimental versions of this work. Some are more brightly colored, others more subdued. Howard continues to work on this piece, and he expects to produce many more variations of this composition before he leaves it alone forever.

The Creative Process

This piece went through a number of distinct phases during its creation.

Phase 1: Source Photography and Sextant Manipulation

The initial photography of the auction items was done with a Pentax K1000 manual 35mm camera, using relatively poor quality film stock, as well as drugstore-quality film processing. The film stock was negative, and, after reviewing the processed film, certain frames were chosen for scanning. Howard scanned the negative strips at 600dpi, using the transparency adapter on the UMAX Powerlook II, which

dS

About the Artist

Biography

Howard's visual art career took shape in the mid '70s when he studied television and film production techniques at City College, San Francisco, and at San Francisco State University. In 1989, Howard studied at the School of Visual Arts, New York, where he spent a few years as a continuing education student. Howard had access to the traditional printmaking studio, as well as access to the newly constructed computer art lab. There, he learned the nuts and bolts of the art of printmaking.

Mort Mechanique and another of his images, *Sonic Color Loom*, a high-color, geometric abstract, were selected in successive years, 1999 and 2000, as finalist images in the Macworld Expo Digital Gallery. As a result of those exposures, both were published in *Digital Fine Art Magazine*. Other images of his have been published in *Design Graphics Magazine*, as well as books on digital art, and displayed in gallery art shows.

● 32.2

resulted in relatively small files at actual 35mm film-frame size.

An image of an engineering sextant was chosen for initial experimentation (32.2).

The first manipulation was the infusion of color into the photo. This was accomplished by adding a layer of a yellow-to-orange color gradient to the sextant image, using the gradient designer in KPT3. The color gradient layer was merged to the sextant file using the Difference mode. Howard experimented in Preview mode so that he could move the slider bars and control the toggles until the image results onscreen were pleasing (32.3).

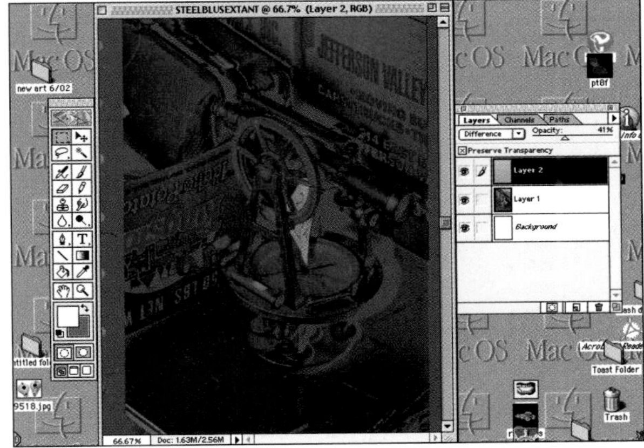

● 32.3

Influences

The Surrealists, Impressionists, and Fauves; the Op-Art movement (which inspires Howard's geometric work); Color Field and Pop artists; video and film artists; and, most recently, ancient artifacts.

Studio

Computer System:
Power Computing Power Tower Pro 225, 225MHz
2GB hard drive
256MB RAM

Monitors:
Power Computing 17-inch

Software:
Adobe Photoshop
Freehand
Kpt 3 and 5 (Old School)

Removable Media:
Syquest 135 EZ Drive
Fujitsu 640 Magneto Optical Drive
Teac CD-R Drive

Archive Media:
MO and CD-R

Tablet:
CalComp Ultra Slate 4 x 5 pressure-sensitive slate

Input Devices:
Umax Power Look II
Pentax K 1000 35mm manual camera with Vivitar Macro/Zoom lens

Printers:
Epson Stylus Color 800

Contact

Howard Berdach
Valley Stream, New York
hberdach@rcn.com

Phase 2: Adding the Skull

The next element chosen for experimentation was a close-up of a head of a skeleton. The skeleton was complete, dating from the time of the Civil War, lying in a wicker casket (a tradition typical of the day). Howard had additional photos of the skeleton which depicted the full length of the skeleton, but, at this point, only a shot of the skull was placed on the new, flattened, colorized version of the sextant. He took the scan of the skull and pasted it into t he frame using the Difference mode set at 92% opacity (32.4).

Once again, Howard experimented with all the layer mode possibilities until he decided on a general look he found appealing. He then applied finer and finer slider adjustments until he was completely satisfied with the result.

At this point, he also began to remove parts of the pasted elements that he didn't want to appear in the final image. This was accomplished by working in the layers with the Eraser tool, using the pressure sensitivity of his stylus to determine exactly how much of the element image that he wanted to leave revealed (32.5).

[TIP]

As a non-destructive alternative to using the Eraser tool, you could paint into the Layer mask, so changes could be made at a later date.

Phase 3: Infusion of Color

At this stage, Howard chose a file from his archive of over 15,000 digital files that had some colors that didn't occur in the image. This file was used to embellish the image and add some reddish-orange coloring, as well as a geometric bluish/purple division in the upper left-hand corner. After this new coloring and design element was fused in, he decided to lighten the entire piece, using Levels controls to give the piece a more electric look (32.6).

Phase 4: Addition of More Elements

In this phase, the image took on its subjective depth by the addition of four new elements, which help to define the story of the piece (32.7).

Layer 1 contains a taxidermy of small, stuffed brown bear, which in the finished image looks more like a snarling dog. The layer, which was set to Difference mode at 43% opacity, appears as a green animal on the top of image, right of center.

Layer 2 features a mannequin, which has price tags hanging from it, standing on grass, leaning against a carved wooden object. This layer's Difference mode is set at 55% opacity. It appears on the right edge of the frame, slightly below center.

Layer 3 is a scientific laboratory glassware in Difference mode at 41% opacity, placed to the left of center.

Layer 4, the Civil War skeleton in a wicker casket, sits in the top left-hand corner of the image. It was pasted in Multiply mode at 100% opacity (32.8).

● 32.4

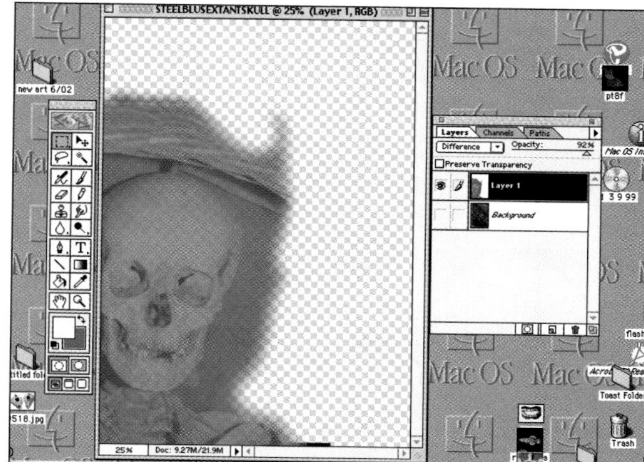

● 32.5

All of these elements were carefully positioned after a long trial-and-error process. Howard also played with the layer Mode settings until he got the results he wanted.

Altogether, about three hours elapsed from the time that Howard placed the first negative strips on the scanner until this point in the construction of the image — this is really quick if you think about how long it would have taken to achieve similar results using traditional photographic collaging techniques.

Phase 5: Final Tweaking and Addition of Mannequin View

Finally, Howard flattened the image and proceeded to tweak the Hue, Saturation, and Levels controls.

He had another view of the mannequin, taken from the side (32.9).

This element was added to the work in just the same manner as all the other elements that preceded

32.6

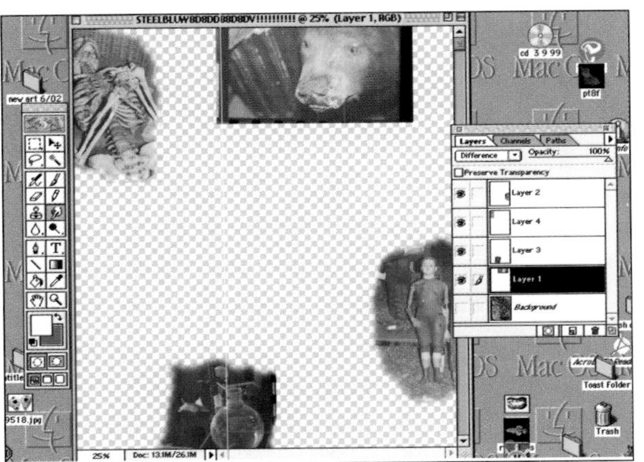

32.7

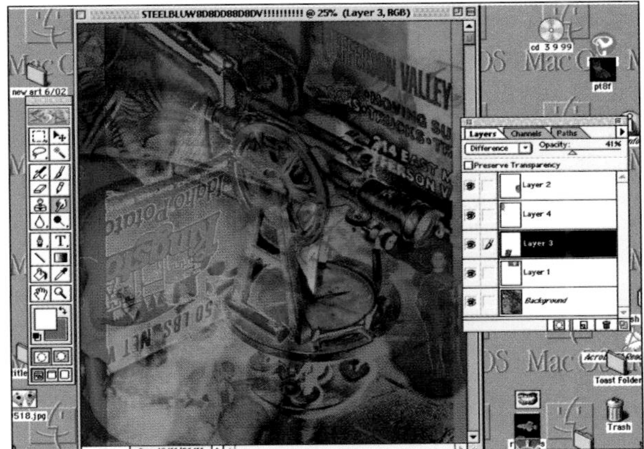

32.8

32.9

it: It was added after extensive sculpting, tweaking, viewing, and tweaking. This particular paste was done in Luminosity mode set at 57% opacity (32.10).

Mort Mechanique was created in the Spring of 1999, and the color tweaking has gone on until this day.

Technique: Building Up a Multi-Layered Collage (Photoshop)

This technique allows you to follow the methodology that Howard applies in building up his multi-layered collages with adjustments to Layer Mode and Opacity for each layer.

1. **Open your base image in Photoshop.**
2. **Open up a variety of source images that you want to compose within the collage above the base image.**
3. **Select the Move tool.**
4. **Drag each source image into the base image.**
   As you drag in each source image, it forms a separate layer.
5. **As each new layer is formed, select Layer Properties in the Layers pop-up menu and rename each layer with a short description of its contents.**

[TIP]

Renaming each layer in this way helps you keep track of which layer is which as you build your multi-layered image.

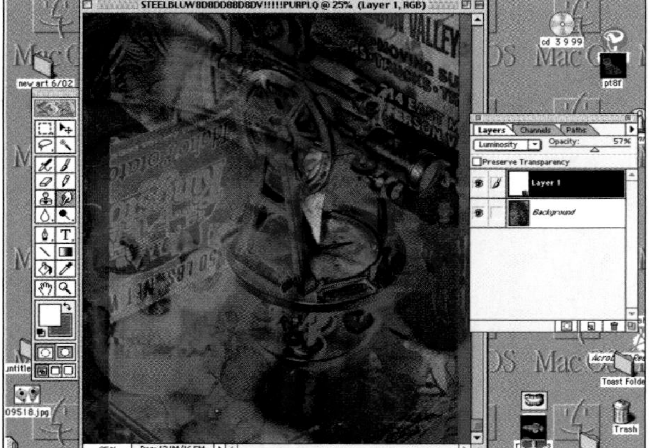

32.10

6. **Select each layer, in turn, in the Layers palette.**
7. **For each layer, experiment with the settings that Howard used in his piece (see the Creative Process description earlier in this chapter).**
   The following steps give an example of the type of tweaking that Howard did.
8. **Select one layer in your image.**
9. **Choose Image→Adjust→Hue/Saturation (32.11).**
10. **Move the Hue slider to the left, for example, to -103, with the Master channel selected in the Hue/Saturation window (32.12).**
    This makes a global hue adjustment to the whole layer.

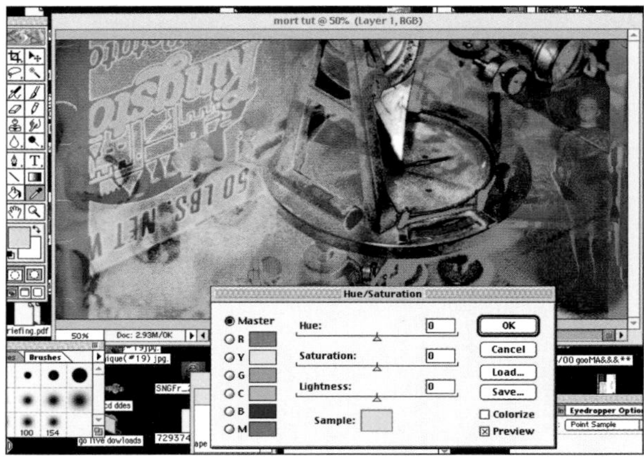

32.11

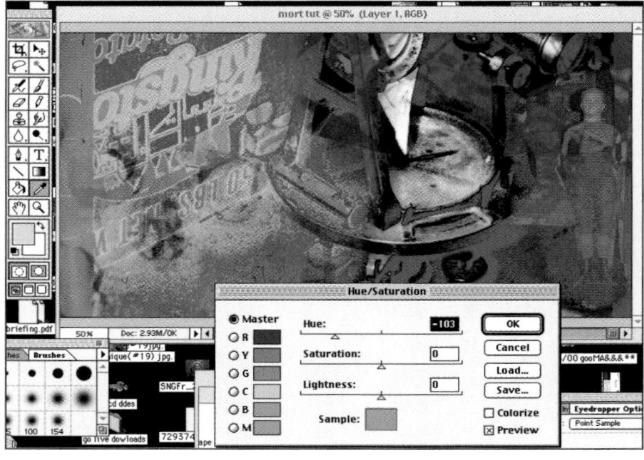

32.12

11. **Move the Saturation slider to the left, for example to -77 (32.13).**

    This makes a global saturation adjustment to the whole layer.

12. **Select the Yellow channel in the Hue/Saturation window.**
13. **Move the Hue slider to the left, for example to -38 (32.14).**

    Doing so has the effect of shifting yellow values to orange.

14. **Select the Cyan channel in the Hue/Saturation window.**
15. **Move the Hue slider to the right, for example to +26.**
16. **Move the Lightness slider to the right, to +29, for example (32.15).**

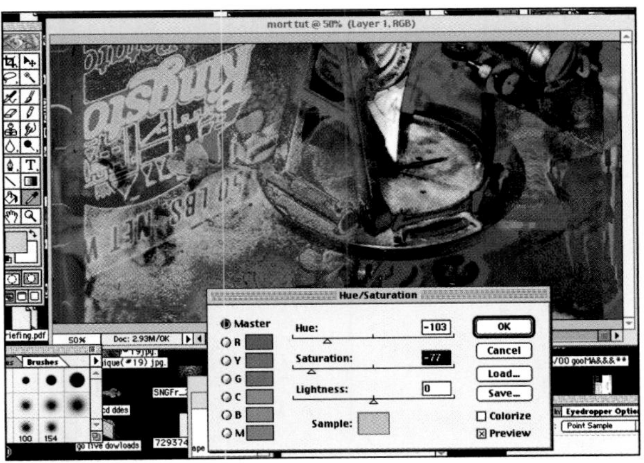

● 32.13

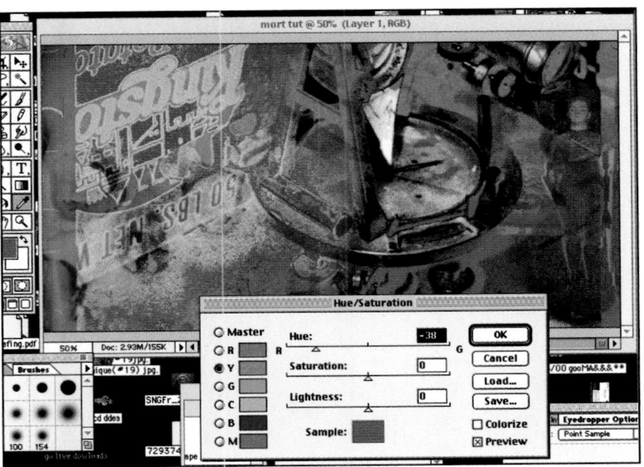

● 32.14

[NOTE]

The slider values given in these steps are completely arbitrary; you should experiment and see what effect you like best. You can also apply the same sort of experimentation to Levels, Curves, and Color Balance (all under the Image→Adjust pop-up menu).

Artist's Creative Insight and Advice

Why Digital?

In the case of *Mort Mechanique,* the computer gave me the opportunity and creative power to achieve a satisfying Rauschenberg-type result in a relatively short time. Using non-digital media to achieve a similar result would have required an extremely difficult and time-consuming series of traditional printmaking processes. With this picture, I felt that I had found my graphic vocabulary. I felt I could, from that point on, manufacture visually anything that I could imagine.

Advice to Artists Working in the Digital Medium

Experiment! This is the key to success: long trial and error experimentation, with every paste, with every element. Exhaust your possibilities. Make many experimental versions of your work.

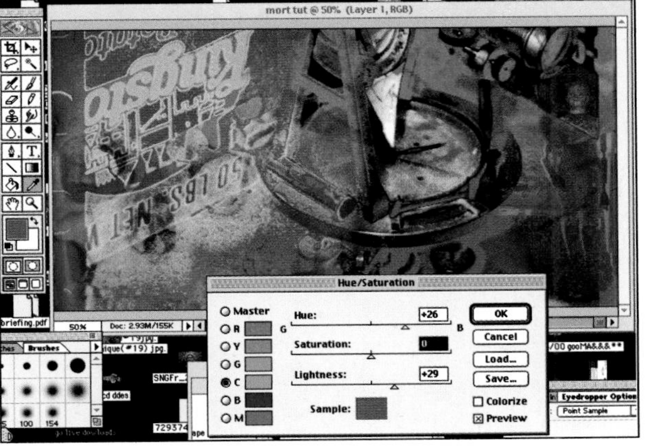

● 32.15

Chapter 33

Digital Ecstasy

by Stephen Burns

Artist's Statement

The genesis of the Chrome-Allusion process, the name I give to the process I use in my artwork, went beyond merely eliciting an emotional response — I aimed instead at the spiritual in art. In expressing the spiritual, I bring out an infusion of energy pulsating through, in, and around my imagery, thus giving each creation a life of its own. Chrome-Allusion suggests a fresh approach to harmony in that it appeals through color, form, rhythm, and void to the sixth sense we all possess yet seldom utilize.

I strive for my work to represent energy composed in such a way that the viewer senses in the work an embodiment of life on a rhythmical scale.

The Story Behind the Artwork

For Stephen, it's important that his creations are contemplated and appreciated in an analytical manner; it is also important that the viewer receives a harmonious experience. The goal of his art is the stimulation of the imagination.

The Creative Process

Digital Ecstasy (33.1) began with a portrait of a model that was originally photographed in Joshua Tree

◀ 33.1

National Park with a Cannon A2E using Fuji 100 F (fine grain) film. (Fuji 100 F uses a grain technology similar to the T-Max films. The actual grains are platelets overlapping one another to give the enlarged image finer detail and sharpness. He finds that this film is wonderful for scanning but suggests experimenting to see what works best with the artist's technique.) He chose Joshua Tree National Park because he was attracted to the dynamic, free flowing stone formations juxtaposed on the softness of the female form. He also chose this location because of its sense of texture; *Digital Ecstasy* had to have texture to be successful.

Stephen's work is based on spontaneity, and the end results depend upon his willingness to listen to his gut instincts. The process described here is not a preset process he follows, but rather the result of an intuitive and spontaneous journey.

When Stephen first began working on *Digital Ecstasy,* he began hunting for objects with dissimilar properties. Also, each object had to be visually degrading, as if time and the environment were taking its toll. He found two objects that fit these qualifications: a bunch of leaves (33.2) that were brown,

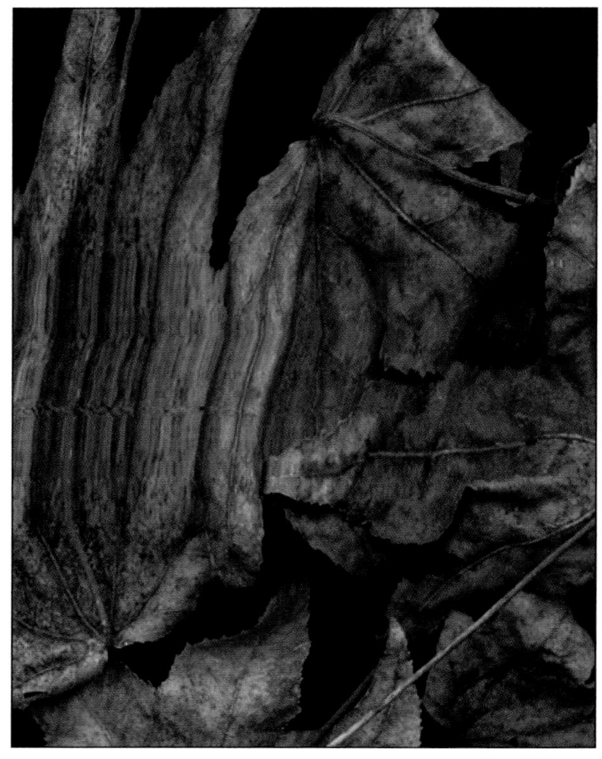

● 33.2

About the Artist

Biography

For the past seven years, Stephen has been an instructor of photography at the Craft Center Extension at UCSD. He teaches subject such as Advanced Darkroom Techniques, Commercial Lighting Techniques, and Digital Cameras. He instructs extensive public and private workshops and presents public lectures on the use of digital as a fine art form. He is also a corporate trainer specializing in the use of digital as an output for both photographic studios and lab use. His work has been exhibited internationally, including the South African Bienalle, Cultural Museum of Tijuana, Tatham Art Museum, Pietermaritzburg (South Africa), and Durban Art Museum, Durban (South Africa) to name a few. He has recently been selected First Place of the prestigious Seybold Seminars Digital Contest.

Stephen is currently the president of the San Diego Photoshop Users Group. He founded the international touring group of fine artists called D-5, Digital Visionaries. He is the annual guest lecturer for the E-Arts International Digital Contest in Del Mar, California, and also the guest lecturer and in-house instructor for the Natural History Museum of San Diego.

Influences

Although his career began as a photographer, his greatest influences were from the great painters, especially those of the early 20th century. Some of these include Jackson Pollock, Franz Kline, Georgia O'Keefe, Joan Miro, Francis Bacon, Roberto Matta, Max Beckman, Arshile

chipped, and cracking from age and lack of water. He found the leaves in his neighborhood. The other object was some newspaper (33.3) that he found laying around the garbage can; the texture was different enough from the leaves, so he thought it would be of use. He then placed the leaves and newspaper on his HP 6300c scanner and scanned them with the maximum resolution of 1200 ppi.

Stephen used a Nikon 4000 scanner to scan the transparency of the model at the maximum resolution of 4000 ppi, giving an image size of 60 megabytes.

He began working with the original portrait and duplicated the base layer of the model so that he always had the original if at any time he wanted to return to the untouched image.

He then added a layer mask in Photoshop to isolate the portrait from its original background. Next, he added an adjustment layer of brightness and contrast to make some subtle luminance changes to the portrait layer.

He then dragged in the leaf scan as a separate layer and applied the same layer mask that was used on the portrait layer. The shape of the leaf layer now

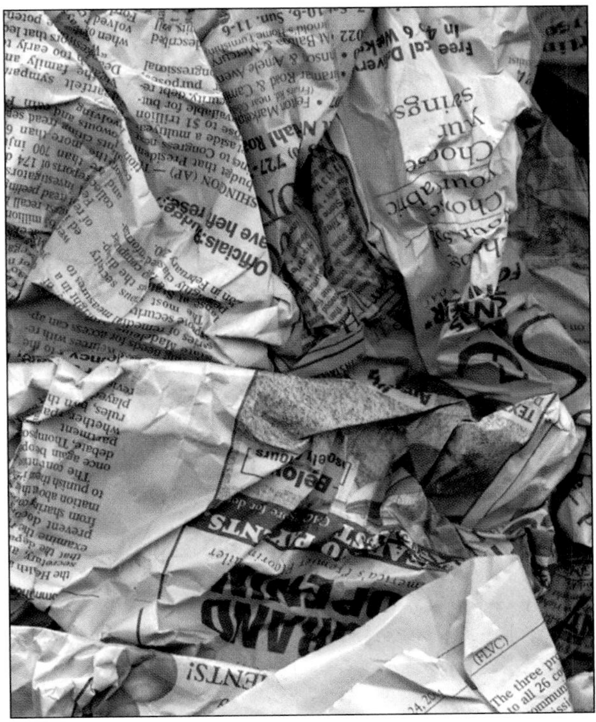

● 33.3

Gorky, Toshitsu Imai, Joel Peter Witkin, Richard Diebenkiorn, Jean Dubuffet, Mark Tobey, Francis Bacon, Robert Motherwell, Mark Rothko, Hans Hoffman, Willem de Kooning, and Paul Klee, to name only a few. One of Stephen's inspirations for his Chrome-Allusion energy principle is Maholy Nagy's Vital Construction Theory, which states that art should reflect the rhythm of life or the energy that brings life.

Some of the influences behind Stephen's fascination with blending the animate and the inanimate are Joel Peter Witkin, H. R. Giger, and Fini Lenor. In his opinion, they have created art works that merge the living and the decaying; however, the dominating message of their use of the technique resonates with death. Burns feels that properly explored, it is one of many approaches to achieving a sense of life and energy on a rhythmic scale.

Studio

Home-Built Computer System:

Dual PIII 850 MHz processors
1.5GB of RAM
6 @ 37GB SCII Cheetas
6 @ 40GB IBM ultra DMA
(All of these are internal drives)

Monitors:

Two 19-inch Viewsonic monitors

Tablet:

Wacom 9 x 12 Tablet

Software:

Adobe Photoshop
Adobe Illustrator
procreate Painter
Lightwave 3D
Newtek Video Toaster
Nik Color EFX
Nik Sharpener

Removable Media:

250 Iomega Zip Drive

Archive Media:

CD Burner

Input Devices:

HPScanjet 6300c
Nikon 4000 Coolscan
Sony VX 2000 Video camera

Printers:

Epson Photo Stylus 1280

Contact

Stephen M. Burns
Encinitas, California
chrome@ucsd.edu
www.go.to/chromeallusion.com

represented the shape of the model's body, which blended the two images together.

After duplicating the leaf layer, Stephen adjusted the opacities of both leaves layers and set the blending mode of both to Multiply. Then he created two new adjustment layers, one for hue and saturation and the other for selective color and tweaked the settings until he got the fungi green color in the leaf layers.

Again he duplicated one of the leaf layers with the mask and dragged the new layer above the working layers. He inverted the mask associated with the layer so that the leaf showed around the perimeter of the model's body, creating an interesting background. To enhance the effect, he added a brightness and contrast adjustment layer to the background leaf to enrich its luminosity.

Next, Stephen added a special effect that he created through his camera. After dragging the effect into the image file, he set its layer mode to Difference (33.4).

He then used layer masking to block the elements of the light streaks that were not important. He also incorporated the scan of the newspaper to add interesting texture to the garment worn by the model (33.5).

Finally, he added some lens flare to give the final image a sense of energy. This was the last touch needed to finish the piece (33.6).

It took Stephen approximately three weeks to create this image. Often, longer periods of creation help him to view the image in a fresh way each time that he comes back to work with it. This gives him the opportunity to break away from any preconceived patterns of creative thought and forces him to become more daring in the creative process.

● 33.4

Technique: Chrome-Allusion Colorization and Overlaying Images (Photoshop)

This technique describes the way Stephen combined different images — in the case of *Digital Ecstasy,* combining the portrait of the model with the scanned leaves, overlaying one above the other and then altering their colorization by means of adjusting layer opacities and blending modes.

For simplicity, we refer to the portrait as the background image and leaves as the image to be combined with the portrait. Naturally, you can use any two

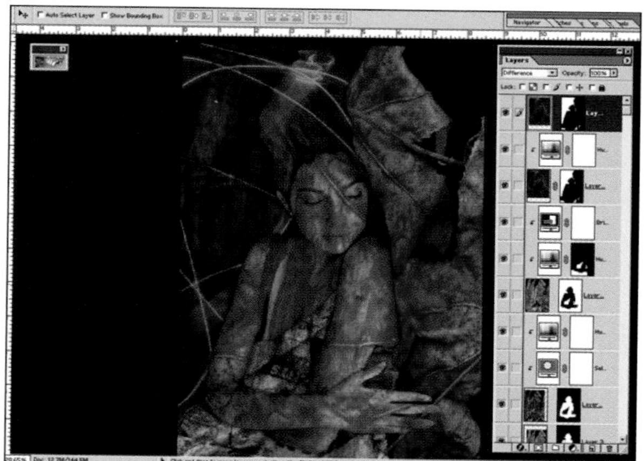

● 33.5

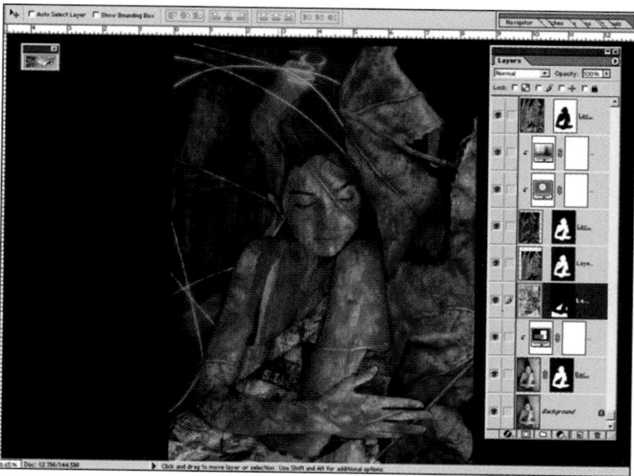

● 33.6

images for this technique, and can expand it for multiple images within the same composition.

1. **Open the original portrait in Photoshop in RGB mode.**
2. **Choose Duplicate Layer in the Layers palette pop-up menu.**
   This duplicates the base layer (Background) of the portrait image. You see a layer generated called Background copy. Doing this ensures that you always have the original if at any time you want to return to the untouched image.
3. **With the Background copy layer highlighted in the Layers palette, click on the second icon from the left in the bottom of the Layers palette.**
   This generates a layer mask associated with the Background copy layer.
4. **Select the Airbrush tool.**
5. **Select black for the foreground color.**
6. **Paint on the layer mask around the model allowing the background to fade away.**
   Painting on the layer mask with black creates transparency on the layer. By painting around the figure, you isolate the portrait from its original background. This allows any background imagery that you drag into the scene to show around the portrait more effectively.

[NOTE]

Stephen always uses a soft edge brush with the edge hardness slider set to zero so that he can make subtle changes along the edges of the mask. Its opacity is usually set to 12% to protect against drastic tonal transitions. The size of the brush changes constantly depending on the size of the area he is working on.

7. **Choose Layer→New Adjustment layer→ Brightness/Contrast.**
8. **Adjust the Brightness/Contrast sliders to make subtle luminance changes to bring more prominence to the portrait layer (33.7).**
9. **Use the Move tool to drag in your additional image elements, in Stephen's case the scanned leaves, as a separate layer.**
   Expect the file size of the document that you are dragging into to increase in size.
10. **Ctrl-left click (Windows) or Cmd-click (Macintosh), clicking on the layer mask icon in the Layers palette that you generated in step 3.**
    This makes a selection of the portrait based on the layer mask.
11. **Making sure that the scanned leaves layer is highlighted in the Layers palette, click (left-click for Windows users) on the second icon from the left at the bottom of the Layers palette.**
    This applies the same layer mask that was used on the portrait layer to the scanned leaves layer. The shape of the scanned leaves layer is now the same shape as that of the model's body (33.8).
12. **Choose Duplicate Layer from the Layers palette pop-up menu.**
    This duplicates the scanned leaves layer.
13. **Set the opacity of the top (duplicated leaves) layer to 68% in the Layers palette.**
14. **Set the opacity of the lower (original leaves) layer to 16%.**

● 33.7

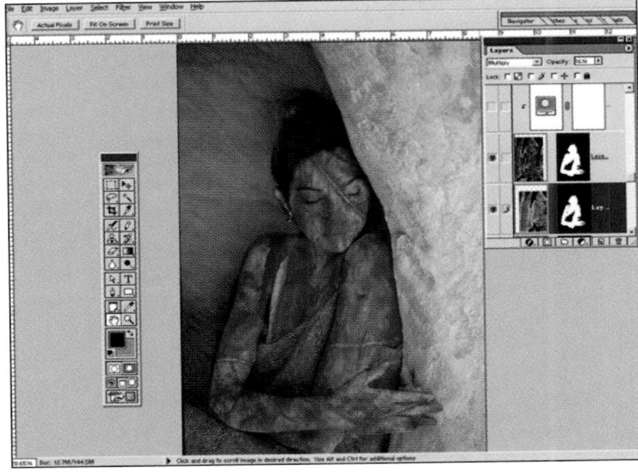

● 33.8

15. **Set the blending mode of both leaves layers to Multiply in the Layers palette.**
16. **Choose Layer→New Adjustment layer→Hue/Saturation.**
17. **Adjust the Hue/Saturation sliders to make visual enhancements to the leaves layers.**
18. **Choose Layer→New Adjustment layer→Selective Color.**
19. **Adjust the Selective Color sliders to make visual enhancements to the leaves layers.**
    In *Digital Ecstasy,* Stephen tweaked the settings until he got a fungi green color in the leaf layers that he liked (33.9).

[NOTE]

Color is extremely important to Stephen because it can evoke certain emotional elements in the human psyche. By varying intensities and contrasts, a spiritual vibration is set up that can generate new awareness in the viewer. On a simple level, colors such as red might denote qualities like will power, freedom, vitality, and action, while blue could reflect love, spiritual enlightenment, and gentleness. If those qualities are accessed in the artwork, the viewer can relate to the work on more of a spiritual and psychological level rather than merely emotional.

When you are tweaking the Adjustment layer settings in your own work, bear in mind the spiritual and psychological influence on the viewer of the colors you select. These color choices are at the heart of the Chrome-Allusion colorization effect.

20. **With one of the leaves layers highlighted in the Layers palette, choose Duplicate Layer from the Layers palette pop-up menu.**
21. **Drag the new layer above the working layers.**
22. **Left-click (Windows) or click (Macintosh) on the mask of the new layer.**
23. **Choose Ctrl-I (Windows) or Cmd-I (Macintosh).**
    This inverses the mask associated with the new layer. Now the leaves show around the perimeter of the model's body, creating an interesting background.
    As a final touch, you can enhance the overall effect by adding a Brightness/Contrast Adjustment layer to the lowest leaves layer, and increase its luminosity (33.10).

Artist's Creative Insight and Advice

Why Digital?

Digital has been a means for me to marry the painting traditions with the pictorial.

Advice for Artists Working in the Digital Medium

Be patient and keep it simple at first. Look at the art of the masters who were innovative in their day and be influenced by them as a means to become unique yourselves.

Most importantly, share with others! This is the first lesson to becoming a master.

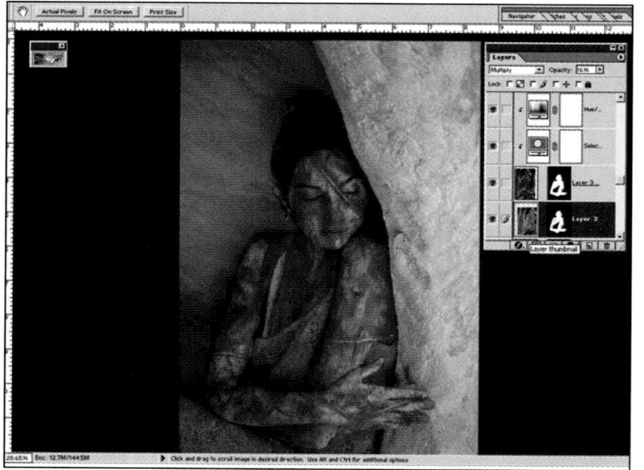

● 33.9

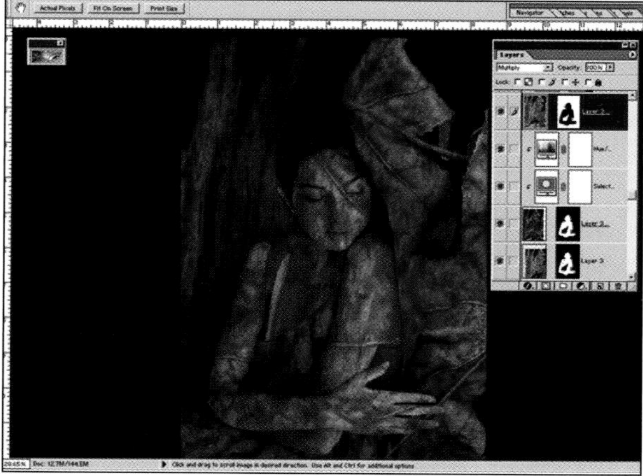

● 33.10

Rick Smolan on Burns' *Digital Ecstasy*

"I enjoyed the dreaminess of the image — the way what surrounded the girl seemed to represent her dreams rather than what was actually around her. The spots of light moving along the cables entangling her were subtle and evoked images of neurons and synapses connecting. The newspaper in which she appeared to be wrapped made it feel like she was plugged into a matrix of information, and the colors of the image were also soothing."

— Rick Smolan, Digital Photographer, Founder, Against All Odds Productions (`www.againstallodds.com`)

Chapter 34

Orrery

by Greg Daville

Artist's Statement

I am a multi-media/mixed-media artist who allows the idea to dictate the medium I work in. As well as interactive/digital and Web-based art, this approach informs all my work, which includes conceptual sculpture and drawing. I am also a writer and am presently working on a surrealist mystery novel entitled *Harbinger's Net.*

The Story Behind the Artwork

Many years ago, at a car boot sale in his hometown of Brighton, Greg came across a small, battered suitcase that contained old letters and photographs. The suitcase contained a scrapbook of intriguing performance photographs that all originated many decades ago.

Greg used these old performance photos as a basis for a body of work called *Spectacles,* the second part of a series called *The Fourth Door. The Fourth Door* refers to the theatrical stage, and how it can be viewed as a door to another world. The initial idea of *The Fourth Door* series was to present the theatrical stage as a setting, not for a performance, but for a tableau or spectacle. He wanted this series of images to have an absurdist flavor.

When he initially began work on this self-initiated project, he wanted it exhibited as a cycle of collages that became more colorful as the viewer moved from one to the next, then gradually receded back to black and white, thus completing the circle.

Spectacles is concerned less with color, and more with the appropriation of old/classic black-and-white photographs (like the ones he came across in the suitcase) as the source material. The more he uses the computer as a creative tool, the less he wants the work to exhibit signs of this particular means of production.

◀ 34.1

One example of the *Spectacles* series is the picture you see here, *Orrery,* (34.1) based on an old photo of a plate spinner (34.2). As the image began to grow, Greg realized that it was beginning to look like an orrery, a clockwork model of the planetary system, named after the 4th Earl of Orrery, for whom one was made.

The Creative Process

Greg constructed the "orrery" (main spiral structure) from one of the spirals, and other elements, in the original image. These select elements were cut out, copied, pasted, and flipped horizontally to form a symmetrical structure. He then selected and copied portions of this structure, duplicating layers over and over again, each time aligning them with the Move tool and distorting them with the Edit→Transform→Distort command until he had constructed the main spiral structure.

● 34.2

Approximately 18 layers of spirals were then individually altered. He carefully deleted sections of the spirals to give the illusion that they circled in front and behind each other as a single continuous spiral. He altered the opacity and feathering of each spiral layer by different amounts to give the impression of three-dimensional perspective (some parts appearing to recede while others came forward). When he was satisfied with the spiral structure, he merged all the layers into a single layer.

All the plates on the spiral were hand cut and copied from the plates on the table. These were then layered onto the spiral structure and individually distorted using the Edit→Transform→Distort and Edit→Transform→Perspective commands. The rods that support the small planet and moon at the top left were hand cut from the runway below the plate-spinner, then copied, pasted, and rotated.

Orrery is by no means perfectly rendered — not everything is completely smoothed out. Greg purposely embraces this low-tech quality as it is closer to the paper collage process and retains a resonance of the original image.

Greg generated a pattern of crosses (34.3) for the floor surface. He hand-made the crosses by simply filling color into squares, which he copied and pasted into crosses (the crucifix and the addition sign). Using layers, he aligned them appropriately until he had a filled square. The layers were flattened and the crosses image was selected and defined as a pattern, which he then used to fill an A4 document.

About the Artist

Biography

Greg obtained a Master of Arts from the Royal College of Art in 1985. He has been a practicing artist since then, working in a variety of media including video, installation, assemblage, and drawing.

He has made digital art for the last ten years. His latest digital piece, (an interactive Dadaist CD-ROM) called *KNOB: [monkey opera],* was a finalist at Milia 2002, Cannes, France, and was purchased by the Biblioteque Nationale de France, Paris.

Examples of his book art are in the collection of the Victoria and Albert Museum, London.

Greg's digital collages have been represented in the top 100 Digital Artists by the I.D.A.A. for the last two years (see `www.worlddigitalart.com`). He has shown his work world wide, including solo exhibitions in London and New York.

He also writes, and examples can be found in *Brought to Book,* edited by artist Ian Breakwell, published by Penguin.

Greg took the flat pattern and then applied perspective from the Transform menu. He used the Move tool to drag this into the main collage, and distorted and resized the crosses layer until it took on the floor-like appearance he was looking for. He duplicated the crosses layer, slightly offsetting one layer, and then reduced the layer opacities to 40%. This gave a blurred look to the pattern (34.4).

Greg also added a herringbone pattern for the back wall. The herring bone pattern originated from a zigzag line that suggested itself when he copied, pasted, and flipped the original image as a starting point. He copied the small runway that runs below the plate man's hand and pasted it onto the other side of the stage. He repeated this hundreds of times, creating a separate layer which he then inverted and reduced in opacity to form the wall texture. He then made a very detailed selection of the plate-spinning man himself and saved it. He used this to cut into the herringbone pattern to accentuate the illusion of it being behind him. He used the same selection to generate his shadow. From this selection he made a small outline of the man's hand, which he used on a separate layer as a fill to create the shadow that falls across the third plate from the left.

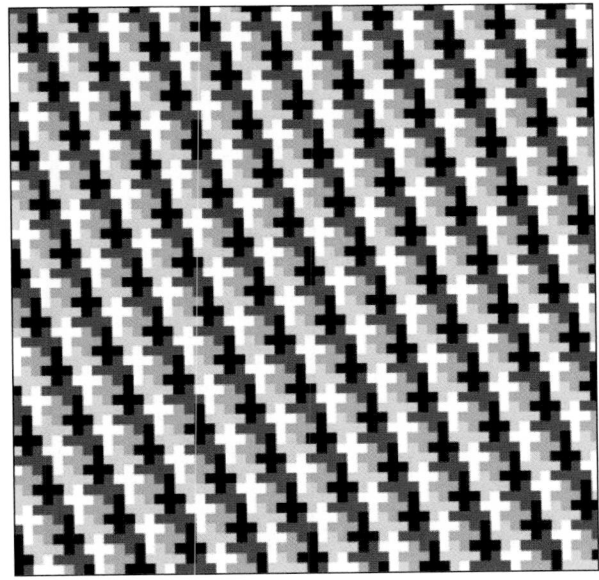

● 34.3

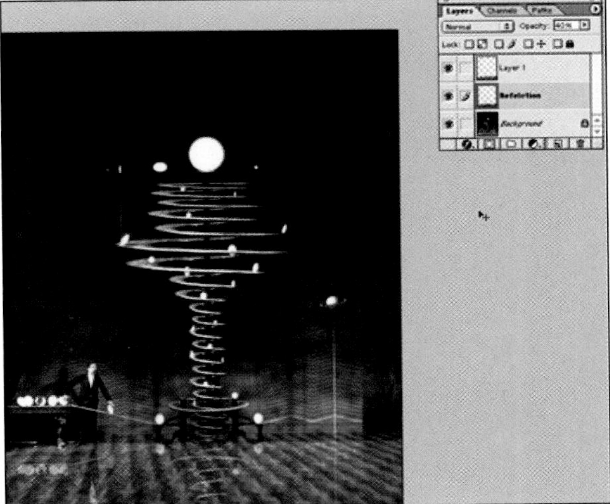

● 34.4

Influences

Marcel Duchamp, Vermeer, Joseph Cornell, Robert Fludd, Bill Viola, Rose English, Cornelia Parker, Leonardo Da Vinci, Marc Bolan, Don Van Vliet, Roland Barthes, and T.S. Eliot.

Studio

Computer System:
Apple Mac G3 laptop
6GB hard drive
512 RAM

Monitors:
Sony 19-inch

Software:
Adobe Photoshop
Macromedia Dreamweaver
Macromedia Director

Removable Media:
Iomega 100MB Zip

Archive Media:
La Cie 20GB portable

Input Devices:
Umax Astra 3400
Fujifilm Fine Pix 4700 digital camera

Printers:
Epson Stylus Photo 1200 (A3+)

Contact

Greg Daville
Brighton, England
art@gallery-daville.co.uk
www.gallery-daville.co.uk
www.site-to-be-destroyed.co.uk

You can see in the early version pictured here (34.5) the floor pattern looking as if it was draped over the edge of a stage.

Greg generated shadows for the large central structure and the man, each shadow on a different layer (34.6).

34.5

To create these shadows, Greg used the Magic Wand tool to select around the orrery (which was by now on a single layer). He inverted and saved the selection, feathered it to 24 pixels, filled it with black, and then reduced the opacity. He duplicated the layer and applied both Edit→Transform→Scale and Edit→Transform→Distort.

He also added an outside pattern that ran around the sides and top of the image (34.7).

This border or curtain suggestion was simply a section of the curtain that rises behind the plates in the original. Greg copied sections of the original curtain, pasted and flipped them vertically, building up the border as he did so.

Greg added reflections of the man and the central object (34.8), giving the floor the appearance of a shiny reflective surface.

Throughout the process of constructing this image, Greg used his "non-digital look" cut-out technique (described in more detail later in this chapter) to isolate various elements in the image. You can see here examples of the alpha channels he generated from the cut-out selections (34.9 and 34.10).

Greg spent many days of painstaking work on this image, while working on many other collages in the *Spectacles* series at the same time.

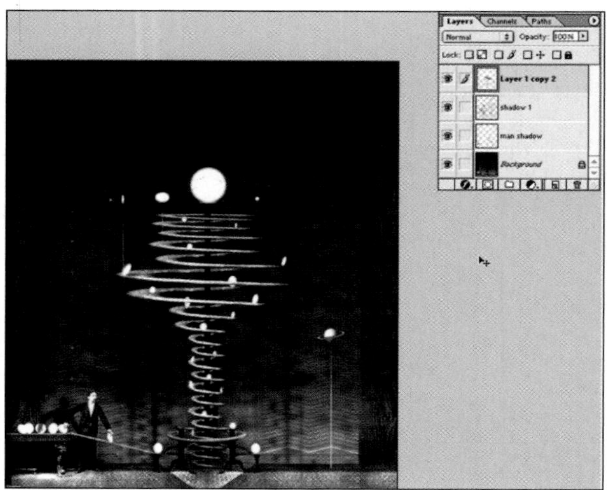

34.6

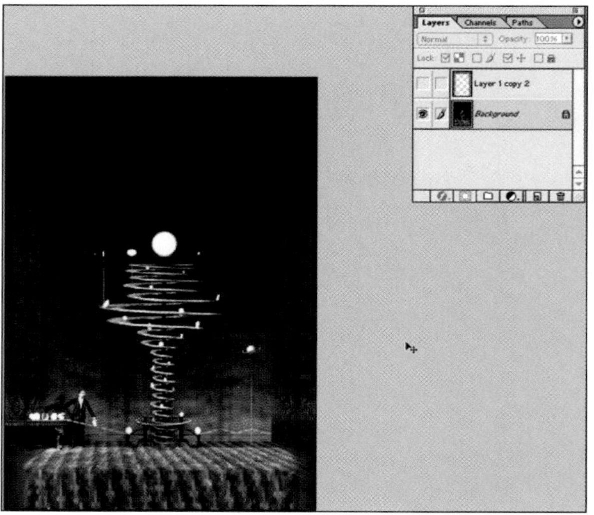

34.7

Technique: Creating the Illusion of an Original Photo from Repeating Cut-Outs (Photoshop)

What stands out in Greg's art is the magical effect he creates using the most simple, basic Photoshop techniques of copy, paste, and flip. He succeeds in creating an illusion that looks like an original photograph of a dramatic and theatrical scene. His is not an image that first conjures up the word *collage*. Yet, in fact, it is a collage.

Photoshop makes it easy to automatically select certain areas, but when dealing with photographic sources, Greg prefers to do it by hand (or mouse). Something as subtle as leaving out the highlights at the edge of a selected area, which might be a figure or object, can often make for a more convincing blend when merged with another layer.

Equally important is a judicious use of feathering. Greg uses it with most selected areas, but usually only at about a couple of pixels on 300 dpi images. Unless the selection requires it, huge feathering can give the image that digital look that he aims to avoid.

This simple technique takes you through the steps Greg used in copying, pasting, and flipping elements from the background source image and putting them together to enlarge the background and make structures.

1. **Open an original source photo in Photoshop (RGB color mode) that you want to use a basis for your collage.**
2. **Select All.**
3. **Choose Edit→Copy.**
4. **Choose Edit→Canvas Size.**

● 34.8

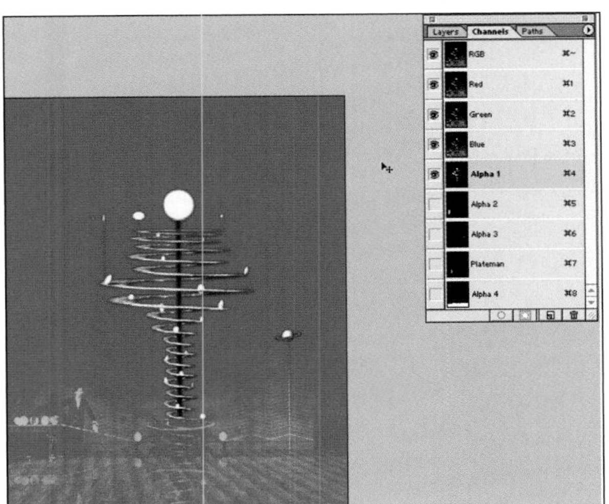

● 34.9

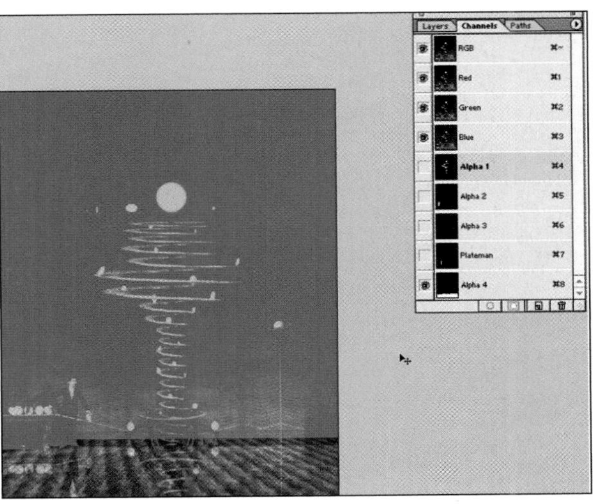

● 34.10

5. **Drag the gray square, (which determines where the original image will stay in relation to the new canvas) to the left and double the width size (34.11). Leave the height as it is.**
6. **Select Edit→Paste.**

   A duplicate version of the original appears as a new layer (34.12).
7. **Choose Edit→Transform→Flip Horizontal.**
8. **Select the Move tool and drag it to the blank area of the canvas (34.13).**
9. **Choose Flatten image from the Layers pop-up menu.**
10. **To enlarge the general working area, repeat all of the previous steps once more.**

    You can expand the canvas size vertically this time (34.14 and 34.15).

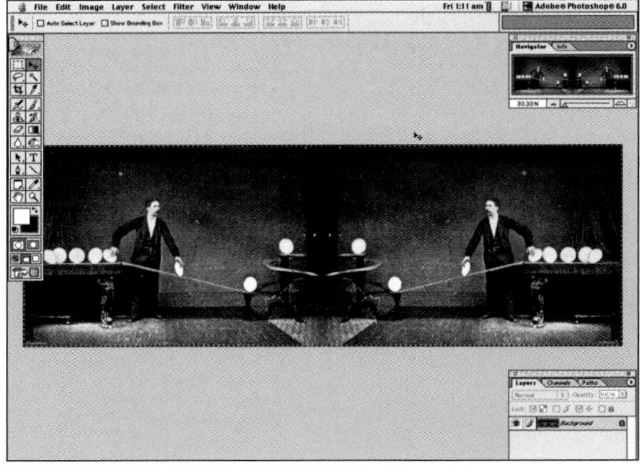

34.13

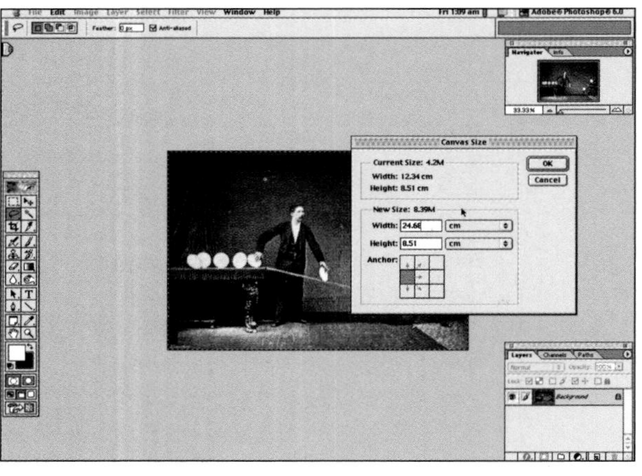

34.11

34.14

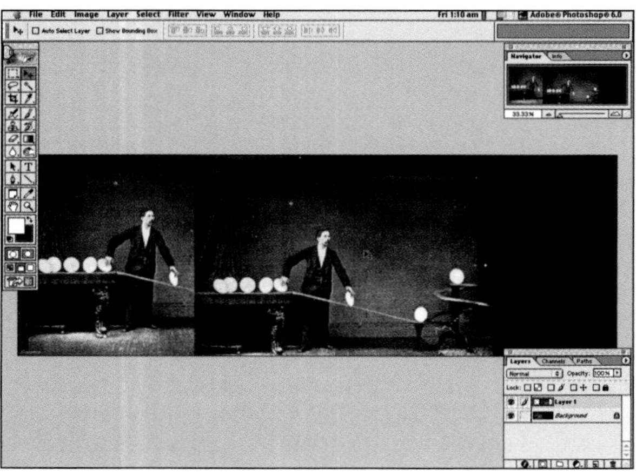

34.12

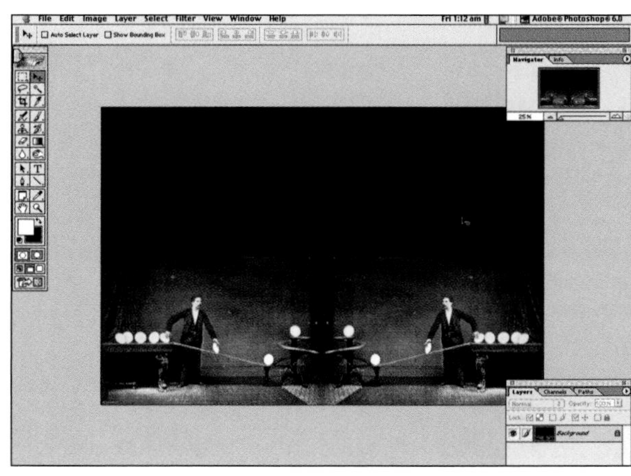

34.15

11. Once again, select all, copy, enlarge the canvas, paste, flip, move, then flatten (34.16 and 34.17).

12. Extend the canvas to your own requirements. Then begin working into the repeated/mirrored areas of the image with the Clone Stamp tool to break down the symmetry (34.18).

You now have a canvas on which to build all the other details of the collage.

13. Begin selecting basic elements with the Rectangle tool.

The illustrations show how Greg selected part of the curtain from the original photograph. This was then feathered by 2 pixels (34.19), copied and pasted to a new layer, then dragged to the other side of the stage (34.20).

34.18

34.16

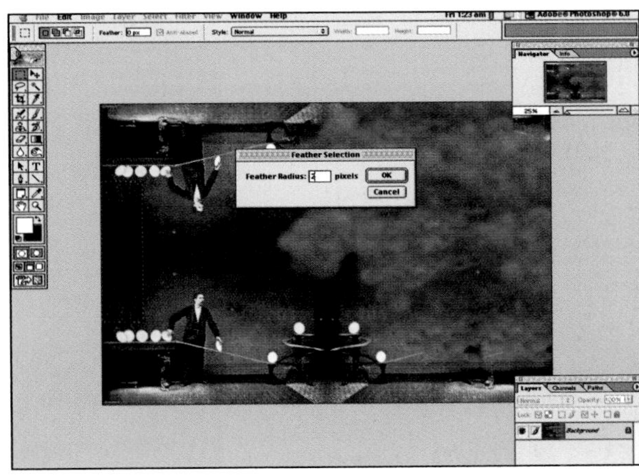

34.19

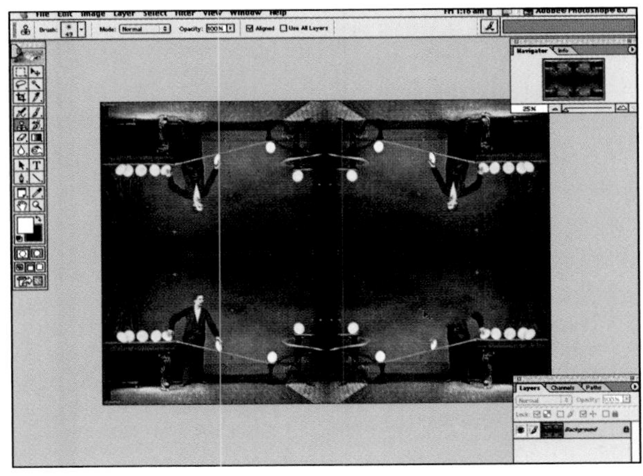

34.17

34.20

This layer was then duplicated and the new length of curtain dragged upwards to extend it, and so on. In Greg's image, once the stage was set, specific elements of the original spiral structure underwent the same procedure, (this time with the Lasso tool) and built up to become the Orrery. You can get an idea of the multi-layered structure of this collage approach by looking at the layers list in this illustration (34.21).

14. **Once you are pleased with the collage as a whole, flatten the image. Then copy and paste the remaining portions of your collage.**

    In Greg's case, he worked on the lower quarter of his image, then flipped the pasted layer vertically, reducing the opacity to 40%. This became the reflection on the stage floor.

[NOTE]

Using elements only from your original image (as described previously), a visual consistency will be obtained in the final image. This simple collage technique gives you generally seamless photographic results.

● 34.21

Artist's Creative Insight and Advice

Why Digital?

I miss the mess of glue, paint, and paper, but I like the fact that you have more control over the stages of the image's development: being able to Undo and Save as. In a way, it's like creating small parallel universes of the same collage, all of which can be visited and edited at the same time.

I think making a collage with real material requires more creative bravery, as actions cannot be undone as on the computer. Perhaps the equivalent digital bravery comes in selecting the final version and sticking to it?

Advice for Artists Working in the Digital Medium

Let *yourself* be the creative director, not the software. Avoid making work that says more about the software effects than the piece itself. Use a minimal amount of effects, sticking to those which are pertinent to evoking a specific ambiance.

Save as you go and always back up your work.

Tips and Insights

I'm not too hot on (or interested in) getting perfect prints. Do not be frightened to experiment. I am getting really interested in printing on non-standard surfaces, like thick watercolor paper (where the inks bleed beautifully) and onto original pages of my notebook and other found documents.

Charmaine Conui on Daville's *Orrery*

"This image provokes nostalgia as well as whimsy. I am reminded of vaudeville stage acts. The images are futuristic, yet vintage in execution. It is a great challenge to combine different elements to create something new, yet old."

— Charmaine Conui, Art Director, Seybold Seminars (`www.seyboldseminars.com`)

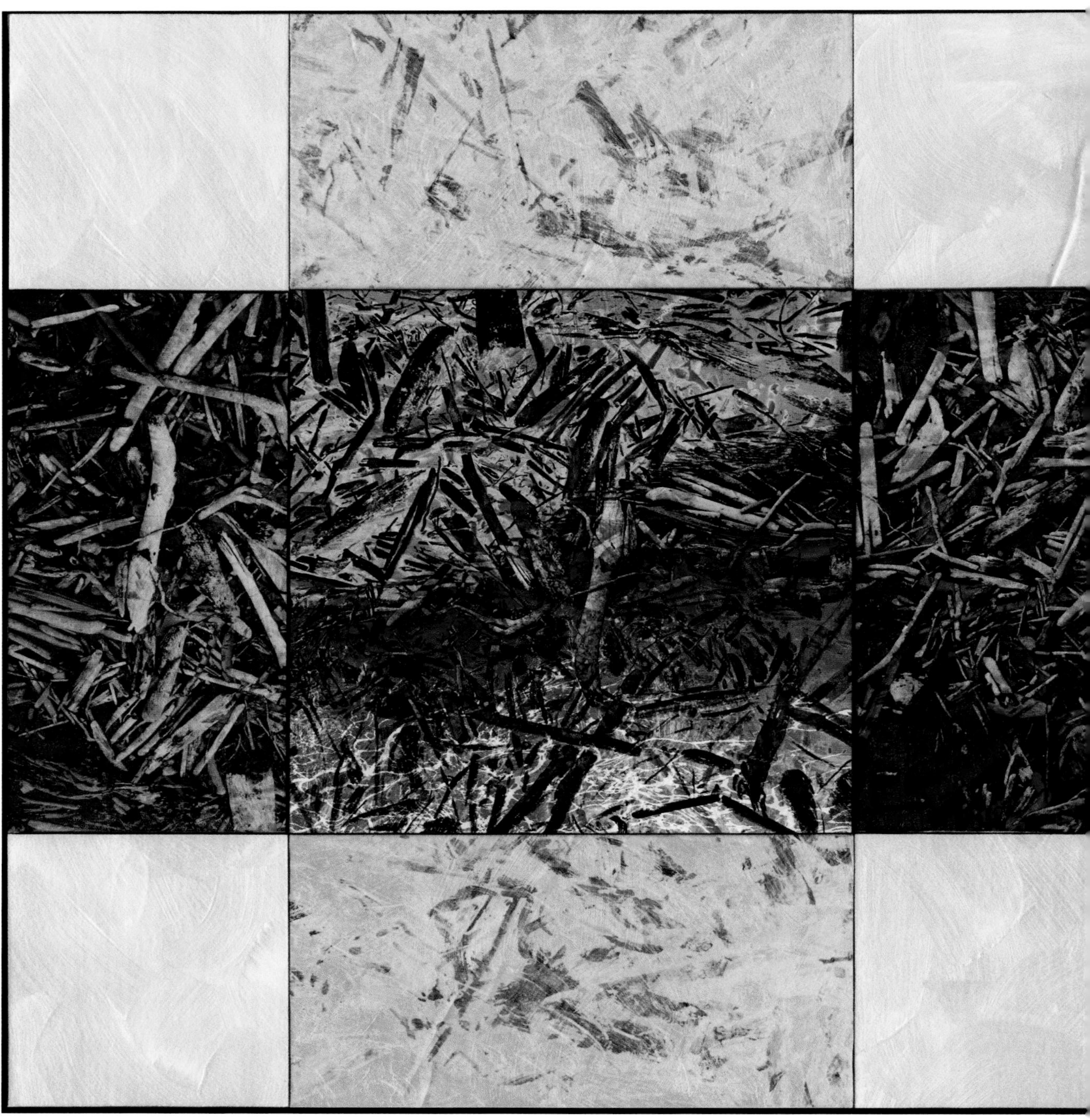

Chapter 35

Tidal Pool

by Karin Schminke

Artist's Statement

Tidal Pool brings the viewer into intimate contact with nature. Subtle textures and patterns are interwoven in a complex manner that is reminiscent of the natural world. The sense of discovery when coming upon a tidal pool is recreated by the center panel's illusion of dimensional shift, which exposes the view beneath the tidal pool surface for exploration.

The illusion of real depth invites viewers to linger and explore, as their movements in front of the image effect their view of the image. The audience employs their own perspective in resolving the elements. In this way, the work becomes a focus of contemplation and meditation, mirroring the role of nature in our lives.

The Story Behind the Artwork

Tidal Pool (35.1) is part of a series of five artworks, collectively called *Xrossings*. The series, which incorporates lenticular technology to give the illusion of three-dimensional depth, deals with opposing forces: of nature, of form, of color, of dimension, and so on.

Tidal Pool is on the borderline between abstraction and representation. The individual imagery is based on photos and scans of wood debris that have been

◀ 35.1

manipulated, distorted, painted on, and transferred until they are barely recognizable. The tiled grid structure of the piece helps abstract and flatten the composition, which complements and contrasts with the three-dimensional realism.

The Creative Process

Tidal Pool consists of nine tiles or panels: a lenticular tile in the center, which gives a sense of three-dimensional depth, surrounded by eight smaller mixed-media tiles. The creative process began with photographic images of driftwood taken by Karin (35.2 and 35.3).

These source images were transferred to a PhotoCD and manipulated in Photoshop. Karin applied a number of different techniques to transform her images and generate variations. One technique was using the Layer Style dialog box to generate a beautiful floating translucent effect (35.4). (This Layer Style manipulation technique is described in detail in the techniques section later in this chapter.)

● 35.2

● 35.3

About the Artist

Biography

Karin Schminke received her MFA from the University of Iowa in 1979 and went on to teach art, design, and digital art classes at the University of Wisconsin-Eau Claire, California State University Northridge, The Art Institute of Southern California, and Shoreline Community College. Since 1994, she has been working full time as an artist. Prior to getting access to digital tools in 1984, Schminke's media was drawing and papermaking. She also was an avid photographer. After a few years of working digitally, she began to integrate all of these media into her art. When she met the other artists of the Digital Atelier in 1994, collaboration began that continues to this day. The exploration of digital technologies for fine artists has resulted in numerous opportunities for regional, national, and international exhibitions, publications, and artist-in-residencies including projects at the Smithsonian National Museum of American Art and The Brooklyn Art Museum.

Influences

Nature has been the largest influence on Schminke's work. Her mentor and graduate

Another technique, used in conjunction with the Layer Style technique, was to change the Layer modes from Normal (35.5) to Overlay (35.6).

In the example shown here, the image generated was one of the component images used for the central tile of the piece. Other variations included a

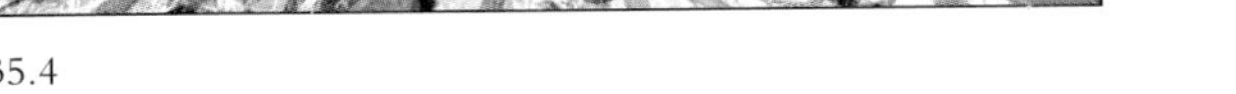

● 35.4

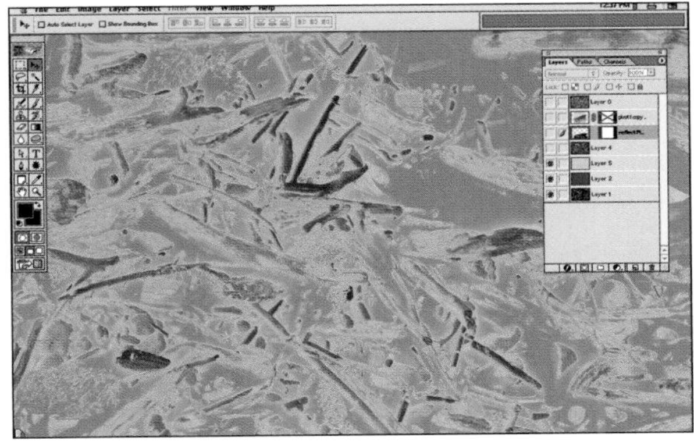

● 35.5

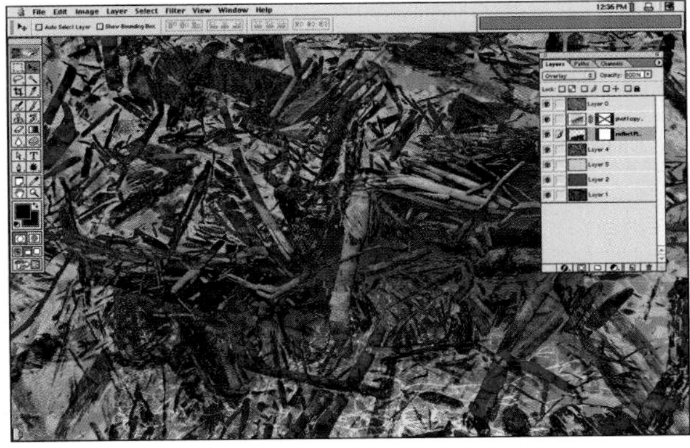

● 35.6

school advisor, Hu Hung Shu, has had a continuing influence upon how she approaches and analyzes her art. She finds inspiration in the purity of the Constructivists and the flat space of Japanese art.

Studio

Computer Systems:

Apple PowerBook Titanium, 500 MHz
20GB hard drive
512MB RAM
Macintosh 8100/100, 200 MHz
8GB hard drive
136MB RAM
Intergraph Extreme Z Windows 2000, dual 300Mhz
18.5GB hard drive
524MB RAM

Monitors:

Apple 17-inch Monitor-Multisync
Intergraph 21SD95

Software:

Adobe Photoshop
Flip!
Quark
Illustrator

Tablet:

Wacom and CalComp, 6 x 8

Input Devices:

Olympus Camedia C-2500L digital camera
Epson Expressions Scanner 836XL

Printers:

Epson Stylus 9500
Encad 880
Textronix Color Laser Printer
Apple LaserWriter IIf

Contact

Karin Schminke
Kenmore, Washington
Karin@schminke.com

predominantly gold one (35.7), used for the top and bottom tiles, and a predominantly blue one (35.8), used for the side tiles. The mixed-media corner tiles were created by painting gold acrylic paint on Tableau paper (35.9).

As the work progressed, the wood turned into thin, delicate forms. Lenticular media, the central media in the *Xrossings* series, was used in *Tidal Pool* to make these delicate forms seem to float in space in separate layers of depth. The result is a playful interaction of form suggesting explorations of deep and colorful tidal pools.

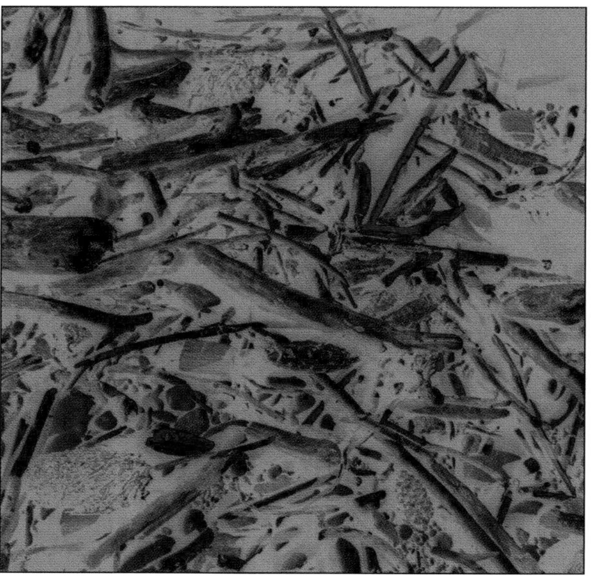

35.7

35.8

Lenticular media allows the viewer to see a series of "frames" sequentially when looking at an image from different angles. By carefully crafting these frames, the artist can create animation, depth, and the morphing of images. A lenticular print utilizes a special lenticular lens, a plastic lens that is made up of many very small lens strips, or *lenticules*, usually oriented vertically, one next to the other. (Please refer to the chapters on the art of Dorothy Simpson Krause and Bonny Lhotka to read about other examples of lenticular technology.)

The individual lenticular layers, or frames, were created in Photoshop. The frames were then interlaced together into a single image (35.10) with Flip! software. The images corresponding to all nine tiles were printed on the Epson Stylus Pro 9500 (35.11).

The central lenticular section image was printed on the 9500 and transferred onto the painted surface of the final piece. Parts of the lenticular image were extended into the surrounding tiles.

Approximately 80 hours were spent creating this work. Many studies were done for both the lenticular and the surrounding panels. It was finished when there was aesthetic continuity among the diverse media.

Technique: Generating Floating Translucent Elements (Photoshop)

In *Tidal Pool,* piles of heavy driftwood were transformed into floating translucent elements. Instead

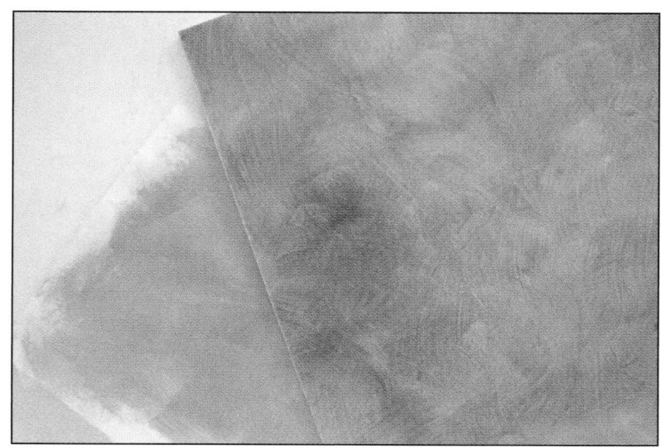

35.9

of working with layer masks to create the transparencies necessary for this task, the Layer Style dialog box provides a simpler and more interactive solution.

1. **In Photoshop, open a RGB file that contains several layers.**
2. **Choose any layer but the background layer.**
   The chosen layer should be highlighted in the Layers palette.
3. **Double-click on the chosen layer in the Layers palette to open the Layer Style dialog box.**
   Notice the area at the bottom center of the dialog box with the label Blend If:, followed by a pop-up menu with the options Gray, Red, Green, and Blue. Leave the default Blend If: Gray selected.
4. **Slide the left (solid black) adjusting triangle to the right in the grayscale slider bar labeled This Layer:, located immediately below the Blend If: label.**
   This begins to eliminate the dark values. You can watch the dark values disappearing in the image as you move the triangle.
5. **Slide the right (hollow) adjusting triangle to the left in the same grayscale slider bar labeled This Layer:.**
   This begins to eliminate the light values. You can watch the light values disappearing in the image as you move the triangle.
   Experiment with these adjustments until you get a look you are satisfied with.
6. **Hold down the Option key while you drag the left side of the triangle apart from the right.**
   This sets up a gradation in the transition from solid form to transparency for that layer (35.12).

[NOTE]

Interesting effects can be achieved by using this technique on several layers. If you have a layer with an image below your chosen layer, you can also determine what areas your chosen image will cover by applying the same technique to the bottom grayscale bar labeled Underlying Layer.

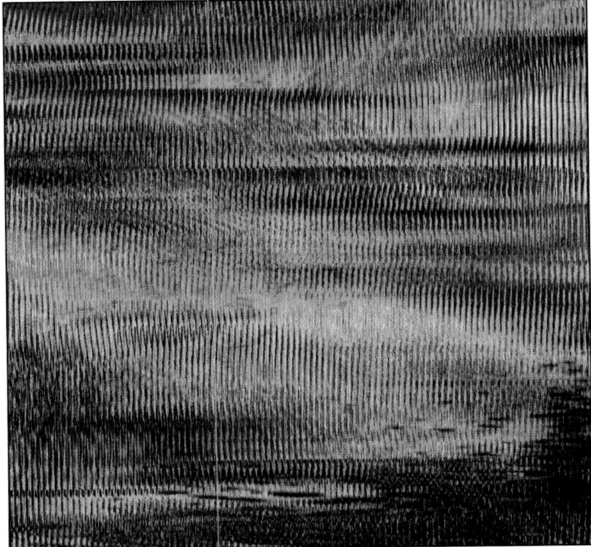

● 35.10

● 35.11

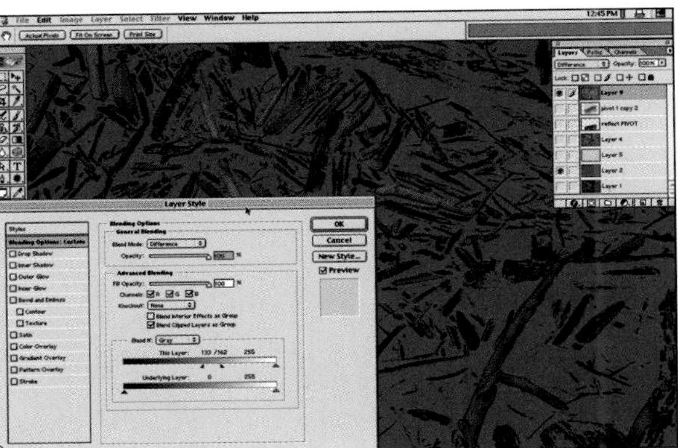

● 35.12

Artist's Creative Insight and Advice

Why Digital?

The computer is a "meta tool" for artists, an umbrella tool that encompasses and enhances all others. It allows the integration of many media in new combinations. It invites the artist to experiment more freely by helping to visualize results, supplying multiples of image elements for testing ideas, and providing a means to break all sorts of rules!

Advice for Artists Working in the Digital Medium

Be experimental and brave!

Don't let concerns with technique overwhelm attention to the art.

Output

Use your artist's eye for color management as every substrate and image created is considered unique. With the Epson Stylus Pro 9500, I find I can predict the color accurately from the LCD monitor on my Macintosh Titanium PowerBook.

My favorite output is mixed media. I really like the effect of layering prints with paints.

Chapter 36

At the Drive-In Theater-of-Consciousness

by Charles Carver

Artist's Statement

I seek to create perceptual forms with a latent potential to unfold into various levels of meanings. I view my art, as well as the process I engage in during its development, as an extension of the creative work performed by the senses and intellect alike — each does not merely copy a ready-made world, but rather, transforms the raw material they receive into new forms and new horizons.

The Story Behind the Artwork

At the time *At the Drive-In* (36.1) was created, Charles was interested in generating a composite image with a somewhat harder edge than his usual body of work, which tended towards an earthy-textural projection of blended forms. He also wanted to develop a composition with an emergent image or figure intimately tied to the background environment.

◀ 36.1

Charles took a series of photographs at a classic car show, in which he focused on abstract shapes and curves (36.2).

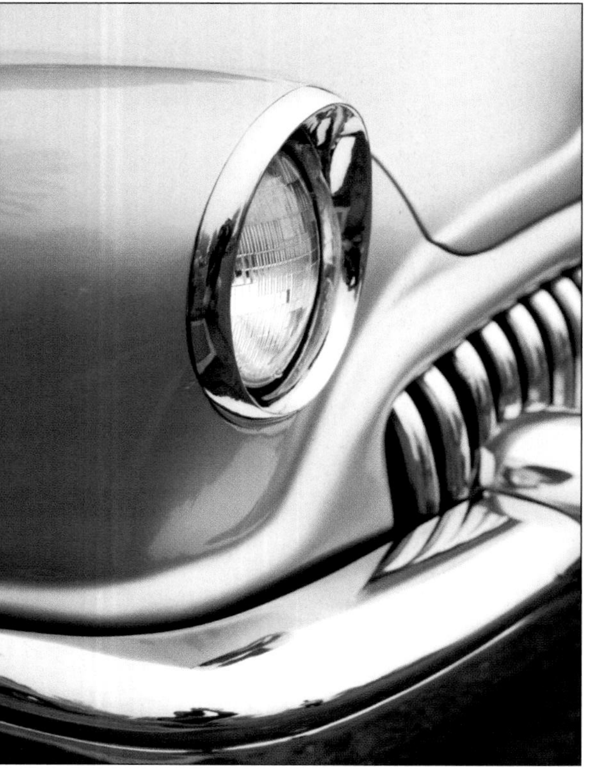

36.2

It took a considerable time for the original visual concept and the final work to emerge. The image matured through a form of dialogue between Charles and the work itself. Charles was receptive to new directions as the composition developed. He created abstract forms by completing shapes suggested by the composition, and by holding on to elements he had initially intended to be temporary guides.

The artwork title, *At the Drive-In Theater-of-Consciousness*, is a play on words. Charles mixed the drive-in theater metaphor, prompted by the classic automobiles that make up this image, with the philosophically false concept of the theater of the mind, a notion where an observer's mind is thought of as a theater in which the observer views the world.

Sweeping forms lead the eye to a central figure: a female form. The structure of the image suggests an overt and tantalizing display of touching and looking through the elements of the car's headlights and strategically placed hands. The central figure seems to delight in the attention it receives from the environment that it has emerged from.

The work is a play on self-awareness. There is a hint that the woman is pregnant. She is a metaphor for a kind of fertile power, which is integral to consciousness. Reflective thought has provided us with the

About the Artist

Biography

Charles Carver started his career as a scientific illustrator and research technician with training in the biological sciences. His work has been featured in *Digital Fine Art Magazine* and has been shown in the United States, Australia, Europe, and Russia through selection into an elite group of digital artists by the 2002 International Digital Art Awards, the 2001 Seybold Seminars Digital Art Awards, and the Macworld Digital Art Contest (years 1998, 1999, and 2000).

Influences

Philosophy of Mind; Phenomenology; time in the natural world.

Studio

Computer System:
Macintosh G4 733
60GB hard drive + 75GB hard drive
1.5GB RAM

feeling that our self is detached from the vehicle of our body. In this composition there is no such clear cut delineation between self and vehicle since the abstraction remains integral to the whole arrangement, just as our thoughts and feelings are integral to our body and our relationship to the world around us.

The Creative Process

Charles is primarily a Photoshop-based artist, so everything preliminary to Photoshop is, to him, preparation, raw material, or outline. In this case, Charles started with a preliminary sketch (non-digital) that he used to generate a preparatory line drawing, or schematic framework, in Adobe Illustrator. In this line drawing, Charles mapped out the main compositional elements.

The original photographs were scanned and opened in Photoshop. Charles experimented with arrangements and juxtapositions (the dialogue with the image) of selected image elements using basic blending techniques. The real trick to the image's formulation was patiently engaging in spontaneous experimentation with the arrangement of forms and how they should blend, as opposed to applying a developed technique or protocol that provided a desired effect.

The central figure was abstracted from a clay figure Charles had previously modeled (36.3). Charles

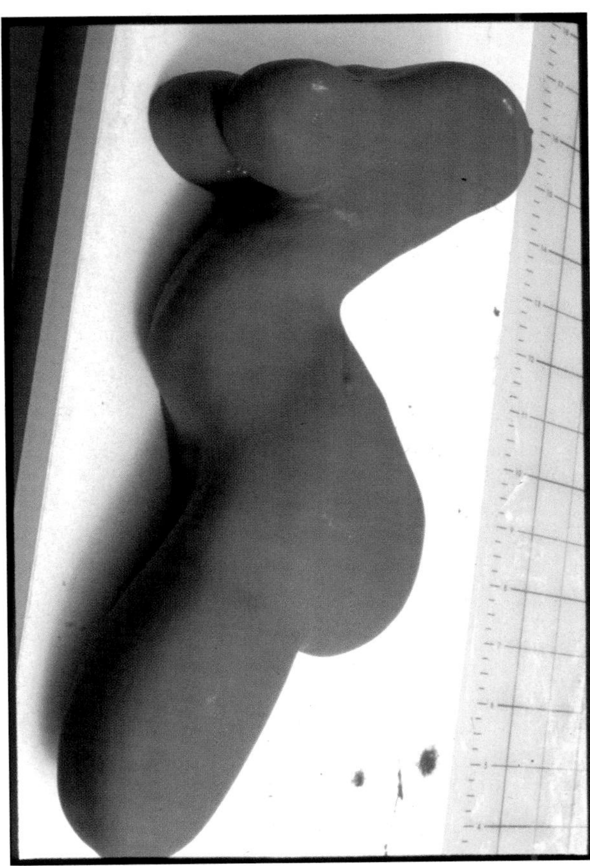

36.3

Monitors:
Apple Display Cinema 22-inch flat-screen monitor

Software:
Adobe Photoshop
Painter
Final Cut Pro
Adobe Illustrator

Tablet:
Wacom Intuos Tablet 9 x 12

Input Devices:
Nikon Super Coolscan 4000 ED
Agfa DuoScan

Printers:
Epson Stylus Photo 2000P

Contact

Charles H. Carver
New Paltz, New York
ccarver@hvc.rr.com
www.eyeandmindstudio.com
www.thecarvergroup.com

made a pencil sketch (non-digital) of the clay figure (36.4).

He scanned this hand-drawn rough sketched figure and opened it in Adobe Illustrator. The sketch was used in Illustrator as a guide for bezier curves to be smoothed out upon it according to its general flow. Thus a bezier line drawing with smooth curves was generated in Illustrator (36.5).

Charles imported the whole Illustrator line image as a bitmap into Photoshop. He used the imported image as a reference template over which he started placing the scanned car forms as new layers. He also generated selections around bounded sections from that bitmap into which he placed images. The figure became the organizing element around which the sweeping surfaces of the car photographs radiated (36.6).

● 36.4

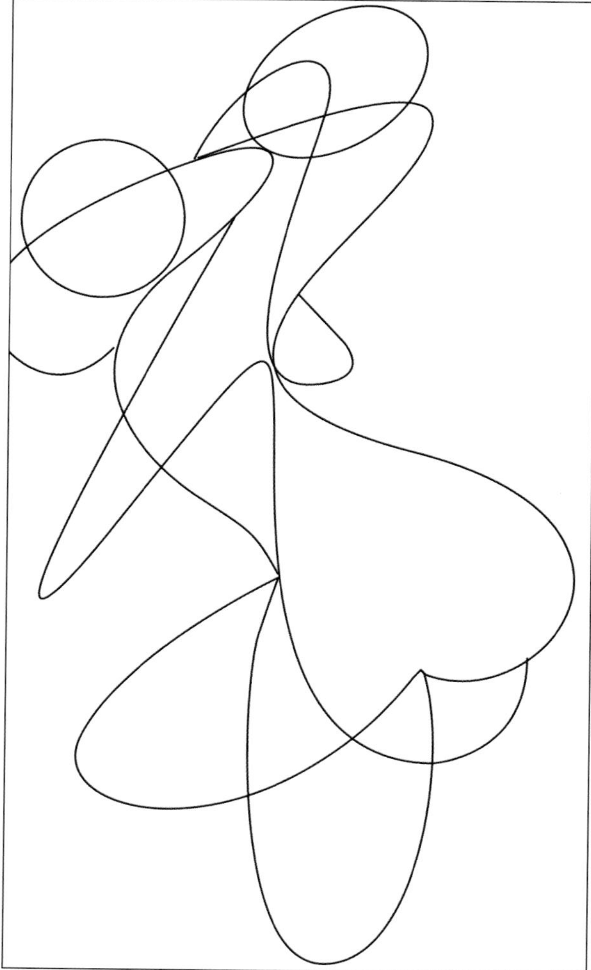

● 36.5

Charles introduced elements of other imagery of the classic vehicles, adjusting opacity, hue, and saturation of the layers as he did (see the technique later in this chapter).

The next step was to add the figurative elements (36.7) and clothing (36.8) taken from a couple of photographs of Charles' wife, Lisa (36.9).

The photos of Charles' wife were introduced as layers. They were duplicated, with the bottom layer being left in normal mode. Charles played with modes and percentages in the stacked layers. He found that selecting either screen mode or soft light mode added a luminous quality to the layers. With these images of Lisa, sections of the different photos had to be moved to the appropriate sections of the developing central figure. Their placement dictated

● 36.6

● 36.7

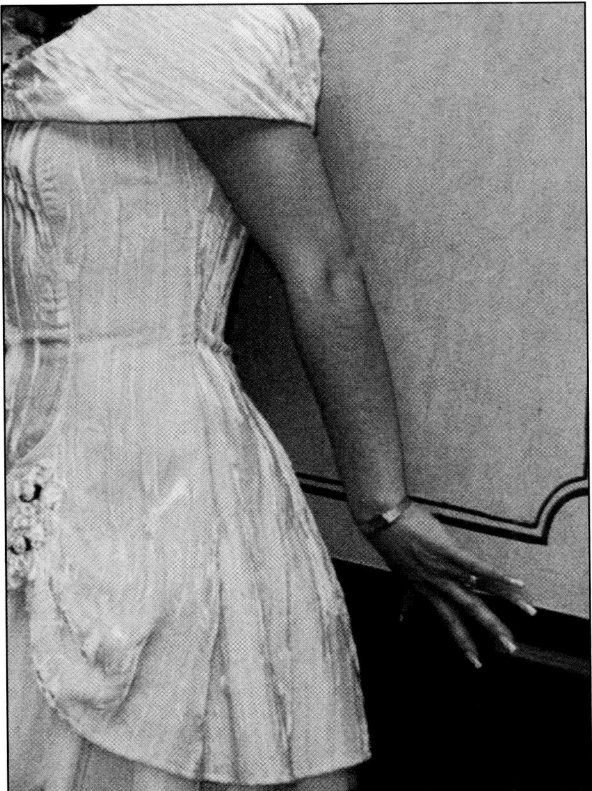

● 36.8

● 36.9

which transparency levels and layer modes to use (36.10).

At that point Charles added reflective references on the surfaces that showed photographs of him taking photographs of his wife (36.11). The newborn baby sketch was added at that point as well.

The composition took approximately two months of working and reworking the surface to the desired balance. Charles knew it was finished when he continued to receive only negative returns for his investment in what-ifs. The very last step was to bring the image into Painter and smooth out portions of the image with a smeary brush for a cohesive look.

36.10

36.11

Technique: Adjusting Layer Opacity, Hue, and Saturation to Blend Photographic Imagery (Photoshop)

The following steps show how Charles weaved different views of the classic vehicles into his composition without the individual source images overpowering the final picture.

1. **Start with your working composition open in Photoshop.**
2. **Open the first image element you want to blend into the working composition (36.12).**
3. **Use the Mover tool to drag and drop the image element into the composition.**
   The image is now a layer in your working composition.
4. **Reduce the layer opacity to about 30% using the Opacity slider in the Layers palette (36.13).**

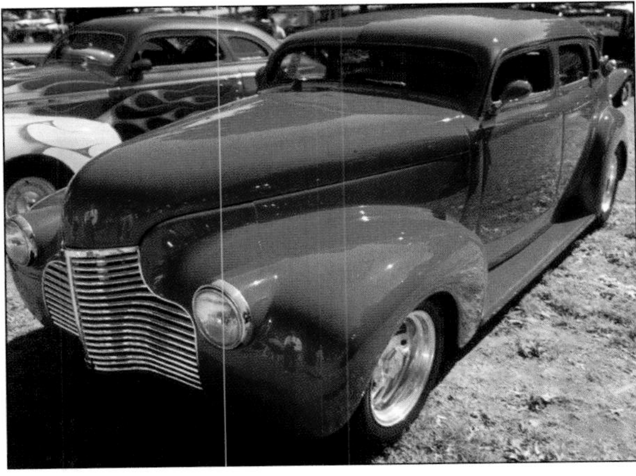

36.12

[TIP]

A convenient shortcut to changing opacity to 30% is to press the "3" key with the selection tool active.

5. **Choose the Move tool and drag the newly pasted image layer into a suitable position for your composition.**
6. **Choose Image→Adjust→Hue/Saturation.**
7. **Adjust the Hue slider to match the background colors.**

36.13

8. **Reduce the Saturation slider to about −50 (36.14).** Charles repeated this technique with a second shot of the vehicle (36.15).
   The layers generated in this manner were inserted into a lower layer position by dragging them down in the Layers palette, so that they would be part of the general background from which the central figure emerges.

Artist's Creative Insight and Advice

Why Digital?

The world of technology is still determined by what we make of it and how we actively employ it, and like any tool, the computer can be an extension of the human eye and mind, like a hand; or it can be simply a device that merely assists our activity, like an appliance. The digital environment is both, but what interests me is its function as an extension of that human power to create by transforming the raw material it receives into a new form, a new horizon to pour into.

Having stated that, however, I do find myself frustrated by the "mediation" it places between the power of the human hand to go about its business in a free flowing style unimpeded by overt thought and hesitation. In that regard, and in the production of tactile paint that is still richer from the point of view of a bodily perception, I believe that traditional painting and sculpture still harbor a qualitative edge that is rapidly diminishing. But in a different manner, that of sheer potentiality and freedom of expression, we have only now merely begun to scratch the surface.

To me, the digital environment is an extension of that creative process nature has initiated in us, for from the very outset our senses do not merely copy a ready-made world but actively transform, enrich, and select its qualities — the very qualities we live. From that scaffolding we live the real meanings we apply to that sensuous world — and so we once again transform, enrich, and select a lived horizon. In my approach to digital art, these are precisely the very same activities with which the digital environment is concerned and makes possible in a manner previously impossible.

Photoshop Strategy

I like to work with photographic element stacking, and then investigate transparency levels and layer modes. Since certain sections come out better than others in terms of the light quality or the form itself, I erase or section out (with a large feathering) what parts I don't like in each layer.

I often jump right into Photoshop with images or textures, and I generate forms that combine well. I just see what develops, and I go from there once a series of forms suggests itself to me. My general approach is to then take a whole section I like and duplicate it into two identical layers. I then combine the two layers, usually by having the bottom layer in Multiply Blend mode at a reduced transparency. The two layers work together and allow the viewer to see through to whatever is underneath; in this case, the

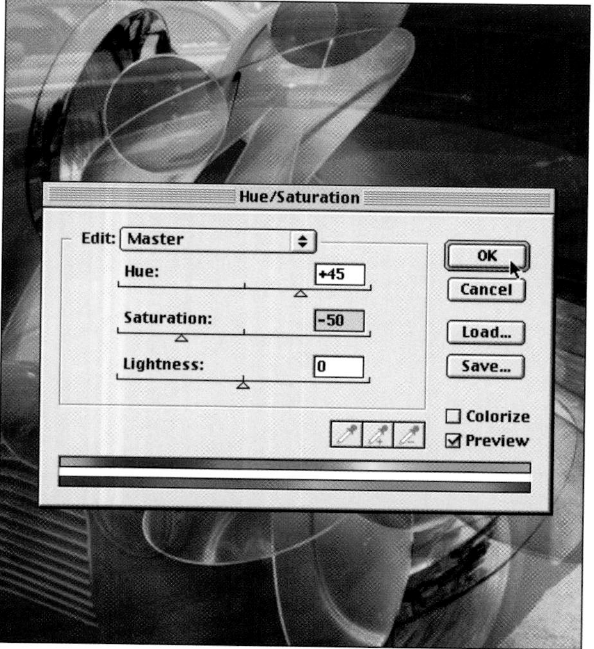

36.14

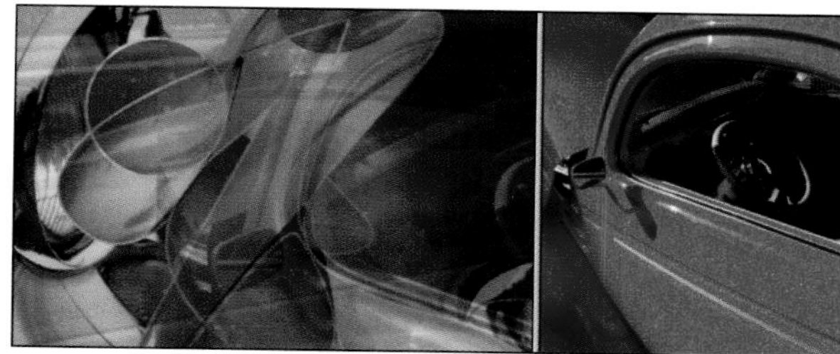

36.15

smooth forms from the car sections that were already placed within the curves that outlined the central figure. The whole idea is that by stacking layers, adjusting transparencies, and playing with layer modes, I like to investigate what nuances develop in terms of their relationship to each other.

Advice for Artists

Keep learning how to listen to what it is you're after, and don't terminate the learning and listening process once a level of "effects" has been mastered. That is merely the starting place.

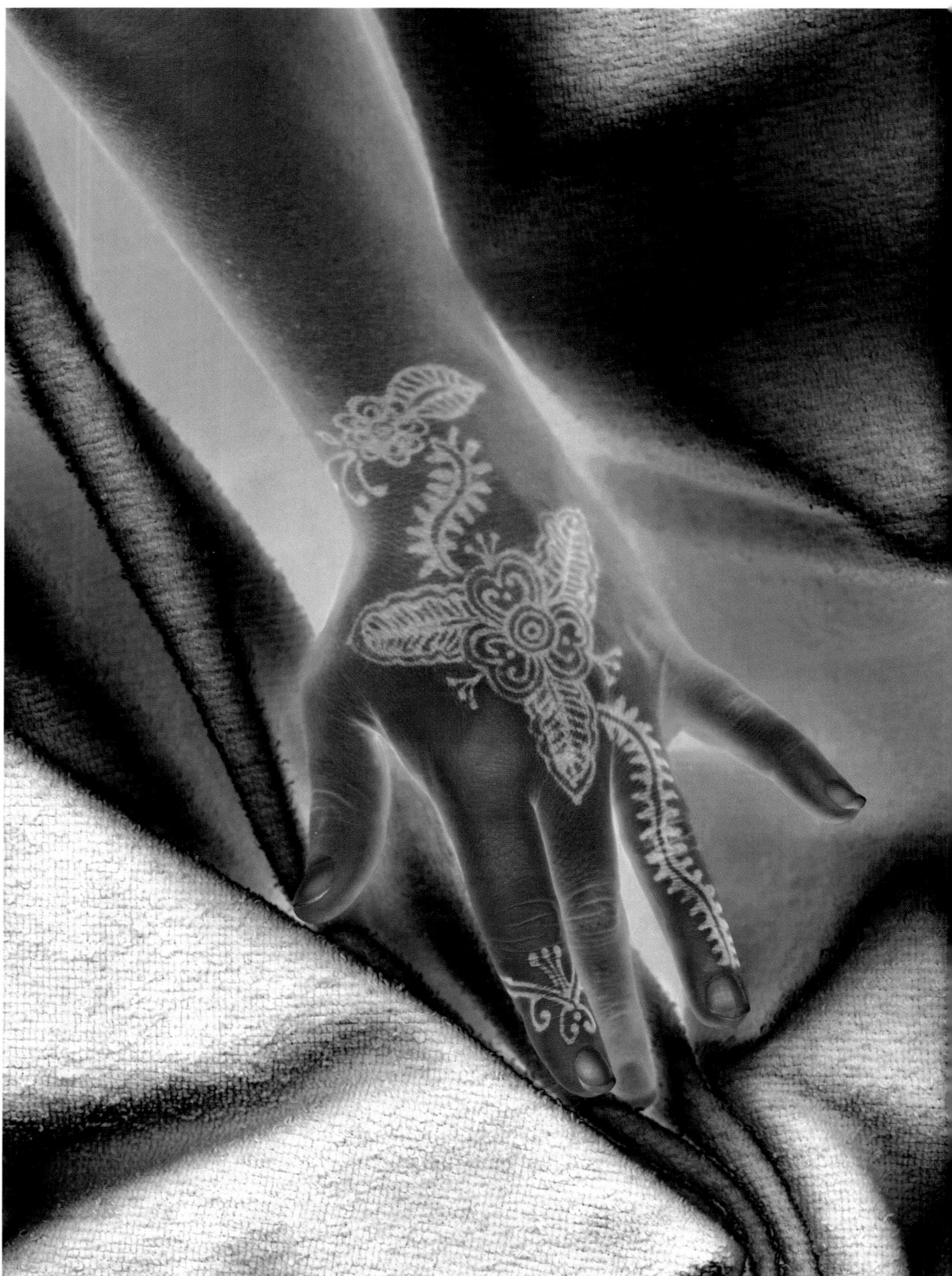

Chapter 37

Gesture V

by Lyn Bishop

Artist's Statement

As we race toward economic and technological advancement in our quest for globalization, we run the risk of sacrificing cultural diversity. My art reflects my desire to preserve the gentle balance between honoring cultural traditions and embracing the future and all that it brings. By combining art, culture, and technology in this way, I weave images and experiences into digital works that speak to the diversity in the world. Making art grants access to worlds that may be sacred, forbidden, enchanting, or threatening. It allows us to see worlds that we may never fully engage in otherwise.

The Story Behind the Artwork

Through the use of the traditional feminine art of body painting, the strong gestural hand motions, and modern technology, *Gesture V* (37.1) symbolizes the beauty of everyday traditions in the worlds' cultures. Lyn's goal was to capture an unexpected interplay between color, texture, and imagery.

The Creative Process

Lyn began by preparing the *mehndi* by following a traditional recipe. The first day, she prepared a strong tea and let it steep overnight. The following morning, she mixed the greenish *mehndi* powder with the tea and a small amount of eucalyptus oil to form a paste similar

◀37.1

to the consistency of toothpaste. That evening, Lyn painted the design onto her hand. The next morning, she brushed off the mud and used a little olive oil to moisturize and remove the stubborn flakes of *mehndi.*

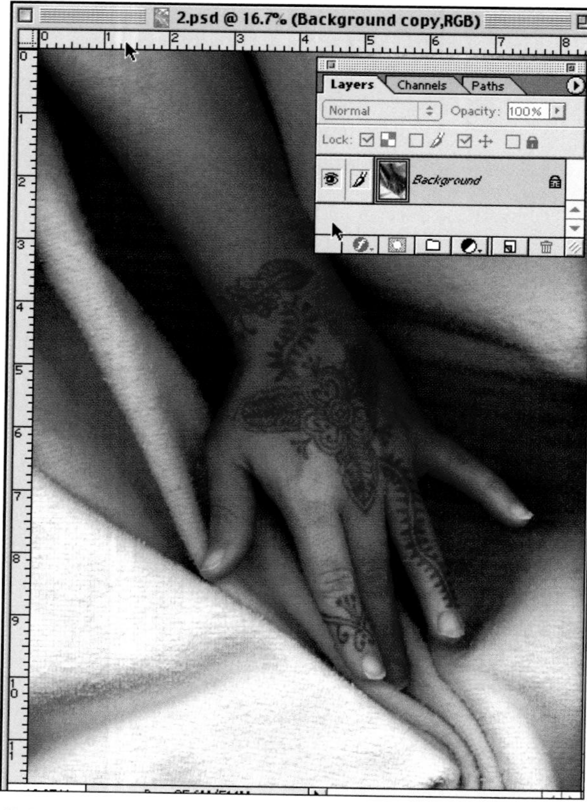

● 37.2

After the stain had a day to darken, she began making a series of direct scans of her arm on a flatbed scanner. Using a white towel as her background, she lay her arm down and draped the towel over. She made several scans of her arm and sorted through them to find the one she wanted to use in this work.

In Photoshop, Lyn opened the chosen scanned image file and duplicated the background layer. This copied layer was inverted, and the layer mode was set to Difference.

The initial process took several days, from beginning the *mehndi* to scanning her arm. Once in Photoshop, the technique was straightforward, and the piece came together within a few hours.

Technique: Creating a Velvety Blue Effect (Photoshop)

This is the technique Lyn followed to add the velvety blue effect to the image.

1. **Scan your hand using a white towel as the scanner's cover (37.2).**
2. **Open the scanned image of your hand in Photoshop.**
3. **Choose Duplicate Layer from the Layers pop-up menu.**
   This creates a copy of the Background layer.
4. **Select Command/Ctrl-I.**
   This inverts the Background copy layer (37.3).
5. **Set Background copy layer mode to Difference using the method pop-up menu in the Layers palette (37.4).**

About the Artist

Biography

Lyn was introduced to the Macintosh and desktop publishing in 1988 when she learned early versions of Illustrator and Pagemaker. She saw the potential for creativity that the computer offered and got excited by the possibilities. Working for Adobe Systems in the 1990s, Lyn was exposed to a wide variety of digital artists who inspired her. After forming a freelance design studio, Zama Arts, she began to explore and create her own digital fine art.

Influences

Lyn's three main influences are art, culture, and technology. Art and artists provide a creative influence to her artistic thinking. Exploring the world's diverse cultures influences her understanding of humanity and the planet as a whole. Technology influences the way in which she creates her art.

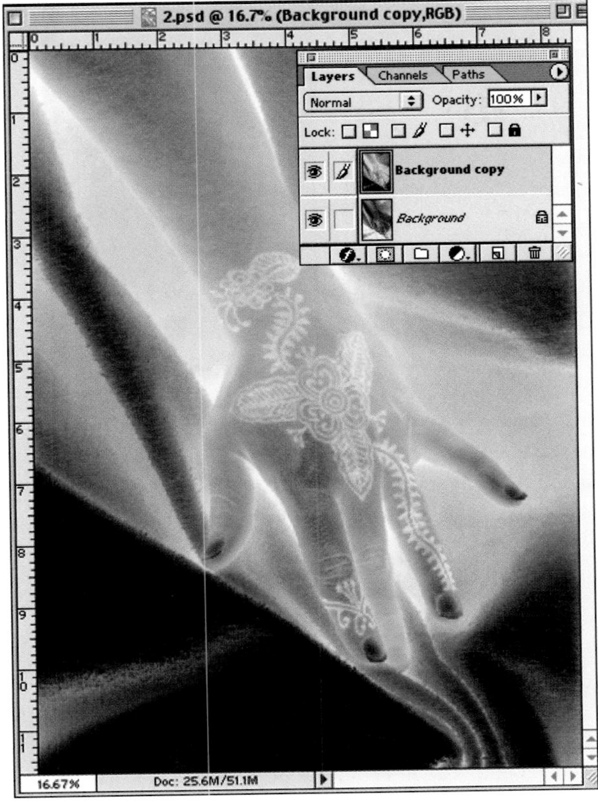

● 37.3

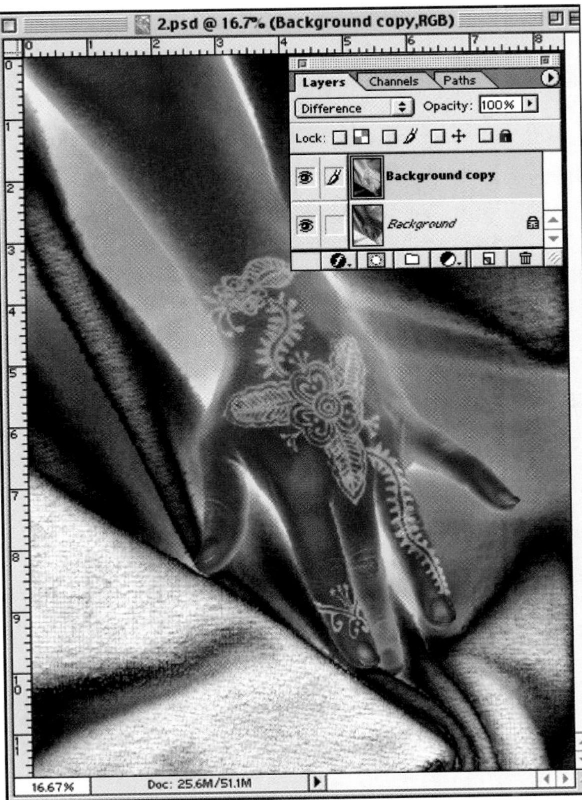

● 37.4

Studio

Computer:
Macintosh G4 dual 450
30GB hard drive
1GB RAM

Monitors:
NEC Multisync 21 inch

Software:
Photoshop
Illustrator
Painter

Archive Media:
LaCie CD-ROM Burner (FireWire)

Tablet:
Wacom 4 x 6 Graphics Tablet

Input:
Epson Expressons 636,
Minolta Quickscan 35 Slide Scanner

Printers:
Epson 3000, Epson 7000

Other:
Traditional artist materials, papers, paints

Contact

Lyn Bishop
Sunnyvale, California
lyn@zama.com
www.zama.com

Artist's Creative Insight and Advice

Why Digital?

Digital is a medium that allows me unlimited experimentation with a variety of elements. I bring together scans of my paintings, traditional and digital photography, and direct digital drawings. The ability to reach for such a rich body of source material is inspiring.

Advice for Artists Working in the Digital Medium

Break the rules.
Believe in yourself.

Color Management

Through using ICC color profiles for a specific ink and paper combination, I've found that I have pretty consistent results when printing my work on my Epson 3000. Using a monitor calibration spider, I'm able to numerically calibrate my screen. This helps to keep the color in line.

Exploring methods that push the digital print into new dimension opens the creative process further. By using techniques developed by myself and other digital artists as a starting point, the mixing of traditional and digital mediums allows the artist to push the digital print into innovative mixed-media directions.

Karen Sullivan on Bishop's *Gesture*

"Lyn Bishop, in her *Gestures* series, uses the traditional feminine art of body painting in a digital form to communicate her desire to see unique cultural blueprints preserved as we move into a globalized technological homogeny. The piece represents a balance of opposites in a unified whole."

— Karen Sullivan, Teacher, Ringling School of Art (`www.ringling.edu`)

Chapter 38

Kimonohawk

by Jaye R. Phillips

Artist's Statement

With the camera, I seek and gather images, much as collecting ideas in journal writing. Photoshop and the computer allow me to combine images that tell stories, often in unplanned and mysterious ways.

I call my work the landscape of motion; I am drawn to the source and evidence of beings moving with the rhythms of nature.

The Story Behind the Artwork

Kimonohawk (38.1) is about persona, with its layers and masks, coverings and uncoverings. The water represents the unconscious, the depths of imagination, the source of the creative impulse. The hawks exist as the shadow guardians of the spirit. The little fish swimming in and out of circles are the sparks of life. The lining of the kimono is a cactus, which thrives on the sun as the source of the illumination of the spirit.

◀ 38.1

The Creative Process

Jaye scanned her photos of a kimono, a tidal pool with fish, several Harris hawks (38.2), and an agave cactus.

She cut the kimono from its original background and placed it on a background of tidal pools. She then used the layer mask of the outline of the kimono to cut out the agave cactus in the same shape as the outline of the kimono. Then she placed the cut-out cactus layer, with 50% opacity, over the kimono layer in Multiply mode. She brightened the lining of the kimono using Image➔Adjust➔Curves, and made the colors more saturated with Adjustment Layers in Saturation.

After selecting the hawk shapes, using the Lasso tool, she feathered the selections (38.3).

● 38.2

● 38.3

About the Artist

Biography

Jaye Phillips has been a Boston-based artist-photographer since 1975. Her work has been exhibited in museums and galleries including the Addison Gallery of American Art, California Museum of Art, and, most recently, Harvard University Mather Gallery as part of Boston Cyberfest. Her photographs are in the Polaroid Collection and the Harvard University Theatre Arts Collection.

She has been the official photographer for the Boston Ballet and numerous modern dance companies. In 1998 she had a book of photographs published by the Museum of New Mexico Press, Zapotec Weavers of Teotitlan. She discovered the joys of the computer as a creative tool in 1988 while designing her artist's book on the rhythms of time, tide, and the sun.

She filled the hawk selections with black, duplicated them, and then flipped, rotated, and resized some of the hawk shapes with the Free Transform tool to give an effect of dancing. She placed the black hawk layer over the water background (38.4).

The hawk layer was then transformed from Normal to Multiply mode. She then lightened the opacity of the hawk layer to about 30% until the hawk shapes read as shadows (38.5).

To finish the image, she colored the water as sunny yellow with the brush tool in Color mode.

The image took about 12 hours to complete.

Technique: Superimposing One Image over Another to Give a Shadowy Effect (Photoshop)

This technique demonstrates the way Jaye superimposed one image — in her case, the cactus image — over another (the kimono) as a shadowy layer that blended with the underlying image.

1. **In Photoshop, open a background image and two other images that you want to superimpose.**

● 38.4

● 38.5

Influences

Corita Kent, David Hockney, T.S. Eliot, and Henri Cartier-Bresson.

Studio

Computer System:
Apple Power Macintosh G3
384MB RAM
8.5GB hard drive
74.5GB external hard drive

Monitors:
ViewSonic CRT, 21-inch

Software:
Adobe Photoshop
Procreate Painter

Removable Media:
Zip drive

Archive Media:
Yamaha CD Writer

Tablet:
Wacom 6 x 9 tablet

Input Devices:
Nikon Super Coolscan 4000 ED

Printers:
Epson Stylus Photo Printers 1270, 1280, and 2000P

Contact

Jaye R. Phillips
Arlington, Massachusetts
Jayelight@yahoo.com

Jaye used the water image as the background and the kimono and cactus as the other two (38.6).

2. **With the background image selected, choose Duplicate Layer in the Layers palette pop-up menu.**
   This operation duplicates the base layer (background). You will see a layer generated called Background copy. Doing this ensures that you always have the original if at any time you want to return to the untouched image.
3. **In the kimono image, make a selection around the outside of the kimono, isolating it from its background, using the Pen tool.**
   The Pen tool offers the most control and precision for making handmade selections around an object. Just create a closed path. You can go back and add, subtract, and alter control points along the path using Photoshop's various pen, path, and point adjustment tools.
   Once you are satisfied with the path, convert the path into a selection by clicking on the third icon from the left in the very bottom of the Paths palette.
4. **Choose Selection→Save Selection.**
   This generates an alpha channel that you can see at the bottom of the channels in the Channels palette. You can activate this alpha channel selection at any time by clicking the left-most icon at the very bottom of the Channels palette.

[NOTE]

As an alternative, just save the path using the Save Path command in the Paths palette pop-up menu. You can then activate the path as a selection at any time by clicking on the third icon from the left in the very bottom of the Paths palette.

5. **Place one of the overlay images over the background layer by dragging the selection into the background image with the Move tool (38.7).**
6. **Going back to the overlay image, open the Channels palette.**
7. **Drag the alpha channel generated in Step 4 into the second overlay image.**
   This automatically adds the same alpha channel to the Channels palette for the second overlay image. You can see this alpha channel listed in the Channels palette. In the illustration here it is listed as "kimonoshape" below the RGB, Red, Green, and Blue channels (38.8).
8. **With the second overlay image active and the imported alpha channel highlighted in the Channels palette, click on the left-hand icon at the bottom of the Channels palette.**
   This activates the same shaped selection you created with the Pen tool. This selection can

● 36.6

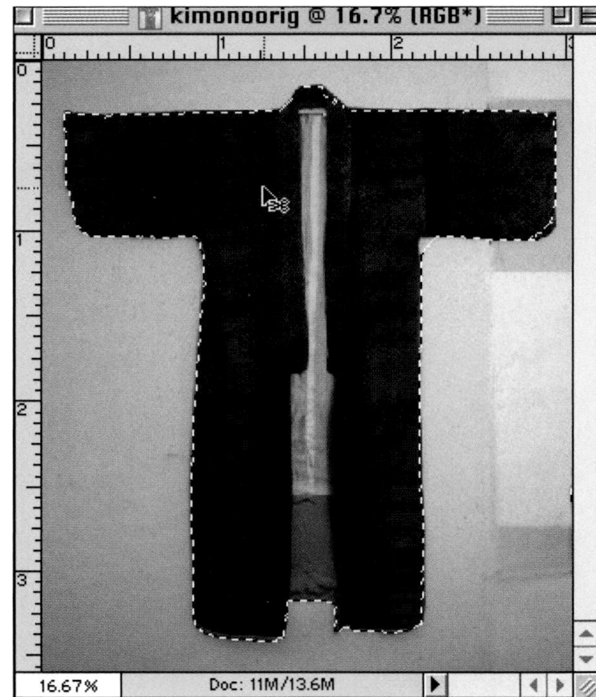

● 36.7

now be used to cut out a shape from the second overlay image (38.9).

9. **Use the Move tool to drag the shaped selection in the second overlay image to the working image.** This generates a cut-out layer positioned exactly above the first overlay layer.
10. **Reduce opacity of the cut-out layer to about 60%.**
11. **Change the layer mode of the cut-out layer from Normal to Multiply.** In this final illustration you can see the result of this technique as applied to the actual composition used in the *Kimonohawk* (38.10).

Artist's Creative Insight and Advice

Why Digital?

The great digital advantage is being able to combine images into unifying montages with all kinds of control of contrast, color, and emphasis. Plus, digital imaging allows for quick sketches of ideas that can be created in real time. With traditional darkroom techniques, you had to spend tedious weeks in the darkroom with multiple enlargers, working with carefully marked easels, cut-out black masks, and copious notes. Also, digital photography frees me from the darkroom and its unhealthy chemicals.

The digital disadvantage, to date, is the distance between what you see on the monitor and what you get as a print in terms of color.

Advice for Artists Working in the Digital Medium

Buy as much RAM as your computer will allow. Take a course if you get stuck often; you will see that you are not alone in having computer glitches and problems, and you will strengthen your own ability to find solutions.

Buy your computer hardware equipment from a retailer that provides a tech-support service and call them for help whenever you need it.

Output

I find that paper selection is very important to the overall aesthetic effect of my final printed image. For archival integrity, I exhibit prints under UV-absorbing Plexiglas. I sometimes draw with colored pencils on the print, especially to add emphasis.

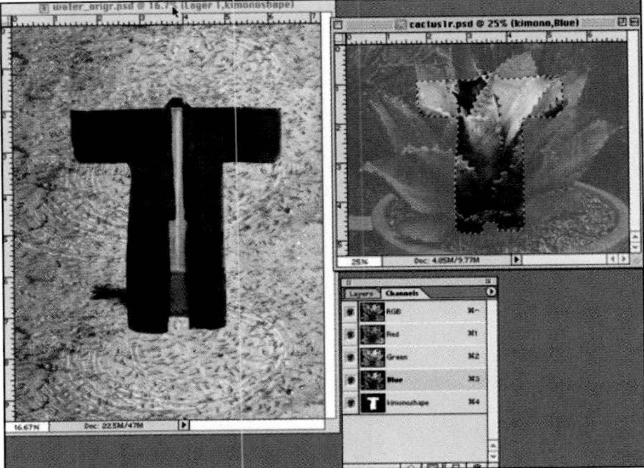

38.8

38.9

38.10

Chapter 39

Lily #4

by Diane Vetere

Artist's Statement

The important thing to me is the ability to create what I want, when I want, and love the process. This is not a job, not just play, but what I do. And it's exhilarating.

The Story Behind the Artwork

This image is an example of how Diane takes something that is to most people ugly, and, through the process of scanning and digital manipulation, transforms it into something totally different — a piece of beauty. The subject of *Lily #4* (39.1) was just a dead flower that had fallen apart and faded; the flower would probably have been put in the garbage by most people. Diane saw the beauty in the curl of the dried petals, the smudges of the pollen from the stamens, and the glorious color and form. This scrap of flower became super-real by being scanned. The even light of the scanner across the whole surface gives it a three dimensional feel. And the green shadow cast on the petals from the scanner beam adds its own charm.

The Creative Process

The flower was placed on the bed of Diane's UMAX Astra 1220S scanner. Diane covered the flower with a box that had been spray painted black inside. The flower, covered by the box, was then scanned at the

◀39.1

highest optical resolution of the scanner, cropped, and enlarged to 12 x 12 inches at 300 dpi in Photoshop.

Diane adjusted the levels of the blacks and midrange colors with Image→Adjust→Levels until it was pleasing. Diane then saturated the color a bit more with Image→Adjust→Hue and Saturation. She then sharpened it with Filter→Sharpen→Unsharp Mask, being very careful not to over-sharpen while achieving a crisp, clean image. The final step was to darken the background by selecting the background with the Magic Wand, selecting Similar, feathering the selection by 5 pixels, and filling with black.

Technique: Scanning a Three-Dimensional Object

The use of a painted box to provide a plain black (or any other color) background is something that anyone can do to scan three-dimensional objects. This is particularly useful when the article to be scanned is fragile.

1. **Find a discarded shoe box.**
2. **Place the shoe box on newspaper in the open air, or a well ventilated environment.**
3. **Spray black paint on all inside surfaces of the box.**
4. **Allow the paint to dry.**
5. **Place a dried flower, or other delicate object, in the center of your scanner flatbed.**
6. **Place the painted shoe box over the object.**
7. **Set the scanner to scan the object at its maximum resolution.**
8. **Scan the object.**

Judge's Critique

"I was impressed with Diane's use of scanning to focus on the intricate complexity of natural form. The subtle coloring and shape of a flower is heightened and magnified by the close-up view. I particularly liked the ballet-like quality within the lily's form."

— JOHN DERRY, Principle Author Painter, Digital Artist

(`www.fractal.com`)

About the Artist

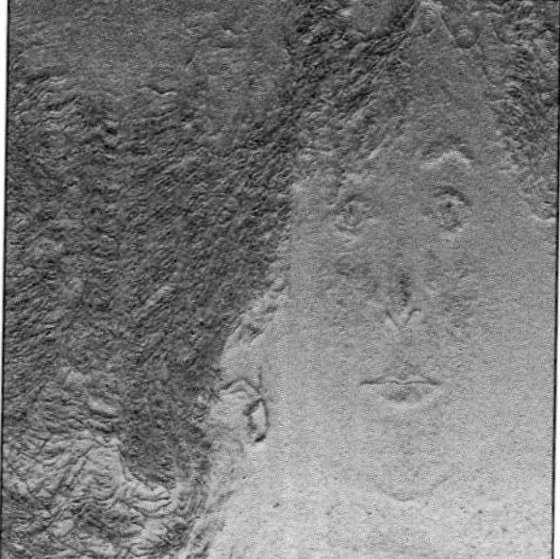

Biography

Educated at University of Waterloo, Department of Fine Arts, Waterloo, Canada, Diane has followed many career paths, only sometimes artistic. Painting and sculpture were her main forms of artistic expression before acquiring a Mac 128 in the mid-80s, after which she concentrated mainly on digital work. *Lily #4* is part of a body of work devoted to seeing the beauty in scans of dried, dead flowers. Diane is currently working with cropped scans of old manipulated Polaroids. Visit her Web site to see examples of both series of work.

Influences

Jan Vermeer and color field painters like Mark Rothko for color; Robert Rauschenberg for sheer audacity and inventiveness.

Studio

Computer System:

Powermac 7500 with a G4 upgrade
1GB RAM
2 internal 36GB hard drives
Orb 2.2GB external hard drive

Artist's Creative Insight and Advice

Why Digital?

From MacPaint in the 80s, to Photoshop today, I've had this ongoing love affair with my computer. The computer allows me to see things in exciting new ways — heightening perceptions and challenging conceptions. I can manipulate color and form in surprising and delicious ways that delight me. There is always an element of surprise and discovery in every piece I do. Sometimes it's as simple as seeing something like this lily through the digital eye of the scanner, and at other times, it's hours and hours of creating a piece from scratch.

Seeing Art

Many years ago, I taught a night course on how to look at art — the main gist of which was that you had to "see" art first, and art could be seen almost everywhere if you just looked. *Lily #4* is an example of this.

Monitors:
19-inch CTX

Software:
Adobe Photoshop

Input Devices:
UMAX Astra 1220S

Removable Media:
Yamaha CD-RW

Archive Media:
CDs and Orb Cartridges

Output Devices:
Epson Stylus Color 1160 with a continuous inking system, MediaStreet's Generations pigmented inks

Contact

Diane Vetere
Toronto, Canada
Diane@dianevetere.com
www.dianevetere.com

Chapter 40

The Digital Divide

by J.W. Fry

Artist's Statement

My work explores the relationship of images by creating layers and juxtapositions of photographs through a variety of weaving techniques. The photographs are cut into vertical and horizontal strips and woven back together to show enough of the different images so that each is recognizable.

The weaving process transforms the sometimes disparate images into a new reality. The resulting artwork is both an object and an image. I hope that people reflect upon their perceptions and reinterpret the various images in their new context in the weavings.

The Story Behind the Artwork

The Digital Divide (40.1) was a personal project to illustrate the theme of the digital divide that is common in our society.

◀ 40.1

The Creative Process

J.W.'s finished artwork is a physical photographic weaving. The computer is an intermediate step in the process. In creating *The Digital Divide*, J.W. first photographed the model (40.2) and the barbwire (40.3). The model was photographed using a Hasselblad and the barbwire with a 4 x 5 camera.

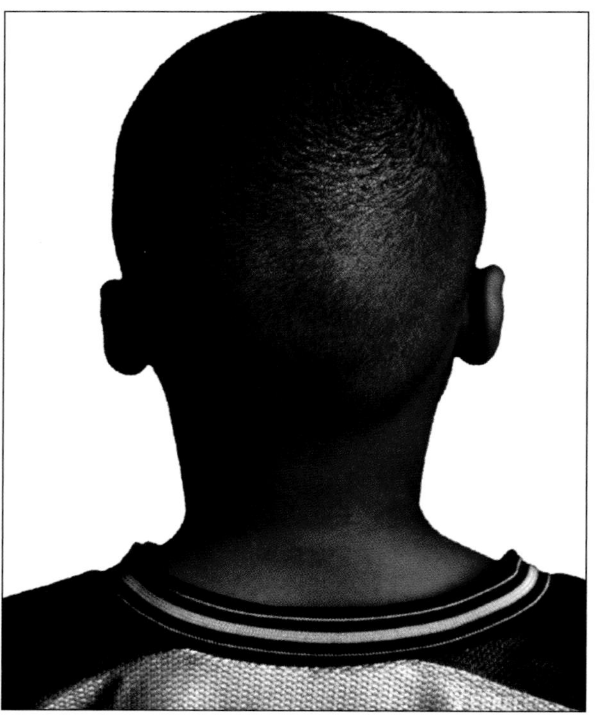

● 40.2

The photos were then scanned into Adobe Photoshop as RGB images at 300ppi. Both source images were then placed over a vertical gradient background (40.4) using the Move tool.

The head and barbwire images each formed a separate layer in the image. The layers were repositioned and resized to suit the composition (40.5).

J.W. kept one version of this image unaltered and then made a second version where he slightly altered the colors and values using the Dodge and Burn tools in Photoshop. He then made a print of each version of the composition. Each print was cut into strips, and these strips were then woven back together. The final weaving was then re-photographed on a white background with a drop shadow, using a 4 x 5 camera. The final result shows a woven texture where the main image comprises a series of small squares, each of which differs slightly in color and value from the adjacent squares. The shifts in color and value

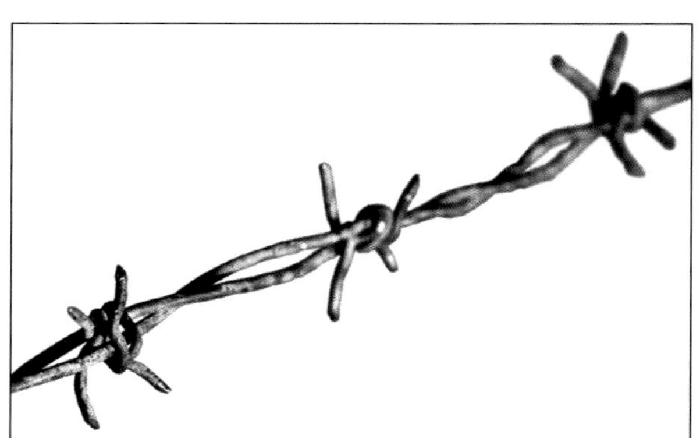

● 40.3

About the Artist

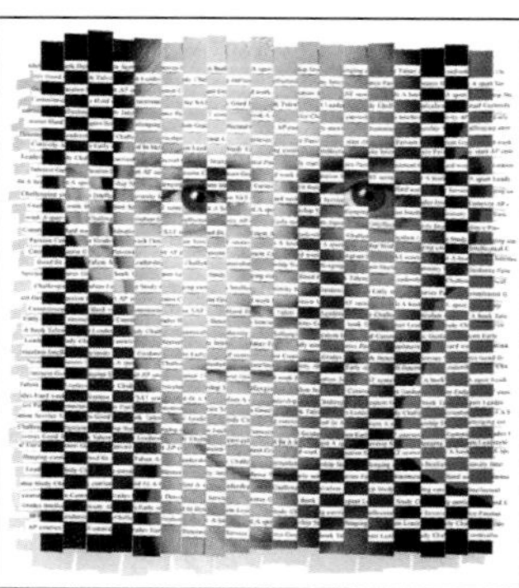

Biography

J.W. Fry began incorporating digital into his traditional work six years ago. He has won awards from Communication Arts Interactive Annual, Graphis New Media, San Francisco Show (Advertising), Print Regional Design Annual, and an Addy Award. His artwork has been included in two books, *A Day In The Life Of Italy* and *The Power To Heal: Ancient Arts and Modern Medicine*. His artwork was also part of the New York International Center of Photography exhibit, Photos from The Power to Heal. This show traveled to over 25 cities throughout the United States and Europe.

Influences

Walker Evans, Paul Strand, Harry Callahan, and Edward Weston.

between adjacent squares results in a checkerboard look to some regions of the image. Where this checkerboard pattern is visible, it is mostly due to the alterations he made in the second image, and partly due to the way light falls differently on those parts of the weave that curve towards the viewer compared to those parts that curve away from the viewer.

J.W. spent approximately three hours photographing the back of the head (with lots of variations), two hours photographing the barbwire, four hours computer time, three hours weaving the images together, and 30 minutes re-photographing the finished weaving on a white background with a drop shadow.

● 40.4

● 40.5

Studio

Computer System:

Mac G3 300
80GB hard drive
768MB RAM

External hard drives:

120GB

Monitors:

ViewSonic 19 inch

Software:

Adobe Photoshop

Removable Media:

Zip drive

Archive Media:

CD burner

Tablet:

Wacom 6 x 9

Input Devices:

Epson Scanner with 4 x 5 transparency unit
Minolta QuickScan 35

Printers:

Epson 1270

Contact

J.W. Fry
San Francisco, California
jw@jwfry.com
www.JWFRY.com

Technique: Weaving Two Images Together (Photoshop)

This technique describes how you can replicate the weaving of two images together in a similar way to that used by Fry in this image.

1. **Open a composition in Photoshop that includes several objects or elements.**
   In J.W.'s case, the objects were the head and the barbed wire. The image should be 300-ppi resolution at the desired print size.
2. **Open an image of one component object or element that appears in the composition you selected in step 1.**
   Choose a second image that is different from the first but contains a common element. The choice of the second image offers room for artistic experimentation. In the case of *The Digital Divide*, J.W. used the same image with slight modifications.
   You can see another example of this "same image, slight modifications" approach in *Red Lips* (40.6). In *Red Lips* he weaved together two almost identical images of the same red lips. He used the Dodge and Burn tools to make slight modifications in some regions of one image. Where you see the checkerboard pattern, such as the central highlighted area between the nose and the upper lip, the images differ from one another. Where the images merge together seamlessly, such as in the center of the lower lip, he left the images identical.
   At other times he uses two or three completely different images, such as in the *Wrench and Saw Blade* (40.7) and *Saw Head* (40.8). To really explore this technique, you should experiment with different possibilities.
3. **If your second image has the same aspect ratio (height to width ratio) but different over all size to the main composition image, use Image→Image Size, with Resample Image checked, to make the object image the same size and resolution as the main composition image.**

[TIP]

If your object image has a different aspect ratio compared to your composition image, then try opening a new image the exact same size as the composition image and paste the object into that new image.

4. **Print both the composition image and the isolated object image.**

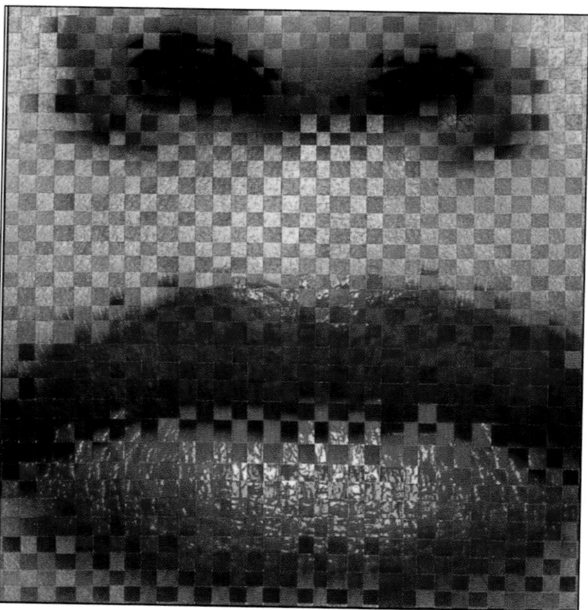

40.6

40.7

5. **Cut one print into vertical strips and the other into horizontal strips.**

[NOTE]

J.W. uses a RotaTrim cutter to cut the prints into strips by hand. The strips are cut without use of a rule so that there is a little variation in the size of each strip. This variation adds to the interest and organic nature of the final image. J.W. specifically avoids creating perfectly even, perfectly straight strips.

6. **Weave the vertical and horizontal strips together so that you combine the two images.**
   J.W. typically sets the vertical and horizontal sets of strips neatly on either side of a clear working space. He then slowly, carefully, and methodically places the top horizontal strip down, gently taping the ends to hold it in place, and then adds all the vertical strips, alternating whether they go under or over the top horizontal strip, taping them into position each time. He then works his way down the image, adding the rest of the horizontal strips, weaving each one alternately under and over all the adjacent vertical strips, taping each strip into position when he's completed the weave.
   In the examples of other weaves shown here, you see that J.W. doesn't always alternate the strips under and over each other. For instance, in the *Wrench and Saw Blade* (40.7) you can see more of the horizontal strips in the wrench, whereas in the *Saw Head* (40.8) you can see more of the vertical strips in the saw.
   When the entire images have been woven together, J.W. lifts the piece from the working surface, turns it over, and tapes the back to secure the weave. He then removes all the tape that has been holding the strip ends in place.
7. **Photograph the finished weaving on a white background with a drop shadow.**
   J.W. raises the finished weave from the white background by placing it on a small book (any small object, or identically sized objects, will do). He then sets up lighting to give the desired drop shadow. His final photographic image has a real shadow, not one generated digitally in Photoshop.

Artist's Creative Insight and Advice

Why Digital?

The computer for me is just another tool, not unlike some low-tech solutions I sometimes use, such as a can of spray paint, scissors, or double stick tape. Digital Art is still in its infancy, and I am very interested to see where it will be going.

Advice for Artists Working in the Digital Medium

Do not be too heavy-handed — it's the artwork that's important, not the medium used to create it.

Give yourself lots of time. The computer is a powerful tool with many features that can consume large amounts of time.

Don't hold your breath. I work mostly with strong primary colors so that there is a little more forgiveness.

● 40.8

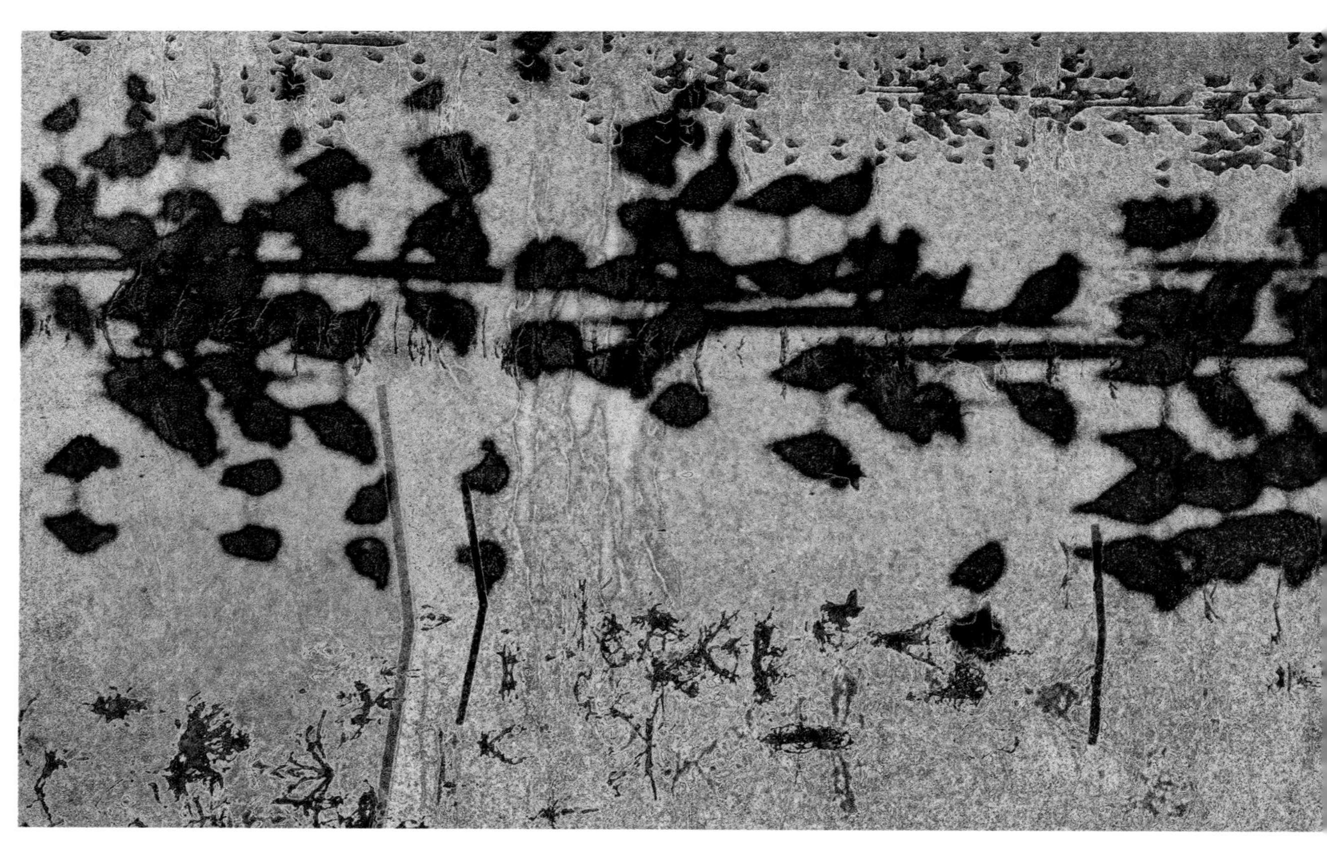

Chapter 41

Dawn at the Baylands

by Helen S. Golden

Artist's Statement

I make art all the time and am obsessively and happily compelled to do so. Working with the computer and its associated sophisticated technologies has empowered me to play, risk, and explore myriad new ideas.

I love transforming something into something else and creating art! I endeavor to create art that will go beyond surface representation and move the viewer to muse and reflect.

The Story Behind the Artwork

Helen was enjoying a nature walk one day in the San Francisco Bay baylands when she was moved to take some photographs. She wanted to record and share some of the delights she experienced while watching and listening to the birds.

One photo was particularly pleasing to her. She began to manipulate this particular photo on her computer using a variety of image refinement and art-making tools and techniques in LucisArt and Photoshop.

Helen didn't follow a pre-planned recipe of techniques. She simply followed a non-linear, non-verbal, and intuitive process. *Dawn at the Baylands* (41.1) was the outcome of this creative process.

The Creative Process

To compose her image, Helen scanned a photograph (41.2) and processed it in LucisArt (a Photoshop plug-in) to get more detail and increase the contrast by using its Klimpt Filter.

Then, in Photoshop, she began to select, copy, scale up, and repeat selected portions of the artwork. After she had created a pleasing structure and composition, she began to make wildly colored versions of the image and then added bits and pieces of those versions back into the image using different layer

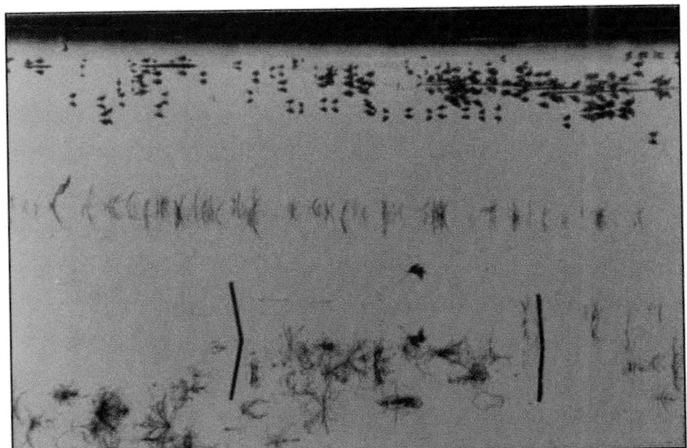

● 41.2

◀41.1

modes, such as Color and Hard Light. The steps she followed, and the stages the image passed through, are described in the technique section later in this chapter.

Next, she used the Rubber Stamp tool in Normal mode to cover cluttered areas; she then used the same tool in Color mode to intensify and balance the image's colors.

Helen spent over 110 hours working on this image, in long and short bouts, over a period of six months. Helen knew when her image was complete when the image stopped "bothering" her.

When the image looked right, she saved it as a Genuine Fractals file in Photoshop and resized it from 6 by 4 inches at 150dpi to 31 by 18.5 inches at 150dpi so it would make a good quality print.

The final image was printed on an HP DesignJet 5000 with UV Pigmented Inks on Hahnemuhle Digital Paper.

Technique: Building a Harmonious Image by Repeating Selections (Photoshop)

Helen selected a small portion of the birds in the background of her chosen scanned photo, enlarged them, and placed them over the basic image. These repeated forms created a rhythm and harmony that she felt captured the feeling of nature that she had when she was walking in the Baylands. This technique shares the way she repeated those selections to build up a harmonious image. The important aspect to note in this process is not so much the detailed settings as much as Helen's overall approach and strategy. She repeatedly copies layers, alters them, groups them, and then merges them to produce new layers.

The LucisArt and Genuine Fractals applications that she used are plug-ins for Photoshop. Once installed on your computer, they are accessible under

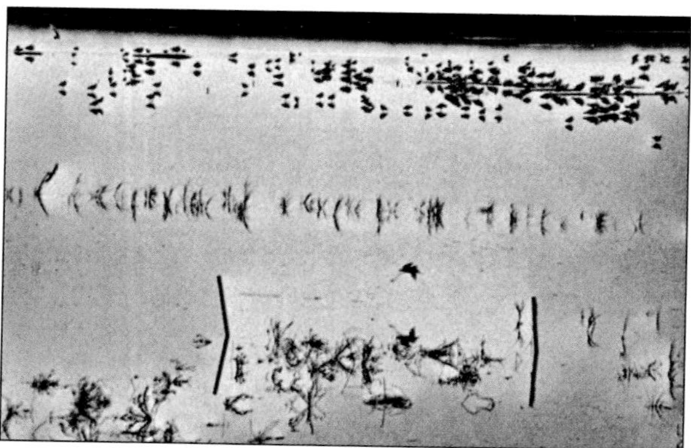

● 41.3

● 41.4

dS.

About the Artist

Biography

Helen began making art with technology tools in the early 1990s, was the first curator/director of Art At The Pond, a San Francisco digital art exhibition space, and worked as a research consultant for technology corporations. She is a founding member of 911 Gallery, of The Main Gallery, and of the pioneering digital art collective Unique Editions, which was an educational, standard-setting, and marketing entity.

Her images are exhibited in virtual and real galleries and are in private, corporate, and museum collections including the National Museum of American Art at the Smithsonian Institution in Washington D.C. Helen is a Laureate of the 1998 Computerworld Smithsonian Information Technology Innovation Distinction and a recipient of the 1998 André Schellenberg Award in Fine Art.

Influences

Helen is affected by the paintings of Goya and Rembrandt; the color in Claude Monet's paintings; photographs by Bill Brandt, Ernst Haas, and Andre Kertesz; sculptures by Isamu Noguchi, Henry Moore, the Photoshop Filters menu, which makes them very easy to use.

1. **Open a scanned photograph (recommended at 300 ppi) in Photoshop in RGB mode.**
2. **Process the photo using the LucisArt filter with the Klimpt filter option.**
   Choose Filter→LucisArt→Klimpt, setting the first button at 100% on the layer named Source Photo (41.3).
3. **Use the Crop tool to slightly crop the altered image.**
   Helen's image evolved intuitively. She kept working to get a composition that felt right. That took a few iterations, and several crops, that were idiosyncratic and not methodological.
4. **Choose Image→Resize and enlarge the altered image.**
   Helen selected a part of the source image, resized it, and placed it on top of the source in order to repeat elements of the image. She tried selecting several different pieces of the main scanned photo image before she found the selection that worked best, echoed elements in the composition, and set up patterns she liked. Therefore, experiment with your image. Try out different selections and, through a process of trial and error, see what feels best to you.
5. **Select a portion of Layer 1 (41.4).**
6. **Scale the selection up so that it becomes the same size as Layer 1.**
7. **Name the scaled-up selection Layer 2.**
   This is part of the process of building an image by repeating selections.
8. **Place Layer 2 (in ColorBurn Mode at 100%) over a copy of Layer 1 (Normal mode 100%).**
9. **Merge Layers 1 and 2 to get an image now named Layer 3 (41.5).**
10. **Make a new copy of Layer 1.**
11. **Alter the colors and contrast in the copy of Layer 1 using the Image→Adjust →Color Adjust and Image→Adjust→Levels commands.**
12. **Name the resulting layer Layer 4 (41.6).**
13. **Place Layer 4 (in Color mode at 100%) over Layer 3 (Normal mode at 100%).**

● 41.5

● 41.6

Barbara Hepworth, and Alexander Calder; the imagination of Pablo Picasso and Max Ernst; the dances of Martha Graham; and the music of J.S. Bach.

Studio

Computer System:
Power Mac 9600/233
8GB hard drive
160MB RAM
Intergraph Extreme Z Windows NT workstation
26GB hard drive
524MB RAM

Monitors:
Intergraph 19-inch Multi-Scan Color Display
Radius PressView 21
Apple 15-inch

Software:
LucisArt
Genuine Fractals PrintPro
Adaptac Easy CD Creator
Deep Paint 3D
Adobe Photoshop
QuarkXPress
Procreate Painter

Removable Media:
ZIP drive
Jaz drive

Tablet:
Wacom Intuos 6 x 8 Graphics Tablet

Input Devices:
Epson Expression 1680 Scanner

Printers:
HP DesignJet 5000PS 42-inch
Epson Stylus Photo1200

Contact

Helen S. Golden
Palo Alto, California
hsgolden@aol.com

14. **Merge Layers 3 and 4 and name the result Layer 5 (41.7).**
15. **Use the Rectangular Marquee tool to select some of the patterns in a copy of Layer 1 (41.8).**
16. **Copy these selections into a new layer.**
17. **Scale up the new layer to the full width of the size of the background image.**
18. **Name that scaled-up layer Layer 6.**
    This is a continuation of the process of building an image by repeating selections.

41.7

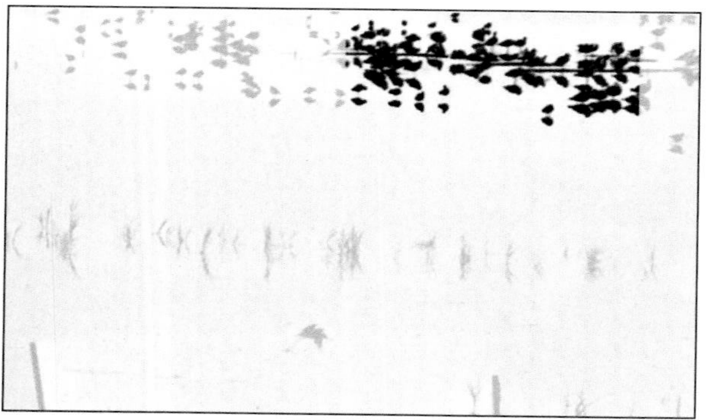

41.8

41.9

19. **Place Layer 6 (in Hard Light mode at 100%) over Layer 5 (in Normal mode at 100%).**
20. **Merge Layers 5 and 6 and name the result Layer 7 (41.9).**
21. **Change and intensify the colors in Layer 7 by experimenting with a variety of operations, such as Image→Adjust→Curves, Color Balance, or Levels.**

[TIP]

You may want to try the following Image→Adjust→ Color Balance settings: Highlights +71, -76, +29; Midtones: -84, +81, -68; and Shadows: -100, +100, +100; or Image→Adjust→ Levels, settings: Red, 51, 1.00, 196; Green: 37, 0.84, 222; and Blue: 52, 0.42, 141.

22. **Copy Layer 7.**
23. **Choose Layer→New Adjustment Layer→Curves.**
    Adjust the curve shapes to get wildly colored results. There are no rules or guidelines here — just experiment. The settings that look best differ for every image.
24. **Group the copy of Layer 7 with a Curves Adjustment layer (41.10).**
    In the example shown here, the copy of Layer 7, grouped with the Curves Adjustment layer, was set in Color layer mode at 90% opacity. This was one of many color variations that Helen generated from Layer 7. She added these color variations selectively to the final image.
25. **Choose Merge Visible from the Layers palette pop-up menu.**
    This merges the copy of Layer 7 with the Curves Adjustment layer.

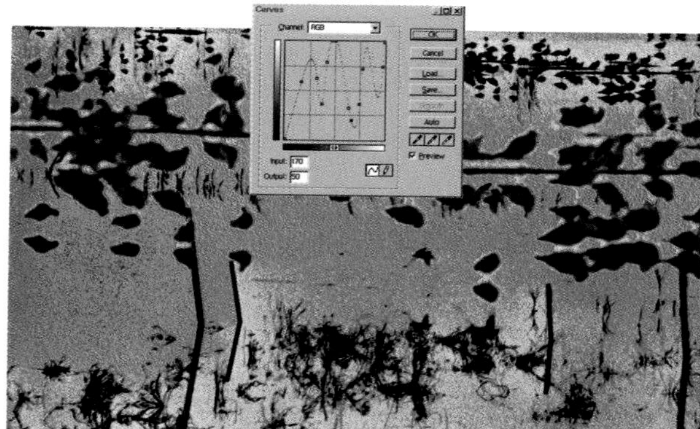

41.10

26. **Choose Filter→Sharpen→Unsharp Mask with the settings Amount: 100%, Radius: 1.0, and Threshold: 0.**
    This helps increase the contrast and sharpness in the image.
27. **Selectively add bits and pieces of the wildly colored image back into Layer 7 (41.11).**
    Using variations of this technique, repeat these steps to build interesting color variations.
28. **Use the Rubber Stamp tool to eliminate unwanted areas and simplify the design.**

Artist's Creative Insight and Advice

Why Digital?

We are just at the beginning of a dazzling and exciting new way of creating art! The advantages in the digital medium are what motivate me to get deeper and deeper into technology. I feel that the tools offer endless, new, and wonderful possibilities and that delights, fascinates, and intrigues me. The disadvantages can be the costs of keeping up with emerging technologies.

Advice for Artists Working in the Digital Medium

I think that artists using technology tools will continue to be subjected to some prejudice against the medium, so I suggest that they be prepared to educate the public and the art world about what they are doing.

The computer is not necessarily a time-saving device! Although I might save time doing some things, I spend more and more time on a piece to achieve greater complexity and to create images that I could barely even have dreamt of before.

Output

Archival integrity is very important to me, and I work with extremely long-lasting papers and inks. I find the digital fine art papers made by Hahnemuhle the best. I have also made many beautiful prints with Hewlett Packard's Designjet wide-format printer.

I call my way of working "tradigital" as it combines the use of new art-making digital tools with traditional ones, such as etching or photography and collaging, sewing, or painting on the work. Blending various media offers infinite creative possibilities.

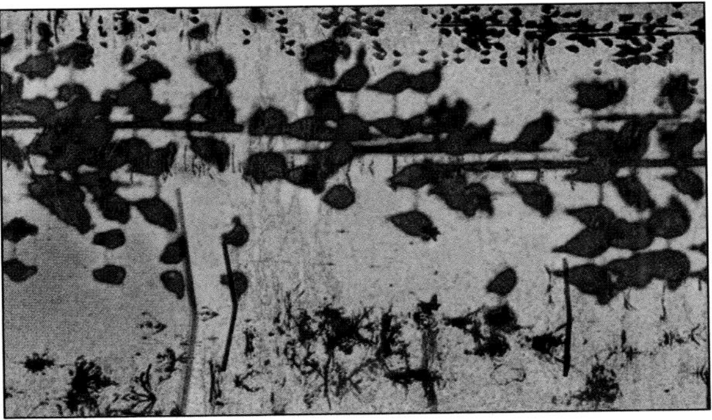

● 41.11

Lynda Lambert on Helen Golden

"Golden captures the essence of what it is to be human. Her work is far beyond surface representation, much deeper. It is the spirit that she is touching, defining, revealing in the work and also in the viewer."

– Lynda Lambert, Assistant Professor in Fine Arts and Humanities, Geneva College, Beaver Falls, Pennsylvania

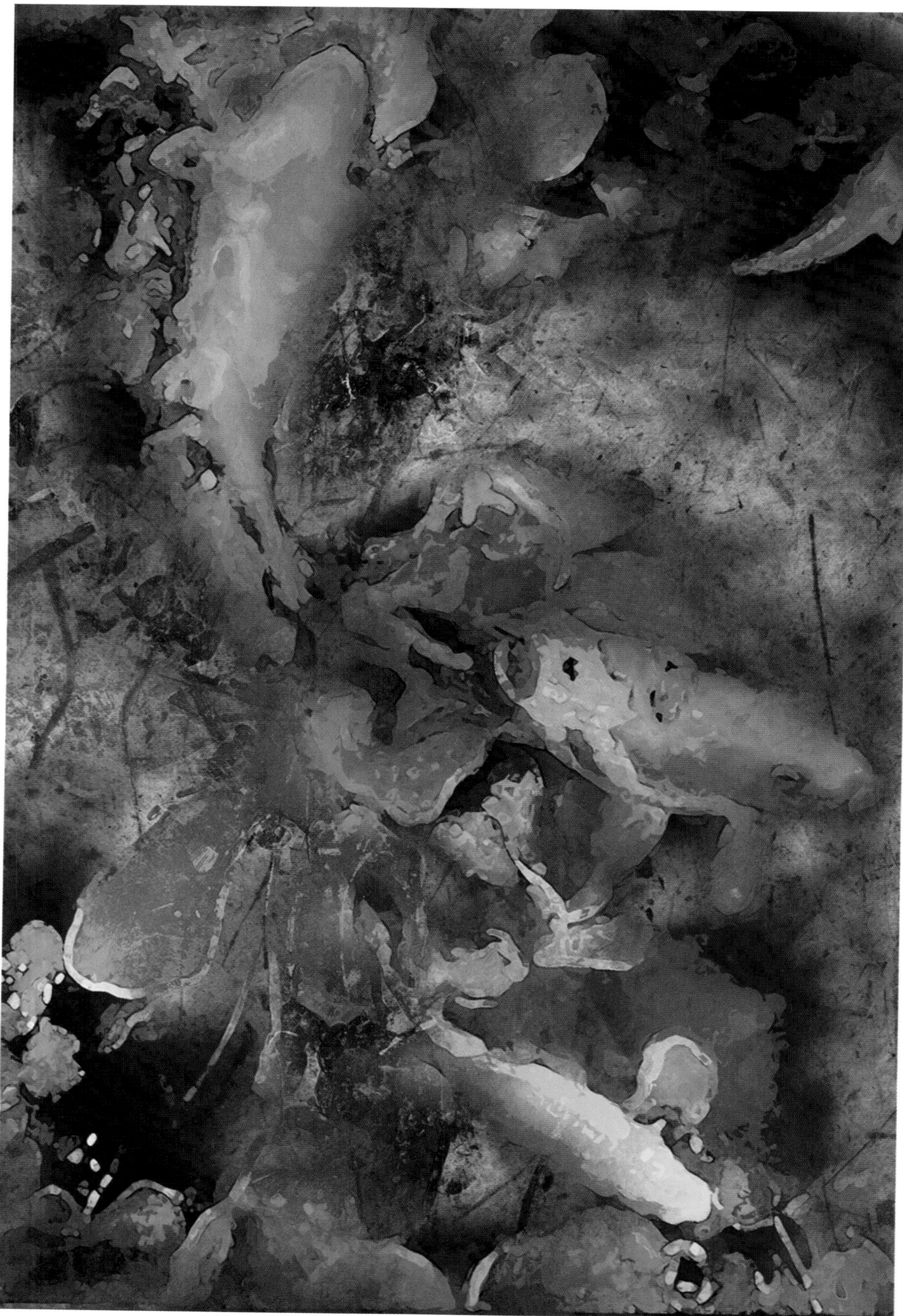

Chapter 42

Koi Pond

by Charles Kacin

Artist's Statement

I love color and the power it possesses to create an emotion. I like my art to visually stimulate and excite the viewer with a bold use of color and images that are out of the commonplace. I like taking the ordinary and making it special through selective color shifts and pairing like and unlike images to create a new visual that questions reality.

The Story Behind the Artwork

Charles wanted to create a piece that exploited color to its fullest and to "break" conventional color usage. He loved the form and shape that elements take in water and has a particular affinity for fish as they react in their watery environment. He also wanted to create a piece that would allow him to experiment with the painterly effects you can achieve with Photoshop filters.

The Creative Process

Charles created *Koi Pond* (42.1) in Photoshop. He started with a base image of random color shapes and applied many artistic filters to the colors to get the

◀ 42.1

distortion he wanted. The Glass filter was particularly helpful in getting a distortion (42.2).

He cut each of the fish out of its respective photo and assembled them onto individual layers (42.3).

Charles also introduced a layer beneath the fish that showed plants he had photographed on the pond surface. He started to experiment with applying different filters, like Paint Daubs, Watercolor, Ink Outline, and the Glass filter, to the different layers, all the time reducing their potency by fading the effects (42.4).

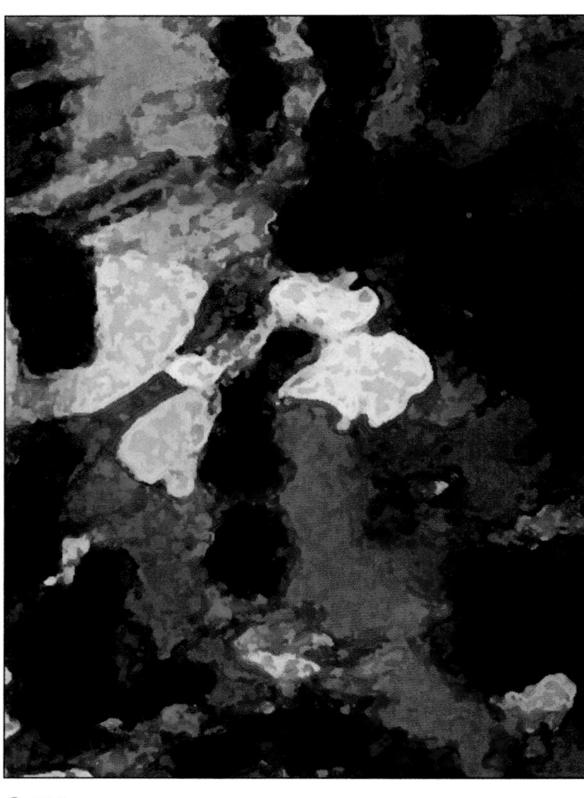

42.2

42.3

About the Artist

Biography

Chuck Kacin has a BA in Journalism/Advertising from Northern Illinois University, DeKalb, Illinois, and a Masters of Adult Education from National-Louis University in Wheaton, Illinois. He is a full-time Graphic Arts professor at College of DuPage.

Influences

While much of Charles' work deals with a surreal environment; it is nonetheless grounded in his reactions to nature and its creativity.

Another influence is art done by others. Charles likes nothing more than to peer over the shoulder of other artists and see first-hand their methods of creation and thinking.

Studio

Computer System:
iMac computer to surf the Web
G4 for serious work

Charles' approach to working with layers and layer masks in this image demonstrates the flexibility of layers for experimentation and for happy accidents to occur. Charles frequently duplicated an image layer, applied a filter or adjustment to the entire image at full strength, and then faded the strength of the filter or adjustment to achieve the desired effect (Edit→Fade), and, if desired, painted through the layer mask to reveal the unmodified layer underneath. For example, Charles adjusted the hue and saturation on a duplicated layer of the original background art and then painted through the layer mask to reveal the original artwork below.

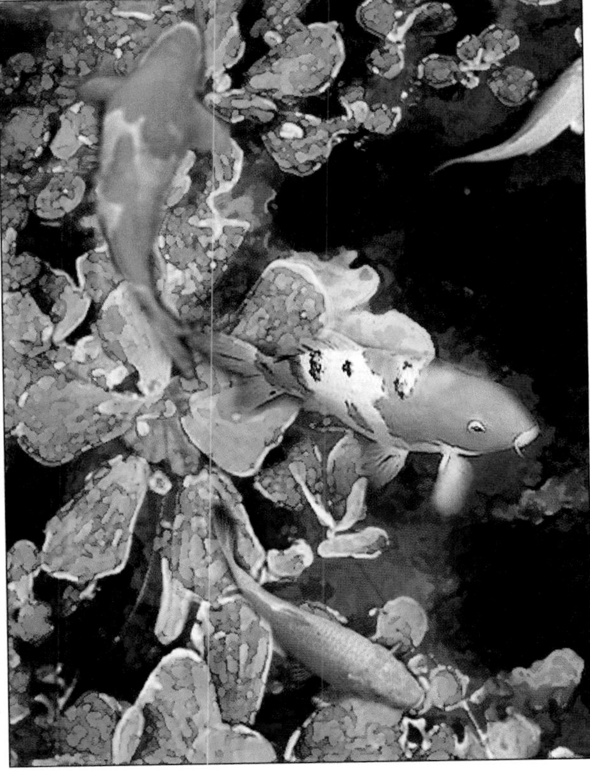

42.4

Charles experimented with the different looks that can be achieved with the various layer blending modes, like Color, Hue, Difference, Luminosity, and Exclusion, to create some exciting color shifts. He double-clicked on the layer name in the Layers palette to reveal the Layer Style dialog box. He used the Advanced Blending sliders to pull one image into another, creating an effect that would be hard to recreate using conventional methods. He selected just one of the slider portions (in the "This Layer" and the "Underlying Layer" sliders) by holding down the option (alt) key to achieve a more subtle blending of the images.

Charles scanned in a piece of hand-made Japanese rice paper; he felt this would unify the composition and tie the subject matter to the Japanese custom of keeping fish as symbols of good fortune. He used a layer mask to adjust the amount of paper in the composition and applied it in the Difference mode. He also used the History Brush to texture and distort the

Software:
Adobe Photoshop
Quark
Illustrator
Painter

Tablet:
Wacom Art-Z

Archive Media:
CD burner with Toast

Input Devices:
Olympus 3040 digital camera

Printers:
Epson photo printer for color output
HP laser for black and white

Contact

Charles A. Kacin
Darien, Illinois
ckacin@aol.com

images, and to revert the painting back to earlier stages in select areas (42.5).

He applied the Lighting Effects filter to soften the intensity of the colors and to add depth. Finally, Charles adjusted the Hue and Saturation and individually tweaked the colors (42.6).

Technique: Using Filters to Modify Imagery (Photoshop)

This technique shows how Charles applies two filters in succession to soften and distort an image — in this case, the plants that were floating on the surface of the pond.

1. **Open the original photograph you want to modify in Photoshop (42.7).**
2. **Choose Filter→Artistic→Paint Daubs and adjust the settings to suit the effect you want.**

   Charles set the Brush Size at 3 and Sharpness at 7 (42.8).
3. **Choose Filter→Distort→Glass and adjust the settings to suit the effect you want.**

   Charles set the Distortion at 4 and Smoothness at 6 (42.9).
4. **Choose Image→Adjust→Hue/Saturation and adjust the hue and saturation settings to enhance the image (42.10).**

Judge's Critique

Seybold Digital Art Contest, New York, 2002

"The painting shows good surface design. There are eroded, splotchy areas. The use of color is bold. All-in-all, it's interesting in nuance."

— MARK ZIMMER, Co-Founder, Fractal Design

(www.fractal.com)

Artist's Creative Insight and Advice

Why Digital?

Working on a computer gives me the ability to be much more spontaneous than I was able to be with traditional media. It also allows me to take more

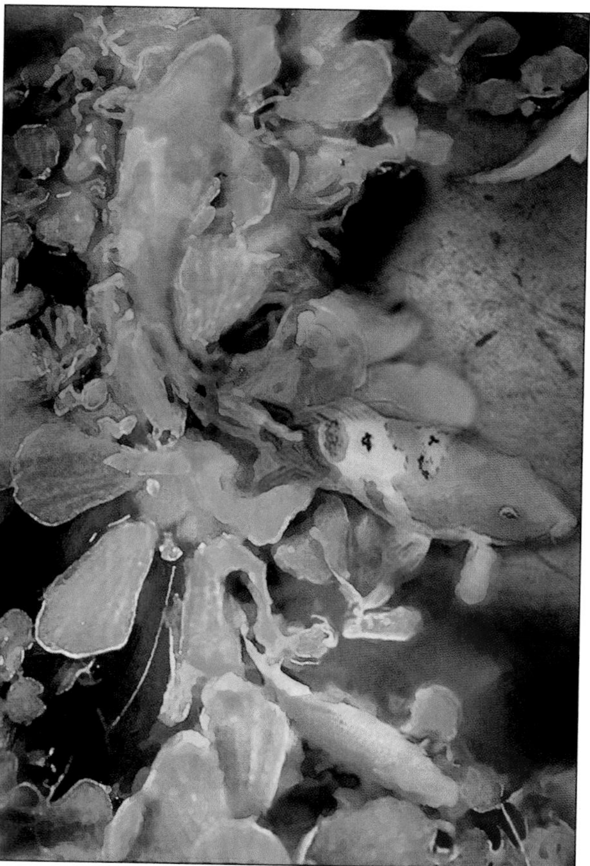

● 42.5

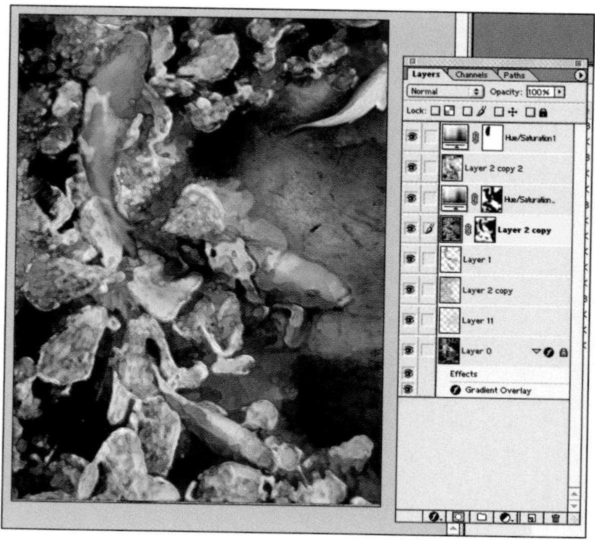

● 42.6

chances — if it doesn't work, I can just erase it. Of course, I am always challenged by the fact that I worked three dimensionally for so long, using clay and paper. So I try to bring that feeling to my digital art.

The most difficult part of painting on the computer for me is to know when to stop. By using separate layers for each stage of a painting, I can backtrack easily, and often in the end, throw away many layers. In other words, my last step is usually to simplify a painting. This is something I could never do when I worked with natural media.

I know that this painting has more of a "digital" feel than a "natural" feel, but to me that is simply the character of the digital medium. I don't try to avoid the digital look. After all, an oil painting looks like it was created with oil paints, acrylic paintings look like they were created with acrylics, and a watercolor definitely looks like a watercolor. To me, a digital painting is what it is, and it's just like using another medium. My digital art looks very much like art I have created in other media, at least in terms of style. It's just a different kind of paint.

Advice for Artists

While the computer is a vital and important tool for both today's art and the art of tomorrow, it is still necessary and essential that persons doing art use some traditional methods, like keeping a sketchbook or thinking ideas out on paper. The computer is a tool and should not be used as a means to generate quick and thoughtless art. The computer doesn't

42.7

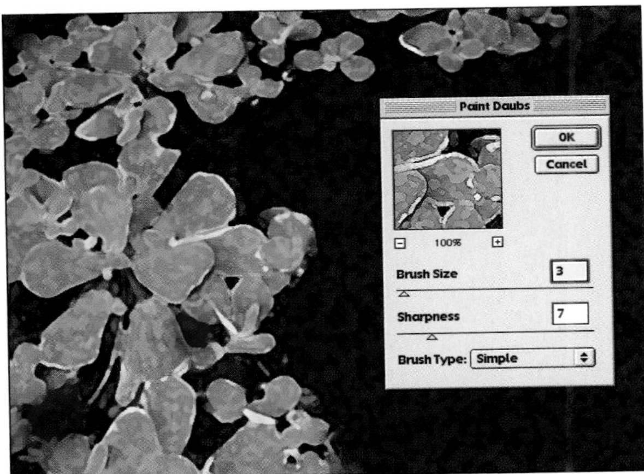

42.8

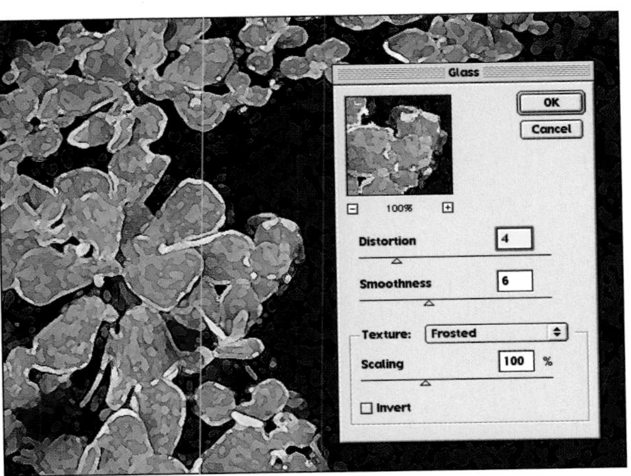

42.9

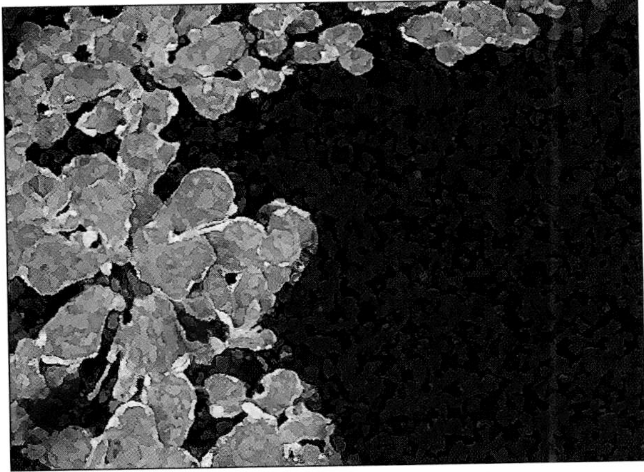
42.10

make art — the artist does. The computer is merely a means to release the creativity within the artist.

Observe, record, and regrow ideas both on paper and in your mind. You will be surprised at how much you can accomplish without ever touching a computer or making a mark on a piece of paper. I have often said the painting is complete in my mind — all I have to do is get it out and onto paper.

Beyond that, learn from your peers; they will be your future competition.

Working with Service Bureaus

Talk to printers before you send them your work. Printers can be a wealth of information that artists often neglect but often blame when their work doesn't appear as they envisioned it. As an artist, quality images created with the final goal of printed output should reflect a respect of the limitations and abilities of the medium.

Chapter 43

Facing Time

by Bonny Lhotka

Artist's Statement

Through life, I gather memories and communicate my emotional response through the use of textural surfaces, real and implied.

My art is a continuum. It is a non-identical reflection of who I am. Each day adds to and changes my past. My art is who I am. Without it I would cease to exist. It is a passionate and compelling reason to live.

It is the excitement of not knowing what new image will appear that takes me to the studio. Each day is a gift. I paint for myself and hope someone else gets my message. It is like sending a message to the universe hoping someone will see.

The Story Behind the Artwork

Bonny became an artist after seeing her first Walt Disney animated film and recalls thinking that images fell out of a brush at the upper-left of the canvas and magically appeared from top to bottom. She finds it ironic that the digital inkjet printer lays down an image in this fashion. The lenticular imaging she uses has direct parallels to the animated cells created in those early films.

Each year, Bonny creates one work at the winter and summer solstice. The day is reserved for creating a work that will reach beyond the last solstice piece, either in concept or process. *Facing Time* (43.1) began in the Winter Solstice of 1999.

Shortly after starting to compose the art, the full moon was visible from her studio on the evening of the new millennium. As the year 2000 arrived, she thought about the disappearance of the time past and the moon and decided to include these themes in her art. The lenticular process allowed her to express the passing of time in a way not possible in any other media.

◀ 43.1

The Creative Process

To understand Bonny's creative process, you first need to understand lenticular printmaking.

Artists throughout the ages have worked on the problem of representing three-dimensional space on a two-dimensional plane. Several of the most effective attempts to capture realistic space rely on human stereoscopic vision; each eye sees a slightly different view. This approach, applied to photography, made stereograph viewers a common site in parlors in the United States 100 years ago. In the 50s, small novelty items in which photographic images flipped from one image to another appeared in cereal boxes and on political pins. After lying dormant for half a century, advances in digital imaging allow the creation of spectacular three-dimensional images using lenticular technology.

A lenticular image allows the viewer to see a series of "frames" (usually 2 to 24) sequentially when looking at an image from different angles. By carefully crafting these frames, the artist can create animation, depth, and the morphing of images.

To create lenticulars, the source images are developed in image-creation software, like Adobe Photoshop. A series of variations on the image are saved as separate files. Each of these variations becomes a frame in the finished lenticular print.

In order to create the illusion of depth in a lenticular image, the artist uses Photoshop to develop a set of frames in which elements in the image are offset to the left or right. Elements which are designed to recede into the background are offset to the left; elements designed to project forward of the picture plane are offset to the right. Elements can also be turned on and off in sequence to give the impression of blinking. To create movement, elements are altered in form and/or position across all frames.

The resultant frame set is then interlaced in linear strips that match the lenticular lens. This lens is a piece of plastic, with a series of parallel lenses, or lenticules, embossed into one surface. After the interlaced image is printed, it is aligned with the lens, so that the viewer sees only one frame at a time. As the viewer moves by the image, all of the frames are seen

● 43.2

dS

About the Artist

Biography

In 1997, along with other members of Unique Editions, Bonny organized Digital Atelier: A Printmaking Studio for the 21st Century at the National Museum of American Art of the Smithsonian Institution. Unique Editions received the Computer World Smithsonian Award. The same year, Bonny and Dorothy Krause helped a group of curators envision the potential of digital printmaking in Media for a New Millennium, a work-tank/think-shop organized by the Vinalhaven Graphic Arts Foundation. At the opening of the Brooklyn Museum of Art 27th Print National, *Digital: Printmaking Now,* Bonny demonstrated digital printmaking techniques along with Digital Atelier artists Dorothy Krause and Karin Schminke.

Her artwork has been commissioned by 100 collections including Lucent Technologies, United Airlines, Johns Space Center, Jones Intercable, Avaya, the U.S. Department of State, Charles Schwab, MCI, and McDonnell Douglas. She is listed in *Who's Who in American Art* and *Who's Who in American Women.*

Influences

Bonny's art is influenced by her experiences. She believes that art comes from an individual's response to what happens in sequence, creating the illusion of movement, depth, animation, morphing, or 3D space that the artist set up in the original frames.

Specialized lenticular software, like Flip!, can interlace 18 or more images and create test patterns that are used to determine the proper pitch or increment (to 1,000th of an inch) to interlace for a perfect match with the lens. Each lens, combined with different printers, inks, and paper, may require a different pitch.

Facing Time is made from a variety of source images that were incorporated into a multi-layered Photoshop file. In this layer, you see a digital photo she took of an antique compass she found in Australia (43.2). This layer is based on a 35mm photo taken by her son, Gregory Lhotka, of a clock at the Musée d'Orsay, Paris (43.3).

Bonny made a series of layers based on a close-up digital photo, taken by her sister-in law, Linda Pierce, of a doll. To make the lenticular print more interesting, Bonny separated the eyes (43.4) from the rest of

43.3

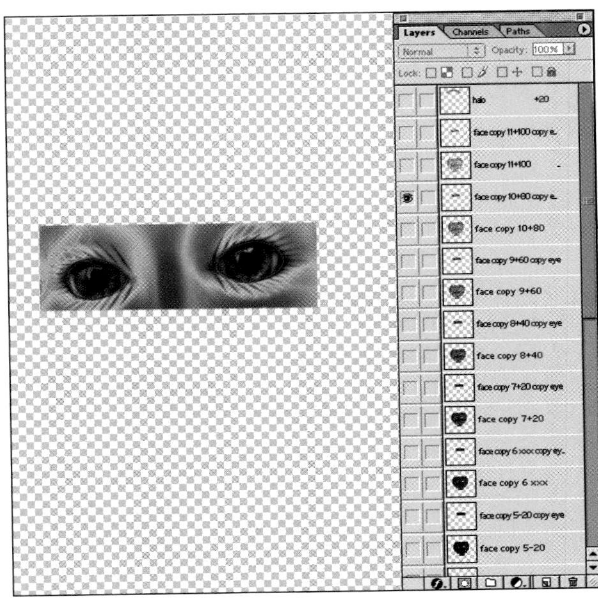

43.4

where they live spiritually, spatially, and intellectually.

Bonny also states that a willingness of companies to sponsor Unique Editions™, and later Digital Atelier®, has provided her with the opportunity to create art in ways that would otherwise not been possible.

Studio

Computer System:
Macintosh Titanium, 500 MHz
20GB hard drive
500MB RAM
Compaq 5330US
(Reconfigured for Win2000 with Nvidia Gforce Ti 500 graphic card)
1.5GB RAM

Monitors:
Radius PressView 21-inch

Software:
Super 3D Genius
Super Flip!
Photoshop

Archive Media:
Pioneer 4.7GB DVD-R superdrive
Yamaha CD-RW

Tablet:
Wacom 4 x 5 GD-0405-U

Input Devices:
Microtek ScanMaker 5
Epson 836XL
Microtek ArtiXscan for 35mm slides

Output Devices:
RJ-8000 Falcon II
Epson 9500
Encad 880 flat bed
Tektronix 780
Hex Pigment Inks with Wasatch Rip
PhotoScript Soft Rip

Contact

Bonny Lhotka
Boulder, Colorado
Bonny@Lhotka.com
www.Lhotka.com

the face (43.5). This allowed her to make the eyes appear to recede behind the eyelids and follow the viewer as they walked around the print.

43.5

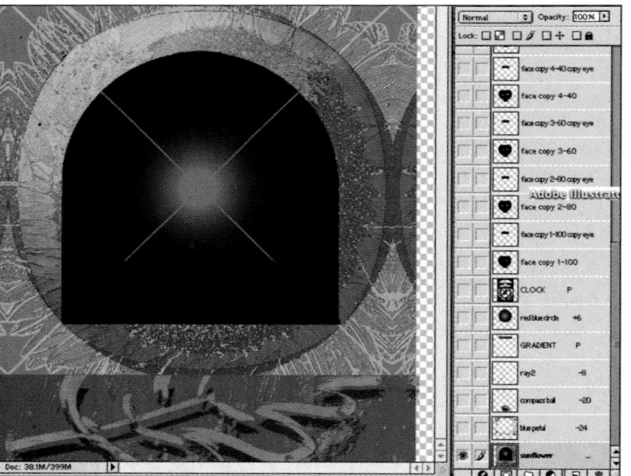

43.6

The bottom layer was a recycled image based on a digital photo of a sunflower grown in her yard (43.6). Bonny added a glowing gold-colored halo (43.7) inspired by the full moon on the winter solstice. Besides these source images, Bonny added additional layers of gradients and shapes, and made a series of layers of the face. This file ended up with 26 layers (43.8).

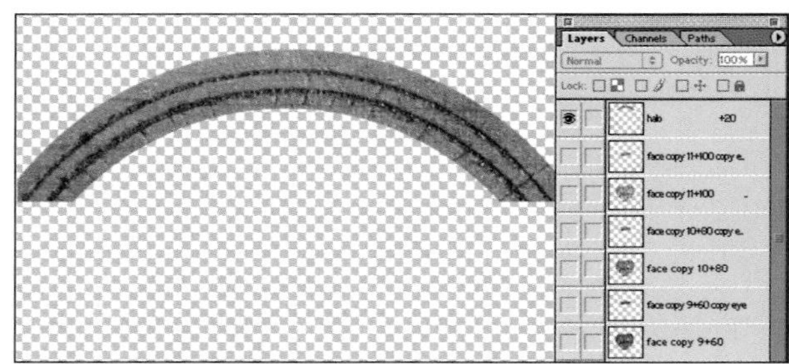

43.7

43.8

The file included all the elements used in the frame shots that were made to create the 3D effect. Selected objects were moved to the left or right depending on whether Bonny wanted the objects to project forward or recede back in space. If an object was animated, she turned it on for at least four of the frames. One example of an animation is the way Bonny modified the brightness of the face so it would appear to fade into the background (43.9).

Bonny spent 40 to 60 hours creating each lenticular image. Her work starts with more elements than needed to tell the story. She then begins removing items until there is nothing left to take out. When she sees the essence of the message in the image, she stops. She uses this process of reduction in both her traditional and digital art.

Technique: Transferring a Digital Print to Wood

This technique explains how Bonny transfers her digital prints to wooden surfaces. You can try this technique at home with just a few supplies.

1. **Open a digital image in Photoshop that you want to print onto wood.**
2. **Choose Image→Rotate Canvas→Flip Horizontal.**
3. **Choose Image→Rotate Canvas→Flip Vertical.**
   These rotations prevent your image from ending up being printed back-to-front.

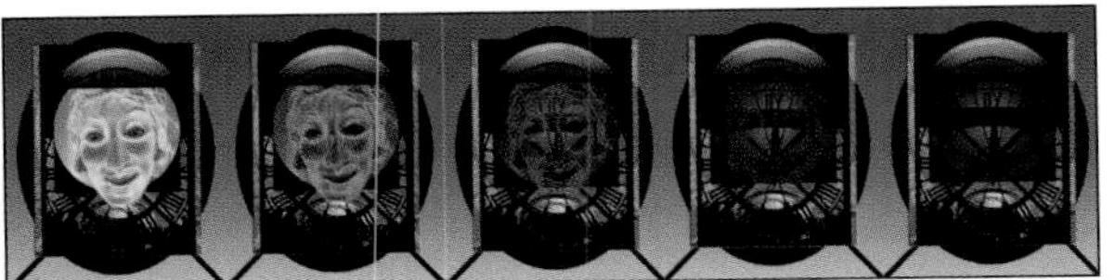

43.9

4. **Choose File→Save As and save the image with a name indicating it has been reversed.**
5. **Make a digital print of that file on clear or white film using pigment inks.**

[TIP]

Bonny recommends Rexam white film or Kimoto Clear Transfer Film, both available from major inkjet suppliers; you must use an inkjet media with a water-soluble coating. It is also recommended that archival pigment inks, as opposed to dye-based inks, are used. They will give much better, longer-lasting results.

After flipping the image right to left, the surround was printed onto Kimoto Clear Transfer Film using the Mutoh Falcon with Pigment inks (43.10).

6. **Prepare a flat piece of wood to receive the print.**
   Bonny recommends Baltic Birch wood. Plywood also works well.

43.10

7. **Use duct tape to form a "lip" (43.11) around the edges of the wooden block to create a tray for holding the glue.**
8. **Warm 1/2 cup (about 2 ounces) of Rabbit Skin Glue in 1 quart of hot water.**
9. **After the glue is dissolved, pour it on to the wooden block (43.12).**
10. **After the glue has set to the consistency of Jell-O, roll the print face down on to the glue surface, with the image facing down and in contact with the glue.**
11. **Wait 5 minutes, then remove the film (43.13).**

The printed image will be transferred to the gel. As the glue evaporates and dries, the image will drop and bond to the wood. (Look at the Studio section of Bonny's Web site, `www.Lhotka.com`, to see an animation showing Bonny doing this transfer process.)

After the glue dries, and the image sinks into and is adhered to the wood, seal the surface with Krylon Crystal Clear to protect it from moisture (43.14).

Artist's Creative Insight and Advice

Why Digital?

The primary disadvantage of the digital medium is the cost of the equipment and the constantly changing technology. Working digitally can also have the effect of inhibiting spontaneous response to accidents that can take the art in exciting, though unanticipated, directions.

The biggest advantage is being able to seamlessly include photography with traditional media.

Advice for Artists Working in the Digital Medium

Use the tools you can afford and concentrate on content. Do not be seduced into thinking digital art is about the latest or newest technology. Spend at least one day a week working with traditional media.

Unless you intend to use the medium as a press to create reproductions of work in other mediums, you should buy a printer you can afford and do you own printing.

● 43.11

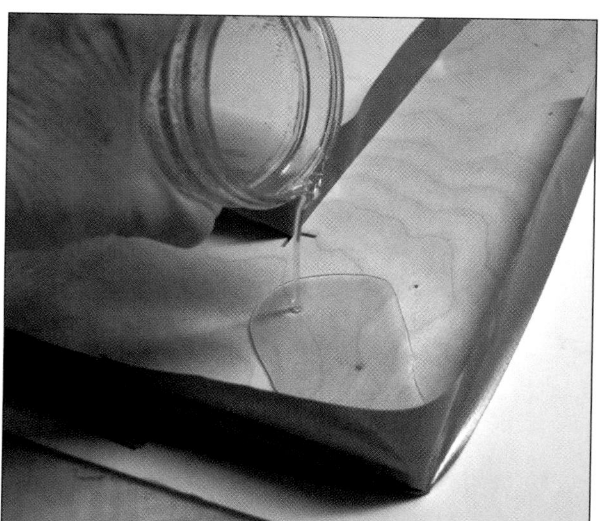

● 43.12

I have developed the digital fresco transfer, which allows me to put a digital image on to any surface. The advantage of this is that I don't have to be restricted to media that can be fed through a printer.

I urge artists to focus on the art and not the technology. Be an artist, not a digital artist.

● 43.13

● 43.14

John Shaw on Bonny Lhotka

"Bonny's graphics, being evaluated in the environment of the André Schellenberg program, are outstanding primarily for her innovative use of printmaking equipment and materials and her application of the developing digital output technologies, to what in fact are images designed for, existing in, and being recognized as, Fine Art. Bonny has been incredibly innovative in applying a developing commercial technology in the world of fine art printmaking. And the impact of her images has been significant, both in the digital fine art community, and also within the commercial large-format digital graphics field in which DPI members operate."

– John Shaw, Managing Director of the Digital Printing & Imaging Association (`www.dpia.org`)

Chapter 44

Autumn Window

by Judy Mandolf

Artist's Statement

There is infinite space in this world for beauty.

The Story Behind the Artwork

Autumn Window (44.1) began as a digital photo taken in natural light in a castle in England with a Nikon 950 camera (44.2). It was October, and England was glowing with intense autumn color, which Judy wanted to capture in this still life.

The Creative Process

Judy's digital images begin as original photographs, which are transferred to a computer, collaged, painted, and otherwise manipulated by various software programs. They are then printed on watercolor paper using archival inks and are sometimes further enhanced by applying various paints and pencils to the surface.

In this case, Judy opened the digital photo in Adobe Photoshop. She cropped the image to create a satisfying composition. She then lightened the overall exposure with Image➔Adjust Levels. She lightened the cyan cast by adjusting the color balance (see Technique #1 later in this chapter).

● 44.2

◀ 44.1

To correct burnout on the left side of the window, Judy copied the right side of the window and pasted it into the left side. Judy cleaned up the central vertical beam by copying and pasting clean portions. She used the Clone Stamp tool (Rubber Stamp tool) to remove traces of the sign in the background of the original photograph.

Judy brightened the gold leaf using the Sponge tool (44.3), which is explained in Technique #2, also later in this chapter. Judy then copied and pasted a pear and two leaves from two other digital photographs (44.4).

Judy adjusted the highlights and shadows on the pear and leaves to match the background. She applied grain and diffusion with the nik Color Efex Photoshop plug-in. As a final touch, she applied a soft edge effect using the Photo/Graphic Edges Photoshop plug-in.

44.3

44.4

About the Artist

Biography

Judy has exhibited her hand-colored photographs and, since 1996, her digital imagery throughout the United States and Europe; her work has also been widely published throughout the world.

She was selected *International Photographer* magazine's Photographer of the Year in 1988, was awarded the Gold Medal Discovery Award by *Art of California* magazine in 1992, and won the New Names/New Faces competition at the prestigious Santa Fe East Gallery in Santa Fe, New Mexico, in 1990. Her digital imagery earned first place awards in the Fallbrook Art and Cultural Competition, the Del Mar Exposition, and *Computer Edge* magazine's art competition. In 2000, she was a winner in the Macworld Digital Art competition, and in 2002 in the Seybold competition.

Technique #1: Compensating for a Color Cast (Photoshop)

Often a photo has a slight color cast, such as too much blue or yellow overall. This technique shares Judy's approach to compensating for this shift.

1. **Open your photo in Photoshop.**
2. **Choose Image→Adjust→Color Balance.**
3. **Use the three tiers of sliders to adjust the color as necessary (44.5).**
   If you are compensating for a cyan cast, as in this case, add some red and some yellow. Midtones is checked by default.
4. **Make adjustments with the Highlights and Shadows checked to see if they help improve the image.**

Technique #2: Enhancing Intricate Areas (Photoshop)

This technique allows you to bring out the brightness, brilliance, and radiance of an intricate element in a photograph — in this case, the gold leaf on the plate.

1. **Open the image in Photoshop.**
2. **Select the Sponge tool (from the same pop-up menu as the Dodge and Burn tools).**
3. **Set the Sponge mode to Saturate and the pressure setting to about 70%.**
4. **Experiment with brush sizes (44.6) to ensure that the Sponge is a suitable size for the region you want to enhance.**

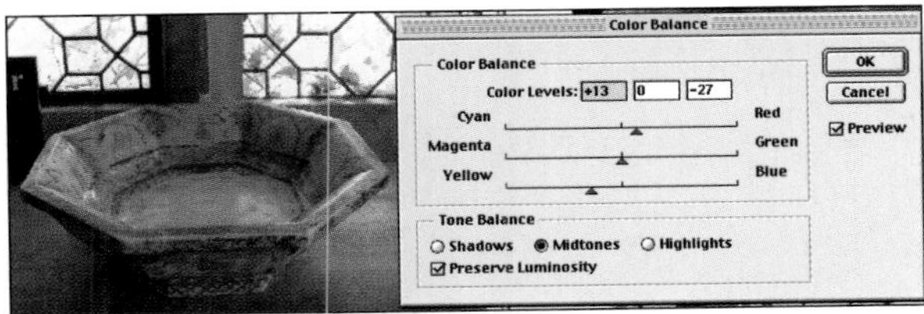

● 44.5

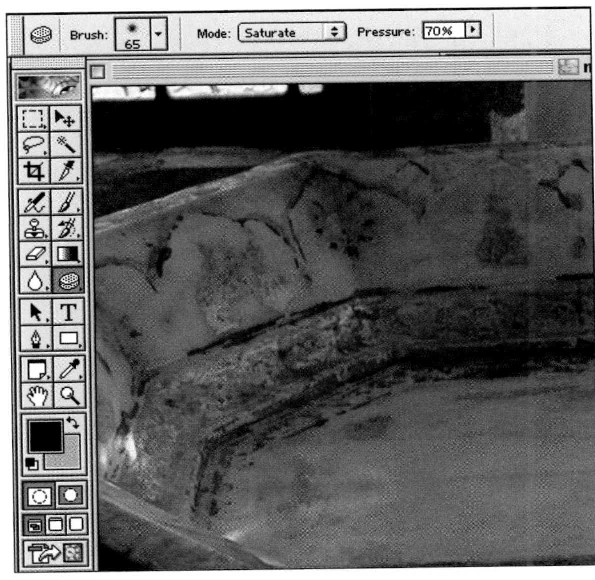

● 44.6

Influences

Georgia O'Keeffe, Jerry Eulsmann, Margaret Nau, Renee Magritte, Dali, and most Northern European masters.

Studio

Computer System:
Macintosh G4 Dual Processor
80GB hard drive
1.5GB RAM

Monitors:
Apple 22-inch flat screen

Software:
Adobe Photoshop
Painter
Studio Artist

Archive Media:
Internal CD Recorder

Input Devices:
Epson 1650

Printers:
Epson 7500 and 1280

Contact

Judy Mandolf
San Diego, California
judymandolf@yahoo.com
www.judymandolf.com

5. **Lightly apply the Sponge tool over the region of interest.**
   Brush back and forth until you are satisfied with the saturation.

Judge's Critique

"I appreciate the use of the restrained monochromatic palette in this piece. There is also a warm translucent quality to the windows that makes one wonder what lies beyond. Nice interplay between smooth and textured objects. Very simple, yet mood invoking."

— DIANE FENSTER, Digital Artist

(www.dianefenster.com)

Artist's Creative Insight and Advice

Why Digital?

I converted from darkroom to digital in 1996, intending it only as an adjunct to my traditional work, namely hand-coloring black-and-white photos. I had never used a computer and didn't really know what could be done. After sitting down with the Apple and Photoshop manuals, I was immediately addicted. I never went back in my darkroom and don't even own one now. There are no smelly chemicals, no long, drawn-out processes, and, best of all, there are no limitations except the extent of my imagination.

Being True to Yourself

Be true to your own style. The one criticism I have with a lot of digital work is the tendency to over create. Filters are heady gadgets and fun to use, but they can easily annihilate a nice image.

Color Management

The slightest change in paper, ink printer, or monitor can throw the color off. And then there is *metamerism,* the phenomenon of pigment-based inks taking on green or magenta casts depending on the ambient light. I have found it well worthwhile to invest in a good profile for each printer paper and monitor combination. I purchase these profiles from www.profilecity.com.

Archival Integrity

It's easy today to achieve archival integrity by using the correct inks and papers. Both of my printers use Epson archival pigmented inks, and numerous archival papers are available. And, of course, it's necessary to follow through with acid-free mounting boards. I output all my work on my Epson 7500 printer.

SUNRISE
MOONRISE
SUNSET
MOONSET
+29 WINTER MOON HIGH
+24 SUMMER SUN
+19 WINTER MOON LOW
−19 SUMMER MOON HIGH
−24 WINTER SUN
−29 SUMMER MOON LOW
HEEL
CENTER
0 10 20 30 40 50

Chapter 45

Primordial Fear

by Dorothy Simpson Krause

Artist's Statement

My work embeds archetypal symbols and fragments of image and text in multiple layers of texture and meaning. By focusing on timeless personal and universal issues — hopes and fears, wishes, lies and dreams, immortality and transience — I challenge myself and the viewer to look beyond the surface to see what depths are hidden.

The Story Behind the Artwork

Primordial Fear (45.1) was a part of the series *timeXposure,* which focuses on how we explore the unknown and master our fears. It incorporates symbols, plans for computing devices, molecular drawings, celestial maps, astrological charts, and photographs of places of power, including the early megalithic sites of Stonehenge and Avebury.

Dot summarizes the underlying philosophy behind the piece, saying, "Although we now have considerably more empirical knowledge than at any other point in history, we understand little more of the mysteries of life and death, time and space than our prehistoric ancestors did. We yearn for connection, but we are essentially alone."

◀ 45.1

The Creative Process

Primordial Fear was composed from six scanned objects: a photograph by Viola Kaumlen of a dramatic sky (45.2); a diagram of Babbage's computing engine (45.3); an early transistor (45.4); a photograph by Jan Doucette of model Linda Serafin (45.5); a drawing of celestial azimuth alignments at Stonehenge (45.6); and a compass (45.7).

45.2

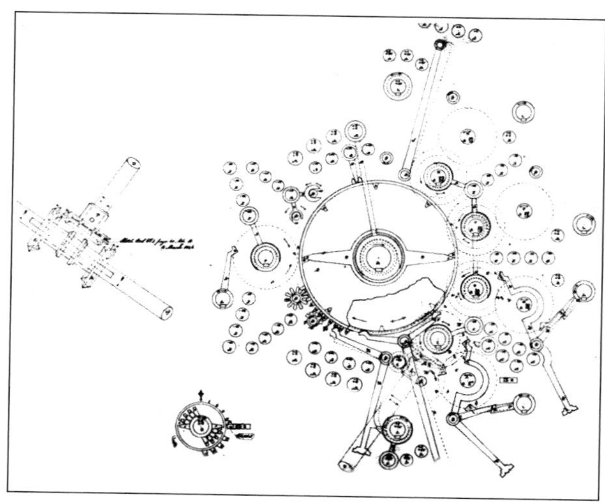

45.3

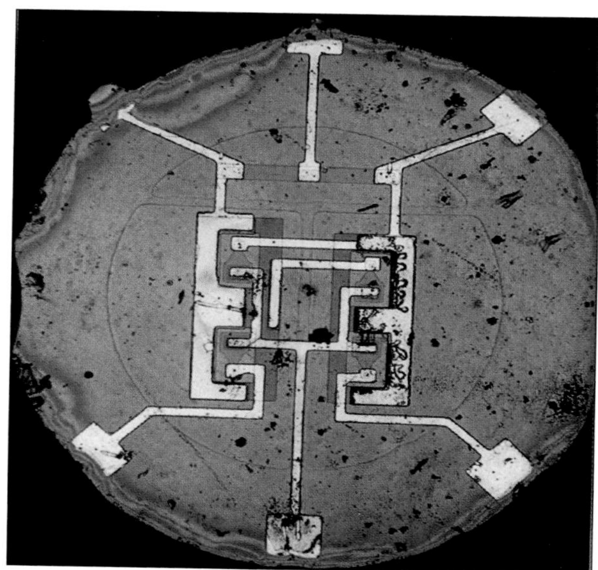

45.4

About the Artist

Biography

Krause is a painter, collage artist, and printmaker who incorporates digital mixed media into her art. Her work is exhibited regularly in galleries and museums and featured in more than three dozen current periodicals and books. She is Professor Emeritus at Massachusetts College of Art, where she founded the Computer Arts Center, and a member of the Digital Atelier® artist collaborative. She is a frequent speaker at conferences and symposia. For her work at the National Museum of American Art she received a Smithsonian Technology in the Arts Award.

Influences

Especially influenced by being able to combine the latest in technology with the humblest of materials, including plaster, tar, wax, and pigment, to evoke the past and herald the future.

45.5

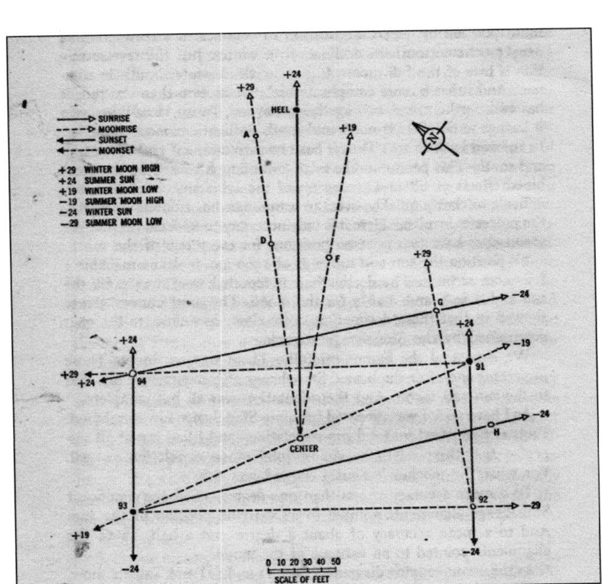

45.6

45.7

Studio

Computer System:

Apple G4, 733MHz
1G hard drive
80G RAM

Monitors:

Radius Pressview 21-inch

Software:

Adobe Photoshop
Procreate Painter

Tablet:

Wacom 6 x 8

Input Devices:

Epson Expression 836XL

Removable Media:

CD

Archive Media:

CD

Printers:

Encad 880
Epson 9500
Mutoh Falcon
Tektronix 780

Contact

Dorothy Simpson Krause
Marshfield Hills, Massachusetts
DotKrause@DotKrause.com
www.DotKrause.com

Dot used lenticular lens technology in this image to make different elements appear to recede or come forward to a viewer walking past. You can see this effect dramatically in an original print of the image.

A lenticular lens (45.8) is a plastic lens that is made up of many very small lens strips, usually oriented vertically, one next to the other. Each miniature lens is known as a *lenticule.* The resolution of a lens is measured in lenticules per inch (lpi). Dot uses lenses with 40 lpi resolution.

Dot uses Flip! software, from `www.FlipSigns.com`, and lenses from `www.MicroLens.com`. The software, Flip!, transforms separate frames into specially interlaced digital images that, when combined with a sheet of uniquely designed lenticular plastic lenses, produces multi-image prints that change with the viewing angle. This produces the illusion of motion, the appearance of an image getting closer or farther away (zooming), the appearance of one picture merging into another (morphing), and a sequence of images that appear to move (animating). In this image, Dot primarily makes use of the animation capability as the planet behind the woman rises and sets.

Within the series of frames generated by Dot for the lenticular print, selected elements were offset slightly in small increments from one frame to the next. To make an object recede, as in the case of the sky, it was moved in small increments to the left. To make an object come forward, as in the lines of the azimuth, it was moved in small increments to the right. The greater the size of the incremental steps, and the larger the number of steps, the more depth was created.

Dot first created a layered file in Photoshop (45.9). She then generated eight frames with the various layers shifted to the left or right in small increments depending on whether she wanted them to recede or come forward, as explained previously. Here are three sample frames (45.10 through 45.12) to give you an idea of the steps. You can see the size of the rising planet increasing in each frame.

The eight frames were interlaced together in vertical strips using the software program Flip! The result was a single, flat, interlaced TIFF image that was then printed using the Mutoh Falcon on Roland PETG white film (45.13). Film substrate was used rather than paper since film holds the high-resolution image more firmly and precisely — paper tends to swell or distort.

45.8

45.9

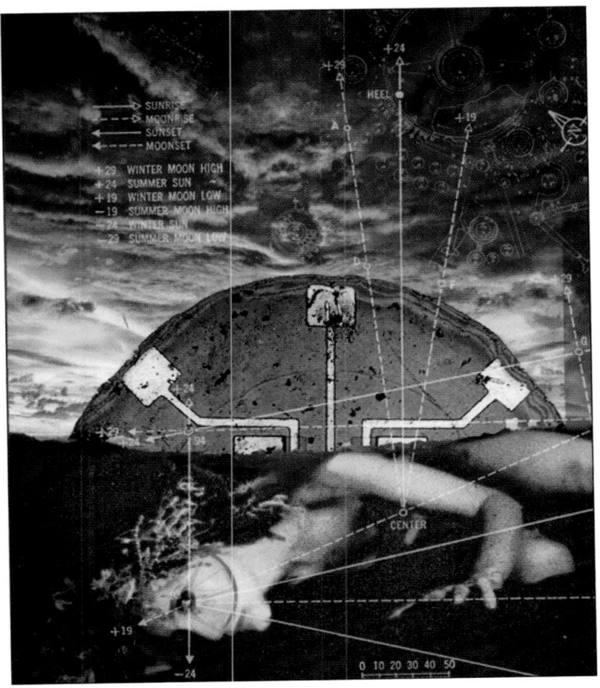

● 45.10

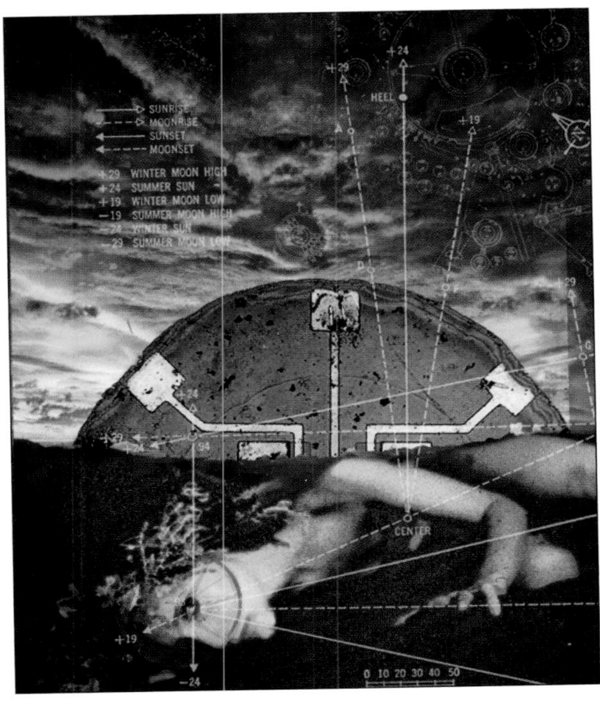

● 45.11

● 45.12

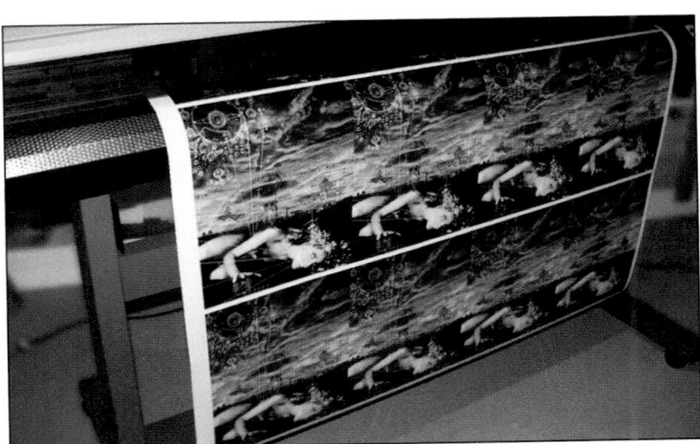

● 45.13

Using a CODA laminator, the print was laminated to the under-side of a plastic 40 lpi (lenticules per inch) lenticular lens from MicroLens (45.14). As you move by the image, you see one frame at a time, which creates the illusion of depth and movement.

More than 100 hours were spent on this project. Both the lenticular process and the emulsion transfer process are complex and time-consuming. The lenticular was the first iteration of this image.

Technique: Making a Two-State Animated Lenticular Print (Photoshop and Flip!)

This technique shows an easy way to apply the principles Dot used in *Primordial Fear* to create your own two-state, animated lenticular print.

Besides Photoshop, you need to invest in the software called Flip!, and also purchase a lenticular lens. The lenses come in 8.5 x 11-inch sheets, which can be cut with a sharp knife for smaller prints. You can obtain the Flip! software from `www.FlipSigns.com`, an organization of artists who promote the illusion arts (702-384-0568; Las Vegas, Nevada), and the lenses can be purchased from `www.MicroLens.com` (704-893-2109; Charlotte, North Carolina).

1. **Open two images in Photoshop, no larger than 8.5 x 11 inches at 300 dpi.**
   These two images should be linked in time; for instance, they could be of the same person with two different expressions, or at two different ages. In the example here (45.15 and 45.16), Dot used two images of the World Trade Center twin towers, one before 9/11 and one after their destruction.
2. **Use the Move tool to drag one image into the other.**
   The image that was dragged now appears as a layer.
3. **Reduce the opacity of the layer to about 50% using the Opacity slider in the Layers palette.**
4. **Use the Move tool and/or the arrow keys to nudge the layer position until it is appropriately aligned over the underlying background image.**
   In the case of a portrait, this may mean aligning the eyes.
5. **Bring the opacity setting for the layer back to 100%.**
   You should now just see the layer.
6. **Save the file as a TIFF image called frame1.**
7. **Click on the visibility icon (the eye) in the Layers palette to make the layer invisible.**
   You should now just see the background image.
8. **Save the file as a TIFF image called frame2.**
9. **Import the two frames into Flip! and generate the interlaced image (45.17).**
   Follow the detailed instructions that come with the software.
10. **Print the interlaced image.**

● 45.14

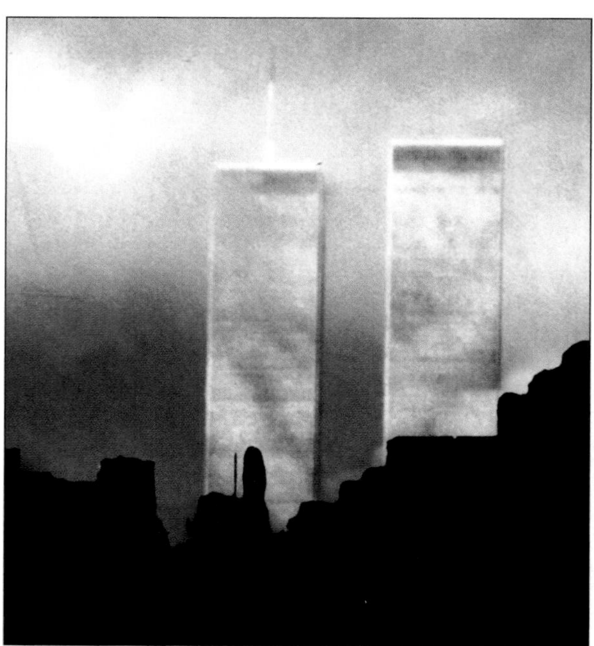

● 45.15

11. **Peel back the protective sheet on the back of the lenticular lens and carefully adhere the print of the interlaced image onto the sticky back of the lens, with the image surface facing the lens.**

[NOTE]

With small images, such as 2 x 2 images, you can attach a pin to the back of the final lenticular print and make badges.

Artist's Creative Insight and Advice

Why Digital?

I've been using a computer since the late 1960s, and it has been my primary art-making tool since the early 1980s when the Apple was introduced. What initially was seen by my colleagues as an insane media choice is now being called visionary — it was, for me, a medium I knew I would never master and always find challenging.

Working digitally, I can scan materials that could not otherwise be used, and alter scale, transparency, and relationships to create seamless collages. I can use traditional materials to build texture and rescan the image to begin the process again.

Advice for Artists Working in the Digital Medium

Mix traditional and digital media. Experiment. Push the boundaries. Break the Rules. Play. Enjoy. If you're not having fun, don't do it.

Some processes have a steep learning curve, but taken a step at a time, any mountain can be climbed. Although prices continue to drop, don't wait for the cheaper price or the newer model; the time you lose in making art is more valuable than money or technical advantage.

Color Management

I use no color management hardware but work backward from the print to the monitor so that all the components look like I expect them to.

Output

I like prints made on and transferred to textured surfaces and often make my own substrates. I work over/under and recursively on prints, rescanning and reprinting for various effects.

Primordial Fear was also used to make a hand-pulled digital transfer print for a USF exchange portfolio, HomeoStatic, organized by Brad Shank. In the case of this print, the Photoshop layers were flattened and the resulting image was sized to 15 x 11 inches, flipped horizontally (since it would be transferred

● 45.16

● 45.17

from one surface to another and automatically get flipped back in the process), and printed with the Mutoh Falcon Jet printer on Roland's domestic white PETG white film. A sheet of handmade lamali paper from Nepal was lightly sprayed with water (45.18) and blotted.

The print was centered on the paper face down and transferred using the CODA laminator as a monoprint press (45.19). When the white film was pulled from the damp paper (45.20), the image remained.

The transferred print, encapsulated in ink jet receiver, sits on the surface of the paper similar to an emulsion transfer. The 20 x 16 digital transfer print is an edition of 34 with 6 artists proofs.

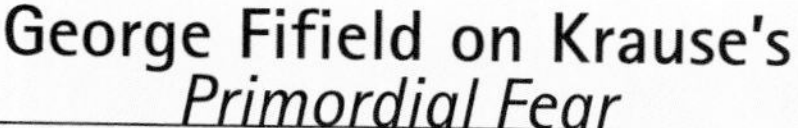

George Fifield on Krause's *Primordial Fear*

"*Primordial Fear* uses the digital technique of layering at its finest. The strata of technical data, the nude, and the landscape compress into a complete whole – colorful, vibrant with story and evocative of mysterious knowledge."

– George Fifield, Director, Boston Cyberart Festival (www.bostoncyberarts.org)

● 45.19

● 45.20

● 45.18

Chapter 46

Follow a Mile

by Graham Huber

Artist's Statement

I like all things disturbing. Or funny. Or better yet, disturbingly funny. I am intrigued by the notions of illusion, deception, and unreality. One could say my hobby is trying to stroke the nerve of oddity.

Pretty things are pleasing, but passive, unremarkable, and often little more than an appeal to the lowest common denominator. Stepping outside the confines of acceptability into what might be considered disturbing is where real innovation is spawned.

The Story Behind the Artwork

Follow a Mile (46.1) is one in a series of concepts that came to Graham after a rather long period of strenuous nonpersonal work. After being tied down for those few months, he set out on a creative binge to relieve the tension. He wanted to develop these concepts into visual ideas.

For this particular piece, the concept alluded to in the title is an amalgamation of the two classic proverbs "follow in my footsteps" and "walk a mile in my shoes." The idea was to depict a wearable foot as realistically and convincingly as possible.

The Creative Process

Once Graham had the idea for this piece, he began planning the photo shoot to capture source material to work with. Setting up the materials and getting the right shot took a considerable amount of time. Graham made rough sketches as reference for the camera angles he needed for things to look right. (When he shoots source images, Graham doesn't try

◀ 46.1

to achieve great photography on the spot; rather, he simply shoots for image potential. The photos on their own may seem rather uninspired in their initial state. The art comes from recognizing something in that picture, and where he goes from there.)

Graham is resourceful with the limited photo studio facilities at his disposal. Graham always works alone, using himself as the model if necessary, as in this case. For this shoot, he ended up dangling a 1000W construction light from a piece of twine, using the timer on the camera to shoot the image while he balanced himself on one foot. The tricky part was maintaining this balancing act while replacing his foot with the shoe, resetting the camera and holding the light. The worn table seen in the image was shot separately.

A working image was constructed in Photoshop (46.2). This image contained separate layers for the background, the table, the foot, and the shoe.

Graham then used layer masks to selectively alter the transparency of the layers until he achieved the desired illusion.

Technique: Applying the Layer Mask for Photo Collage (Photoshop)

Layer masks in Photoshop provide a convenient means of controlling the transparency of a layer. Thus you can brush out parts of a layer to smoothly blend one image into another or juxtapose one image over another.

Layer masks are an invaluable tool for the digital artist, especially when compositing two or more photographs together in a single image, as in this case. In this technique, Graham shares the beauty and power of working with layer masks to construct and control a photo-composite image.

1. **Open your working image in Photoshop.**
2. **Introduce your photographic image elements into your working image as separate layers.**

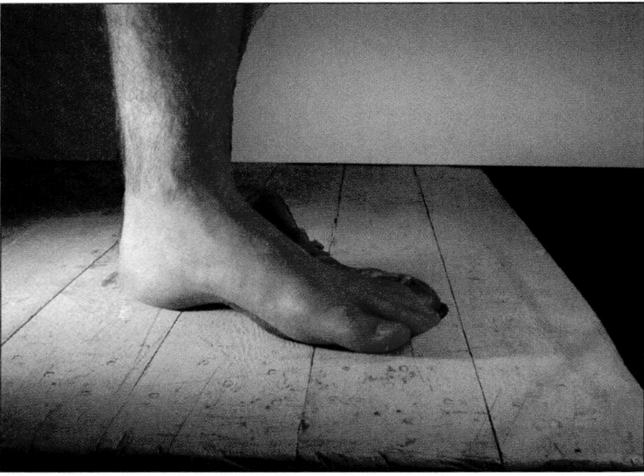

● 46.2

About the Artist

Biography

Graham has a B.Des Honours from the York University/Sheridan College Joint Design Program. Born to parents of a science background, Graham grew up on the unlikely diet of traditional art (favoring black pen and ink) until discovering Photoshop as a teenager. Cautioned against becoming a starving artist, he sought his formal education in design. His professional clients have included Labatt, Molson, Bass Ale, Löwenbräu, the City of Toronto, and the York/Sheridan Design program.

Influences

Derek Lea, Dave McKean, David Ho, and David Carson. Musically, the work of Tool and Dredg. Classically, the visual punning of Rene Magritte and MC Escher.

Studio

Computer System:
AMD Athlon, 1.4GHz
512MB RAM
30GB hard drive
Windows XP Professional

[TIP]

Use the Move tool to drag images from your source files into your working image. The source images form layers. If any layer needs rescaling or distorting to suit the composition, then choose Edit→Transform→Scale. Drag on the control handles to distort or rescale the layer.

[TIP]

For the best printed results, your imagery should be at a high enough resolution for the final image to be 300 dpi at its final printed size.

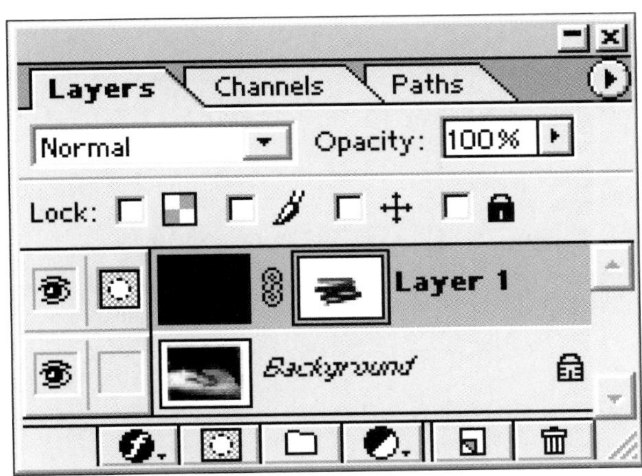

● 46.3

3. **Select a layer in the Layers palette that you want to selectively modify the transparency of.**
4. **Choose Layer→Add Layer Mask→Reveal All or click the "add layer mask" icon in the bottom of the Layers palette.**
   A new thumbnail box appears beside the original thumbnail in the Layer window (46.3).
5. **Click this new Layer mask thumbnail box.**
   The paintbrush icon beside the thumbnails in the Layer window changes to a dotted circle icon.
6. **Select the Paintbrush tool.**
7. **In the Paintbrush options palette select a large soft-edge brush for the smoothest results.**
8. **Change the foreground color to black.**
9. **Draw on the canvas.**
   Wherever black is drawn, the image is erased (46.4).

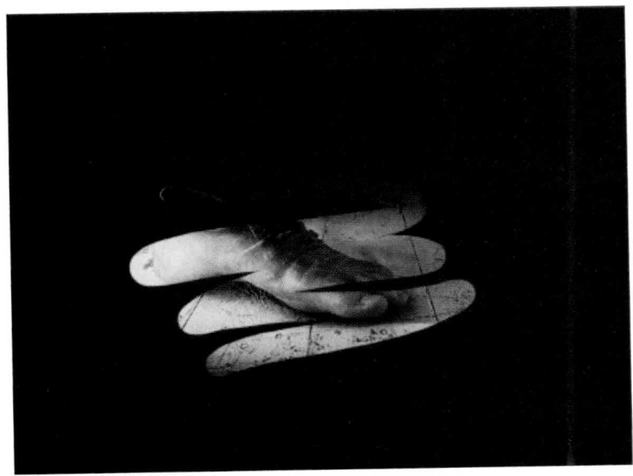

● 46.4

Monitors:
Samsung SyncMaster 900NF 19-inch
Acer 77C 17-inch

Software:
Adobe Photoshop

Tablet:
Wacom 4-x-5-inch Graphire2

Input Devices:
Microtek Scanmaker 6x
Nikon Coolpix 990 digital camera

Removable Media:
Kodak and Memorex CDRs

Printers:
Epson Stylus 640

Contact

Graham Huber
nowonmai@yorku.ca
nowonmai.capnasty.org/portfolio

[TIP]

To restore any part of the erased image, change the foreground color to White. Then draw on the canvas to restore parts "masked" out. You may also use the Eraser tool for this.

For subtle effects, play with the opacity of your brushes or use the Clone tool to make a mask from parts of other images. The value of using layer masks is that information in a layer is never permanently lost. You can go back at any point and restore a section or the whole thing in its original form.

Rick Decoyte on Huber's *Follow a Mile*

"An unusual approach to color and layering combined with an innovative cropping technique give this image a sense of psychological depth appropriate to the portrait format."

— Rick Decoyte, Owner and Curator, Silicon Gallery (`www.fineartprint.com`)

Artist's Creative Insight and Advice

Why Digital?

One of the great advantages to working digitally is the highly malleable workspace. Undo commands, file duplications, cut and paste, and (most of all) layers allow an artist to escape the fear of commitment to one approach over another that can plague traditional work.

I work primarily with the digital medium because of this, and also because it fits into the lifestyle I lead. I am able to roll my three areas of creative focus (photography, design, and illustration) into the all-encompassing realm of digital art.

Critics are willing to concede that with strong work, the distinction of digital or not is no more relevant to the validity of the piece as art than the distinction between oil and acrylic paint. It is the concept and execution that is important, digital or otherwise.

Of course, there are naturally some disadvantages. For instance, even against my own advice, I find it difficult to set aside the time for traditional work because it is not a part of my regular work habits. Fortunately though, technologies like graphic tablets can help bring the two together more. I've grown up as part of a tech-savvy generation. This is just the nature of my life.

Advice for Artists Working in the Digital Medium

Keep up your traditional skills. Try not to get caught in the trap of labeling yourself as a digital artist, assuming that means you don't need to know how to sketch. Neglect to pick up a pencil for long enough and you just might forget how to hold it.

Everyone needs inspiration, but letting yourself just copy another's style if you feel you don't have one of your own is a good way to run yourself into a creative dead-end. The popularity of online art communities is great for seeing what else is out there, but also very prone to this problem. I've learned not to get so swept up in user ratings and rankings that I forget why I am doing the work I am.

I know when an image is finished when the work I continue to put into it starts to detract from the overall piece. The effectiveness of a finished piece comes out of the refinement — not exhaustion — of the concept. Knowing when to quit is part of the game.

Output

My best tip for outputting digital work is to just accept the reality that it will likely *never* come out looking the same as onscreen. However, that doesn't mean there's nothing you can do about it. I learned the techniques for accurate color reproduction by getting to know the employees of a print shop and insisting on being there when the paper comes out of the printer. The sooner you know the limitations, the easier it will be for you to work around them constructively *before* you finish your work and realize there's no way it can ever be printed as you've created it.

Chapter 47

Agave Meadow

by Cher Threinen-Pendarvis

Artist's Statement

The computer is not the source of my art. It does not make digital paintings with the push of a button. The artist breathes life into an artwork, whether traditional or digital, from a heart filled with inspiration.

The Story Behind the Artwork

Cher volunteers on a citizen's committee whose focus is preservation of the native plants and sculptured cliffs in a natural park near her home in San Diego, California. Pendarvis was inspired to paint *Agave Meadow* (47.1) because she discovered that the Agave Shawi, a native of the California Maritime Succulent Scrub Habitat, was a threatened species. *Agave Meadow* is from a series of paintings that she created of the hills and coastline near her home in San Diego.

Creative Process

Cher began the work on location by making several colored pencil reference sketches. She made one general sketch and also several smaller sketches of details such as the agave plants and foreground grasses.

Back in her studio, she arranged the colored pencil sketches so that she could look at them all simultaneously. In Painter, she first made a loose composition sketch (47.2) using the original drawings as visual reference. She frequently used the Sharp Chalk from the Dry Media brush category to create this initial line sketch, which went through several transformations to get to the point of having the graceful flowing lines of the hills.

● 47.2

◀ 47.1

Once the initial line sketch was completed, Cher continued to work over the sketch. As she added pastel under-painting (layering pastel on top of it itself) in several places, the forms and details gradually emerged (47.3 and 47.4).

● 47.3

Remembering the morning light and looking at her reference sketches helped Cher to keep the painting loose while working in Painter to rough out the composition. Then she added many layers of colorful, textured strokes, creating a lot of movement. Cher established the basic color theme using the Square Chalk, then painted in more detail with a custom Artist Pastel Chalk and the Large Chalk variants.

To blend areas, such as smoothing the clouds in the sky, softening the horizon, and blurring the distant shrubbery (47.5), she used a low-opacity Grainy Water variant from the Liquid brush category. The Grainy Water variant mixes paint by dragging through existing color on the image, while adding a subtle indication of paper grain at the same time.

● 47.4

● 47.5

About the Artist

Biography

A traditionally trained artist, Cher has created fine art, illustration, and design on the Macintosh since 1988. Her earliest digital paintings were made in black-and-white using Image Studio, and she has been a devoted user of Painter, Photoshop, and the Wacom pressure-sensitive tablet since these electronic art tools were first released. Cher received a BA with Highest Honors and Distinction in Art in 1974, from San Diego State University, specializing in painting and printmaking, and since then she has worked in design, illustration, and fine art.

Cher's digital art has been exhibited as large-format, hand-worked prints worldwide. Her work has been featured in numerous publications, books, juried art exhibitions, and traveling shows. Cher is also the author of all editions of *Painter Wow!* (PeachPit Press).

Influences

The importance of art in Cher's life came to her when she discovered pencils, paper, and crayons as a child. Her mother, Wanda (also an artist), encouraged her to draw. Together they enjoyed sketching

After blending areas, she returned to some of the chalk variants and pressed lightly on the stylus while adding more cross-hatching and broken color to areas of the image. The lighter she pressed with the stylus, the lower the opacity of her chalk marks. Thus she could build up soft, subtle brushwork. All the while, she kept the feeling of the breezy early morning in her mind while she painted, an atmosphere that emerged especially in the later stages (47.6 through 47.8) of *Agave Meadow*.

Cher was lost for hours while creating *Agave Meadow*, busily layering color over color using various Chalk brushes and blending tools. Completing the painting took several creative sessions in the studio. Between painting sessions, she returned to the location to have a fresh look at the subject.

47.6

Technique: Emulating Traditional Pastel (Painter)

This technique shows you how Cher created her colorful painting that emulates the look and feel of a traditional pastel layered on paper.

47.7

47.8

and painting landscapes when living in Japan when Cher was seven years old. She is also influenced by the work of John Constable, Jean Gustave Courbet, Eugene Boudin, Edgar Degas, Claude Monet, and Wayne Theibaud.

Studio

Computer System:

Mac G4, 450MHz
40GB hard drive
512MB RAM
Titanium laptop with combo drive; G4 550
30GB hard drive
512MB RAM

Monitors:

La Cie 22 Electron Blue

Software:

Painter
Photoshop
Illustrator
Fireworks

Tablets:

Wacom Intuos 6 x 8

Input Devices:

Umax flatbed scanner

Printers:

Epson 2000P
Epson 3000

Contact

Cher Threinen-Pendarvis
San Diego, California
cher@pendarvis-studios.com
www.pendarvis-studio.com

[TIP]

Cher suggests that you do a series of traditional (non-digital) color sketches, using colored pencils or pastel on paper, before beginning your subject in Painter. Doing so gives you a firm foundation for your digital work and helps the finished piece retain a certain non-digital look. Carefully analyze your subject as you draw, adding the appropriate amount of detail where necessary. Keep your marks loose and lively. Use your choice of colors and character of pencil marks to express your feelings about your subject. You can use this information later as you create the subject digitally.

1. **Choose File→New (Cmd/Ctrl-N) and open a new canvas in Painter.**
   Set the size and resolution of the new canvas to suit the scale and size of your source sketches and your desired output. Most printers require a file resolution of 300 ppi at the final size for the best quality prints.
2. **Choose a neutral gray color in the Standard Colors color picker (47.9) in the Colors section of the Art Materials palette.**
   Bring the cursor in the Saturation/Value triangle to the center left of the triangle to create a neutral gray (about half way up the left side, or about 50%). This gray is a convenient color with which to map out a rough compositional sketch, which you can then paint over.
3. **Choose the Sanded Pastel Board texture (47.10) in the Papers section of the Art Materials palette.**
   Cher selected this paper texture (also referred to as paper grain) and then kept it as the paper texture throughout the painting process in Painter. She used "grainy" brushes that are influenced by the paper grain and thus embued her image with a consistent paper grain. This helped build up the effect of a traditional pastel drawing where the paper grain generally shows through.

[NOTE]

You can try this technique using other paper grains, too. Painter comes with vast resources of ready-to-use Art Materials, and you can also customize your own Art Materials. For instance, you can scan and save paper textures from your own favorite papers. For more details on doing this, refer to the Painter User Guide.

4. **Choose the Sharp Chalk variant (47.11) of the Dry Media brush category in the Brushes palette.**
   The size of the chalk depends on the overall size of your canvas. For a rough compositional sketch, you don't have to worry about fine detail, so a brush size of about 10 or so is usually fine.
5. **Make a composition sketch that sets out the main shapes and lays the groundwork for the overall composition, mapping out what goes where.**
6. **When you are happy with the composition sketch, choose the Square Chalk variant in the Dry Media category and roughly color over your image.**
7. **Blend areas using a low-opacity Grainy Water variant from the Liquid brush category.**

[TIP]

Experiment by using 20% to 40% opacity.

8. **Keeping your subject, lighting, and the atmosphere in mind, choose the Artist Pastel Chalk (47.12) from the Dry Media brush category and make light brushstrokes over areas of your image that you would like to be more defined.**
   You can see here the way Cher customized the Artist Pastel Chalk. Using the sliders in the

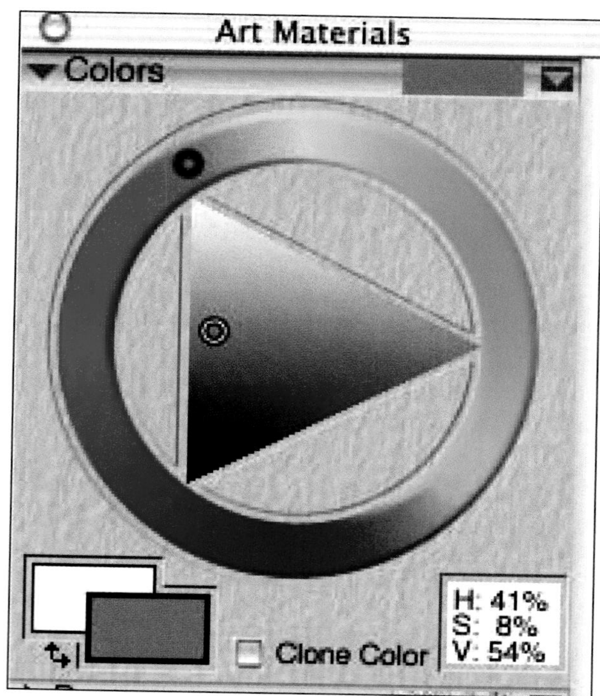

● 47.9

Controls:Brush palette, she increased the size from 10 to 27.4 and decreased the opacity from 100% to 72%.

You can also see here the simple arrangement of palettes that Cher uses. Arranging your palettes in a simple layout like this, hiding those palettes you don't need, makes Painter much easier to use.

[TIP]

You can save your palette arrangements by choosing Window→Arrange Palettes→Save Layout. Name your layout and click OK. Your arrangement is then added to the Arrange Palettes layout list, and you can recall it at any time in the future.

For more activity in the brushwork and color, practice varying the size of your brush as you work, using the Size slider in the Controls:Brush palette.

Remember that objects close to the foreground (such as the foreground plants in *Agave Meadow*) are usually more detailed and more brightly colored than distant objects.

9. **When you are satisfied with your painting, choose File→Save As and save the flattened image in Photoshop or Tiff format for print and Web use.**

Artist's Creative Insight and Advice

Why Digital?

I begin my paintings by sketching from life with colored pencils and paper, or by drawing on location with a laptop computer, pressure-sensitive tablet, and Painter. With the computer, I can combine media that would be impossible to combine traditionally — such as oil paint, chalk, and watercolor — and this flexibility has allowed me to push my work to new limits.

Also, with the computer, you can draw over an area several times without reworking it, and you can save several stages and clone portions back in if you need to.

Advice for Artists Working in the Digital Medium

If you don't already have a solid background using traditional tools and techniques, pick up a good art history book and see which master artist's work most appeals to you. Then go to museums to look at their art or find additional books on your favorite subject to study. Experiment with traditional tools and also their electronic counterparts on the computer.

Printing and Color Consistency

Find a service bureau that is willing to work with you to achieve the best prints possible from your digital files. To achieve better, more consistent color

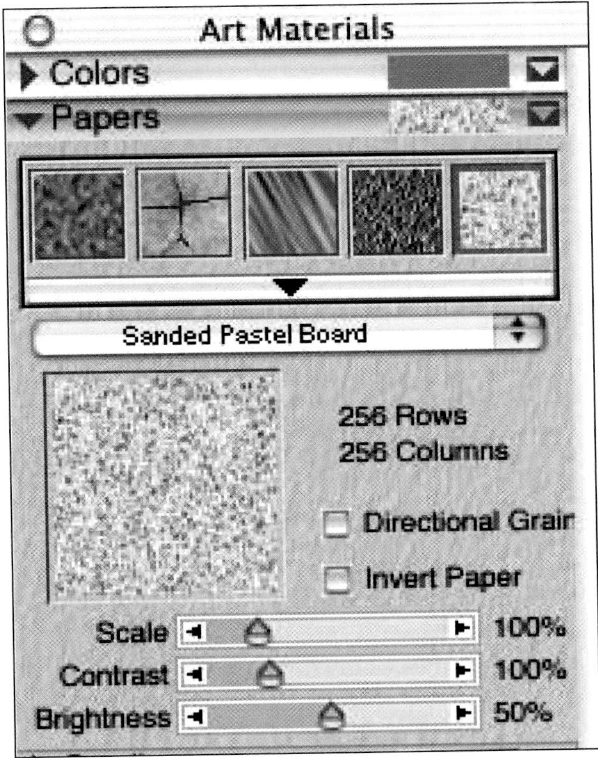

47.10

47.11

form your images, work with the service bureau to create custom color tables and then load them into your computer so that your system is calibrated to their output devices.

For making smaller prints, I enjoy working with an Epson 2000P printer that uses archival inks and papers. This printer makes very good quality prints with bright colors. The prints are amazingly color accurate, right out of the box.

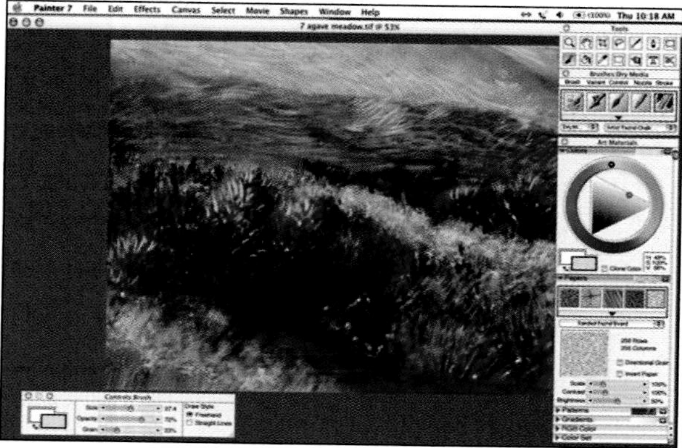

● 47.12

Index

B

C

Continued

G

H

Continued

N

O

P

Continued

R

S

T

U

V

W

Y

Z

About the Authors

Jeremy Sutton, artist, educator, and author, grew up in London and lives in San Francisco. His publications include *Fractal Design Painter Creative Techniques* (Hayden Books, 1996), *Total Painter* (Total Training, 1998) and *Painter Creativity: Digital Artist's Handbook* (Focal Press, 2002). Jeremy has a degree in Physics from Oxford University, England, and is a former faculty member of the Academy of Art College, San Francisco. He has drawn and painted all his life and has been creating art on the computer since 1991. He currently teaches Painter at training seminars and workshops throughout the world. You can view examples of his colorful portraits and learn about his classes and workshops on his Web site at `www.portrayals.com`.

Daryl Wise's involvement with digital art started in 1992 when he had the pleasure to work at Fractal Design, the makers of the software Painter. At Fractal Design, he worked with the press and artist communities and was responsible for the company's special events. He presently runs a small PR and event company in the central California coast city of Watsonville. He coordinates digital art contests for Macworld Conference and Expo and the Seybold Seminars. He is also the managing director of the Santa Cruz Digital Arts Festival.

Colophon

This book was produced electronically in Indianapolis, Indiana. Microsoft Word 98 was used for word processing; design and layout were produced using QuarkXPress 4.11 and Adobe Photoshop 5.5 on Macintosh G3 and G4 computers. The typeface families used are Bembo, Orator, Rotis Sans Serif, Rotis SemiSans, Rotis SemiSerif, and Zapf Dingbats.

Acquisitions Editor
Michael Roney

Project Editor
Mary Goodwin

Technical Editor
Colin Smith

Editorial Manager
Rev Mengle

Vice President and Executive Group Publisher
Richard Swadley

Vice President and Executive Publisher
Bob Ipsen

Vice President and Publisher
Barry Pruett

Project Coordinator
Nancee Reeves

Graphics and Production Specialists
Melanie DesJardins, LeAndra Johnson, Gabrielle McCann, Laurie Petrone, Ron Terry

Quality Control Technicians
Andy Hollandbeck, Linda Quigley

Proofreading and Indexing
TECHBOOKS Production Services

Cover Image
Anthony Bunyan

Special Help
Cricket Franklin